TERRORIZING OURSELVES

EDITED BY BENJAMIN H. FRIEDMAN,
JIM HARPER, AND CHRISTOPHER A. PREBLE

TERRORIZING OURSELVES

WHY U.S. COUNTERTERRORISM POLICY IS FAILING AND HOW TO FIX IT

CATO INSTITUTE
WASHINGTON, D.C.

Library of Congress Cataloging-in-Publication Data

Terrorizing ourselves : why U.S. counterterrorism policy is failing
and how to fix it / edited by Benjamin H. Friedman, Jim Harper, and
Christopher A. Preble.
    p. cm.
Includes bibliographical references and index.
ISBN 978-1-935308-30-0 (hardback: alk. paper)   1. Terrorism—
United States.   2. Terrorism—Prevention—Government policy—United
States.   3. Terrorism—United States—Prevention.   4. National security—
United States.   I. Friedman, Benjamin H.   II. Harper, Jim, 1967–   III.
Preble, Christopher A.

    HV6432.T4786 2010
    363.325'160973—dc22
                                                            2010005480
Printed in the United States of America.

CATO INSTITUTE
1000 Massachusetts Ave., N.W.
Washington, D.C. 20001
www.cato.org

Contents

Acknowledgements

One might think that three coeditors could manage to assemble the chapters in this volume without much help. Far from it.

For starters, we are grateful to our contributors. We thank them for taking time out of their busy lives to write the chapters. We wish to express special thanks to Brandi Dunn, a tireless worker and perceptive critic who kept us on schedule, solved nettlesome problems, expressed her opinion, and otherwise made this entire project productive, rewarding, and ultimately fun.

The Cato Institute is more than just the publisher of this book. It is our intellectual home, a place that stimulates original thinking and allowed us to dedicate considerable time and effort to its completion. We want to thank Ed Crane, Bob Levy, William Niskanen, and David Boaz for their leadership. Cato vice president Gene Healy reviewed all of the chapters, offered timely feedback, and pressed us to live up to the highest ideals of sound scholarship and clear writing. The quality of the finished product is a testament to his tireless work. Charles Zakaib provided invaluable research assistance, as well as insightful comments, at various stages. We also appreciate the help of Peter Bandyk, Nicholas Brooke, Matt Fay, Jordan Gazit, and Adam Lamothe.

Others at Cato provided essential assistance. David Lampo kept us on track to meet our deadline. Robert Garber and Camille Cooke put together the marketing plan, and Jon Meyers designed the cover. Harrison Moar helped with media outreach. Copyeditors Joanne Platt and Ashley Young of Publications Professionals reviewed all chapters and played a particularly helpful role in reconciling the stylistic idiosyncrasies that are inevitable in a work combining the contributions of 13 opinionated scholars. We are grateful to all of these individuals for their contribution to this project.

Finally, this book is just one of the tangible outputs produced as part of Cato's strategic counterterrorism initiative, an ambitious three-year project made possible by the generous support of the

Atlantic Philanthropies, with additional support from the Open Society Institute. The initiative develops and publicizes sophisticated, strategic responses to transnational terrorism and works to replace some of the flawed paradigms that bedevil current U.S. national security policies arising from terrorism. We want to thank both organizations for their support.

Benjamin H. Friedman
Jim Harper
Christopher A. Preble

January 2010

Introduction

Measured in lives and dollars, government reactions to terrorism often impose greater costs on the societies attacked than terror attacks themselves. Overreaction does the work of terrorism. Ignorance of this cardinal fact is why U.S. counterterrorism policy is failing.

As we approach nearly a decade of aggressive U.S. government action, the results that counterterrorism policy should seek still elude us. Americans are neither as secure as they should be, nor do they feel that their lives and liberties are well protected.

Instead, terrorism is very much with us. Though they pale in comparison to 9/11, new attacks, both successful and failed, remind us that terrorists seek ways to harm us. And the nation's politics remain in thrall to the specter of terrorism. Rather than dispassionately addressing true threats, our national leaders often hype implausible threats and jockey for political advantage in anticipation of terrorist strikes.

This struggle to address terrorism exists for good reason: Policymakers, the media, and the public lack a strategic understanding of terrorism. And they lack awareness of appropriate, strategic responses to it.

This book contains the dispassionate, analytical thinking about terrorism so needed if the United States is going to develop successful counterterrorism policies. It aims to foster new understanding and new approaches to terrorism that center on resisting overreaction. By addressing terrorism forthrightly and confidently, we can take control of our security, drain power from terrorism, and make it ineffective.

The first step in a conventional account of strategic counterterrorism is to understand its practitioners. Terrorists have motivations, there is a strategic logic to their actions, and examining these things can reveal strategies that frustrate and dissipate their efforts.

But we begin with a chapter highlighting the goal of counterterrorism. "[T]he best way to formulate grand strategy," begins U.S.

1

National War College professor of strategy Audrey Kurth Cronin in her chapter, "Defeating al Qaeda," "is to look beyond the war to the nature of the peace."

In many ways, terrorism draws power from the state, turning state power toward the accomplishment of terrorists' aims. Aware of the gifts overreaction gives terrorists, Cronin illustrates how states can deny terrorism the oxygen and nutrients that sustain it. She explores the seven patterns by which terrorist groups meet their demise.

Of course, deepening our understanding of how terrorism arises will enable us to counter it earlier and better. James Forest, director of terrorism studies and associate professor at the United States Military Academy, investigates terrorism's roots in his chapter, "Terrorism as a Product of Choices and Perceptions." Along with activities aimed at weakening terrorist groups and ameliorating the conditions that spawn or justify terrorism, Forest argues, strategic communication, public diplomacy, and counterideology are leading elements of a robust counterterrorism strategy.

Mia Bloom, associate professor at Penn State's Schools of International Studies and Women's Studies and a fellow at Penn State's International Center for the Study of Terrorism, similarly explores inchoate terrorism. In her chapter, "Are There 'Root Causes' for Terrorist Support? Revisiting the Debate on Poverty, Education, and Terrorism," Bloom takes a fresh look at old assumptions and at recent analyses of what may "cause" terrorism.

The links that analysts have sought between socioeconomic conditions, political grievances, and terrorism exist, though they may better be thought of as soil in which terrorism can grow. And Bloom's chapter serves as a warning against overreliance on external conditions as causes of terrorism. "[A] focus on external influences on behavior robs the individual of agency; specifically of choosing to engage in terrorism." From whatever background circumstances, many individuals may choose terrorism because they perceive it as a way to expand their influence and power—similar, perhaps, to the way an arsonist thrills at watching the destructive fire he set. For others, overreaction advances articulated organizational goals— imposing costs on the victim state, for example, or promoting the cause of a terrorist group to key audiences. Denying terrorists such gratification is a way to mute the attractiveness of terror tactics.

One way of thinking about overreaction is to divide it into categories, common forms of error that make gifts to terrorists and advance their goals:

- Waste of Blood and Treasure: Terrorist attacks—or well-placed threats of attack—can prompt victim states to waste their own resources, both the blood of their soldiers when they go to war and the wealth of their people when countermeasures cost more than they provide in security.
- Recruitment and Sympathy Gains: A strong power victimized by terrorism is likely to do violence or take other responses that engender sympathy for terrorists' causes and aid their recruiting and support.
- Delegitimization: Terrorism can cause victim states to come loose from their ideological moorings, reducing their credibility and authority with various audiences. A state claiming a liberal, tolerant credo, for example, may appear hypocritical to allies and domestic constituencies alike when its response to terrorism appears illiberal and intolerant.

War making, of course, is the response to terrorism most likely to expend the most blood and treasure. War is also the most likely to drive support to terrorism, and the most likely to draw a state's moral authority into question. Paul Pillar, professor of security studies at Georgetown University, and Christopher Preble, the Cato Institute's director of foreign policy studies, look at military responses to terrorism in their chapter, "Don't You Know There's a War On? Assessing the Military's Role in Counterterrorism."

Obviously, military force is a powerful tool, for good or ill. The "potential effect on terrorist capabilities is immediate and unqualified," they observe, though they find that the "limitations and drawbacks of using the military are more numerous and collectively quite substantial."

Their chapter also examines the role of the word "war" in the terminology of counterterrorism. The phrase "war on terror" incorrectly implies that the military is the leading instrument of our counterterrorism efforts, they say, and that counterterrorism has a definite beginning and end. The war frame can also cause us to "conflate the disparate threats posed by terrorist organizations," they

3

argue. It "plays into the terrorists' own rhetoric that the West is engaged in a war against Islam."

James Lewis of the Center for Strategic and International Studies recognizes and reaffirms the importance of knowing what counterterrorism activities communicate in his strategy-oriented chapter, "Assessing Counterterrorism, Homeland Security, and Risk." "For the United States," he writes, "the most important political aspect of counterterrorism is not reform or development overseas but the political message it conveys through its actions."

Given states' predilection toward overreaction, Lewis argues that the central challenge in homeland security is risk assessment. Terrorism invites the spending of enormous sums to secure every potential target against every conceivable vector of attack. Terrorism works its will as public accounts drain and valuable economic functions such as international trade slow down.

Ohio State University professor John Mueller provides a dose of the clinical, green-eyeshade work that should imbue counterterrorism in his chapter, "Assessing Measures Designed to Protect the Homeland." Mueller holds the calculus of defensive overreaction up to the light: Targets are essentially infinite and interchangeable, meaning that securing any one of them transfers risk to the next one. Accordingly, most target-protective security measures add little or nothing to national security.

Among his recommendations is to consider the negative effects of protection measures—not only costs but inconvenience, enhancement of fear, negative economic effects, and reduction of liberties. Mueller cites a study suggesting that armed guards, high walls, and barbed wire, which reduce fear in the context of crime, actually increase fear in the context of terrorism—"exactly the negative emotional effect terrorists themselves hope to induce."

Veronique de Rugy, senior research fellow at the Mercatus Center at George Mason University, continues with this theme in her chapter, "The Economics of Homeland Security," by analyzing homeland security spending. "Homeland security should be about wise choices, not just increased spending," she says as she begins her walk through the economic problems involved in finding optimal security levels. For example, de Rugy shows how public choice economics explains why political actors pursuing their parochial interests promote collective overreaction—excess security spending that harms the country.

When policymakers engage in such behavior, they often cite the threat of "WMDs"—weapons of mass destruction—a chief driver of terror concerns. Chapters on nuclear terrorism and bioterrorism assert that terrorist use of such weapons is not near at hand, contrary to what we often hear.

In "The Atomic Terrorist?," John Mueller examines the likelihood that terrorists could access and deploy a nuclear weapon. States with the wherewithal to build nuclear weapons have strong self-preservation-based incentives not to give them to terrorists; if "loose nukes" ever existed, they have deteriorated into "radioactive scrap metal"; building a bomb of one's own requires facilities and engineering prowess beyond the wherewithal of most nation-states. Stateless actors are even less capable. These facts make the risk of nuclear terrorism vanishingly small.

Milton Leitenberg, senior research scholar at the University of Maryland's Center for International and Security Studies, similarly takes on bioterrorism and bioweapons in his chapter, "Assessing the Threat of Bioterrorism." Examining state biological weapons programs, bioweapons proliferation, state assistance to nonstate actors, and efforts to develop biological agents or weapons by terrorists, he finds, among other things, that "exaggeration, propaganda, and alarmism about [bioweapons] are counterproductive, inducing interest by nonstate actors in precisely the kinds of activities that the United States would like to prevent and generating a dangerous set of overreactions at home."

Even a small chance of mass casualties deserves protective measures, and neither Mueller nor Leitenberg dismiss threats as nonexistent. The job is to find the security measures that cost-effectively address genuine threats. Protective measures should not be premised on terrorists' intentions or on theoretical possibilities or worst-case scenarios. They should focus instead on the likelihood that terrorists can access and deploy any particular weapon.

With this knowledge available to the public and policymakers, why would fear so dominate and our public policies be so inclined toward overreaction? Ben Friedman of the Cato Institute answers this question in his chapter, "Managing Fear: The Politics of Homeland Security."

"Americans want more homeland security than they need," writes Cato's research fellow in defense and homeland security studies, for two reasons. "[C]ognitive biases cause people to worry more about terrorists than they should," says Friedman, and "U.S. citizens' information about terrorism comes largely from politicians and government organizations with an interest in reinforcing excessive fears."

Counterterrorism policies that fail cost-benefit analysis—overreactions—are good politics. "Overreaction is then highly probable for the foreseeable future," he predicts.

Is this our fate? A cycle in which terror attacks draw overreactions, which draw further terror attacks against a progressively weaker, more terrorized, and more overreactive nation? It doesn't have to be.

"[I]f analysts attack overwrought statements, their authors might think twice about fearmongering," says Friedman. The Department of Homeland Security should think of itself "not just as a risk manager but also as a fear manager."

Communications policies around terrorism are an essential tool in the fight against overreaction, and against terrorism itself. Controlling excessive responses can control the effect of terrorism, reduce its utility to terrorists, and ultimately help reduce terrorist incidents.

The final two chapters begin to answer the call for better terrorism communications. In a chapter titled "The Impact of Fear on Public Thinking about Counterterrorism Policy: Implications for Communicators," Priscilla Lewis, codirector of the U.S. in the World Initiative, presents research conducted for her organization by the Topos Partnership.

"By understanding how fear affects public thinking and by learning how to counter some of fear's negative effects," she writes, "influential communicators may be able to help prevent strong public emotions from being channeled in unconstructive directions." She presents a variety of perspectives on fear's influence, with specific recommendations for communicators.

William Burns's concluding chapter, "Communicating about Threat: Toward a Resilient Response to Terrorism," is written in the same vein. Burns, a research scientist at Decision Research, a nonprofit organization that investigates human judgment, decision-making, and risk, discusses the factors that influence fear in communities.

Fear is often amplified as people communicate about attacks, but fear can be mitigated if the public has good base-line information and if natural community coping mechanisms are allowed to operate. Burns prescribes a model for devising communications about specific threats like a "dirty bomb" (exploded radioactive material). Subject-matter experts should collaborate with researchers in advance to survey public understanding and to devise messages that are factually informative and that give the public a sense of control. This approach can dissipate the frustrating and terrifying effects of ignorance.

Communications policies that suppress instinctive fears and over-reactions to terrorism are not a substitute for direct counterterrorism activities, of course. Infiltrating terror cells, disrupting terror networks, frustrating planning, and interdicting attackers are all essential activities. Communicating soundly about terrorism is a policy that, in calming public debate about terrorism, will draw support to programs and activities that directly and effectively address terrorism. It will foster the worldwide sense that such programs and activities are balanced, just, and fair. This is an essential element of counterterrorism; terrorists benefit from the perception that they fight an unjust actor.

If it has taken nearly a decade to discover that cool, phlegmatic counterterrorism meets the challenge of terror, so be it. The flawed, reactive approach that began on 9/11 and that largely continues today is often counterproductive, and it should be abandoned.

U.S. counterterrorism policy must be recentered on the idea that overreaction does most of the work of terrorism. Instead of exalting and fearing remotely possible—or impossible—threats, the nation should address real threats steadfastly and confidently. The new world of globalized communications will convey this confidence quickly, showing would-be terrorists that terrorism cannot be successful.

The alternative is more of the same: spending huge sums on dubious security measures, shedding liberties, and sacrificing American lives to attack overhyped threats. The danger of terrorism is real, but so is the danger of excessive reaction to it. Instead of indulging fear and overreaction, we must stop terrorizing ourselves.

1. Defeating al Qaeda

Audrey Kurth Cronin[1]

More than 50 years ago, Basil Liddell Hart observed that the best way to formulate grand strategy is to look beyond the war to the nature of the peace. In the same way, the United States can look beyond the international terrorist campaign inspired by al Qaeda, beyond the short-term steps the West has embarked on to answer it, and toward a broader vision of how it will end.

The United States is learning from hard experience that understanding war termination is more important than dissecting the causes of war. Similarly, the processes by which terrorist groups end hold within them the best insights into which strategies succeed and which fail, and why. Thinking about the end is crucial, not just because it provides a new perspective on what al Qaeda is doing but because it provides a much-needed, fresh framework for what the United States and its allies are doing. Studying how terrorism ends is the best way to inoculate society against the strategies of terrorism, avoid a dysfunctional action/reaction dynamic, reframe counterterrorism, and know what it means to win.

Objective research demonstrates that many common assumptions about the endings of terrorist campaigns are wrong—or at least incomplete and misleading. An analytical framework for how terrorist campaigns have *actually* ended sets forth the core elements of a comprehensive counterstrategy for hastening the end of al Qaeda and its associates.

The Strategies of Terrorism

There are five classic strategies of terrorism, and understanding them is essential to devising an effective counterstrategy. These strategies—compellence, provocation, polarization, mobilization, and delegitimization—are not mutually exclusive. Three of them are strategies of leverage that seek to draw enough power from the nation-state to accomplish terrorists' aims. What a government does in response is at the core of their efficacy. Unfortunately, democracies with a Western strategic tradition have particular difficulty understanding them, not to mention constructing an effective strategy to respond to them.

The first time-honored strategy is compellence. Compellence is the use of threats to influence another actor to stop doing an unwanted behavior or to start doing something a group wants it to do. Terrorism has been used in support of many causes, but targeted governments naturally tend to assume that the goal is compellence. Fitting terrorist group activity into the same mental framework used for state activity is instinctual, and sometimes it is appropriate. For example, terrorists may try to force states to withdraw from foreign commitments through a strategy of punishment and attrition, making the commitments so painful that the government will abandon them. And at times, this approach has appeared to work. Examples include the U.S. and French withdrawals from Lebanon in 1983, the U.S. withdrawal from Somalia in 1993, and the Israeli withdrawal from Lebanon in 2000.

Some see terrorism in Iraq as a foreign-inspired plan to force the United States to depart both Iraq and the region.[2] Many also argue that terrorism succeeded in the 2004 bombings in Madrid, leading to a change of government in Spain and the withdrawal of troops from Iraq. Of course, this is an oversimplification in each case. But terrorism is meant to oversimplify complex situations: the interpretation is persuasive to many audiences, not least those in the West, and that is a major reason why it is put forth on the Internet and over the airwaves.

Compellence targets a state's policy and tries to change it. Given their 20th-century experience with air power and nuclear deterrence theory, Western policymakers and strategic thinkers find the logic comfortably familiar. As a result, they tend to focus exclusively on compellence, blinding themselves to the other typical strategies of terrorism and their practical implications. Groups that rely primarily on terrorism do not have the luxury of behaving as if they were small states. In formulating an effective counterstrategy, this state-centered mindset is not a promising way to end terrorism.

Instead, we must be cognizant of the other strategies that terrorists have used, especially strategies of leverage. Strategies of leverage go beyond the dichotomous, state-versus-interloper models that are so ingrained in the Western strategic mindset. The relevant actors instead are a kind of triad of state, opposing group, and audience. This turns traditional ends/ways/means formulations of strategy on their head: in terrorism, strategy is not just the linear application of means to ends because the reactions of other actors and audiences can be a group's means, ends, or both.

Strategies of leverage come in three forms.[3] The first, provocation, tries to force a state to react, to do something—not necessarily to undertake a specific policy but to engage in vigorous action that works against its interests. The Russian group Narodnaya Volya, for example, had provocation at the heart of its strategy, a firmly established purpose for terrorism during the 19th century. Narodnaya Volya attacked representatives of the czarist regime, seeking to provoke a brutal state response and inspire a peasant uprising. More recent cases of provocation include the Basque group ETA's early strategy in Spain, the Sandinista National Liberation Front's strategy in Nicaragua, and the FLN's early strategy in Algeria.

Provocation is a difficult strategy to apply effectively, because terrorist groups often cause a state to behave in unforeseen or erratic ways. A terrorist attack may provoke a government into unwise or emotion-driven action that serves no one's interests. This is what happened with the outbreak of World War I, for example. The assassination of Archduke Franz Ferdinand was in itself an unimportant act. Assassinations had been endemic in the West for decades, including the assassinations of the Russian czar, the French president, the Spanish prime minister, the Italian king, and, in 1901, U.S. President McKinley, among others. But because of conditions in place at the time, not least Austro-Hungarian paranoia about Serbian nationalism, the act had huge implications. Gavril Princip, the consumptive 19-year-old who pulled the trigger, never meant to set off a world war and was utterly bewildered by the global conflagration that followed. Terrorism on its own is comparatively insignificant, but when it provokes a state, it can be a catalyst that indirectly kills millions. In this case, terrorist activity "ended" when it set off a cascade of state actions that resulted in a long and bloody war.

The next strategy of leverage is polarization, which tries to divide and delegitimize a government. Terrorist attacks affect the domestic politics of a state, often driving regimes sharply to the right and forcing populations to choose between the terrorist cause and brutal

11

state repression. The goal is to pry divided populations further apart, fragmenting societies to the point at which it is impossible to maintain a moderate middle within a functioning state.

Polarization is a particularly attractive strategy against democracies, and it appeared regularly during the 20th century. But like the strategy of provocation, it often results in unintended consequences. Examples include the Tamil Tigers in Sri Lanka and the Provisional Irish Republican Army in Northern Ireland. Terrorist activities in Germany, Austria, and Hungary after World War I were likewise meant to polarize, and they played a role in the onset of World War II. Anarchist activities in Spain played an important role in the coming of the Spanish Civil War (1936–1939), and a similar scenario occurred in Portugal in the 1920s, leading to an authoritarian regime.

But the archetypal example of a polarization strategy gone awry is the Tupamaros in Uruguay beginning in the early 1960s. At a time of economic stagnation in Uruguay, the ultraleftist Tupamaros drew inspiration from the Cuban revolution and set out to target symbols of the "imperialist regime," such as businesses and airports. Uruguay had a robust party system; an educated, urban population; and an established democratic tradition. If democracy were an antidote to terrorism, Uruguay should have been immune. But the campaign polarized society, driving politics to the right. In response, the government suspended all constitutional rights and eventually turned to the army, which by 1972 had crushed the group. Even though terrorist attacks had ended, the Uruguayan army then carried out a coup, dissolved Parliament, and ruled the country for the next 12 years. In their short preeminence, the Tupamaros had executed one hostage and assassinated eight counterinsurgency personnel in a widespread campaign of kidnappings, robberies, and terrorist attacks. The right-wing authoritarian military regime that came to power from 1973 to 1985 killed thousands. A polarization strategy drove the government to destroy itself.

Another strategy of leverage is mobilization. Its purpose is to recruit and rally the masses to a cause. Terrorist attacks may be intended to inspire current and potential supporters of a group, again using the reaction of the state as a *means*, not an end. This is what the campaign of bombings and assassinations in the late 19th century did for the anarchist movement and the 1972 Munich Olympics massacre did for Palestinian nationalism.

When terrorist attacks are used to mobilize, they are not necessarily directed toward changing the behavior of a state at all. They aim instead to invigorate and energize potential recruits and to raise a group's profile internationally, drawing resources, sympathizers, and allies.

A strategy of mobilization is well suited for the 21st century's globalized international community, which allows movements to gather together on a scale and at a speed never before witnessed in history. It also gets to the heart of why so many see the struggle with al Qaeda as a multigenerational "long war."

Mobilization has been al Qaeda's most effective strategy thus far. A global environment of democratized communications has increased public access to information and has sharply reduced the cost. Through the growth in the frequency of messages and an exploitation of images, groups like al Qaeda can use "cybermobilization" to leverage the effects of terrorist attacks in an unprecedented way.[4] If a group is truly successful in mobilizing large numbers, this strategy can prolong the fight and may enable the threat to transition to other forms, including insurgency and even conventional war.

These four strategies may be joined by a fifth, related strategy: to erode a state's fundamental legitimacy at home and abroad in order to weaken and isolate it. Eroding legitimacy undermines a state's other foreign and defense policy goals and may change the fabric of the state itself in ways that complicate its ability to develop alliances with other states or governments. France in the first Algerian war and Russia in the first Chechen war are two examples.[5] In the Algerian war, prominent Americans, including then senator John F. Kennedy, supported the FLN, not least because the U.S.-allied French were allegedly engaging in torture. And the Russians' initial response to the Chechens was considered so brutal that the international community soundly condemned it.[6]

Because relatively weak nonstate actors are the primary practitioners of terrorism, there are far more examples historically of strategies of leverage used by terrorist groups than any other type. A group may use a combination of several, or even all, of these strategies, but what a government does in response to terrorist attacks is what matters. Reactions by a state in the narrow framework of one strategy may be counterproductive with respect to the others.

Democracies are not well designed to handle strategies of leverage, especially in the short term. They tend to make decisions that directly or indirectly reflect their constituencies. At a time when the people are hurt, angered, and may be clamoring for justice or revenge, dispassionate strategic calculation can be virtually impossible, particularly if a state has little experience with terrorist attacks and thus no historical context within which to place them. The natural brakes on democratic war making are actually *accelerators* in counterterrorism. Counterterrorism strategies that are designed to prevent a state from being compelled by a group break down if the goal is to provoke a state, polarize a population, or mobilize a constituency. The result is that the campaign may be unwittingly extended.

But unless they grossly overreact and lose the support of their constituencies, democracies have a crucial advantage in dealing with strategies of leverage over the long term: the capacity to survive and learn from trial and error. Of course, even better is for states to skip the trial and error and gain from someone else's experience of ending terror campaigns. That is what we will examine next.

Myths about the Ending of Terrorism

There are several common beliefs about how terrorist campaigns end that are either flatly wrong or at the very least based on incomplete and misleading information. In examining the closing phases of hundreds of groups as part of a multiyear research project undertaken for my book, *How Terrorism Ends*, I was surprised by what emerged.

The first myth is that dealing with the causes of terrorism will always lead to its end. There is in fact a weak relationship between beginnings and endings, and the historical record contradicts the belief that the causes of a terrorist campaign persist throughout its course and are crucial to ending it. Far more often, a group's motivations to launch attacks evolve over time. The original objectives sought in a particular campaign are often only loosely related to why it stops. Terrorist campaigns rarely achieve their initial goals, and as the campaigns unfold, evolving dynamics within a group often eclipse external factors.

The launching of a campaign alters the strategic landscape in ways that are irreversible. Most often, the strategic or "outcome goals" (in economic parlance) that first spark a campaign, like popular suffrage, self-determination, minority rights, control over territory, a new

14

system of government, and so forth, are overtaken by tactical "process goals," such as revenge, retaliation, protecting sunk costs, consolidating a group, and the need to show strength.[7] When a campaign is already under way, it becomes imperative for policymakers to be aware of the give-and-take, to recognize their part in it, adapt to it, and focus on a conclusion.

It is also crucial that they be aware of the audiences that are observing the campaign and how they are reacting to events, because they are often the key to the end. Understanding the causes of terrorism may be no more important to ending a campaign than understanding the causes of war is to ending it: naturally, the question has relevance, but it is overshadowed by the dynamic of the conflict itself as it unfolds.

A second myth is that terrorism is entirely situation dependent and can only be understood in the specific context of a particular group or cause. This one has pervaded the post-9/11 analysis of terrorism in the United States: when al Qaeda appeared, many analysts argued that it was unique. It is true that the particulars of a given campaign are vital, including its historical, political, social, and economic circumstances, not to mention its ideology, tactics, constituency, motivations, structure, and so forth. There is no shortcut for in-depth, even painstaking analysis of each organization. But terrorist campaigns often display a kind of contagion effect and are designed with the lessons of predecessors or contemporaries in mind.[8]

In al Qaeda's case, for example, there are scores of cross-cultural, cross-regional "lessons learned" studies that have been done by members of the movement and then shared among the group. Those translated into English alone cover predecessors as disparate as the Red Army Faction and the Red Brigades, Harakat al-Dawla al-Islamiyya in Algeria and the Islamic Army of Aden Abyan in Yemen, the Janjaweed movement in Southern Sudan, and leftist movements in Central and South America. Especially in our globalized age, groups that use terrorism study and mimic other groups that use terrorism. Naturally, there are differences between them, but the value in comparatively studying groups consists in determining what the similarities and differences *are*.

A third myth is that today's brand of terrorism is especially dangerous and more likely to persist in the present era than in earlier times. Some people argue that what's important and impressive about terrorism is not that it ends but that it endures.[9] Quite a few scholars in recent years have written about the effectiveness of terrorism in manipulating state action.[10] But are groups that use terrorism really so successful?

In doing the research for my book, I studied hundreds of groups.[11] I was very careful about how groups were selected, omitting those that had only one attack or one small set of attacks, for example. Of the 475 (of 873) groups in the RAND/MIPT (Memorial Institute for the Prevention of Terrorism) database that deliberately targeted noncombatants and engaged in a series of attacks (thus a campaign), the average life span was only about eight years.[12] Estimates given by others are even shorter: long-standing terrorism expert David Rapoport argues that 90 percent last less than a year.[13] And the degree to which they have failed to achieve their aims is even more remarkable: in my study, only a small minority, about 5 percent, have by their own standards succeeded in achieving their aims.

Terrorism is not a promising vocation: it always ends. The challenge is to determine how a given group is most likely to end, and then consciously push it in that direction by confounding its strategies as they unfold.

Patterns of Endings for Terrorist Groups

Seven general pathways out of terrorism emerge from careful study of the modern history of the phenomenon. As I have explained in other writings, these include the destruction of the leadership, failure to transition between generations, achievement of the cause, a process of negotiations, military or police repression, loss of popular support, and reorientation to other malignant behavior, such as criminality or conventional war.[14]

Of course, not all of these seven are equally probable for each group, and they are certainly not all applicable to al Qaeda. For example, it is obvious that al Qaeda will not end if Osama bin Laden is killed. While there are ample other reasons to target him, groups that have ended through decapitation have been hierarchically structured, reflecting to some degree a cult of personality and lacking a viable successor—none of which describes al Qaeda. It will also not die out between generations, as al Qaeda has already shown itself to be a multigenerational threat.

Likewise, achieving the cause will not happen. Groups that histori-cally have achieved their ends have done so by setting forth a clear and limited aim. At least as articulated in recent years, al Qaeda's aims are to mobilize the *umma* to rise up, throw off the influence of the West, eliminate its support for so-called apostate Arab regimes, and establish a new order (sometimes called a caliphate). These objectives could not be achieved without overturning the interna-tional political and economic system, and there is no evidence that the group has moved closer to achieving them. In short, these three pathways to the end are irrelevant to al Qaeda.

But the other four patterns bear closer examination. Negotiations, for example, can lead to the achievement of some aims of a group and the short-term decline of terrorist activity, the Provisional IRA's 1998 Good Friday Agreement being the best-known example. But of course, this pathway to the end is always much more complicated than the mere pursuit of a negotiated agreement. Parties on both sides of the table may splinter as a result of talks. Indeed, dividing groups can be a purpose of negotiations, potentially strangling the most radical factions. The problem is that splintering may just as easily occur on the status quo (usually pro-government) side, as happened with the Ulster Volunteer Force in Northern Ireland when the British government entered the negotiations. The decision to negotiate is a tricky calculation for any government.

Close examination of the historical record indicates that transition-ing to a negotiations process as a means to the end requires feasible terms and a sense of stalemate in the struggle. And members of groups favoring negotiations typically seek a way out of what they consider to be a losing cause. Even if policymakers could stomach talking to the leaders of al Qaeda (which is frankly impossible), none of these factors describe the situation we are in with this group. Negotiations with the core of al Qaeda are highly unlikely.

But there is a small caveat to this statement: "Al Qaeda" is not a unified group. Negotiations with local affiliates that have only recently joined the movement may be unavoidable. Many local nationalist groups have associated themselves with a broader move-ment whose aims are so sweeping that they cannot possibly repre-sent local grievances, some of which may have some merit.

Not all the organizations that are labeled "al Qaeda" share the narrow vision of its Egyptian- and Saudi-dominated leadership. The movement is full of discord. It would be foolish to act as if groups as disparate as the Bangladeshi Jihad Movement, Abu Sayyaf (the Philippines), the Eastern Turkistan Movement (Xinjiang, China), and Allah's Brigade (Palestine) all share exactly the same goals.[15] The United States and its allies must disaggregate the al Qaeda threat, enlarge its internal inconsistencies, and deal with local issues on a local level—in short, policymakers must stop generalizing about the movement, learn to tolerate complexity, and use it to advantage.

Military or police repression can nudge a group toward the end, as was the case with Russia's Narodnaya Volya and Peru's Sendero Luminoso. Yet while the military campaign against al Qaeda has yielded some important gains, driving the core of the organization into hiding and sharply reducing its operational capacity, the limitations of this approach have been amply demonstrated.

Democracies find it difficult to sustain a policy of repression: the approach carries high resource and opportunity costs, often undermines civil liberties, and erodes domestic support over time. While the use of U.S. military force overseas has demonstrated Western strength, killed many of al Qaeda's leaders, and prevented some attacks, it cannot single-handedly drive al Qaeda toward its end. That would require a kind of scorched-earth policy that a democracy like the United States (not to mention American allies) would never tolerate.

The loss of popular support leads to the demise of many campaigns, and this is a promising scenario for al Qaeda. Popular support may dissipate for a number of reasons. There may be harsh government counteraction, the offer of a better alternative, removal of state sponsorship, or a sense that the ideology has been rendered irrelevant. Another possibility is that a group fails to present a positive image of its goals, or palpable progress toward those goals, both of which apply to al Qaeda.

But the most important way to lose popular support is through the group's own miscalculations, especially targeting errors. Poorly targeted violence has backfired against groups as disparate as the Real Irish Republican Army (the Omagh bombings), Egypt's GAI (the Luxor killings), and Italy's Red Brigades (the killing of Aldo Moro). Attacks may cause revulsion among a group's actual or potential public constituency: at least one-third of the victims of al Qaeda–claimed attacks have been Muslims, the very people that al Qaeda claims to be championing.

Finally, terrorist groups can morph into something else. They may transition out of terrorism toward mainly criminal behavior or even escalate toward full insurgency or conventional war (especially if they are supported by—or are perceived as supported by—a state). Some argue that a transition to insurgency has already happened with al Qaeda.[16] If that is so, it would be a bad outcome. Insurgencies have longer average life spans than terrorist campaigns, and in recent history, insurgents have also won more frequently.

It is counterproductive to speak of the al Qaeda movement as a "global insurgency," because the phrase bestows legitimacy, emphasizes territorial control, glosses over huge disparities in the movement, and puts the United States into an unfortunate strategic framework that precludes clear-eyed analysis of the time-honored strategies of leverage that the al Qaeda leadership is effectively using against the United States. In this connection, it is worth remembering that al Qaeda has already catalyzed two conventional wars.

Conclusion

The al Qaeda movement is most likely either to implode or to transition to another form of violence. Which path it takes depends at least in part on what the United States and U.S. allies do. The al Qaeda movement can still do serious damage, but treating it as a new, monolithic threat like the Communist menace is profoundly counterproductive and makes it seem stronger and more united than it is. The most effective way to nudge it toward implosion is to confound the classic strategies of leverage being employed by the leadership. The United States can exploit the ample weaknesses of this movement, enlarging its inconsistencies and hypocrisies so as to confound its ability to mobilize, for example, even while engaging in a carefully constructed counterthrust of our own.

A grand strategy of countermobilization would have five key elements: First, it is crucial to clarify to global audiences what "al Qaeda" is and what it is not. Western policymakers must stop applying the al Qaeda name to each group that claims an association with the movement or whose attacks al Qaeda claims. The core, broader nebula, localized factions, and individuals each have a plethora of aims and local interests. These disparate groups have only rage and humiliation in common; beyond that, they share no common concept of the future.

Second, the United States must work with local governments to exploit the internal cleavages in this movement, employing nuanced policies that hive off local constituents. On a case-by-case basis, this may even involve negotiating with some, or at least demonstrating a far more sophisticated understanding of their specific grievances.

Third, the United States must spotlight al Qaeda's mistakes. When groups claiming an association with al Qaeda use human shields, kill women and children, damage the economy, undermine the stability of the community, and slaughter Muslims, the United States must do a much better job of publicizing it. Al Qaeda's command-and-control over local activities is poor: Stupid actions committed in its name should be labeled "al Qaeda" and advertised. The movement is providing ample ammunition to use against it this way, more powerful in its potential strategic effects than scores of counterinsurgency operations and confirmed kills in this "war," yet we are missing it.

Fourth, we must facilitate or work with the backlash that is under way against this movement, or at least avoid making our own mistakes that prevent it. Our goal should not be "winning hearts and minds" but facilitating al Qaeda's tendency to lose them. Held up to the light, al Qaeda's strategy is self-defeating: it is killing the very people on whose behalf it claims to be acting.

Fifth, in this time of huge budget deficits and overstretched military assets, American policymakers must move beyond open-ended commitments and arguments over metrics in the "war on terrorism" and focus on a pragmatic plan for defeating al Qaeda. From September 12, 2001, our aim should have been to end al Qaeda's ability to do us harm. Instead, we inflated our goals, committing the elementary errors of failing to clarify our strategic objective, align ends and means, and adhere to the principle of conservation of enemies. Now we are paying the price.

The important question for policymakers in the midst of this terrorist campaign is not "how are we doing?" but rather "how will it end?" And the second vital question is not "When will the next attack be?" but rather "What will we do after that?"

The strategies of terrorism emerge from and reflect unique historical, political, and social contexts that are constantly evolving. But terrorist groups end in certain consistent ways. The crucial challenge is to determine which of the patterns of endings fits a given group, hasten the process as it unfolds, and push it further in that direction.

Policymakers who become caught up in the short-term goals and spectacle of terrorist attacks relinquish the broader historical perspective that is crucial to the reassertion of state power and legitimacy. Terrorism's classic strategies of leverage are deliberately designed to exploit such mistakes. Consciously driving a terrorist campaign like al Qaeda's toward its end is much better than answering the tactical elements of the movement as it unfolds, and it is also far more likely to result in success.

2. Terrorism as a Product of Choices and Perceptions

James J. F. Forest

Throughout the past several decades, and particularly since the attacks of September 11, 2001, much has been written and said about the root causes of terrorism. In fact, an entire field of study has developed to help us understand why this complex phenomenon emerges in some contexts (and not others) and what the major contributing factors to terrorism appear to be.[1] Drawing from these studies, this chapter addresses the need to understand the mechanisms and tools that frame the relationships between the individual, the organization, and the environment. The chapter then offers several propositions to describe these relationships, highlighting the importance of strategic communication, public diplomacy, and counterideology as critical components of a robust counterterrorism strategy. It concludes by suggesting some implications for U.S. policymakers, focusing on how the United States might become more effective at influencing street-level perceptions and interpretations of policies and conditions that terrorist groups have used to justify their violent actions.

Two Frames of Analysis

There are two frames of analysis for considering the motivations that animate terrorists. First, the "static frame" of analysis identifies individual and organizational characteristics, the environmental conditions that produce grievances among members of a population, and the environmental conditions that facilitate opportunities to conduct violence (including weapons trafficking and porous borders). The second frame describes an individual's engagement in (or disengagement from) terrorist activities as a process involving complex interactions between individuals, organizations, and environments, as well as the perceptions and convictions generated by these interactions. This "dynamic interactions" frame suggests that understanding the processes of action and reaction—structurally framed by relationships (political, socioeconomic, ethnic, etc.)—between individuals and organizations within a particular environment is a necessary first step toward identifying situational, contextually relevant counterterrorism strategies.

For this discussion, the terms "terrorism" and "terrorist activity" are used interchangeably to indicate a broad category of actions that range from the kinetic (e.g., bombings, kidnappings, hijackings, and other kinds of violence that kills or destroys property) to funding, recruitment, safe haven, and other types of activity on which violent groups depend. In essence, these activities are viewed as a product of characteristics and conditions combined with interactions between the choices of individuals, organizations, and their environmental dimensions. Constructing our analysis in this way can help illuminate patterns of interaction that are consistent across several contexts and can yield insights for what can be described as "influence warfare"—efforts by states to influence the choices individuals make toward (or against) engaging in any kind of terrorist activity.[2]

Examinations of the so-called root causes or risk factors of terrorism have pointed to a variety of individual and organizational characteristics, and to the effect of both political and socioeconomic conditions.[3] Gifted scholars like Martha Crenshaw, Jeffrey Ian Ross, and Assaf Moghadam have offered typologies and models that help clarify and categorize these factors, highlighting similar precipitant conditions, triggers, and opportunities for actions, both locally and globally.[4] Efforts to summarize and synthesize these typologies and other studies can yield different visual representations of how various risk factors and levels of analysis intersect and overlap.

To begin with, there is ample research on individual characteristics—including psychological influences, kinship, belief system, and grievances (like revenge or perceptions of injustice)—that contribute to a person's motivations for engaging in terrorist activity. There are also numerous studies on the leadership, membership, history, and ideology of terrorist organizations. But perhaps the broadest category of research on "root causes" or "risk factors" of terrorism examines the structural risks for terrorist activity (e.g., socioeconomic, political, and other conditions that give legitimacy to an individual's grievances), as well as the triggering events and facilitators involved. Figure 2.1 attempts to capture at least the primary

Figure 2.1
THE STATIC FRAME: OBSERVATIONS OF CHARACTERISTICS AND
CONDITIONS THAT CONTRIBUTE TO THE RISK OF TERRORIST
ACTIVITY (♦)

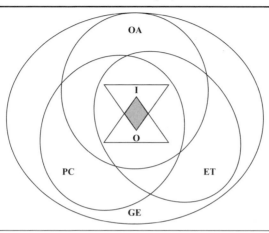

CODES	INCLUDES ITEMS SUCH AS:
I Individual characteristics	Personal motivations for action, including psychological influences, kinship, belief system, and grievances (like revenge, perceptions of injustice)
O Organizational characteristics	Leadership, membership, history, an ideology that articulates seemingly legitimate grievances, along with strategies to mitigate them
PC Precipitant conditions	Structural reasons why an ideology resonates; socioeconomic, political, and other conditions that generate (or give legitimacy to) grievances
ET Environmental triggers	Specific actions, policies, and events that enhance the perceived need for action (very dynamic and time relevant) within a particular environment
OA Opportunities to act	Facilitators like access to weapons; freedom of movement; funding; safe haven/state sponsorship; weak governments; and porous borders
GE Global environment	Interdependent economies, interstate conflicts, diaspora, transnational criminal networks, the Internet, etc. that influence local conditions and opportunities

SOURCE: author.

25

categories of risk factors that terrorism scholars have examined over the past several decades. While an exhaustive account of the research in each of these categories far exceeds the scope of this chapter, what follows provides some highlights from the individual, organizational, and environmental levels of analysis.

While studies have illuminated multiple factors contributing to a greater risk of terrorism, they are often brief snapshots in time and are thus unable to adequately account for elements of time, perceptions, and the nature of dynamic interactions between individuals, organizations, and their environment. More importantly, this research may lead to overly simplistic explanations of how a given factor "causes" terrorism, while minimizing the dimension of individual agency. Since terrorism is "caused" by an individual's choosing to conduct terrorist activity, it is important to understand the interpretations and influences on which individuals make choices. Thus, a second frame of analysis, illustrated in Figure 2.2, can be combined with the previous frame to help account for the variables of time, perceptions, and interpretive influences.

Using these two frames together, one can explore the phenomenon of terrorism through a sort of bifocal lens, one focused on characteristics and conditions, the other focused on perceptions and dynamic interactions. This analysis helps us understand the means (including ideologies, myths, symbols, social networks, and the Internet) that frame the relationships between the individual, the organization, and the environment. The following propositions can illustrate these relationships, which emphasize the importance of perceptions and influences behind an individual's choice to engage in (or disengage from) terrorist activity.

Seven Propositions from a Dual-Frame Analysis of Terrorism

1. Individual choice (even if reluctant or coerced) is the primary "cause" of terrorist activity. Some individuals choose direct involvement in actions that kill, whereas others choose to engage in support activities, like providing funding, safe haven, or ideological support. But whatever a given person does that is terrorism related, the chances are good that that person chose to do it.[5]

2. Psychological and socioeconomic traits influence an individual's decision to engage in (or disengage from) terrorist activity.

Figure 2.2
THE DYNAMIC INTERACTIONS FRAME: INCORPORATING TIME, PERCEPTIONS, AND INTERPRETIVE INFLUENCES

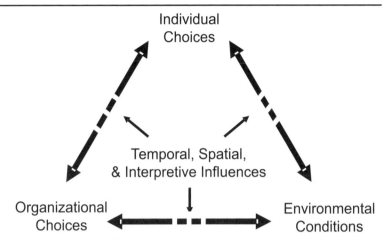

Individual
Choices

Temporal, Spatial,
& Interpretive Influences

Organizational
Choices

Environmental
Conditions

Terrorism as product of choices informed by dynamic interactions between individuals, organizations, and environmental conditions, influenced by time and space considerations and by whoever and whatever help us interpret the world around us.

SOURCE: author.

These factors also influence his or her perceptions toward and interactions with specific organizations and environmental conditions. In other words, an individual's involvement in or disassociation from terrorist activity occurs at the intersection of ideas, perceptions, and opportunities. Further, the nature of these characteristics, perceptions, and interactions change over time. From a counterterrorism standpoint, the importance of this line of reasoning is that ideas and perceptions about environmental conditions, opportunities, and organizations can be influenced.

3. An individual's family, peers, role models, and others who help interpret and contextualize local and global conditions influence his or her perceptions toward and interactions with a terrorist organization and the surrounding environment. These are examples of the kinds of interpretive influences or credible

voices that must play a role in a government's strategic communications effort.[6]

4. The members of terrorist organizations influence an individual's decisions about terrorist activity by providing ideological justification for violence, along with training and expertise, material support, and connections with others. This proposition emphasizes the importance of understanding terrorist ideology, especially where and why a particular organization's ideology resonates.

5. Individual decisions (within and outside the organization) shape an organization's choices with respect to what constitutes acceptable terrorist activity. The organization swims in a sea of people; without individuals, there is no organization. An important point here is that perceptions of an organization's leadership, especially its competence and personal agendas, are vital and can be undermined.

6. The motivations and opportunities for individuals to engage in terrorism are framed by their views toward environmental conditions and policies (domestic and foreign), some of which are used to legitimize an organization's ideology. Addressing perceptions of environmental conditions—including triggers, precipitant conditions, opportunities, and the impact of the global environment—is an important aspect of a strategic communications effort.

7. And of course, the actions of individuals and the organizations they compose produce a wide range of effects on their surrounding environment. The simple laws of physics—action and reaction—affect the trajectory of all armed conflicts.

The next part of this chapter provides support for these seven propositions and is organized around the three levels of analysis (individual, organizational, and environmental conditions) described earlier.

On Individuals

To begin with, it must be reiterated that the *primary cause* of terrorism is a human being's decision to commit some form of terrorist activity. Some individuals choose direct involvement in actions that kill, while others choose to provide funding, safe haven, or ideological support. Although a variety of factors influence a person's decision to engage in terrorist activity—from kinship and ideology to the availability of weapons and criminal network connections—the dimension of individually *choosing* to commit a terrorist act is central. Even the relatively few known "reluctant" terrorists had to decide at some point whether to pull that trigger, detonate that bomb, transfer those funds, or perform some other specific act that would lead to death and destruction. Thus, a considerable amount of research in this field examines the personal motivations behind an individual's choice to engage in terrorist activity, including psychological influences, kinship, belief system, and grievances (like perceptions of injustice). Scholars have cited the importance of a person's hatred of others, desire for power or revenge, despair, risk tolerance, unbreakable loyalty to friends or family who are already involved in a violent movement, prior participation in a radical political movement, thirst for excitement and adventure, and many other types of motivations.

Research in this area typically focuses on background characteristics of individuals who have engaged in terrorist activity (e.g., emphasizing the role of psychological traits, gender, age, socioeconomic status, and religiosity).[7] Thus, academic disciplines that study human behavior, particularly the field of psychology, can contribute much to our understanding of what motivates individuals to choose terrorism. According to renowned psychologist Max Taylor, much of this research has attempted to describe personal characteristics of terrorists, on the assumption that terrorists can be identified by these attributes.[8] Surely, many have argued, terrorists are individuals with anti-social or other personality disorders that drive them toward terrorist activity, and, therefore, we can derive some form of "terrorist mindset." For example, Jerrold Post's research led him to coin the term "psycho-logic" to describe how terrorists construct a personal rationalization for acts they are psychologically compelled to commit.[9] In essence, a polarizing and absolutist "us versus them" rhetoric employed by terrorists reflects their underlying views of "the establishment" as the source of all evil and provides a psychologically satisfying explanation for what has gone wrong in their lives; a "psychopolitics of hatred."[10]

Proponents of similar psychological explanations for terrorism describe individuals consumed by hatred toward others and willing to kill without remorse or regard for those who may die from their terrorist act.[11] Walter Lacquer has argued that "madness, especially paranoia, plays a role in contemporary terrorism. Not all paranoiacs are terrorists, but all terrorists believe in conspiracies by the powerful, hostile forces and suffer from some form of delusion and persecution mania."[12] Others have suggested that an emphasis on rote memorization and an unwillingness to challenge authority may contribute to an individual's susceptibility to indoctrination by terrorist groups.[13]

Overall, these and various other studies in psychology have sought to illuminate a unique set of attributes that contribute to terrorism. There is clearly a demand for it among policymakers and the general public who seek clarity in what is in fact a very complex problem.[14] However, the most common result of research in this area actually reveals a pattern of "normalcy"—that is, the absence of any unique attribute or identifier that would distinguish one individual from another.[15]

Clark McCauley has observed that "30 years of research has found little evidence that terrorists are suffering from psychopathology,"[16] and Marc Sageman concurs, noting how "experts on terrorism have tried in vain for three decades to identify a common predisposition for terrorism."[17] Sociologist Martha Crenshaw also agrees with these scholars in declining to ascribe abnormal pathology to terrorists, arguing instead that terrorists' actions are the product of a strategic, rational choice.[18] Overall, there is no single psychology of terrorism, no unified theory.[19] The broad diversity of personal motivations for becoming a terrorist undermines the possibility of a single, common "terrorist mindset." Thus, profiling individuals based on some type of perceived propensity to conduct terrorist attacks becomes extremely difficult, if not altogether impossible.[20]

This inability to profile reinforces the importance of individual choice; that is, individuals from virtually *any* background can choose to engage in terrorist activity. Thus, an especially promising area of research on the individual risk of terrorist activity uses phrases and metaphors like "pathways to radicalization" and "staircase to terrorism" to describe a dynamic process of psychological development that leads an individual to participate in terrorist activity.[21] In one particularly noteworthy example, Max Taylor and John Horgan offer a framework for analyzing developmental processes—"a sequence of events involving steps or operations that are usefully ordered and/or interdependent"—through which an individual becomes involved with (and sometimes abandons) terrorist activity.[22]

Each day, countless individuals grapple with situations and environmental conditions that may generate feelings of outrage and powerlessness, among many other potential motivators for becoming violent. But an individual's view of these situations and conditions—and how to respond to them appropriately—is clearly influenced by his or her family members, peers and personal role models, educators, religious leaders, and others who help interpret and contextualize local and global conditions. Because these interpretive influences play such a key role in how an individual responds to the challenges of everyday life, we sometimes see a contagion effect, whereby an individual's likelihood of becoming involved in terrorism is increased because he or she knows or respects others who have already done so.

An individual's interpersonal connections also help frame the potential legitimacy of an organization that has adopted terrorism. According to Michael Leiter, director of the National Counterterrorism Center, friends, family members, and authority figures in their community are among those who introduce individuals to the fringes of violent extremist groups.[23] For example, psychologist Sageman has argued that social bonds play a central role in the emergence of the global Salafi jihad, the movement whose members compose organizations like al Qaeda and Jemaah Islamiyah.[24] As described in the next section, an organization that is perceived as legitimate can influence an individual's perceptions of environmental conditions and what to do about them. In sum, a central component of any terrorism analysis should be an understanding of the dynamic nature of an individual's interactions with and perceptions toward his or her environment and specific organizations, along with the many developmental processes into, through, and out of terrorist activity.

On Organizations

For many years, esteemed scholars like Martha Crenshaw, Bruce Hoffman, Louise Richardson, Daniel Benjamin, and Steve Simon have illuminated the special qualities of terrorist organizations that help develop an individual's will and ability to kill.[25] Within these organizations, the most salient attributes include ideology, strategy, leadership, history, and membership—especially individuals who bring practical knowledge about (and possibly connections to others who can assist with) acquiring weapons, funds, and intelligence for the group. These and other attributes contribute to operational success, increase the group's chances of achieving at least some of its objectives, and subsequently help determine the likelihood of attracting recruits and various forms of support. Organizations can play a critical role in shaping an individual's trajectory toward terrorism by interpreting environmental conditions and events in particular ways. They also offer ways and means to engage in terrorist activity. Few individuals have all the requisite knowledge and connections to be effective terrorists, and this is a primary motivator for joining a group or social network within which their terrorist aspirations can be achieved. Of course, while individual terrorists like Carlos the Jackal or Theodore Kaczynski have caused considerable suffering, they are the exceptions; in general terms, it is difficult to overstate the importance of group membership or affiliation in the world of terrorism.

Terrorist experts like Ehud Sprinzak and Ariel Merari have demonstrated how these organizations recruit individuals who evolve gradually into terrorists through a radicalization process involving a disengagement of moral self-sanctions from violent conduct.[26] In exploring this "moral disengagement," renowned psychologist Albert Bandura identified several developmental processes that can disengage morality from an individual's conduct, such as reconstruing conduct as serving moral purposes, obscuring personal agency in bad activities, disregarding consequences of actions, and blaming or dehumanizing victims.[27]

A terrorist group's ideology can play a particularly vital role in an individual's decision to engage in terrorist activity by sanctioning harmful conduct as honorable and righteous. These ideologies typically articulate a set of grievances (including socioeconomic disadvantages and a lack of justice or political freedoms) that are seen as legitimate among a target audience, along with strategies to mitigate them.[28] Usually, but not always, the strategies they put forward require joining or at least supporting the organization—thus, an ideology also provides a group identity and highlights the common characteristics of individuals who adhere to, or are potential adherents of, the ideology. According to Assaf Moghadam, "Ideologies are links between thoughts, beliefs and myths on the one hand, and action on the other hand . . . [providing] a 'cognitive map' that filters the way social realities are perceived, rendering that reality easier to grasp, more coherent, and thus more meaningful."[29]

Research by Andrew Kydd and Barbara Walter indicates that terrorist organizations are usually driven by political objectives, and, in particular, "five have had enduring importance: regime change, territorial change, policy change, social control and status quo maintenance."[30] Terrorist groups view violence as an effective vehicle for political change, often pointing to historical examples of terrorism playing a key role in driving the United States (and later Israel) out of Lebanon and convincing the French to pull out of Algeria. Ethnic separatist groups like the Liberation Tigers of Tamil Eelam in Sri Lanka, the Abu Sayyaf Group in the Philippines, and the Euskadi Ta Askatasuna in Spain all want the power to form their own recognized, sovereign entity, carved out of an existing nation-state, and they believe terrorist attacks can help them achieve this objective. Groups engaged in the Middle East conflict—like the Al Aqsa Martyrs Brigades, Hamas, the Palestinian Islamic Jihad, and the Palestine Liberation Front—want the power to establish an Islamic Palestinian state. Other groups want to establish an Islamic state in their own region, including Ansar al-Islam in Iraq, Al-Shabaab in Somalia, Al Gamaa al-Islamiyya in Egypt, Islamic Jihad Union in Central Asia, and Jemaah Islamiyah in Southeast Asia.[31] In all cases, these groups seek the power to change the status quo and forge a future that they do not believe will come about peacefully, and they are determined to use terrorism to achieve their objectives.

There are also important psychological and other reasons that draw individuals toward membership in a terrorist organization. For example, as Jerrold Post argues, the need of individuals to belong and exercise control in their own lives is intensified in communities where segments of the population are ostracized or persecuted based on ethnic, religious, or social backgrounds. By belonging to a radical group, otherwise powerless individuals become powerful. Group identity provides a foundation of relative stability on which disenfranchised or isolated members of a society build a base of commonality and join together.[32] Bard O'Neil and Donald Alberts have described how organizations provide a blend of ideological and material incentives that meet an individual's need for belonging, identity, and rectifying perceived injustice. Once individuals have joined or otherwise actively supported terrorist groups for ideological reasons, it is difficult to win them back because of the psychological and emotional investments they have made.[33] Other reasons individuals join these groups include a perception of rewards for participating in terrorism, friendships and camaraderie that lead to and are solidified within the terror cell or organization, and the perceived opportunity to attain a higher social status derived from group membership.

A terrorist group's ideology plays a central role in all this, but an ideology has no power unless it resonates within the social, political, and historical context of those whose support the organization requires. The resonance of an organization's ideology is largely based on a combination of persuasive communicators, the compelling nature of the grievances articulated, and the pervasiveness of local conditions that seem to justify an organization's rationale for the use of violence in order to mitigate those grievances. When an organization's ideology resonates among its target audience, it can influence an individual's perceptions and help determine the form of his or her "decision tree," a menu of potential options for future action that may include terrorism.

Support for terrorism among community members can rise and fall over time, and the ideologies of many organizations have not had long-lasting resonance. Over the past two decades, ideologies that have seen a significant decline in support include the nationalist/separatists and the Marxist/Communists, while there has been a significant increase among Islamist and other religious groups, environmentalists, and right-wing extremists. Resonance and support are also influenced by the choices made by individuals within an organization about the kinds of terrorist activity they conduct. How organizations choreograph violence matters; in particular, terrorist groups must avoid counterproductive violence that can lead to a loss of support from the community. From this perspective, it is particularly useful to incorporate research on how organizational dynamics influence the various forms of terrorism chosen by that organization. For example, Mia Bloom has demonstrated how suicide terrorism can be thought of as a competitive strategy, where individual terrorist organizations contend for the attention of various audiences and, consequently, resources (both money and members).[34] Similarly, this research has shown how groups can become more radical in response to environmental and policy changes (including new threats from security forces) and internal competition and/or tensions (e.g., pressures from charismatic leaders to take more violent action).

Overall, successful terrorist organizations capitalize on an environment in which their ideology resonates and their grievances are considered legitimate by smart, competent individuals who are then motivated to act either with or on behalf of the organization. The likelihood of ideological resonance is greater when members of a community are desperate for justice, social agency, human dignity, a sense of belonging, or positive identity (especially when surrounded by a variety of depressingly negative environmental conditions) and experience intense outrage or hatred of a specific entity because of its actions (real or perceived). How a local environment sustains a terrorist organization depends largely on how individuals within the community view the opportunities for that organization's success. The past also matters: Is there a history of political violence either locally or within the surrounding region? Are there regional examples of success or failure of terrorism? As discussed in the next section, terrorist organizations thrive in an environment where they can find weapons and safe haven, communicate, transport humans and materiel, attract financial and other forms of support, and provoke a draconian government response that further validates their ideological rationale for violent action. Environmental and structural conditions (and perceptions thereof) influence both organizational and individual characteristics and direct their strategic choices and rationales toward violence. Indeed, the old maxim that "all politics is local" holds true for political violence as well. Thus, the third and most expansive—and from a counterterrorism perspective, perhaps the most important—level of analysis examines the environmental conditions surrounding existing or burgeoning terrorist movements.

On Environmental Conditions

Environmental conditions can be a primary source of legitimacy and resonance for a terrorist group's ideology and a central factor behind an individual's willingness to participate in terrorist activity.

The relevant environmental conditions can be loosely organized around four somewhat overlapping categories: precipitant conditions, environmental triggers, opportunities to act, and global environmental factors (see Figure 2.1).[35]

Precipitant conditions are described as structural reasons why a terrorist organization's ideology resonates among a particular audience. Here, scholars have drawn links between terrorism and local conditions, like government oppression or corruption, foreign occupation, poverty, discrimination (ethnic, racial, religious), injustice (real or perceived), and a lack of political or socioeconomic opportunities.[36] Researchers have collectively assembled a broad and colorful landscape of the many structural issues that must be addressed by governments seeking to reduce the risk of terrorism. How local communities perceive these issues must also be addressed, as oftentimes politically violent groups will seek to convince others that things are far worse than they truly are.

Environmental triggers are specific actions, policies, and events that enhance the perceived need for action among members of a community. These triggers are very dynamic, time-relevant, and seized on by the propagandists of terrorist organizations in their attempts to enhance the resonance of their ideology. Types of triggers include a change in government policy, the suspension of civil liberties, a banning of political parties, the introduction of new censorship and draconian antiterrorist laws, an erosion in the security environment, a widely publicized incident of police brutality or invasive surveillance, or a sudden regime change, like an assassination.[37]

A trigger is not necessarily a relatively quick or contained event. For example, research by Paul Ehrlich and Jack Liu suggests that persistent demographic and socioeconomic factors can facilitate transnational terrorism and make it easier to recruit terrorists.[38] Similarly, the National Intelligence Council's 2025 Project report notes that pending "youth bulges" in many Arab states could contribute to a rise in political violence and civil conflict.[39] Any potential triggers are far more likely to enhance a terrorist organization's ideological resonance when the structural conditions described earlier are already a source of grievances and when individuals and organizations perceive ample opportunities to engage in terrorism.

Opportunities to act can encompass the structural or temporary conditions at the community or regional level that facilitate various forms of terrorist activity. Examples include significant access to weapons and explosives, a general sense of lawlessness, freedom of movement, availability of funding and safe haven, state sponsorship, a weak government, or incompetent security apparatus. Countries with a robust "shadow economy" (economic activities that are underground, covert, or illegal) can provide an infrastructure for terrorist organizations to operate in, whereby financing becomes easier and detecting it becomes more difficult.[40]

On a global level, the Internet provides numerous new opportunities for terrorist groups to influence and draw support from a global audience.[41] Al Qaeda is a pioneer of online terrorist-oriented activity, from soliciting and moving funds to disseminating propaganda videos and military instruction manuals in multiple languages. Terrorists use thousands of websites as virtual training camps, providing an online forum for indoctrination as well as the distribution of terrorist manuals and instructions. They can also capture information about the users who browse their websites, which can be useful for the early stages of recruitment.[42] Indeed, al Qaeda leaders view those at the center of their information strategy—the website designers, bloggers, and video editors—as important mujahideen. As Abu Yahya al-Libi recently declared, "May Allah bless you lions of the front, for by Allah, the fruits of your combined efforts—sound, video, and text—are more severe for the infidels and their lackeys than the falling of rockets and missiles on their heads."[43]

Certain kinds of physical and cultural geography can also provide opportunities for terrorist groups to thrive. Urban population growth, where jobs and educational opportunities are increasingly unavailable, can result in greater levels of discontent, crime, and urban instability that terrorist groups can capitalize on.[44] An environmental trigger may also create an opportunity to act. For example, a sudden regime change may create an anarchic environment in which groups find greater freedom to obtain weapons and conduct criminal and violent activity. Terrorist groups will capitalize on events from which they could benefit strategically, tactically, or operationally. Certainly, political instability provides many such opportunities.[45]

A terrorist group's opportunities to act are greatly enhanced by the availability of small arms and light weapons.[46] Small-arms proliferation has allowed armed groups to challenge the primacy of the state and to create conditions of instability that provide aid and comfort to criminal and terrorist communities. In Yemen, in the North-West Frontier Province of Pakistan, in the slums of urban Jamaica, and in the Caucasus Mountains and countless other places, trafficking in drugs, humans, and weapons cohabit with warlords, militia leaders, and political opportunists in an environment that precludes good governance and judicial oversight.[47]

Finally, one must not overlook the global environmental factors that contribute to both the opportunities and grievances perceived by organizations and individuals interested in terrorist activity. Regarding globalization, a good deal of animosity—particularly in the developing world—may stem from a perception of victimization by corrupt governments backed by powerful nations and multinational corporations.[48]

The global media also influence perceptions in many ways, including whether they choose to describe a particular event as an act of terrorism. Globally dispersed diaspora communities provide funding to militants back home (e.g., Tamils in Canada, or Pakistani-Kashmiris in Denmark and the United Kingdom). And as research by Paul Pillar demonstrates, a nation's foreign policies can significantly influence foreign perceptions and contribute to the threat of international terrorism.[49]

These are just some of the many elements of the global environment that can influence an individual's views toward terrorism. Together with the aforementioned three categories (precipitant conditions, environmental triggers, opportunities to act), the research clearly links environmental conditions with the risk of terrorism. Further, a local population's perceptions about these conditions are important attributes that can be exploited by ideologically motivated groups intent on convincing the locals that they cannot make a positive effect on their environment without resorting to violent means. The following section offers recommendations based on this analysis of risk factors and the interplay between them.

Implications for a New Counterterrorism Strategy

This chapter illustrates the centrality of perceptions and beliefs in the study of terrorism and counterterrorism. An individual's choice to engage in—or disengage from—terrorism occurs at the intersection of ideas, perceptions, and opportunities. Successful terrorist organizations capitalize on an environment in which their ideology resonates and their grievances are considered legitimate by smart, competent individuals. From this perspective, it becomes clear that a counterterrorism strategy focused on killing or capturing individuals and interdicting finances will not lead to victory unless combined with a concerted effort to discredit the organization, its leaders, and its ideology and to influence the perceptions of potential supporters within the community targeted by the organization.

Effective counterterrorism strategy should focus on at least three areas: organizations, environmental conditions, and perceptions. First, we should attack terrorist organizations and their members, degrade their functional capabilities, encourage "leaving" alternatives, and support sociopolitical entities that draw support away from them. Second, we need to work with other countries to mitigate sociopolitical conditions and other grievances that terrorist organizations have historically used to justify their use of violence. Here, the U.S. Agency for International Development, along with the Departments of Agriculture, Commerce, and Education, is just as important in helping combat terrorism as the Departments of Defense and State. We also need to continue working collaboratively to confront enabling opportunities, things that facilitate terrorist activity, like safe havens, weapons proliferation, weak border controls, and illicit financial networks. Third, we must actively influence perceptions and interpretations of conditions, opportunities, and organizations. We have done quite a lot in the first two areas, particularly since 9/11, but this third area requires greater attention and action.

At a minimum, policymakers need a greater understanding of the contexts in which the risks of terrorism are considered significant. To develop context-appropriate counterterrorism strategies, an extensive body of research is needed on situation-specific factors that contribute to political violence in a particular location. We need to identify the most prominent influences in a community and determine how and where youth congregate and learn from peers; how social networks develop and evolve in different cultural contexts; what groups enjoy strategic influence, and why; what interactions matter most in motivating individuals to conduct violence; and other central questions.

With this knowledge, counterterrorism strategists should craft appropriate ways to assess the resonance of a terrorist organization's messages, themes, and communication mechanisms and should determine ways to reduce the resonance of these messages and themes within a given context.[50] As support for terrorism wanes, intelligence tends to increase on terrorist activities, penetrations occur, and operations become more difficult.[51] Reducing an organization's ideological resonance requires addressing an array of environmental conditions that may span a broad socioeconomic and political landscape.[52] For example, many analysts have described the need for the United States to support democratization, or at least a more equitable distribution of sociopolitical opportunities to participate in governance, to express grievances peacefully, and to congregate freely.[53] The relegitimization of state authority in the Middle East and North Africa should be based on the adoption of democratic procedures that will apply pressure on authoritarian regimes.[54]

How we frame the need for political reforms is just as important as the reforms themselves. Our rhetoric should focus on issues of social and political justice, as well as government transparency and accountability. Our emphasis should be on demonstrating how an environment that allows for *respectful* debate and nonviolent disagreements should be a point of civic and national pride. Overall, we need to make better use of what Joseph Nye calls "soft power" in ways that alter the conditions that breed discontent and terrorists.[55] Addressing these environmental conditions can also enhance the resonance of our counterideology messages and improve the potential success of our information operations and public diplomacy efforts. Transparency and justice should be a hallmark of any government with which we do business; if they are not, we should find ways to compel changes in behavior through our words, policies, and actions. Applying soft power—particularly in the realm of diplomacy, politics, and finance—to change environmental conditions is in our own national security interests.

In addition to addressing ideological resonance, we must attack the "street perception" of a terrorist organization, with particular focus on how critical support communities view its leadership and members, its strategies and tactics, and the lack of transparency in its financial dealings. As clandestine organizations, terrorist groups face a considerable challenge in maintaining operational security. Terrorist groups are increasingly relying on the Internet to engage in heated debates about strategies and tactics, and that provides a unique window into what an organization's members indicate are major concerns and vulnerabilities.[56]

We must also engage radical ideologues with counterarguments and diminish the credibility of their ideology. For example, as Assaf Moghadam has recently observed, al Qaeda attacks have killed and injured far more Muslims than non-Muslims, which they justify by using a logic of the ends justifying the means. Thus, "the United States and its allies should grasp every opportunity to highlight the disastrous consequences that Salafi-jihadist violence has wrought on the everyday lives not only of Westerners, but first and foremost on Muslims themselves."[57] Further, leaders of the al Qaeda movement preach about the benefits of martyrdom, but they rarely if ever conduct suicidal operations themselves or send their loved ones on such missions. U.S. counterterrorism policy should call attention to this hypocrisy.

In support of this effort, the United States needs a more robust public influence infrastructure, one that incorporates the strategic purpose of the Department of State's new Counterterrorism Communications Center and engages the Internet in a meaningful way. As we begin to assess and improve the street-level resonance of our own messages and themes, we must engage the Internet as part of a broad public influence effort. The Internet plays an increasingly important role in connecting individuals with terrorist organizations and should be equally important in connecting citizens with their governments.[58] However, while some government agencies have been monitoring radical websites and blogs for years, authorities are legally constrained in how they can intervene in these forums. This is, in part, because the Smith-Mundt Act prohibits the government from posting material that could be construed as propaganda. Congress needs to examine the Smith-Mundt Act and provide a new legal basis for a robust online counterideology effort that should fracture terrorist organizations and their supporting communities and force the propagandists to defend their deficient ideology and strategy.[59]

And finally, we should recognize the limitations of the nation-state in the information domain and embrace the new and innovative ways in which individuals are increasingly empowered to confront hostile ideologies. One recent example is the Radical Middle Way— an organization of young British Muslims who have rejected the

Salafi jihadist interpretation of the Koran and are trying to consolidate a mainstream response to fundamentalist Islam. Its public events and Internet activities are funded by the sale of music videos and are being touted as an example of how to weaken the resonance of al Qaeda's ideology among youth.[60] Similarly, in Indonesia, Ahmad Dhani—the leader of the immensely popular rock band Dewa—has used music to influence millions of fans, encouraging them to resist the tide of religious extremism. As Kyai Haji Abdurrahman Wahid—a former president of Indonesia—observed, "Dhani and his group are on the front lines of a global conflict, defending Islam from its fanatical hijackers [and helping] to rescue an entire generation from Wahhabi-financed extremists whose goal is to transform Muslim youth into holy warriors and suicide bombers."[61]

Egyptian Amr Khaled, who runs one of the Arab world's most popular websites and hosts a regular show on a Saudi-owned religious satellite channel, is a moderate who encourages Muslims to transform their lives and their communities through Islam while also getting along with the West. He explains: "[Osama] bin Laden is saying he is talking on behalf of Muslims. Who asked him to talk on behalf of us? Nobody."[62] And in Saudi Arabia, Ahmad al-Shugairi, a moderate preacher who is quite popular among a young audience that is hungry for religious identity but deeply alienated from both politics and the traditional religious establishment, uses his satellite TV program *Khawater* (*Thoughts*) to preach that Islam's greatest strength is its diversity and its openness to new ways of thinking.[63] Private initiatives like these are generally more effective at countering the influence of al Qaeda than any U.S. public diplomacy strategy and deserve our support. Terrorism will not likely be defeated without the use of kinetic force, but it will certainly not be defeated without a commitment to a broad spectrum of effective communication and strategic influence efforts.

Conclusion

Terrorism is a product of interactions between individual choices, organizational choices, and the environmental dimensions that influence those choices. Combining the two analytical frames when analyzing terrorism reinforces the critical importance of the information battleground and the need to develop a supreme ability to conduct influence warfare.[64] Combating terrorism requires knowledge, intelligence, and an ability to influence others through nonkinetic means. Our need to communicate effectively, contextually, situationally, and in culturally relevant themes—in order to influence perceptions and choices—has never been more urgent.

DISCLAIMER
    The views expressed herein are those of the author and do not purport to reflect the position of the United States Military Academy, the Department of the Army, or the Department of Defense.

3. Are There "Root Causes" for Terrorist Support?: Revisiting the Debate on Poverty, Education, and Terrorism[1]

Mia Bloom

For nations like Afghanistan, Pakistan, Indonesia, or much of the Middle East, young men have no opportunities. The only education they are receiving is that provided to them by religious schools that may not provide them with a well-rounded view of the world. They see poverty all around them and they are angry [sic] by that poverty. They may be suffering under oppressive and corrupt regimes and that kind of environment is a breeding ground for fanaticism and hatred. . . . It's absolutely critical that the U.S. is engaged in policies and strategies that will give those young people and these countries hope and make it in their self-interest to participate and create modern, open societies like we have in the U.S.

—Illinois State Senator Barack Obama,
Chicago Defender, October 17, 2001

Islamic governments assert that a critical reassessment of counterterrorism policies and the need to address the "root causes" of terrorism are necessary to improve relations between the Islamic world and the West. Heeding this advice, President-elect Obama indicated in December 2008 that he would address the Muslim world in hopes of improving America's relations with both friends and foes in the Islamic world.

In anticipation of President Obama's overtures, ambassadors from several Muslim countries put forward recommendations that they said would help. In particular, they focused on the need to identify and address the "root causes" of terrorism as paramount, and they placed the Israeli-Palestinian conflict high on the list of grievances that required the president's attention. Further, in an open letter to the president coinciding with his inauguration, the Organization of the Islamic Conference attributed terrorism to "deprivation, poverty,

45

despair and, most importantly, political injustice."[2] The statement by then Illinois state senator Barack Obama in the aftermath of 9/11 echoes these sentiments.

Notwithstanding these widespread beliefs of a linkage between terrorism, socioeconomic conditions, and political grievances, two questions remain: First, are there root causes for terrorism? And second, to the extent that there are, would addressing such causes undermine the appeal of terrorist organizations? This chapter surveys the existing literature on root causes in an attempt to answer these two questions. It finds that the debate over the existence of root causes, specifically of a connection between poverty, education, and political violence, is inextricably linked with the underlying weaknesses in the study of terrorism and reflects in many ways our limited understanding of the dynamics at work. After an exploration of the existing scholarship on the subject, the chapter will suggest an alternative framework for considering underlying causes, preconditions, and risk factors related to terrorism.

Background

It would be comforting to believe that by addressing root causes, we can combat the appeal of violent organizations. However, simplistic assumptions of cause and effect do not take into account that involvement in terrorist violence is a complex phenomenon. Accordingly, a far better understanding of terrorism and the motivations of people who join violent movements remains a paramount concern for U.S. policymakers.

The "root cause" debate pits those who say that terrorism is the result of national issues—such as poverty and economic injustice, the Palestinian and Kashmiri conflicts, and the wars in Iraq and Afghanistan—against those who argue that it is driven by a jihadist ideology rooted in Islamic teaching. While some root causes (e.g., the relationship between poverty and violence) have been easily dismissed—perhaps too easily—the idea of a magic bullet that might end terrorism remains. Since terrorism has not evolved as the result of any one impulse, it is unlikely to be resolved easily or quickly. However, the issue of root causes might provide a better understanding of the context in which terrorists recruit, operate, and draw support from a given population. This approach might be better at assessing populations at risk for radicalization and recruitment in terrorist organizations.

The terrorism literature suffers from a dearth of primary-source field research. This shortcoming is largely due to researchers' reluctance to enter the field to conduct interviews with active or disengaged terrorists. "As a result, much of our knowledge and understanding about terrorist movements comes from news reports and other secondary sources," explains John Horgan, an applied psychologist and director of the International Center for the Study of Terrorism at Pennsylvania State University. "This contributes to a systematic bias in data analysis and skewed findings that do not correlate with the reality of terrorist behavior."[3]

This defect in the literature has resulted in narrow, prescriptive frameworks that limit our understanding of terrorist behavior and of the root causes of terrorist violence. Despite some limited progress, most analyses of terrorism remain short term, incident driven, politicized, and narrowly focused. According to psychologist Colin Wastell: "We are absolutely in need of research that engages with the phenomenon, with the problem as it really exists. Not as we would characterize it, or caricature it."[4] For psychologist Jeff Victoroff, the field "is characterized by theoretical speculation based on subjective interpretation of anecdotal observations."[5] Terrorism expert Marc Sageman, author of *Leaderless Jihad* and other works, complains that "the lack of solid ethnographic work is compounded by the self-promotion of an army of self-appointed experts, who rely exclusively on Internet propaganda from terrorists. This is a bit like studying the nature of the Nazi state through its published and broadcast propaganda."[6]

Much of the terrorism literature also suffers from the fundamental attribution error.[7] "This error is a basic human tendency," explains Paul Gill, a fellow at Pennsylvania State University's International Center for the Study of Terrorism, "to use dispositions as an explanatory variable for behavior while underestimating the powerful impact of the situational context within which the behavior is carried out."[8] Research focuses on the actions of the terrorist rather than on the processes through which he or she became a terrorist. By focusing on the individual's actions in isolation, scholars fail to interpret the influences of the social and economic environment on the individual as intervening variables. Moreover, by focusing on just one part of a terrorist organization, the operative, we completely miss the complexity of involvement in terrorist organizations. Put simply, involvement in the organization is multifaceted, and different things motivate different people at different times. Gauging whether a root cause or root causes exist is very much a moving target. What might have motivated someone at the outset of involvement might be very different from those things that sustain his or her involvement over time.

The scholarly literature is replete with attempts to identify root causes and assess to what extent root causes explain the phenomenon of terrorism. These studies inevitably begin with questions of poverty, education, culture, religion, and human dignity. In his seminal book on the subject, Tore Bjørgo challenged the very notion that such root causes for terrorism even exist. Instead, Bjørgo listed a number of preconditions (not root causes), which included among others the following:

- Lack of democracy, civil rights, and the rule of law;
- Failed or weak states;
- Rapid modernization;
- Illegitimate and corrupt governments;
- Extremist ideologies (secular or religious); and
- Powerful external actors holding up corrupt regimes.[9]

Other research has called into question the explanatory value of root causes. For example, Ariel Merari studied 32 suicide bombers but found no specific socioeconomic factors (or personality factors, such as depression or suicidal symptoms) to account for their recourse to violence. Merari, a professor of psychology at Tel Aviv University, noted that terrorist groups appeal to piety or patriotism but concluded that neither fanaticism nor nationalism is "necessary or sufficient" to explain their behavior. The key ingredient, Merari posited, may be the individuals' susceptibility to indoctrination.[10]

As such, an understanding of root causes is useful in order to structure effective countermeasures and develop competing ideologies. It also has broad political appeal. Unlike divisive issues like support for Israel or the occupations of Iraq and Afghanistan, the issue of fighting a war on poverty can unite people across the ideological spectrum. Policymakers and scholars are interested in alleviating poverty, independent of whether doing so will or will not reduce terrorism.

Root Causes and U.S. Counterterrorism Policy

Policymakers in the United States and elsewhere have long operated under the assumption that terrorism is by and large a byproduct of poverty and a lack of education. Indicative of this belief is a 2002 U.S. State Department memorandum, in which then Secretary of State Colin L. Powell wrote, "I fully believe that the root cause of terrorism does come from situations where there is poverty, where there is ignorance, where people see no hope in their lives."[11] In 1995, former Israeli prime minister Shimon Peres told the United Nations, "We have to address ourselves to the young generation and to education, so that neither poverty nor ignorance will continue to feed fundamentalism, poverty, disillusion [sic] and hatred."[12] After the attacks on September 11, 2001, President George W. Bush said, "We fight against poverty because hope is an answer to terror."[13] Former World Bank president James Wolfensohn reasoned, "The war on terrorism will not be won until we have come to grips with the problem of poverty and thus the sources of discontent."[14]

The assumption that poverty and terrorism are intimately linked unites both sides of the aisle in the United States. Echoing President Bush and Colin Powell, former vice president Al Gore said in 2002 that there is "another axis of evil in the world: poverty and ignorance; disease and environmental disorder; corruption and political oppression," all of which lead to terrorism.[15] The presumption of a relationship between education, poverty, and terrorism may be said to constitute the prima facie justification for economic development as a key component of counterterrorism policy. As much as today's "war on terror" is a military one, it is also being waged as a "war on poverty" and a war against illiteracy, which are presumed to exacerbate the conditions from which terrorism emerges.[16]

Recent scholarship is creating an academic consensus around a very different set of assumptions. According to the RAND Corporation's Claude Berrebi, "The empirical evidence collected so far gives little reason to believe that materialistic or educational improvements would help reduce terrorism."[17] Increasingly, scholars argue that the terrorism-poverty connection is nothing more than a popular misconception. At the individual level, the leaders of militant movements are better educated and of higher status than most of the population from which they come. In fact, the operatives are usually better off financially and educationally from the society as a whole.

49

According to President Obama's assistant treasury secretary for economic policy, Alan Krueger, the relationship between poverty and
terrorism is an inverse one. Indeed, Krueger's research suggests that
not only are poverty and poor education unrelated to terrorism, but
that wealth and higher levels of education actually correspond to
participation in terrorism *positively*.[18]

Terrorism scholar Walter Reich attempted to sound the final death
knell to the notion that there was any relationship between poverty
and terrorism, saying: "The belief that poverty is a root cause of
Islamist terrorism has been thoroughly discredited. Numerous studies of terrorism have debunked the notion."[19] These conclusions
strongly suggest that reducing poverty and improving education
are unlikely to yield much by way of counterterrorism policy.

Where did the misconceptions about a linkage between socioeconomic factors and terrorism originate? Much of the preliminary
research on the relationship inadvertently miscoded the poverty
variable by using gross national product, not an individual terrorist's
particular socioeconomic status. To further complicate matters, the
GNP figure often used was based on the location of the attack, rather
than the country from whence the perpetrator came. The potential
distortion is clear in cases such as an attack, for example, by a
Palestinian militant in Israel, since Israel has a far higher GNP than
the Jordanian refugee camp where the attacker originated.

This confusion over coding GNP was addressed in the subsequent
literature by focusing on the individual insurgent and assessing to
what extent he or she was poor or uneducated compared to his or
her community as a whole. This approach likewise poses a host of
possible faulty correlations between poverty (or the lack thereof)
and terrorism.

Terrorist organizations desire the most qualified candidates to
carry out violent acts on behalf of the organization. Therefore, while
the base of support or "applicants" may be poor and uneducated,
only the most qualified applicants—the frontline activists—are
likely to be educated and to come from backgrounds of socioeconomic privilege. While wealthier and better-educated members of
a population might *participate* in terrorism, current research finds
that *support* for terrorism shows the opposite trend.[20] This datum
reinforces the existence of a selection effect (identified by Ethan
Bueno de Mesquita) that the "demand side" of terrorism accounts

for some of the confusion surrounding possible linkages between poverty, education levels, and political violence.[21] Though the actual terror operatives tend to come from privileged backgrounds (relative to their larger populations), a significant factor in understanding political violence, this finding cannot rule out a relationship between poor education, poverty, and terrorism. In addition to terrorist leaders' seeking the most qualified candidates, they are selecting against those likely to self-immolate by accident and those whose literacy skills might hinder their ability to carry out a mission. In particular, terrorist leaders know that college-educated operatives will likely speak more than their native language and will be better able to blend with the target population. A university-educated Palestinian will likely speak Hebrew and a university-educated Saudi will undoubtedly speak English. This acquired skill set will be invaluable in field operations, which might include trying to board an Egged bus in Israel or a U.S. airliner.

Here, too, we should be cautious. Rather than focus on the individual terrorists, it is important to examine the larger contexts from which they emerge. To this end, scholars and policymakers should study the community that provides support and sustenance to the frontline terrorist operative. A greater understanding of the environmental conditions could clarify the connection, if any, between preferences for violence and poverty or a lack of educational opportunities.

Who supports terrorism? Numerous scholars have asked this question in recent years, though a paucity of public opinion data from relevant cases, coupled with questionable methodologies, has left the answer incomplete. Much of the work on this subject has focused on supporters' levels of education and standards of living. Several researchers have addressed the question of education, poverty, and terrorism directly, and conclude that not only is this relationship unfounded but an inverse relationship exists. For example, Alan Krueger and Jitka Maleckova find that members of Hezbollah are more educated and have a higher standard of living than the Lebanese Shia population as a whole; Claude Berrebi replicates these results with respect to Palestinian terrorists in Hamas and the Palestinian Islamic Jihad.[22]

Their findings should be treated with caution due to limitations within the data. Both studies employ estimation techniques susceptible to producing biased results. To date, all such studies rely on nonrandom lists of terrorist participants, based on available information.[23] The creation of large data sets on terrorism is a useful tool for students and scholars alike. However, each study combines data on terrorist participants with available demographic data from the target population to estimate the likelihood of participation in terrorism. The dependent variable—participation in terrorism—is strictly determined by the list of terrorists collected. Such sampling from the dependent variable, even in the presence of weighting, produces results of unknown bias.[24]

This is not to say that Krueger and Maleckova's and Berrebi's findings, as well as other studies that support their conclusions, should be completely discounted. Charles Russell and Bowman Miller's compilation of demographic data on 350 terrorists from 18 revolutionary groups engaged in urban terrorism produced a similar finding: higher education and better standards of living characterized right-wing and European terrorists compared to the populations from which they were drawn.[25] According to one study, not only are better-educated individuals overrepresented among terrorists: they are also drawn increasingly from engineering and the hard sciences.[26] Al Qaeda and many other Middle Eastern and Islamist organizations attract engineers, doctors, and scientists to their ranks and particularly to leadership roles. These studies appear to show empirically that education and wealth positively predict *participation* in terrorism; the relationship between socioeconomic characteristics and *support* for terrorism, however, remains an open question.

Indeed, the case studies from which the existing literature draws do not include those terrorist organizations that would challenge their hypotheses or invalidate their findings; for example, the Liberation Tigers of Tamil Eelam in Sri Lanka; the Provisional Irish Republic Army; the Kurdistan Workers' Party, or PKK, in Turkey; the Basque separatist group ETA in Spain; and, to a lesser extent, the Taliban in Afghanistan. In many of the ethnonationalist conflicts in which terrorism emerges, the target group for terrorist recruitment is often severely disadvantaged socioeconomically vis-à-vis the ethnic majority. The minority tends to be excluded from the benefits of the state, and thus these disparities become part and parcel of the terrorist group's raison d'être. The selection model of terrorist recruitment explains the discrepancies observed in the literature but has not been subjected to empirical testing.

Other studies examine the relationship between the occurrences of terrorism and the pervading socioeconomic conditions of a population. Alan Krueger and David Laitin and, separately, James Piazza find no relationship between poor economic conditions and the prevalence of terrorist acts.[27] Alberto Abadie finds only a qualified relationship between poverty and terrorism. Terrorism is more likely in poorer countries, but this relationship disappears when political freedom and geographic characteristics are factored in. It is countries undergoing a political transition, Abadie concludes, that have more to fear from terrorism than either established democracies or entrenched autocracies.[28]

Interestingly enough, Abadie's finding invalidates yet another set of alleged root causes, those pertaining to a lack of democracy, civil rights, and the rule of law. According to this school of thought, the absence of alternative mechanisms to voice dissent creates pressures for violence. Proponents of this view allege that people turn toward terrorism when there is no political space in which to assert their grievances. Given that autocracies suffer from terrorism less than democracies, the absence of political freedoms cannot be a unifying root cause.

Going back to supposed links between poverty and terrorism, Brock Blomberg and others argue that while high-income and democratic states have higher incidences of terrorism compared to other states, periods of economic downturn increase the likelihood of terrorist acts.[29] While this research theorized that increased terrorism is the rational response of those adversely affected by economic contraction yet unable to affect governing institutions, their study does not show that economically repressed and disenfranchised individuals are in fact supportive of, or responsible for, increases in terrorist violence.

Studies of public opinion and terrorist participation, distinct from studies of general socioeconomic conditions, provide a more conclusive examination of the possible connection between an individual's socioeconomic status and support for political violence. A number of scholars examine the demographics of terrorist participants to reach their conclusions that support for terrorism is positively related to better education and higher standards of living.[30] This method ignores, however, a selection effect that may be at work in the recruitment patterns used by terrorist leaders. As explained above, these organizations are likely to prefer the most capable applicants of a pool to carry out attacks. Thus, it may not be that education and wealth positively correspond to terrorist participation for the reasons these scholars suggest, namely, that the educated and wealthy are more politically active, committed, and possess greater opportunities for violent political involvement.

This supposition is corroborated by a 2005 news story out of Great Britain. The *Sunday Times* carried a front-page story exploding the myth of a causal relationship between terrorism and poverty among Muslims. The newspaper reported on leaked Whitehall documents that show "Al-Qaeda is secretly recruiting affluent, middle-class Muslims in British universities and colleges to carry out terrorist attacks" in Britain. The targets of the "extremist recruiters," the *Times* reported, are students with "technical and professional qualifications."[31] The recent attempt against Northwest 253 by Umar Farouk Abdul Muttalib provides yet another example of highly educated and skilled operatives coming out of elite academic institutions in Britain.

Yet the terrorist "selection effect" usually goes untested, or its implications are downplayed in the academic literature. If a selection effect does exist, the proposed relationship between support for terrorism and an individual's socioeconomic characteristics may be undone. Indeed, traditional notions that lack of education and poverty correspond with support for terrorism—due to frustration from lack of opportunity—may be closer to the truth.

John Horgan observes, "Explanations that seek to privilege one *kind* of explanation over another miss the essential point about conceptualizing terrorism as a process, and tend to commit the logical error of confusing causation with correlation."[32] Furthermore, becoming a terrorist is not an overnight metamorphosis. An individual aggrieved malcontent does not emerge from a chrysalis newly formed and reinvented as a terrorist; in fact, the process of involvement in terrorism might be incremental and gradual. This complexity is captured by Taylor and Quayle's description of involvement in terrorism:

> No different from any of the other things that people do. In one sense, embarking on a life of terrorism is like any other life choice. . . . To ask why an individual occupies a particular social, career or even family role is probably a deceptively

easy but essentially unanswerable question. What we can do, however, is to identify factors in any particular situation that helps us understand why particular life choices have been made. This same analysis applies to the development of the terrorist. [33]

What motivates the individual to join a movement in the first place might not be what sustains his or her involvement over time. The implication is that answering questions about why people become involved in terrorism may have little bearing on the answers that explain what they do as terrorists, or how they remain involved in terrorist activity over a long period. Similarly, answering questions about what keeps people involved with a terrorist movement may have surprisingly little if any bearing on what causes them to disengage from terrorist operations or from the organization (and/or broader movement) altogether.[34]

Swati Parashar, a research associate in the International Terrorism Watch Project at the Observer Research Foundation in New Delhi, corroborates this perspective: "Convenient root causes like poverty, illiteracy, backwardness, fundamentalism, authoritarianism are hardly the considerations in sustaining terrorism or in winning recruits."[35]

In an effort to address the paucity of data about terrorists and the groups to which they belong, Horgan undertook a project to interview scores of terrorists to ascertain motivation and whether one could identify whether root causes existed. After a decade of conducting personal interviews with the operatives themselves, he concludes:

> Even when an individual him or herself suggests the perceived presence of such a catalyst, we ought to interpret its significance with great caution since personal accounts often obscure acknowledgement of the expected positive features of involvement. We run the risk of forming quite an incomplete and biased interpretation of an already biased account. When we are in a position to consider accounts from activists around the world, different qualities are certain to emerge, with different emphases on particular "push" and "pull" factors, reflecting different roles held by different people under different degrees of ideological content, social, ideological and organizational control, commitment, etc.[36]

Finally, in addition to the fact that a better understanding of root causes cannot provide insight into *why* some members of a population choose violence while the majority does not, a focus on external influences on behavior denies the individual the capacity for choice; specifically, of choosing to engage in terrorism. In essence, if specific conditions are presumed to be determinative, then an individual's particular motivations can have little influence. The individual terrorist could not choose his or her path; rather, the structural conditions of the root cause made violence the inevitable result of the process begun by someone else. Akin to the sex offender who claims he was beaten as a child, the root causes debate shifts responsibility away from the individual who chose a certain path in the first place. "Although we can develop potential models of terrorist behavior," Horgan explains, "the progress of psychological research is unsatisfactory as long as the data is insufficient to inform theories and test basic hypotheses."[37]

Michael Radu explains that the need to uncover the root causes of terrorism might be driven by a desire to understand how people could make such choices, but the practical effect is to oversimplify what is a complex, even messy, process. "Framing the question as 'What are the root causes of terrorism?' leads too easily to looking at the usual suspects: 'poverty,' 'injustice,' 'exploitation,' and 'frustra-tion.' Like the man in the parable who looks for his lost keys under the streetlight instead of where he lost them because 'the light's better,' it's easier to look in these familiar areas than to face and address the real problems."[38] However, the search for root causes as a means for countering terrorism ultimately depends on the ability to discern what *particular* factors caused a *particular* individual to engage in violence. Scholars and policymakers must either identify intervening variables or else better understand the diverse pathways of involvement. This approach will enable them to find ways to intervene in a process, not a blanket fix-all.

Walking Away

Again, Bjørgo's study allows us to examine factors that help sus-tain involvement. First and foremost, Bjørgo and Horgan agree that the factors that sustain terrorism are not necessarily those that pro-duced terrorism. Factors such as cycles of revenge and the need for the group to maintain its survival sustain involvement. For Bjørgo, if the individual operative has no way out of the movement, that too sustains involvement. Other mechanisms that sustain involvement include changes in the individual's priorities or engagement in criminal activities (e.g., kidnapping, drug trafficking, bank robbery) that have their own attraction, independent of any connection to political violence.[39] Under such circumstances, the individual involvement may be less about an ideological or religious belief than the pulls associated with the profitable illicit enterprise. When terrorists become profit seekers rather than power maximizers, we tend to observe a shift in priorities. Groups such as the FARC in Colombia, Abu Sayyaf in the Philippines, and others become far more involved in moneymaking. For analysts like Audrey Cronin, this might portend the end of the group as a result of implosion.[40]

One of the major findings of Horgan's *Walking Away from Terrorism: Accounts of Individual Disengagement from Radical and Extremist Movements* is that across cases as diverse as the Irish Republic Army, al Qaeda, and Jamiat Islamiyya in Indonesia, what ultimately caused his interviewees to leave the movements (or walk away from terrorism) was the significant discrepancy between what they expected their life to be like in the movement and what it actually was.[41] It is this discrepancy between expectations and realities that offers the most convenient counter to radicalization or at least involvement in violence. If the academic researcher on terrorism is expected to make terrorism known and dispel myths, he or she can identify these discrepancies and exploit them for counterterrorism purposes. Ultimately, Horgan's distinction between deradicalization and demobilization is an important one. The fact that many people who might walk away from engaging in terrorism (and participate in highly publicized deradicalization programs) persist in their views means that they can (and will) continue to impart these views to others— inspiring both the attacks at Fort Hood and against U.S. passengers on Northwest 253.

Root causes remain important to our understanding of the context against which terrorist movements legitimize their claims and replenish recruits. Although such research might have only modest utility in helping to understand an individual's motivation, the issue of underlying root causes or preconditions to terrorism deserves greater attention. First, an attention to root causes recognizes that terrorism is often rooted in legitimate grievances (especially those that have the supportive voice of a community). Second, it is crucial to understand how the interplay of state counterterrorism policies feeds into the cycle of revenge. In essence, state actions can be a catalyst for more terrorism and more violence.

However, the search for root causes does not imply that there is a simple cause-and-effect relationship between the roots and the outcomes. Attempts to identify root causes are not based on the assumption that terrorists are merely passive actors and that the structural element (humiliation, occupation, poverty) makes terrorism the only option available. We should also remember that terrorism can be based on imagined or virtual grievances. Terrorist organizations are adept at manipulating events to their own benefit. Third, perceived grievances have a tendency to shift over time. Even if one were to identify what might be considered a root cause at the outset of a terrorist campaign, that might be very different from what sustains the campaign along the way.

While addressing issues such as the Israeli-Palestinian conflict might very well undermine some of the propaganda available to terrorist entrepreneurs, a holistic approach is needed to understand motivation at the individual level, the group level, and the societal level. Addressing root causes might not be a bad idea, but it will likely have very different results from those that are anticipated.

For example, identifying root causes may help undermine the general appeal of the terrorists' message to the larger public but have less effect on the true believers who engage in violence. Although it is not difficult to identify the broad sociopolitical and socioeconomic preconditions for a climate conducive to the emergence of terrorism,[42] it remains the case that very few people will actually engage in terrorism. More than anything else, this factor alone cautions us against the root cause approach as a panacea to terrorism. Because whatever root causes will affect the target population as a whole, the fact that only a small fraction rise up to engage in terrorist violence requires us to rethink whether a root cause or a series of root causes exists at all. Rather than identifying a singular magic bullet, whether it is poverty, lack of education, culture, religion, or some other structural condition (e.g., occupation and the presence of foreign troops), understanding how and why people choose terrorism requires a nuanced appreciation of the complex processes of involvement. In effect, rather than consider root causes a form of path dependence of an inevitable outcome, the elements often associated with root causes might be better understood as risk factors for radicalization and involvement in terrorism.

4. Don't You Know There's a War On?: Assessing the Military's Role in Counterterrorism

Paul R. Pillar and Christopher A. Preble

Nine days after the 9/11 terrorist attacks, in a speech before a joint session of Congress watched by tens of millions on television, President George W. Bush pledged to use all instruments of U.S. power—"every means of diplomacy, every tool of intelligence, every instrument of law enforcement, every financial influence, and every necessary weapon of war"—to destroy and defeat the al Qaeda network. The U.S. "war on terror begins with al Qaeda, but it does not end there," he explained. "It will not end until every terrorist group of global reach has been found, stopped and defeated."[1]

At the time, few Americans questioned President Bush's conscious framing of U.S. counterterrorism efforts as synonymous with the wars of the 20th century. Likewise, few doubted that the United States would use its enormous military power—and soon—to take the fight to al Qaeda. Indeed, less than a month after Bush's speech to Congress, U.S. personnel were on the ground in Afghanistan coordinating with local warlords in the campaign that swiftly brought down the Taliban regime.

In this chapter, we review the leading arguments for and against using military force in counterterrorism operations and conclude that the military instrument is useful in certain unique circumstances. We will also show, however, that the risks of military action often outweigh its benefits. Further, we explore the rhetoric surrounding counterterrorism and specifically question the utility and wisdom of characterizing counterterrorism efforts under the broad metaphorical rubric of war. Consciously framing counterterrorism as an either/or proposition—either as warfare or as a criminal justice problem—is equally unhelpful. Counterterrorism is a whole-of-society enterprise, combining not merely government agencies but also the private sector and an alert and engaged citizenry. In this context, it is neither a purely law enforcement function nor a war, strictly speaking, and policymakers and opinion leaders should avoid implying otherwise. Indeed, given the need to carefully manage public expectations and to calm public anxiety, we conclude that it is inappropriate to cast such efforts as synonymous with warfare.

The Military and Lethal Force

States use military force for several different counterterrorist purposes. The purposes have waxed or waned in apparent importance over time and have played widely differing roles in the counterterrorist efforts of different states.

One purpose that has applied less to the United States than to other countries has been to supplement police resources in securing the homeland. The British Army, for example, was used extensively to combat terrorism during "the Troubles" in Northern Ireland. The United States has been spared Ulster-type entrenchment of potent terrorist groups on its own territory. It also has longstanding *posse comitatus* restrictions on the military's performance of any domestic law enforcement functions. Apart from the Coast Guard's protection of shores and ports, the military's role in defending against terrorism in the U.S. homeland has consisted of limited and discrete functions, such as the provision of certain standby response capabilities at major events.[2]

Go back 25 years and the main thought that would probably come to mind about the military and counterterrorism was the rescue of hostages. This function has shaped specialized counterterrorist military units in several countries. Israel's Sayeret Matkal has been the pioneer and model. Germany, after its failed handling of the Palestinian terrorist attack at the 1972 Olympic Games in Munich, created a commando unit that proved its worth five years later with the rescue of hostages aboard a Lufthansa airliner in Mogadishu. For the United States, the incident comparable to Munich was the failure of an operation to free U.S. hostages at the U.S. Embassy in Tehran in 1980. That episode led directly to the establishment of the U.S. Joint Special Operations Command.

The Joint Special Operations Command's hostage-rescuing capability has gone largely unused, and the evolution of terrorist tactics and objectives since the takeover of the embassy in Tehran has made the classic hostage-taking incident seem increasingly quaint. The terrorism about which we worry most today involves attacks in which terrorists kill people straightaway, rather than capturing people and threatening to kill them if demands are not met. Hostage taking is still in the terrorist repertoire, however, and maintaining a military capability to respond to such incidents is still useful. The U.S. Navy Seals' brilliant rescue of a captive American merchant ship captain off Somalia in April 2009—although the abductors were pirates motivated by pecuniary concerns rather than terrorists with political motives—was a reassuring demonstration of some of the skills that that capability entails.

Even with the awesome abilities of special forces as illustrated by the rescue of the merchant captain, decisionmakers need to be cautious about applying force to ongoing terrorist incidents in which the lives of captives are in the balance. There have been spectacular successes, such as what the Germans accomplished at Mogadishu and what the Israelis did in a now-legendary operation in 1976 involving a hijacked airliner at Entebbe, Uganda. But there have also been big failures. When Egyptian commandos attempted a similar rescue involving a hijacked Egypt Air plane in Malta in 1985, 60 of the 96 passengers and crew aboard the aircraft were killed. Russia's use of force to end incidents in which Chechen terrorists have taken hostages has twice resulted in heavy death tolls for the hostages. At a theater in Moscow in 2002, where the Russians used a toxic aerosol to disable the terrorists, 129 of the hostages died, mostly from the effects of the chemical.[3] Two years later, Russian commandoes stormed a school in Beslan, North Ossetia, where Chechens had taken hundreds hostage. At least 334 hostages, most of them children, died in the ensuing gunfire, explosions, and fire that engulfed the building.[4] Even the Israelis, who have the most experience in hostage rescue and whose capabilities in executing such operations are second to none, have had their share of failures, in which many hostages as well as rescue team members have been killed.[5]

Those failures reflect the inherent difficulty of using force when the terrorists have the advantage of being willing and able to use their own deadly force against their captives. The difference between success and failure in such operations is slight, with luck playing a major role. The smallest complication could turn triumph into tragedy.

63

Retaliation

Prolonged hostage dramas dominated the first couple of decades of the modern era of international terrorism, including the spate of airplane hijackings in the 1970s. By the 1990s, the counterterrorist use of military force had come to mean something different for the United States: responding to a bombing or some other terrorist attack that was over and that had never involved hostages. This is the use of military force for retaliation, not rescue.

The United States has used military force for this purpose four times. In response to a Libyan-instigated bombing in 1986 of a nightclub in Berlin patronized by off-duty U.S. service personnel, the United States used 100 combat aircraft flown from carriers or from the United Kingdom to strike a variety of military targets in Libya. After Iraq unsuccessfully tried, using paid agents, to assassinate former President George H. W. Bush during a visit to Kuwait in 1993, the United States retaliated by firing 23 Tomahawk cruise missiles at the headquarters of the Iraqi intelligence service in Baghdad. After al Qaeda's bombing of the U.S. Embassies in Kenya and Tanzania in 1998, the United States fired several dozen cruise missiles against sites associated with Osama bin Laden. Most struck a complex of training camps in eastern Afghanistan; a few were fired at a pharmaceutical plant in Sudan suspected of a role in the possible manufacture of chemical weapons. The fourth such use of military force was Operation Enduring Freedom, the U.S.-led intervention in the Afghan civil war in late 2001, following the 9/11 attacks in the United States. That operation was by far the largest use of the U.S. military following a terrorist attack; it has since transformed into a much broader mission involving other counterterrorist purposes of military force. But its principal initial purpose, in direct response to al Qaeda's attack on 9/11, was to roust al Qaeda from its haven in Afghanistan and to oust its Taliban ally from power.

Exactly what does one accomplish by using military force to retaliate for a terrorist attack? The most substantive, and perhaps the most persuasive, answers to that question arise when the use of force goes beyond retaliation per se and includes material effects designed to reduce the future use of terrorism—purposes to be discussed further below. Certainly this was true of Operation Enduring Freedom, even in its initial phase. Deprived of its Afghan safe haven and the hospitality of its ideological kinfolk in the Taliban, al Qaeda might become less capable of conducting major terrorist attacks against U.S. interests. A hope to crimp capabilities for future terrorist operations also shaped some of the earlier, smaller operations. U.S. policymakers selected the plant in Sudan as a target in 1998, despite the fragmentary and inconclusive nature of the intelligence about it, in the hope that by destroying it they were reducing the capability and thus the chance of a future chemical attack by al Qaeda. But with the Tomahawk strike against the Iraqi intelligence service headquarters, it would be hard to identify even a hoped-for physical impairment of future terrorist capabilities. The strike was a military pinprick, carried out at night to reduce likely casualties. It was pure retaliation.

A political reality is that populations—and this certainly is true of the American public—demand that their leaders "do something" in response to a terrorist attack against their interests. The particular effects or secondary consequences of the response are less important to the public than the assurance that their nation is not just having to sit there and take it from terrorists. The public wants to strike back, somehow and somewhere. Military force has the attraction of being an especially emphatic and demonstrative way of striking back. Satisfying the popular urge to "do something" undoubtedly has been a motivation for past retaliatory U.S. use of force.

If enough of the citizenry places enough value on revenge—if it enhances collective emotional satisfaction—one might argue that this alone is reason enough for military retaliation. But as a matter of sound policy, it is hard to justify revenge for the sake of revenge. A somewhat more defensible argument is that military retaliation demonstrates the seriousness of the government's commitment to counterterrorism and can stimulate a similar commitment among its citizenry. This argument probably had more validity before 9/11 but has less now, with the national priority placed on counterterrorism not in doubt.

Retaliation can send the same message to foreign audiences about determination in pursuing counterterrorist objectives, perhaps stimulating other governments to enhance their own counterterrorist efforts. The U.S. airstrike on Libya had this effect on some European governments, including ones that opposed the strike. The Europeans' concern about what additional unilateral action the Reagan administration might take led them to go further than they had gone before in curtailing contacts with Libya and in expanding their own counterterrorist efforts. The U.S. lead on the ground in Afghanistan was an essential stimulant to broader participation in that country by the North Atlantic Treaty Organization.

Deterrence of future offenses is often regarded as the prime reason for retaliating against past ones. The reasoning can apply to terrorists as well as to other adversaries. It is not true, as is sometimes supposed, that terrorists cannot be deterred.[6] And in practical terms, the cases discussed here dealt with state sponsors of terrorism, which, presumably, can still be deterred. Several considerations, however, make the deterrence of terrorism through military retaliation substantially more problematic than the deterrence of other unwanted behavior by foreign adversaries.

International terrorism today is far more the work of nonstate actors (such as al Qaeda, the most familiar and feared terrorist group) than of states. One of the most salient trends in international terrorism over the past quarter century has been the trend away from terrorism by regimes toward terrorism by groups. Even Muammar el-Qaddafi's Libya, such a big terrorist concern in the 1980s, now cooperates with the United States against their common Islamist enemies. The biggest difference between a state and a transnational group, as far as military retaliation and deterrence are concerned, is that the former has a return address and the latter does not. It is substantially more difficult to identify sites that are feasible military targets and are of significant value to groups than is the case with states.

Even a group that enjoys a physical safe haven, as al Qaeda did in Taliban-ruled Afghanistan, offers few if any targets that are so valuable to the group that feared destruction of them would be likely to influence the group's decisions appreciably. The training camps that the United States hit with cruise missiles in 1998 were the best possible military targets that could have been selected for their association with bin Laden and al Qaeda, but their rudimentary nature meant their destruction was not much of a loss.

Rather than causing terrorist tears over lost facilities, retaliatory strikes have been at least as likely to be welcomed by terrorist leaders because of other consequences. One is a rally-around-the flag effect of increased support for a leader, whether of a group or a state, in the face of a foreign threat. Qaddafi enjoyed such an effect in the immediate aftermath of the 1986 strikes against Libya.[7] Iranian rulers would enjoy the same effect in the event of a U.S. (or Israeli) military strike, for whatever reason, against Iran. Another consequence, especially important for groups, is to elevate the group to the status of a belligerent engaged in war against a major power. Yet another is the possibility of added support and recruits as a response to revulsion over the damage inflicted by the retaliation. This last effect corresponds to a common objective of insurgents in a guerrilla war, in which insurgent attacks are intended to provoke the government side into counterattacks that will alienate the civilian population.

The record of the use of military force to retaliate for terrorist attacks is not promising as far as deterrence of further terrorism is concerned. Israel's repeated uses of its military to retaliate for terrorist attacks by its Palestinian and Lebanese opponents have been part of a seemingly unending cycle of attacks and counterattacks. Qaddafi—although later combinations of carrots and sticks would entice him onto a much more constructive path—did not slacken his use of terrorism in the aftermath of the 1986 air strike. The bombing of Pan Am Flight 103 in 1988 was probably his specific response to the U.S. attack. As for al Qaeda and the other radical Islamists who constitute the chief terrorist concern of today, the nature of their goals, their use of destructive confrontation with the United States as a means of pursuing those goals, the ostensibly divine basis of their motivations, and the role of martyrdom in their methods all make them resistant to being deterred from their operations by military attack, or the threat of attack.

The dominant counterterrorist uses of military force by the United States have now moved beyond incident response and retaliation to encompass two other basic purposes, reflected in the expansion of Operation Enduring Freedom in Afghanistan. One is the use of military force to directly degrade the capability of terrorists and terrorist groups to conduct operations. The other is stabilization intended to prevent a state from becoming a terrorist haven and sponsor, as Afghanistan was under the Taliban's rule. These two purposes overlap, and much of the counterinsurgency effort in Afghanistan is aimed at both. To extract general observations about the counterterrorist use of military force, however, it is useful to consider these purposes seriatim.

U.S.-led operations in the Afghanistan-Pakistan theater constitute today the largest, though not the only, use of military force to attack terrorist capabilities directly. Those include operations on the ground in Afghanistan and, increasingly, strikes from unmanned aerial vehicles over northwestern Pakistan. The targets include al Qaeda and other largely Arab extremists, the Taliban and other Afghan militias, and to a lesser but growing degree, elements of the Pakistani Taliban. During the Bush administration, the use of military force in this mode included a fraction of the remaining U.S. military operations in Iraq and isolated missile strikes in Yemen and Somalia.

The Obama administration has continued some of these tactics but has demonstrated considerable sensitivity to minimizing civilian casualties. For example, in September 2009, one of Africa's most wanted terrorists, Saleh Ali Saleh Nabhan, was killed in a raid in southern Somalia, approximately 155 miles south of Mogadishu. The precise details of the assault remain shrouded in secrecy, but U.S. officials confirmed that it involved forces from the U.S. Joint Special Operations Command. Nabhan, wanted in connection with an attack on a beach resort that killed 13 people and a nearly simultaneous failed attack on an Israeli airliner in his native Kenya, was presumed to have been killed by commandos deployed from helicopters. The *New York Times* reported that "the decision to use commandos and not long-range missiles in this case may reflect a shift by the Obama administration to go to greater lengths to avoid civilian deaths."[8]

The role of the military in counterterrorism operations is not limited to kinetic operations against suspected terrorists and their training facilities. U.S. advice and assistance also have facilitated operations for the same purpose by foreign military forces. Perhaps the most successful recent example of this approach has occurred in the Philippines, where fewer than 1,000 U.S. military personnel have worked with government officials and local military and law enforcement to deliver a serious blow to the Abu Sayyaf Group and other terrorist organizations with suspected ties to al Qaeda.[9] Comparable missions in Iraq and Afghanistan—which between them consume more than $15 billion every month and employ more than 200,000 U.S. military personnel, plus additional tens of thousands of civilians—have been less effective so far even though they have received far more attention, in part because of the enormous resources that have been dedicated to the effort.

Pros and Cons

The biggest advantage of the military instrument over other counterterrorist tools is that the potential effect on terrorist capabilities is immediate and unqualified. Forcefully putting a terrorist hors de combat does not depend on anyone else's cooperation, and it does not depend on the terrorist's, or anyone else's, calculations or psychology. A potential secondary benefit is disruption of terrorist activity going beyond immediate physical destruction. Being the target of armed attack can interfere with planning and induce terrorists to devote more attention to operational security and less to preparing their own attacks. A tertiary attraction is the demonstration that the use of force provides, to those at home and abroad, of one's own determination and the priority being given to counterterrorism.

The limitations and drawbacks of using the military are more numerous and collectively quite substantial, even though the indirect nature of some of the drawbacks may make them less visible. The number one limitation is the paucity of good military targets associated with terrorism. For all the focus on training camps having some association with a group such as al Qaeda, or through which some people associated with the group have passed, the attention has more to do with a camp's being a physical facility that one can locate on a map and can attack with armed force. It has nothing to do with such camps' being critical to the preparation and conduct of terrorist operations. They are primitive facilities that are easily replaced. And the preparations that matter most for the terrorism that can harm us the most occur in places that are not conducive to the use of force, including heavily populated cities, or the territory of well-governed states that understandably object to military operations by foreign states on their soil.

Using military force to attack terrorist capabilities really means attacking people rather than facilities. This is what the most visible recent expansion in the counterterrorist use of U.S. military force—the strikes with air-to-surface missiles fired from Predator drones over northwestern Pakistan—is all about. It is the overt use of military force that commonly bears the label "targeted killing," otherwise known as assassination.

The use of military force for this purpose entails the same limitations and drawbacks of assassination accomplished through other means, as well as some additional drawbacks of its own. Israelis, who have repeatedly used (or attempted) assassinations of leaders of Hamas, believe the technique has kept that Palestinian group off balance and curbed some of its operations. Among the more high-profile operations was the assassination in March 2004 of Sheik Ahmed Yassin, the wheelchair-bound founder of Hamas. Killed by a missile strike from an Israeli helicopter that also claimed the lives of nine others, Yassin's funeral drew an estimated 200,000 Palestinians, who looked on him as a leader and martyr on par with South Africa's Nelson Mandela.[10] These and other attacks have probably contributed to the slackening of Hamas's terrorist operations within Israel. They have not crippled the group, however, and it is difficult to disentangle the effects of the assassinations from the effects of other developments and other measures, especially the security barrier Israel has erected along the West Bank.[11]

A basic limitation to the efficacy of assassination as a counterter-rorist tool is that terrorists—even senior ones—are replaceable. The replacement might not represent an improvement from the counter-terrorist perspective. The Israelis discovered this when they assassi-nated the secretary-general of Hezbollah in 1992. The new secretary-general was the charismatic and politically gifted Hassan Nasrallah, who has since led the group to even greater influence. A strength of al Qaeda is its ability to quickly replace any lost cadre. With bin Laden and his number two, Ayman al-Zawahri, still at large, other members of the group who have been killed or captured have vari-ously been described as al Qaeda's "number three."[12] This partly reflects a tendency by U.S. officials to exaggerate the significance of the latest scalp bagged, but it also reflects a real ability of the group to regenerate. The pattern extends beyond Hezbollah or al Qaeda. Experience in Iraq and the Afghanistan-Pakistan theater provides little support for the idea that the killing of specifically targeted individuals discernibly reduces subsequent terrorism.

Assassination, through either military or clandestine methods, requires timely and precise intelligence, which is often difficult to obtain. (And, of course, killing rather than capturing a terrorist precludes any possibility of obtaining from the captive additional intelligence about his group and its future operations.) It also requires delicacy in execution. Much can go wrong, as has happened with several Israeli operations. In one of them, mistaken identity resulted in the Israelis killing an innocent Moroccan waiter rather than the Palestinian terrorist they were seeking. In another, a botched attempt to assassinate Hamas political leader Khalid Mishal in Amman produced a political crisis with Jordan.[13]

The use of military rather than covert means to kill a wanted terrorist accentuates another hazard of such operations: collateral damage and the anger and recriminations resulting from it. Innocent people have been killed as byproducts of assassinations using military force. This has occurred in Israeli operations aimed at Hamas figures. More recently, some of the missile strikes in Pakistan and Afghanistan have caused collateral casualties. Such unintended consequences contribute to further untoward indirect effects of the use of military force against terrorists, discussed below.

The disruptive effect of military strikes on the operations of terrorist groups—that is, the disruption that extends beyond the killing of individual members of the group—is real but limited by the groups' capacity to adapt. That bin Laden and Zawahri have been on the run as high priority targets of the U.S. military almost certainly has impeded their ability to function as operational commanders. The limitation is demonstrated by the fact that bin Laden was already on the run within Afghanistan after the embassy bombings in 1998 and the subsequent U.S. missile strikes (which U.S. officials hoped would catch him at the training camp complex the missiles struck). After 1998, he probably did not sleep in any one place more than a couple of nights in a row. But that clearly did not stop al Qaeda's preparation for the 9/11 attacks. The adaptations that have enabled a group such as al Qaeda to operate without a fixed and secure headquarters have included the use of modern telecommunications as well as organizational structures and procedures that do not require the top leaders to be in constant contact. Bin Laden and Zawahri's current roles in international terrorism are less that of operational commanders than of ideologists and propagandists. Being hunted men evidently has not significantly impaired that latter function—especially for Zawahri, with his frequent dissemination of taped messages.

The United States' use of military force to reduce terrorist capabilities has the same, less direct, but still damaging and counterproductive consequences as the use of force to retaliate for past terrorist attacks. The consequences may be all the greater insofar as this use of force is more sustained than simple retaliation and perhaps is seen as less justified as memories of past terrorist provocations fade.

71

One such consequence is to incur the wrath of civilian populations over the U.S. use of military force and the destruction resulting from it. This unfortunately has been in evidence in Afghanistan, which had been a rare oasis of goodwill toward the United States within a Muslim world in which anti-American sentiment is the norm. That goodwill has been significantly lessened by the collateral damage from U.S. military operations. Afghan President Hamid Karzai's "first demand" of Barack Obama was for the president-elect "to put an end to civilian casualties."[14]

Similar resentment—amid a population that was already less friendly toward the United States—has been evident in Pakistan in reaction to the missile strikes in the northwest.[15] The pattern repeats that seen after similar strikes in 2005 and 2006 against forces of the Union of Islamic Courts in Somalia, which did kill some militants but also instigated public anger against the United States and a resulting increase in the popularity and extremism of the Islamists.[16]

The tradeoff here is not between counterterrorism and popularity. It is between immediate tactical counterterrorist objectives and longer-term strategic ones. Anti-American sentiment impairs counterterrorism. It affects the willingness of a civilian population to cooperate with U.S. counterterrorist efforts, its willingness to support its own government's efforts, and the inclination of individual civilians to condone, support, or even join the efforts of anti-American terrorist groups.

That does not mean the broader and longer-term effects should always take precedence over the immediate tactical ones, but it does mean the former should always be considered even if they are less visible and measurable than the latter. It means taking into account that while the strikes using drones over Pakistan have killed some militants who were targeted, the same strikes have killed far more civilians—leaving that many more friends and family members of the deceased who might be willing to support anti-U.S. causes. And it means resisting the temptation to employ a technologically potent military capability because it is available and because alternative means for dealing with a problem are not. There is evidence that, at times, the United States has fallen to this temptation in its use of the drones; it has tended to see nails because the handiest tool available to it has been this very impressive hammer.

Negative consequences extend even more broadly, beyond populations that feel the immediate physical damage of military operations to ones that are nevertheless angered by them. Here, the United States bears the burden of being the world's sole superpower. Its use of military force is more likely than that of any other country to be resented as contemptible bullying by the big kid on the global block. Here too, the issue is not merely one of being liked or disliked; the potential effects on terrorism, counterterrorism, and the likelihood of future terrorist attacks on U.S. interests are substantial. The use of U.S. military force within the Muslim world has probably done more than anything else to sustain bin Laden's bogus narrative of a United States that is out to kill and subjugate Muslims and to plunder their resources.

Counterterrorism is a global enterprise, requiring the active cooperation and assistance of international actors—both state and nonstate. The most important cooperation is likely to come from the communities in which terrorist organizations attempt to recruit new followers and who are the intended audience for much of the organization's propaganda. Terrorist attacks are newsworthy and therefore attract the most attention to the organization's cause. By the same token, the effects of these operations often fall disproportionately on the very population that the organization is attempting to reach. The use of terrorism, therefore, is a double-edged sword. Terrorist organizations attempt to induce a targeted society to lash out, in the hopes that these reactions will cause harm to innocent civilians, engender hostility and hatred of the country carrying out the retaliatory acts, and drive more sympathy to the terrorists. We can prevent falling into the terrorists' trap by carefully limiting our responses.

Afghanistan, Iraq, and the "Global War on Terror"

It is in the larger strategic context of the "global war on terror" that the use of military force, and the associated language of warfare, can have a detrimental effect. Within a few months of 9/11, U.S. military personnel had dislodged al Qaeda from Afghanistan and overthrown Osama bin Laden's allies, the Taliban. That much of the on-the-ground fighting was done by Afghans, not Americans, and that they were advised and supported by nonmilitary personnel generally escaped public scrutiny. Devastating "daisy-cutter" bombs dropped on the al Qaeda stronghold at Tora Bora and images of

Special Forces personnel on horseback fit well within the "war on terror" paradigm crafted in the days immediately after 9/11.[17]

The requirements for achieving the U.S. objective in Afghanistan of preventing a terrorist safe haven will continue to be subject to discussion and debate. For our purposes, which concern the use in general of military force on behalf of counterterrorism, the pertinent questions are to what extent Afghanistan represents a phenomenon likely to arise elsewhere and to what extent physical safe havens are important in international terrorism.

There has been nothing else quite like Afghanistan under the Taliban, and nothing else at all like the alliance between the Taliban and al Qaeda. That alliance was not state sponsorship but instead a partnership in which the group helped the regime (in prosecuting the civil war) at least as much as the other way around. Whatever one's assessment of the advisability of maintaining a large-scale and effectively open-ended military presence in Afghanistan, our difficulties there have demonstrated just how costly and time-consuming such missions are likely to be. Leaving aside, therefore, that Afghanistan under the Taliban was an exceptional case, it is unclear whether the U.S. government would seriously contemplate a repeat of the Afghanistan experience elsewhere, even if another place could be shown to be a safe haven for al Qaeda.

These lessons have become clearer with the passage of time. In 2002, long before they had sunk in, the Bush administration, tragically and ironically, came close to creating another Afghanistan in Iraq. The supposed alliance between the previous Iraqi regime and al Qaeda was a figment of war-selling imagination, but the U.S. invasion itself triggered a new jihad in Iraq. It also became the single most conspicuous U.S. military action in recent years to sustain bin Laden's narrative and to accentuate broader resentment over alleged U.S. predations against the Muslim world. The aftereffects of the jihad against the Soviets in Afghanistan have manifested themselves for years in subsequent global jihadist terrorism. We can expect to see for many years ahead the terrorist aftereffects of the jihad against the United States in Iraq. The Iraq War, supposedly launched as part of a "war on terror," was a highly counterproductive use of military force as far as counterterrorism is concerned.

In contemplating possible intervention and stabilization operations in any other country that starts to show Afghan-like qualities, some questions about terrorist safe havens need to be addressed. One is whether, even if such a haven were important to terrorists, it needs to be in whatever country we happen to be contemplating. The question can be posed today about Afghanistan. If terrorists were denied haven there, could they not go instead to, say, Somalia? And as we think about such possibilities, where and how do we limit our military intervention?[18]

Even if convinced that a particular country is of unusual importance, both intrinsically and with regard to terrorism—as many regard Pakistan today—a further question is what this means in terms of military targets. In particular, what does it mean when terrorists live and plan and work in cities, where military force is apt to be an especially blunt and mostly unusable counterterrorist instrument? Terrorist activity that may eventually hurt us is more likely taking place in Karachi or Lahore than in a rural district in northwestern Pakistan.

Related to that question, and to the larger pattern of terrorism's presenting few good military targets, is the issue of how important are physical safe havens of any kind.[19] The cities in which terrorists do their preparations do not have to be in states that are hostile or, like Pakistan, unstable. They can be in the West. The preparations that mattered most in the 9/11 operation did not take place at training camps in Afghanistan but instead in apartments in Germany and Spain and at flight schools in the United States. We should worry more about extremists researching transportation schedules on a computer—and the computer could be anywhere in the world—than about ones practicing in a hand-to-hand combat pit somewhere in South Asia. We can bomb a training camp, but we cannot bomb the computer.

A response to this last point is that terrorist organizations such as al Qaeda rely on secure physical infrastructure, such as training camps, as part of their recruitment and indoctrination process, as well as of the general maintenance and management of the organization. Yet that does not speak to how essential any part of a group's existing organizational maintenance functions is to the activity that matters most to us, which is terrorist attacks. More importantly, terrorist threats—even just Sunni, Salafi, jihadist terrorist threats— do not emanate only from al Qaeda, or from any other established, infrastructure-laden organization. With increasing fractionation and decentralization of the jihadist movement, the threat in the coming years will more likely come from individuals, groups, and cells that are unburdened by any such physical infrastructure. It is a threat that emerges from alienated populations in places like Muslim communities in Europe, where military force is unemployable.

Another unintended consequence of military force is to contribute to the widespread perception that a group such as al Qaeda is a bona fide belligerent rather than a band of outlaws. Whatever else U.S. military efforts against bin Laden and his group have accomplished, they have conformed to his portrayal of a civilizational war between the Judeo-Christian West and the Muslim world, with the United States leading the fight for the former and bin Laden and his group doing so for the latter. As with an insurgent force confronting superior government forces in a guerrilla war, merely being able to survive in a military conflict becomes a sort of victory for the insurgents. In similar fashion, the more counterterrorism is seen as a military contest, the more terrorists can win merely by not losing.

Talking about Terrorism: Fighting a War or Managing a Problem

It is in talking about terrorism that the terminology of counterterrorism becomes particularly relevant. Just as the use of the military tool often has counterproductive effects, so too does casting the fight against al Qaeda and other terrorist groups of global reach as a "war" often undermine long-term counterterrorism objectives. When policymakers refer to a "war on terror," the term incorrectly implies that the military is the leading instrument of our counterterrorism efforts, and it further suggests that the challenge has a definite beginning and an equally definitive conclusion.[20] There is also the illogicality of declaring war on a tactic. It makes no more sense than the British and French declaring war on blitzkrieg in 1939, or the Americans declaring war on kamikazes in the Pacific in 1944. In both cases, strategy was appropriately directed toward an adversary—the Germans and Japanese, respectively—and not to the means they employed.

Other interrelated problems flow from the imprecise evocation of a "war on terror." The phrase has the effect of conflating many different entities into a supposedly monolithic threat; it complicates allied cooperation, and it gives legitimacy to terrorists as combatants.

Accordingly, the Department of Homeland Security in 2008 advised policymakers to "accurately identify the nature of the challenges that face our generation." "If senior government officials carefully select strategic terminology," the paper published by the Office for Civil Rights and Civil Liberties averred, "the government's public statements will encourage vigilance without unintentionally undermining security objectives."[21]

In general, referring to a "war on terror" tends to conflate the disparate threats posed by terrorist organizations, and it likewise has the effect of uniting different groups with very different aims. It also plays into the terrorists' own rhetoric that the West is engaged in a war against Islam. The problem was certainly exacerbated by President George W. Bush's ill-considered reference to an American crusade,[22] but the perception of an inevitable clash of civilizations would still be a problem even if senior government officials were more careful in their choice of words.

The danger of declaring a "global war on terror" (GWOT), and in conflating many disparate entities into a single monolithic threat, warned Jeffrey Record in a paper for the Strategic Studies Institute at the U.S. Army War College, was that it subordinated strategic clarity to moral clarity. Record cautioned that, by declaring a GWOT, the United States had embarked "on a course of open-ended and gratuitous conflict with states and nonstate entities that pose no serious threat to the United States."[23]

Moral clarity can lead to sloppy policy by uniting our enemies; it can also complicate relations with allies who are instrumental to combating a prototypical transnational threat. A report published by the Pentagon's Defense Science Board amplified these concerns. Evocative phrases such as "global war on terror," and "fighting them there so we don't fight them here," the DSB conceded, "may have short-term benefits in motivating support at home." However, this "polarizing rhetoric," the board went on to say, "can have adverse long-term consequences that reduce the willingness of potential allies to collaborate, and give unwarranted legitimacy and unity of effort to dispersed adversaries."[24]

Fighting the Terrorists on Our Terms, Not Theirs

Yet another problem associated with framing counterterrorism as a global war on terror is that it elevates and legitimizes terrorists as combatants. Some contend that the terrorists declared war on us and that it therefore makes no sense for us to temper our rhetoric.[25] But the opposite is closer to the truth. We should not let our adversaries set the terms of the debate, any more than we should allow them to pick and choose when and where we will fight them. Supporters of the GWOT mindset often cast terrorist leaders as the modern-day incarnation of Hitler or Stalin. But while Osama bin Laden or Ayman al-Zawahri might seem like Hitler or Stalin in their willingness to kill, and while they share the megalomania, they are very unlike the butchers of the 20th century who were, after all, the leaders of major nation-states and capable of mobilizing tens of millions of people on short notice. By contrast, modern-day terrorists can only dream of unleashing the scale of violence and chaos visited on the globe during World Wars I and II. We do not advance our broader objectives of diminishing their appeal to their target audience and otherwise rendering them to the margins of history—where they belong—by portraying them as being on par with the leaders of major industrial states.

But while experts on counterterrorism, including many in this volume, stress the need for carefully limiting our response to terrorism—both through the discriminate and rare use of military force and also through the careful employment of language—the impulse to overact and lash out will remain strong. In the emotional aftermath of a terrorist attack, political leaders and opinion makers will be strongly inclined to exaggerate, even if inadvertently, the nature of the threat. We can over time, however, erode the political utility of hyping the terror threat by patiently documenting what military actions have or have not worked in the past and by drawing attention to the multifaceted nature of counterterrorist efforts, which include military, but chiefly nonmilitary, initiatives. In this way, the war metaphor will become progressively less popular.

A sound and comprehensive counterterrorism strategy aims to calm public fears of terrorism by informing the intended targets of terrorism—the public at large—about the terrorists' actual capabilities to do harm. Suggesting that relatively minor and ultimately containable threats posed by disconnected terrorist organizations must be handled as we would a war with an industrial nation-state grossly overstates the nature of the terrorist threat and therefore undermines attempts to assuage public anxiety through dispassionate assessments of the terrorists' actual capabilities.

Rhetoric, and the shaping of expectations, are more important in the context of counterterrorism operations than in traditional wars. Victory or defeat in most wars is determined by armies on the battlefield, or fleets at sea. By contrast, because terrorists aim specifically at breaking the public will, measures intended at shoring up public resolve are a crucial element of effective counterterrorism strategy.

Despite the widespread skepticism toward the "war on terror" terminology—including some of the Bush administration's own agencies and advisory committees noted above, who warned against using the term—critics pounced when President Barack Obama appeared to move away from his predecessor's rhetorical framing of U.S. counterterrorist efforts. Former vice president Dick Cheney led the charge, expressing "serious doubts" about President Obama's conduct of U.S. counterterrorist efforts, "especially about the extent to which he understands and is prepared to do what needs to be done to defend the nation."[26] Former Speaker of the House Newt Gingrich, commenting on the Justice Department's decision to investigate the use of enhanced interrogation techniques on suspected terrorists, declared that "the Obama administration, still in the middle of a war with the radical wing of Islam, [was] waving a white flag of surrender."[27]

The bitter partisanship and institutional wrangling of the past eight years over the framing and conduct of U.S. counterterrorist efforts have clouded rather than clarified our understanding of the role that military force should play. In this context, the dispute over whether to continue with Bush administration policies concerning, for example, targeted assassinations and the use of unmanned aerial vehicles to kill suspected terrorists often obscures a fundamental point about how we should characterize counterterrorism overall. If most counterterrorist work will involve the use of the military, then it might be appropriate to cast these efforts—not merely rhetorically but legally—as warfare. If, by contrast, the military tool is often irrelevant, and occasionally counterproductive, to combating terrorism, then policymakers should consciously steer the conversation away from warfare per se and should focus the public's attention instead on the range of tools employed to advance public safety.

Americans broadly support the concept of using military operations to combat terrorism but are growing weary of specific large-scale missions—including those in Iraq and Afghanistan—where the costs appear to have outweighed the benefits. For example, a poll conducted in 2008 by the Chicago Council on Global Affairs found that strong majorities approved of "U.S. air strikes against terrorist training camps and other facilities," (79 percent) "attacks by U.S. ground troops against terrorist training camps and other facilities," (72 percent) and "assassination of individual terrorist leaders" (68 percent). The same poll showed deep reservations about the war in Iraq: 76 percent of respondents expressed regret that money spent on the Iraq venture could have been spent on needs at home, and nearly 6 in 10 said that the war had not reduced the threat of terrorism.[28] By the summer of 2009, doubts about the efficacy of the military force had crept into public attitudes toward the war in Afghanistan, which since 9/11 had enjoyed broad bipartisan support. In August, the *Washington Post* reported that, for the first time since they began asking the question, a majority of Americans (51 percent) believed that the Afghan war was "not worth fighting."[29] It is too soon to say whether this weakening of public support for these particular missions will apply generally to other major military interventions associated with counterterrorism, but it is clear that such support cannot be taken for granted.

Conclusion

The war on terror metaphor has obscured the nature of the terrorist challenge and at times undermined our ability to combat it effectively. Our resort to military force to deal with particular terrorist threats that might be better addressed by nonmilitary means likewise complicates our efforts. The two problems go hand in hand.

The Bush administration devised the GWOT framework partly to provide a rationale for using military force to remove Saddam Hussein from power in Iraq. The questionable rationales for that war—including the dubious linkage between Iraq and al Qaeda—combined with the chaos that ensued after the collapse of Hussein's rule, invited condemnation of many U.S. policies lumped under the GWOT and discouraged other countries from openly cooperating with U.S. officials.

As a political tool, a weapon wielded to discredit one's opponent, the GWOT remains potent. One of candidate Barack Obama's campaign slogans stressed "Hope over Fear," but few other political leaders have been so willing to dial down their rhetoric pertaining to terrorism, ever fearful of being perceived as having not done everything in their power in the event of another attack.

But the GWOT concept was also harmful in shaping thinking on counterterrorism, elevating the military in the policymakers' toolbox at the expense of other instruments of power that have proved more effective. Policymakers must appreciate the particular salience of nonmilitary means for addressing the terrorist challenge, and they should not be shy about calling attention to such measures—including, for example, information sharing among law enforcement and intelligence agencies, and lawful electronic surveillance of suspected terrorists—even at the risk of being portrayed by critics as being "soft" on terrorism. To steer clear of the language of warfare does not mean, as noted in this chapter, that the military cannot and should not play a role in combating terrorism. The key is in balancing the costs and risks of direct military action and, when such operations are deemed essential, combining them with operations that advance a broader agenda to diminish the gruesome appeal of terrorism in communities that have been willing to support or tolerate it. Reframing the nature of our counterterrorist efforts away from the military mindset—and confining military missions to those rare instances when the precise application of force can deliver significant benefits—will pay long-term dividends.

5. Assessing Counterterrorism, Homeland Security, and Risk

James A. Lewis

Homeland security and counterterrorism are not the same thing. In fact, since much of homeland security is aimed at preparing for highly improbable events, those efforts contribute little to reducing the threat of terrorist attack. Terrorism is a means—which we rightly regard as illegitimate—to obtain a political end. The end sought by Islamist terrorists is the recession of Western ideas and the spread of a polity based on sharia. We are in a political struggle with a theologically based insurgency that has global reach. Attacking civilian populations to create shock, distress, and fear is one of the most important tactics for this insurgency, with the goal of destroying the will of its opponents to resist. Effective counterterrorism ultimately depends on winning this political struggle.

The terrorists argue that their tactics are justified by Western indifference to their suffering, by the indiscriminate use of modern weapons against their civilian populations, and, perhaps, because they view their effort as sanctioned by some divine authority. It is also likely that many of the people who carry out these tactics are psychotic, that the violence fulfills some deep personal craving, and that they act out their fantasies of violence and revenge in the context of a justifying ideology and as part of a long-term strategy to achieve their political goals. The political nature of terrorist violence is an important factor, often overlooked, in assessing the risk of terrorism.

Terrorism is not new. The groups we face now are the inheritors of a violent legacy that stretches back to the anti-colonial struggles of the 1950s. What is new is the global nature of these attacks. World-spanning networks for trade, travel, and finance allow groups to project force globally. Porous borders, the immense migration of the last 30 years, and the ease with which immigrants flow between birth country and new home create new opportunities for violence.

The global context for terrorism, the stateless nature of the opponents, porous national borders, and the willingness to inflict unbounded violence against civilian targets greatly increase the risk of a successful attack in Western "homelands." Unfortunately, this risk is difficult to measure or assess. Assessing the risk of terrorist attack is a challenge for which the United States lacks extensive precedent and experience. Terrorism touches the civilian population directly, creating a heightened sense of fear and vulnerability. Our opponents' methods can seem irrational (although, in the main, they are not). The knowledge of having been surprised (in New York, London, or Madrid) and of having had many other narrow escapes haunts Western governments. Risk appears unbounded.

September 11, 2001, was a shock—it should not have been, as it was the third massive blow aimed at U.S. territory by al Qaeda in eight years—and this shock continues to drive U.S. policy in unhelpful ways.[1] A pervasive sense of vulnerability has shaped thinking on counterterrorism and "homeland security." The sense of vulnerability is compounded in the United States by a response, the set of policies we call homeland security, that has been organizational and mechanistic, almost willfully ignoring the larger political context in order to fret over specific threats. This response is largely irrelevant to counterterrorism. To understand this, it is useful to sketch out the elements of an effective counterterrorism strategy.

Elements of Counterterrorism

Counterterrorism has the immediate goal of preventing attacks and disrupting terrorist plans and organizations. Its long-term goal is to eliminate these groups by shrinking support (in terms of money and recruits) for terrorism. An effective counterterrorism program combines intelligence, law enforcement, military action, diplomacy, and economic activities to achieve these goals.

Effective counterterrorism has some resemblance to counterinsurgency, and the experience of the British in Malaya and the French in Algeria provides an instructive comparison for any effort to end terrorism. Insurgents in these countries, who used terror tactics, were split from their supporters, infiltrated, criminalized, and (in the case of Malaysia) ultimately destroyed. The core of an effective strategy is to identify and locate terrorists, disrupt their plans, cut off their sources of support, remove them from action, and discourage new recruits from joining their effort. Other activities (including many of the activities taken in the name of homeland security) make only an indirect contribution to counterterrorism.

The first essential component of effective counterterrorism is intelligence. Gathering information on terrorist groups, their members, supporters, intentions, and plans is essential to an effective defense and to eventually removing the terrorist threat. It involves recruiting human agents from the terrorist groups or their supporters. In today's environment, human intelligence collection must take place both domestically (conducted by the Federal Bureau of Investigation) and internationally (conducted largely by the Central Intelligence Agency). It also involves signals intelligence. Terrorism depends on global communications networks, and communications surveillance has been one of the most useful tools of the U.S. counterterror effort.

The second essential element is aggressive enforcement of criminal law against terrorists. Some aspects of the law enforcement effort are in fact intelligence activities conducted domestically—the recruitment of informants and the surveillance of communications. However, it is the ability of police forces to arrest, try, and imprison that degrades terrorists' effectiveness and creates a powerful deterrent to terrorist action. Treating terrorists like criminals rather than as combatants helps delegitimize and deflate their cause and is an important part of the political struggle.

Law enforcement activities that contribute to counterterrorism also include the interdiction of financial networks. This specialized activity is important for dealing with global opponents who operate across many states and who are willing to use the financial networks developed for international commerce. Successful interdiction has forced groups to move back to *hawala* (traditional financial networks) or to couriers, complicating planning efforts and creating some deterrent effect.

Law enforcement for counterterrorism also includes border control and customs, missions assigned in the United States to the Department of Homeland Security. We know from experience that terrorists will exploit weak controls on the entry of people. We should avoid, however, overemphasizing the importance of border controls in preventing terrorism. Sealing borders against terrorists is not possible at reasonable cost. The scale of illegal immigration into the United States suggests that a trained terrorist would have a good chance of success in walking across one of the land borders. And as the continued inflow of narcotics demonstrates, it is possible with ingenuity and enough money to get anything into the country.

Controls on the entry of goods have focused spending and effort on preventing the entry of weapons of mass destruction (WMDs) disguised as licit shipments, but this is unrealistic. Acquiring a nuclear weapon or radiological material would be a major coup for a terrorist group, and it would be unlikely to let it out of its control, so the notion of terrorists placing the weapon in a container in some overseas port and waving goodbye makes little sense—they would be likely to accompany it to the target. Terrorists will seek to avoid customs inspections and immigration checkpoints and will rely on illicit means of entry for both people and goods, or rely on domestic recruitment and acquisitions to evade border controls.

Law enforcement also provides "point defense" against terrorism. Police patrols, border inspections, and airport checkpoints all complicate terrorist planning. But as the last line of defense, such measures come into play only if the terrorists have succeeded in evading other efforts and have approached their target. If we catch a terrorist trying to board an aircraft, it means that the CIA and FBI have failed.

Counterterrorism requires an expanded use of police and intelligence powers by a country, but that creates normative and practical difficulties. From a normative perspective, effective counterterrorism raises civil liberties concerns. The need to ensure greater cooperation between intelligence and law enforcement agencies amplifies these concerns, particularly in the United States, which has a greater degree of separation between domestic law enforcement and intelligence than is found in other countries.

In fact, some suspension of civil liberties has been a part of almost all anti-terror campaigns in every country. Even if terrorism is treated as a crime and is prosecuted under normal criminal law, many nations have found it necessary to pass legislation providing police with additional investigative authorities that are less constrained by civil liberties safeguards. Anti-terror programs invariably make it easier to surveil and investigate, to detain, and to suppress certain political activities. The issue is not whether to restrict civil liberties to some degree but rather the scope, duration, and rationale of the intrusions.

The precedent in the United States has been to overreact. The Palmer raids of the 1920s, McCarthyism in the 1950s, and the various intrusions of the 1960s (such as the FBI's COINTELPRO program, which was designed to penetrate and disrupt dissident groups) suggest some consistent weakness in American governance. When it came to civil liberties, those overreactions eventually proved to be self-correcting. Overreaction can also inflict lasting economic damage. An astute terrorist might seek to use attacks to trigger this overreaction to damage a state. The greatest damage from the nation's inability to assess risk accurately may not come from resources squandered on irrelevant programs but from unnecessary losses for the national economy.

If intelligence and law enforcement form the core of effective counterterrorism, military force plays only a supporting role. There is no capital city to bomb, no port to blockade. Terrorist groups are not connected to any nation, although the goal of some groups is to create a new state. If they connect to a state, as al Qaeda did with the Taliban government, they become much more vulnerable because they provide a convenient target for retaliation.

The use of conventional force carries political risk of escalating or prolonging the conflict. The use of massive force brings collateral damage, and we know from experience that harm to innocent bystanders (e.g., an air strike against a wedding party or the accidental shooting of a relative) are among the best recruitment tools for our opponents. Such mistakes are not the result of malevolent intent (although they're portrayed that way by terrorists and their supporters) but an unavoidable part of combat with heavy weapons. Minimizing the role of conventional military forces and heavy weapons could actually increase the effectiveness of counterterrorism.[2]

The United States benefited when it used military force (albeit paramilitary groups from the CIA, supported by Army Special Forces and air power) to dislodge al Qaeda from Afghanistan. The subsequent action in Iraq inflamed many potential recruits and detracted from the more important counterterrorism effort in Afghanistan. If one primary measure of effective counterterrorism is the effect on the political environment that produces terrorism, then, on balance, the effort in Iraq probably increased the terrorist threat by giving political advantage to our opponents and by increasing their popular support and the supply of recruits from the Islamic community both in the region and in Europe and North America.

Diplomatic activity—working with foreign partners and shaping the policies and responses of other governments—is crucial for countering global terror. This activity involves obtaining the support, open or tacit, of other governments to pursue terrorists and for these governments to undertake their own anti-terror operations. It can involve gaining permission for U.S. agents to operate in a country, encouraging a country to undertake its own anti-terror operations, or securing its agreement to cooperate with U.S. efforts.

The diplomatic task is extremely difficult. The terrorists we face have some sympathy in the Middle East, making governments there less willing to crack down. Saudi Arabia, for example, will move swiftly and effectively against terrorist groups that threaten its stability, but it is much less forceful in moving against wealthy Saudis who finance terrorism abroad. In the current, religion-based struggle, diplomatic engagement that appears serious in trying to address the Israel-Palestine issue can help reduce support and recruits for terrorism, reduce the appearance of legitimacy of terrorist groups, and encourage other governments in the region to be more active.

Counterterrorism resembles counterinsurgency, but there are crucial differences. In counterinsurgency, economic development and political reform are crucial components of a successful effort, as they help reduce support for the insurgents and reduce the flow of new recruits. In a global campaign, however, they are less effective. The United States cannot restructure the political systems of other countries—the attempt in Iraq was a disaster—and we cannot provoke quick economic growth without political reform. Incremental improvements that may bring prosperity to the Middle East a generation hence will not protect us against terrorism today.

The goal of promoting economic development and political reform is to change the calculus for potential recruits: join the terrorists and face the increased probability of death or imprisonment or decide to remain a noncombatant and take advantage of increasing economic and political opportunities.[3] In an international conflict, however, it is easier for the United States to increase the disincentives.

This is not to say that engagement and aid do not have a role, but we must be careful not to overestimate their benefits or their chances of success. We are dealing with a large cadre of hardened opponents who are persuaded of the righteousness of their cause. They come from societies and political regimes that are resistant to change, including change needed for economic growth. Increased aid and engagement are intended to change the political dynamics that produce terrorism, but in fact, most of this political dynamic lies outside of U.S. control. One uncomfortable element of counterterrorism is that in the near and medium term, U.S. security may benefit more from efficient repression in foreign countries than from the messy process of liberalization. There is no black or white answer, and an effective program will need to calibrate the mix of long-term support for reform against the immediate benefits of support for existing regimes.

The ultimate goal is to change the political calculus of terrorists and their recruits as to the justification and benefits of terrorist action. If terrorists and their supporters are persuaded that the risk of action is too high, that there are other avenues for dissent, and that the justification for terror is wrong, the number of opponents will shrink to a hard core that will need to be removed from action.

For the United States, the most important political aspect of counterterrorism is not reform or development overseas but the political message it conveys through its actions. Actions that reinforce the perception of Middle Eastern audiences that the United States is hostile help terrorism. The treatment of immigrant populations is also crucial. The failure in Europe to integrate Middle Eastern immigrants and to inculcate in them Western political norms has created a discontented population that is fertile ground for recruitment. Expanded enforcement and intelligence activities against terrorists by the United States must balance the need to identify and disrupt domestic terrorism while avoiding efforts that could unfairly single out and alienate this immigrant population.

Counterterrorism in the past was usually a domestic law enforcement activity or, at most, a cross-border activity involving sanctuaries in neighboring countries. The conflict we are in now is the first global episode of terrorism, with disparate attacks on many continents, and an effective response requires broad international engagement by the United States. What is unusual in the U.S. response since 9/11 is the heavy emphasis on homeland security, essentially civil defense. There is an almost despairing assumption that terror attacks are unstoppable and the United States must prepare for the worst—chemical, biological, or radiological attack, or in the most extreme case, the detonation of a fully functioning thermonuclear device. These efforts have largely been divorced from probability, creating immense problems for homeland defense and counterterrorism strategies in the United States.

The core of the U.S. counterterrorism effort rests with the Central Intelligence Agency, the National Security Agency, and the Federal Bureau of Investigation. The Department of Defense and the Department of State also have important roles. The work of those agencies to detect and disrupt terrorist plans and actions is America's primary line of defense. If the Department of Homeland Security had never been created, its absence would not have reduced the effectiveness of this primary counterterrorism effort or greatly increased the risk of a successful terrorist attack. This does not mean that there is no role for the Department of Homeland Security, but its primary mission is not counterterrorism.

Homeland Security

After the cold war's end, a growing consensus argued that the United States would face new kinds of threats, including terrorism, unconventional uses of WMDs, and attacks on the domestic population and infrastructure. That assessment proved to be correct, but its corollary, that opponents would use unconventional weapons, remains doubtful.

A series of reports in the 1990s called for a new approach to national defense, which would secure critical infrastructure and cyberspace to deal with terrorism and WMDs.[4] One of these reports called for major reorganization to meet the new threats. The third report of the Hart-Rudman Commission, released in January 2001, called for the creation of a new independent National Homeland Security Agency (NHSA) with responsibility for planning, coordinating, and integrating various government activities involved in homeland security." The new agency would combine Customs, Border Patrol, and the Coast Guard with new Directorates for Critical Infrastructure Protection and Emergency Preparedness and Response.

It remains unclear whether any of these suggested changes would have happened without the 9/11 attacks. The attacks provided the political energy for massive federal reorganization, sweeping new legislation, and, at least temporarily, a new emphasis on vigilance at all levels of government to detect and prevent terrorist attacks on the territory of the United States.

We still live with the result of this change, from the signs in airports announcing that the threat level is unchangeably orange (raising it leads to immense expense; lowering it is politically risky) to massive federal spending to protect against a range of potential threats. It is useful to ask, however, how much this reorganization and the associated efforts protect against terrorism. They are defensive measures, preventive actions, things the United States does to itself rather than to terrorists. The desired effect on terrorists is to change their calculations of the benefits and difficulties of a potential attack. These measures do not stop terrorists from attacking, they make terrorists adopt other (and we hope less damaging) weapons and tactics.

An equally damaging problem lies with the assessment of risk. DHS's priority missions are border protection and preparedness. The emphasis on preparedness is the product of the many reports from the 1990s, which identified domestic attack by terrorists using WMDs as one of the greatest new threats the nation would face. That this has never occurred in the two decades since the warnings began has not decreased their frequency or volume.

Counterterrorism, Homeland Security, and Risk Assessment

Risk assessment is the greatest problem for planning in homeland security. The problem has three elements. First, the WMD preparedness mission involves very low probability events that have potentially large consequences. The tendency has been to overestimate both probability and consequences (evidentiary standards and methodology for risk assessment are weak). The second element is that terrorists, who seek asymmetric advantage and surprise, will devote considerable effort to planning attacks for which we have not prepared. This observation does not mean that we should not prepare, but it imposes a kind of ceiling on how much effort to expend, to avoid building a Maginot Line that terrorists will bypass. The third element is that many assessments of risk routinely underestimate the "collateral damage" to the economy as a result of heightened security efforts; if we screen all containers entering the country, it will disrupt supply chains and increase company costs, all to prevent the very low risk of a dirty bomb being smuggled in this way.[5]

Improving predictive capability is probably beyond our capacity as a nation. Politically, it is more convenient to express grave concern over a lack of preparation and then spend heavily on preparations. There is no immediate penalty for overspending, and support can always be found to justify massive expenditure. Nor is there any accounting of the economic losses created by overzealous defense. Because the threats we are defending against are so improbable, we have little ability to measure the benefit of a program other than by how much is spent on it. We can spend large sums of money without substantially reducing the risk of an attack.

The model used by the United States for risk assessment says that risk is determined by threat, vulnerability, and consequences. DHS considers all areas of the nation equally vulnerable to a successful terrorist attack and assigns every state and urban area the same level of vulnerability in its risk analysis model.[6] In practice, the focus is on consequences rather than vulnerability, while the probability of a particular form of attack is generally ignored.

The difficulty of assessing risk is not entirely a new problem for the United States, where for many years expenditure has been equated with security. We spend more than most other nations combined to prepare for attacks. Long experience and planning guide defense expenditures, but some investments, such as missile defense, involve threats whose probability is difficult to assess. Unlike defense, homeland security is intimately linked to domestic activities and to the economy—it involves regulation and interference with transport and travel. A defense program may channel resources to unproductive areas, but a homeland security program will not only consume resources, it can also damage the economy.

One CIA advisory group, for example, concluded that the 9/11 attacks demonstrated how an adversary could cripple the United States by attacking nontraditional, primarily private-sector targets. This conclusion is inaccurate but could be more accurately phrased as "9/11 demonstrated that a shrewd opponent could use attacks to precipitate actions where the United States would injure itself." This suggests that the goals of counterterrorism and homeland security could conflict in some circumstances. If our opponents are looking for unconventional attacks, what could be more enticing than to trigger antibodies that lead the U.S. to attack itself?

A neutral approach to estimating risk would examine the causes and consequences of previous attacks. It would estimate the likelihood of a potential attacker selecting a target and which weapon or kind of weapon an attacker would be likely to use against it (and this involves an understanding of the attackers' motives, preferences, strategic rationale, goals, capabilities, and experience). It would attempt to match attacker goals and capabilities against potential infrastructure vulnerabilities, in effect duplicating the analysis and planning process of potential attackers, as they identify targets and estimate the likelihood of success in achieving their goals using a particular weapon and tactics.

America's political culture shapes analyses of risk. The federal government has become progressively more risk-averse since the 1970s.[7] The reasons for this include a loss of confidence among political elites, decreased public trust of government, and partisanship. This political change is important for understanding counterterrorism and homeland security. A risk-averse government will estimate the probability of a damaging attack as higher than a more neutral approach might suggest.

More importantly, politics drives spending on homeland security. Preparation has become an important source of federal subsidies. It goes beyond the mild conundrum of researchers who stand to benefit from increased funding by being the most vocal about looming vulnerabilities; the greater problem is the politicization of homeland security grants. This is a well-known story that immensely distorts U.S. counterterror strategies. In theory, a grant allocation "reflects the intelligence community's best assessment of areas of the country and potential targets most likely to be attacked,"[8] but it is easy to deride agency efforts, from rural states getting preference over major urban areas to the Amish Country Popcorn Company of Berne, Indiana (population 4,200) or Florida's Weeki Wachee Springs ("City of Mermaids") being designated as critical infrastructure and thus eligible for grants. A grant to a Kentucky state agency helped prevent terrorists from using bingo games to fund their operations.[9]

These examples are symptoms of a larger problem. The Department of Homeland Security is too weak to withstand congressional pressure (any agency would find this difficult). The weak linkage between probability and threat makes it difficult to distinguish between many minor risks and a few major threats. A rigorous approach would limit risk to outcomes that affect the macroeconomic performance of the United States or that reduce U.S. military capabilities.

Every society has the ability to absorb a certain amount of death and destruction without serious consequence. To put risk in perspective, 16,000 Americans were murdered in 2007.[10] That did not lead to the collapse of the state or the end of our way of life. Those murders were not centrally organized or politically motivated, nor did they occur simultaneously in the same location, but they suggest a degree of national resilience that is usually underestimated. Horrific overestimates of casualties and their consequences have become part of the national discourse on homeland security. This imprecision and exaggeration do a disservice to the nation. As one op-ed by a prominent group of authors proclaimed:

> Shame on our leaders and on us if the lamentations of the next blue-ribbon panel will be intoned over the graves of hundreds of thousands of Americans, the collapse of our economy, and perhaps a fatal blow to our way of life.[11]

What kind of terrorist attack would kill hundreds of thousands of Americans? The only plausible scenario would involve the detonation of a nuclear weapon in a city. The detonation at Hiroshima, for example, killed about 70,000 people immediately and an equal number thereafter from the effects of the blast and radiation. No other weapon would have a similar effect. Deaths from radiological "dirty" bombs are limited to the blast area—at most a few blocks. Those who escaped the initial blast would be unlikely to suffer harm. Chemical and biological weapons are difficult to produce, weaponize, and deliver on target—we know this from the extensive experimentation undertaken by the United States and the Soviet Union during the cold war. If terrorists could acquire a crop-duster, and if the weather conditions were right and the operation unhindered, they could deliver a chemical or biological weapon in sufficient quantity to cause mass casualties—but the odds are heavily against them.

The op-ed confidently asserts, "There is little doubt that al Qaeda intends to and can detonate a weapon of mass destruction on U.S. soil." That the intention exists is clear (although it might better be described as a wish than a strategy), but there is no evidence that al Qaeda has access to nuclear weapons. Radiological, biological, or cyber weapons all create risk, but the likelihood of attack and the potential for damage vary widely from weapon to weapon. The more exotic the attack, the less likely it is to occur or to succeed.

Fear of a pandemic also appears exaggerated—the World Health Organization estimated that 2 to 7 million people could die in an avian flu pandemic, for example.[12] But since 2003, there have been 467 cases of avian flu, resulting in 282 deaths.[13] The source of the exaggeration may be the assumptions that medical research and treatment have not progressed since 1919 and that the government would lack the will to impose strict quarantine regulations (which are surprisingly effective in limiting the spread of disease).[14]

What explains this discrepancy between risk and perception? During the cold war, analysts became accustomed to thinking about horrible things that never happened—from nuclear winter to atomic war. This willingness to suspend disbelief has carried over to the war on terrorism. There are also important differences between policy experts and terrorists. Experts imagine exotic attack scenarios. Terrorists are conservative. They prefer reliable weapons that are easy to acquire and use. Terrorists know that bombs work and that in civilian settings bombs cause terror. Attacks using exotic, untried weapons are more likely to be detected and more likely to fail. Our enemies in Iraq and Afghanistan are innovators, creating new and deadlier bombs every month, but there has yet to be a casualty from a dirty bomb or biological weapon. Terrorists have researched bioweapons, but they appear to have set them aside as unlikely to work without major investments and the creation of vulnerable infrastructure.[15] It is difficult to weaponize and deliver biological agents, even more difficult if the goal is mass casualties, as they can be degraded by exposure to rain, sunlight, air, and wind. Our opponents seem to have decided that it is better to stick with those weapons they know will work.

Politics and Legitimacy: Fragile or Robust?

The counterargument to a more risk-tolerant approach is that it ignores the political effects of a successful attack. A successful attack damages a government's credibility and influence and creates the risk of an overreaction by security forces that does more damage than the attack itself. Some war games even contemplate nonstate actors' launching attacks with the knowledge that while the actual damage would be limited, overreaction would do much more damage (the history of the Transportation Security Agency and the air passenger business, where large costs to consumers and taxpayers are traded for a modest reduction in risk, demonstrates this effect). While the "self-inflicting strategy" may not appeal to the most violence-prone attackers in the various jihadi groups, it is the most likely scenario for a terrorist attack that could trigger long-term economic damage.

Nevertheless, the political consequences of an attack can backfire against the terrorists if their intent is to break the will of the target country to resist. In many instances, the effect of an attack is to harden resistance and increase support for an incumbent government. Even unpopular governments tend to benefit politically.[16] Political leaders who put forth the right message of steadfast resolve in the face of attacks will actually improve their standings. This support can be lost if the response to an attack is seen as an overreaction or as ineffective. But a government may limit political harm if it offers the right messages, avoids self-inflicted damage, and is seen as making progress in reducing risks of further attacks.

Avoiding Maginot on the Potomac

Tired of being invaded by the Germans every few years, France hit on the ideal solution. It would build a mighty wall of fortifications to block the route of the next invasion. By fortifying France, by securing its borders, it would bring safety to the Third Republic. Everyone knows that the Germans simply went around the Maginot Line. It has become a symbol for a mindless defensive mentality. Few strategists would recommend a Maginot-like approach for defense, but there are powerful, Maginot-like tendencies in our thinking about homeland security.

The Maginot Line experience shows that an inventive opponent will simply go around a massive defense. More importantly, what the Maginot Line should teach us is that those who are active, nimble, and unafraid are most secure. The real point of the Maginot Line is that building the best defenses in the world can make a nation less safe. That there have not been any mass terror attacks since 9/11, even though, according to some critics, our borders are open, our ports insecure, and our preparations inadequate, is suggestive. The brunt of the battle is borne by the CIA, the National Security Agency, the FBI, and the military. Their efforts, in cooperation with foreign partners, to capture terrorists and disrupt their plans are the most successful means to prevent attacks and eventually defeat terrorism.

For fiscal year 2010, the president requested more than $55 billion for the Department of Homeland Security.[17] That is more than the military budgets of all other nations except China. We are either very safe or very inefficient. These expenditures, combined with the political unease generated by some of the counterterrorism and homeland security measures, help explain the general sense that the effort is overextended and needs to be refocused with regard to spending, mission, and intrusions into public life. A focused counter-terrorism effort faces two major obstacles, however: a highly politi-cized threat assessment process, unhelpfully linked to subsidies for local governments, and imprecise and overly expansive definitions of risk and mission.

An effective counterterrorism strategy would use expanded intelli-gence and law enforcement activities to disrupt terrorist operations and erode terrorism's political underpinnings. An effective protec-tion strategy would prevent terrorists from accessing nuclear weap-ons, accelerate medical research, and create the rules and organiza-tions that would allow governments to respond swiftly to incidents, using quarantine and other public health measures as needed. All other activities, to the extent that they divert resources and attention from the central missions or harm the American economy or polity, work against the national defense.

6. Assessing Measures Designed to Protect the Homeland[1]

John Mueller

Some 34 percent of homeland security outlays are devoted to making potential targets less vulnerable to terrorist attack—to protecting what the Department of Homeland Security calls "critical infrastructure" and "key assets" or "key resources."[2] I seek here to set out some general parameters for coming to grips with this homeland security concern and to supply a framework for analysis. As illustration, I then apply the parameters to forge something of an assessment of which targets it may make sense to seek to protect and which ones might best be left unprotected.

My concern, then, is with *protection*—measures constituting what the military might call passive defense, such as posting security guards, hardening targets against explosions, screening people entering an area, setting up barriers, and installing security cameras.[3]

I do not deal with *policing* or other active defense measures—efforts to hunt down and detain terrorists after they have committed violent acts or (preferably, of course) before they have done so. Nor am I focusing on *mitigation*—measures that seek to reduce the consequences of a terrorist attack after it happens, such as establishing emergency procedures for evacuation, measures that might contain the damage, or facilities to provide medical treatment to the injured. Nor do I seek to assess the promotion of *resilience*—the ability to absorb and respond sensibly to a terrorist attack.[4] The costs and benefits of policing, of mitigation, and of resilience promotion should be subjected to a similar analysis, but, except incidentally, that is not the focus here.

Policy Considerations: Premises

There seem to be at least eight premises that should be considered when formulating policy for protecting the homeland or seeking to reduce its vulnerability.

1. The Number of Potential Terrorist Targets Is Essentially Infinite
Terrorists seek to kill people and/or destroy property in pursuit of a political goal.[5] They may exercise some discrimination in selecting targets, but because people and vulnerable property are everywhere in the United States, they have a wealth of potential targets—there are about 5 million commercial buildings alone.[6] Nothing can be done to change this fundamental condition. Indeed, it is difficult to think of something that *couldn't* be a target. Even a tree in the woods, after all, could be ignited to start a forest fire.

2. The Number of Terrorists Appears to Be Exceedingly Small and Their Efforts and Competence Rather Limited
Since terrorism of a considerably destructive nature can be perpetrated by a small group, or even by a single individual, the fact that terrorists are few does not mean there is no problem. However, many homeland security policies were established when the threat seemed far larger, and those perceptions may still be fueling, and distorting, current policy.

Thus in 2002, intelligence reports asserted that the number of trained al Qaeda operatives in the United States was between 2,000 and 5,000.[7] And on February 11, 2003, Robert Mueller, director of the Federal Bureau of Investigation, assured a Senate committee that al Qaeda had "developed a support infrastructure" in the country and had achieved "the ability and the intent to inflict significant casualties in the US with little warning."[8] By 2005, however, after years of well funded sleuthing, the FBI and other investigative agencies concluded in a secret report that they had been unable to uncover a single true al Qaeda sleeper cell anywhere in the United States,[9] a finding (or nonfinding) publicly acknowledged two years later.[10]

Al Qaeda deserves special attention here because, as stated by Glenn Carle, a 23-year veteran of the Central Intelligence Agency, where he was deputy national intelligence officer for transnational threats, it is "the only Islamic terrorist organization that targets the U.S. homeland."[11] However, if one looks at attacks worldwide outside of war zones since 9/11 not only by al Qaeda but also by its imitators, enthusiasts, look alikes, and wannabes, the number of people killed amounts to some 200–300 per year.[12] That, of course, is 200–300 too many, but it suggests that the threat is rather limited. Moreover, the rate of terrorist mayhem outside of war zones may, if anything, be declining.[13]

In assessing dangers presented by international terrorists, then, policymakers should keep in mind Carle's warning: "We must see jihadists for the small, lethal, disjointed and miserable opponents that they are." Al Qaeda "has only a handful of individuals capable of planning, organizing and leading a terrorist organization," and "its capabilities are far inferior to its desires."[14]

In testimony on January 11, 2007, Director Mueller suggested that "we believe al Qaeda is still seeking to infiltrate operatives into the U.S. from overseas," but even that may not be true. Since 9/11, well over a billion foreigners have been admitted to the United States legally, and many others have entered illegally.[15] Even if border security was so good that 90 percent of al Qaeda's operatives were turned away or deterred from trying to enter, some should have made it in—and some of those, it seems reasonable to suggest, would have been picked up by law enforcement by now. The lack of true al Qaeda attacks inside the United States combined with the inability of the FBI to find any potential attackers suggests that the terrorists either are not trying very hard or are far less clever and capable than usually depicted.

It follows that any terrorism problem within the United States principally derives from homegrown people, often isolated from one another, who fantasize about performing dire deeds. In the same testimony, Mueller stressed that his chief concern about terrorism within the United States is now with homegrown groups. From time to time, some of these people may manage to do some harm, though in most cases their capacities and schemes—or alleged schemes—seem to be far less dangerous than initial press reports suggest.

Although they someday might conceivably rise to the cleverness of the 9/11 plot, far more likely to be representative is the experience of the would-be bomber of a shopping mall in Rockford, Illinois, who exchanged two used stereo speakers (he couldn't afford the opening price of $100) for a bogus handgun and four equally bogus hand grenades supplied by an FBI informant.[16] Had the weapons been real, he might actually have managed to do some harm, but the threat he posed was clearly quite limited. Political scientist Michael Kenney has interviewed dozens of officials and intelligence agents and has analyzed court documents, and he finds homegrown Islamic militants to be operationally unsophisticated, short on know how, prone to making mistakes, poor at planning, and severely hampered by a limited capacity to learn.[17] Another study documents the difficulties of network coordination that continually threaten operational unity, trust, cohesion, and the ability to act collectively.[18]

By contrast, the image projected by the DHS is of an enemy that is "relentless, patient, opportunistic, and flexible"; shows "an understanding of the potential consequence of carefully planned attacks on economic transportation, and symbolic targets"; is a serious threat to "national security"; and could inflict "mass casualties, weaken the economy, and damage public morale and confidence."[19] That description may fit some terrorists—the 9/11 hijackers among them—but not, it seems likely, the vast majority.

3. In Many Cases, Target Selection Is Effectively a Random Process

Homegrown terrorists—and, as Director Mueller suggests, they seem to be the most likely prospective perpetrators of terrorism in the United States—are likely to select targets for their convenience. Thus the would be bomber targeted the Rockford Mall because it was nearby. Similarly, the two men who sought to ram a car loaded with explosives into the Glasgow, Scotland, airport in 2007 presumably selected that target because they happened to live nearby. This process, together with other internal motivating mechanisms stressing group cohesion and camaraderie more than grand planning,[20] effectively makes terrorists' target selection something like a random process. Efforts to determine terrorist "intent" in advance become, then, highly problematic.[21]

4. The Probability of Any Specific Target Being Attacked Is Extremely Small in Almost All Cases

Despite the attention it garners, terrorism is rather rare, comprising incidental, isolated acts of mayhem perpetrated by individuals or by small groups, violence that generally does a comparatively limited amount of damage. Even under quite dire scenarios, in a country like the United States, the chance of an individual target being hit is vanishingly small. Indeed, at present rates, and assuming another 9/11 every several years, the lifetime probability that a resident of the globe who lives outside a war zone will die at the hands of international terrorists is about 1 in 80,000.[22] For that number to change radically, terrorists would have to become *vastly* more capable of inflicting damage: in fact, they would pretty much need to acquire an atomic arsenal and the capacity to deploy and detonate it.[23]

Given that it can be carried out by a single individual or by a very small group, terrorism, like crime, can never be fully extinguished. Therefore, it is, of course, essentially certain that terrorists will strike *some* target *somewhere*. However, the chance that any individual target will be attacked is exceedingly small in almost all cases. Protection measures may effectively reduce this likelihood further by deterring the terrorists or by reducing the target's vulnerability to attack. But for the overwhelmingly vast number of targets, they do so by nudging that likelihood from near zero to even more near zero.[24] And the question is, as risk analyst Howard Kunreuther puts it, "How much should we be willing to pay for a small reduction in probabilities that are already extremely low?"[25]

5. If One Potential Target Enjoys a Degree of Protection, the Agile Terrorist Can Generally Readily Move on to Another One

There is also something that might be called "the displacement effect." Terrorists can choose, and change, their targets depending on local circumstances. This process, of course, does not hold in the case of natural disasters: a tornado bearing down on Kansas does not choose to divert to Oklahoma if it finds Kansans too well protected. In stark contrast, if the protection of one target merely causes the terrorist to seek out another from among the near infinite set at hand, it is not clear how society has gained by expending effort and treasure to protect the first. The people who were saved in the first locale gain, of course, but their grief is simply displaced onto others.

There have been instances in Israel in which suicide bombers, seeing their primary targets, shopping malls, rather well protected, blew themselves up instead on the street.[26] The Israelis count this as something of a gain since they claim that fewer people died as a consequence, a fact likely to be of little comfort to the victims' families. Actually, however, if the goal of terrorists is to kill, a shopping mall is generally not that lucrative a target because people inside tend to be fairly widely dispersed, something that is often less true on the sidewalks outside.[27]

It also seems essentially impossible, due to the massive number of lucrative targets the country presents, to protect them enough so that international terrorists are directed in frustration to visit their violence on other countries. Measures that make it sufficiently difficult for outside terrorists to get into the country may conceivably do so, but not those devoted to protection.

6. To the Degree Protection Measures Make One Target Safer, They Make Other Targets Less Safe

An inference deriving from the displacement effect should be specifically pointed out and considered. Building hurricane shelters in one area does not increase the likelihood of another place being struck by the hurricane. But in the case of terrorism, the displacement effect essentially means that any effort to protect, or to deter a terrorist attack on, a potential target puts other targets more at risk.[28] Obviously, this would be of no concern if all potential targets could be protected, but that is clearly impossible. Protection policy, therefore, necessarily requires making choices about what to protect, and this, equally necessarily, means that targets left off the protection list become more attractive to the terrorist.

For example, there is a program to protect bridges in the United States, and a list of about 200 of the most important bridges has been drawn up. There seems to be no evidence that terrorists have any particular desire to blow up a bridge, due in part, perhaps, to the fact that it is an exceedingly difficult task under the best of circumstances and that the number of casualties would likely be much lower than for many other targets.[29] The hope of the protectors apparently is that, after security is improved for all these targets, any terrorists who happen to have bridges on their hit list will become disillusioned. If so, however, they might become inclined to move on to the 201st bridge or, more likely perhaps, to another kind of bridge: the highway overpass, of which there are some 590,000 in the United States.[30] If the terrorists' attention is drawn, further, to any one of a wide array of multiple overpass bridge networks, they might be inclined to destroy one of those. The financial and human consequence, not to mention the devastating traffic inconvenience, that could result from such an explosion might well surpass the destructive consequences of one directed at one of those 200 bridges. The issue then is, how has society benefited from the protection of the bridges?

7. Most Targets Are "Vulnerable" in That They Are Fairly Easily Damaged, but They Are "Invulnerable" in That They Can Be Rebuilt Fairly Quickly and at Tolerable Expense

On the one hand, most—probably almost all—potential terrorist targets are "vulnerable" in the sense that they can be damaged, in many cases badly, even by a simple explosion. On the other hand, if a damaged target can be readily repaired or replaced at an acceptable cost in time and money, including reasonable compensation to any victims—that is, if the effect of the violence can be readily absorbed—there is a sense in which one could say that the target is not vulnerable. (This discussion focuses entirely on material targets; people are also highly vulnerable and, if killed, cannot, of course, be "repaired.") For example, the considerable damage inflicted on the Pentagon on 9/11 was repaired fairly quickly, as were the tourist facilities destroyed in the Bali attack in 2002.

8. It Is Essentially Impossible to Adequately Protect a Wide Variety of Potential Terrorist Targets Except by Closing Them Down Completely

Veronique de Rugy has drawn an important lesson from Britain's experience with terrorism during the July 2005 attacks on the London Underground.[31] In part because of previous experience with Irish Republican Army terrorism in the city, the London Underground is normally fairly well policed. Then, after the terrorist attacks of July 7, 2005, those prevention and protection measures were, of course, vastly enhanced. Despite those enhanced measures, terrorists successfully infiltrated more bombs into the Underground a mere two weeks after the first attack. As it happened, the bombs did no damage because they were poorly constructed and did not actually explode. But this fortunate result, of course, stems entirely from terrorist incompetence, not from the protective measures. As she concludes, this experience strongly suggests that the quest to make targets like that adequately secure is essentially hopeless. Protective measures may complicate the situation for the terrorist somewhat, but in many cases only marginally so.

Policy Considerations: Implications

Five policy conclusions or implications can be derived at least in part from these premises.

1. Compare Any Protective Policy with a "Null Case": Do Nothing, and Use the Money Saved to Rebuild and to Compensate the Victims

Working from the premises outlined above, the cost-effectiveness of any policy that seeks to protect potential targets—to make them less vulnerable to terrorist attack—should routinely be compared with a null alternative. This alternative would hold that—given the (exceedingly) low probability of any individual target being hit, given the essentially random nature of much target selection, given the ability of terrorists to redirect their focus from one of myriad potential targets to another, and given the often rather modest costs of rebuilding an attacked target—it is incumbent on the policymaker to consider whether the proposed policy is more cost-effective than refraining from spending anything on a particular target or set of targets and then using the money saved to rebuild, to repair, and to compensate in the unlikely event that an attack on the target actually happens.[32] Included in the calculation should be a consideration of the emotional and psychological costs potentially inflicted by the terrorist act.

2. Abandon, or at Least Greatly Scale Back, Efforts to Imagine a Terrorist Target List

The Department of Homeland Security has made considerable effort over the years to imagine which targets terrorists might prefer to attack, and this inventory now reportedly runs into the hundreds of thousands.[33]

It is true that not every potential material terrorist target is equally valuable, equally vulnerable, or equally costly to protect or to repair or replace. However, numbers begin to look much alike when they are multiplied by one very close to zero.

Conceivably, one might compile a *very* short list of targets that might enjoy special appeal to terrorists—the next section of this chapter has some suggestions. However, because of the multiplicity of targets (especially if killing people is the terrorists' goal), because of the exceedingly low likelihood that any particular target will be struck, and because of the semirandom and perhaps quite limited nature of the terrorism enterprise, the process of target identification can quickly become one of imaginative, and even obsessive, worst-case-scenario thinking. Moreover, as Frank Furedi notes, such a "vulnerability-led response" can "foster a climate that intensifies people's feeling of insecurity and fear," and this in turn "invariably leads to the discovery of weaknesses that have the potential to turn virtually any institution in any place into a terrorist target."[34]

Partly in consequence, once a short list is established, the logic of protection can become overtaken by the effusive, self-generating, and self-perpetuating reality of the pork barrel. Because essentially anything can be a target, those seeking funds can easily imagine themselves on the list in a determined pursuit of shares of the largesse. Thus, Senator Patrick Leahy (D-VT) complained that the Bush administration wanted "to shortchange rural states," even as Senator Hillary Clinton (D-NY) faulted that same administration for the opposite perceived defect: "The reality is that they don't have a constituency in big cities."[35]

The quest for funds has also contested big cities against smaller ones. But it is difficult to see a plausible way in which this debate can be adequately adjudicated. It is true that cities like New York, London, Madrid, and Washington have been attacked by terrorists in recent years, but so has remote Glasgow, as well as resort areas in Egypt and Indonesia that are far from cities. And plotters and suspects apprehended within the United States have variously been accused of planning to inflict (or at least of vaguely thinking about inflicting) mayhem not only on the Brooklyn Bridge and Kennedy Airport in New York but also on targets in such places as Baltimore, Maryland; Seattle, Washington; Portland, Oregon; Detroit, Michigan; Boston, Massachusetts; Chicago, Illinois; Minneapolis, Minnesota; Ft. Dix, New Jersey; Columbus, Ohio; Miami, Florida; upstate New York; and Rockford and Peoria, Illinois.[36]

3. Temper Worst-Case Thinking

In developing terrorist risk assessment scenarios for fixed targets, the DHS applies what it calls "reasonable worst-case conditions."[37] Although it sensibly warns against compounding "numerous unlikely conditions" into such thinking, that process can become almost inevitable.

If the likelihood of a given target being struck is exceedingly low, to assume the attack will in addition be massive substantially compounds the probability issue. That is, given the limited nature of the terrorist enterprise and the multiplicity of potential targets, the likelihood of a specific target being hit is breathtakingly low, and given the quite modest capacities of most terrorists, the likelihood is also extremely low that any hit will even remotely correspond to "reasonable worst-case" possibilities, such as a duplication of the 1995 Oklahoma City attack when a vehicle-borne device delivered an explosion equivalent to 4,000 pounds of TNT.

Moreover, not only does worst-case thinking compound (or bedevil) the likelihood (or unlikelihood) estimation, it can undermine probabilistic thinking entirely. If the results of an attack are assumed to be potentially catastrophic, a special kind of "probability neglect"[38] takes over: under such circumstances, there is a tendency to conclude that no protection cost would be unbearable no matter how unlikely the prospect of an attack.

In addition, since funds are limited, it is not at all clear that protecting a relatively small number of potential targets from extreme (if perhaps "reasonable") attacks makes more sense than protecting a much larger number against lesser attacks.

4. Consider the Negative Effects of Protection Measures: Not Only Direct Cost but Inconvenience, Enhancement of Fear, Negative Economic Impacts, Reduction of Liberties

As terrorism inflicts not only direct but indirect costs, it is elemental that any sensible anti-terrorism policy proposal must consider both the direct and indirect costs that might flow from the policy.

Clearly, there are sizable direct economic costs to seeking to protect the homeland. Some of them accrue in direct protective expenditures. For example, to deal with the extremely unlikely event of a direct replication of the anthrax attacks of 2001, the U.S. Postal Service has spent some $1 billion for each fatality suffered in those attacks.[39] But costs can also accrue in indirect form, such as deterring inconvenienced customers from entering protected shopping centers.[40]

Sometimes, security measures can even cost lives. Increased delays and added costs at airports due to new security procedures provide incentive for many short haul passengers to drive to their destination rather than fly. Since driving is far riskier than flying, the extra automobile traffic generated by increased airport security screening measures has been estimated to result in 400 or more extra road fatalities per year.[41]

Protection and other policies can also enhance fear unrealistically. One preliminary study finds that visible security elements like armed guards, high walls, and barbed wire made people feel less vulnerable to crime. However, when these same devices are instituted in the context of dealing with the threat of terrorism, they make people feel tense, suspicious, and fearful, apparently because they implicitly suggest that the place under visible protection is potentially a terrorist target.[42] In other words, the protective measures supplied exactly the negative emotional effect terrorists themselves hope to induce. By the same token, security measures that do reduce fear may be beneficial.

5. Consider the Opportunity Costs of Protection Measures

Any sensible policy analysis must consider what else could have been done with the effort and money being expended on the policy proposed.[43] One study assesses increased post-2001 federal homeland security expenditures, much of them devoted to protective measures. It then compares that with expected lives saved as a result of these increased expenditures. It concludes that some 4,000 lives would have to be saved per year to justify the increased expenditures and that the cost per life saved ranges from $63 million to $630 million (or even more), greatly in excess of the accepted regulatory safety goal of $7.5 million per life saved. Not only do these expenditures clearly and dramatically fail a cost-benefit analysis but their opportunity cost, amounting to more than $31 billion per year, is considerable. It is highly likely that far more lives would have been saved if the money (or even a portion of it) had been invested instead in a wide range of more cost-effective risk mitigation programs. For example, an investment of $200,000 per year in smoke alarms will save one life, and similar examples can be found in other risk reduction measures or regulations.[44] Any analysis that omits such considerations is profoundly faulty, even immoral.

Application: Situations in Which Protection Is Essentially Futile

These considerations lead to a set of specific policy proposals about protection measures. One very large category includes situations in which protection is unlikely to be cost-effective.

Weapons of Mass Destruction Attacks

It is difficult to imagine protecting a potential target against an atomic bomb explosion because of the bomb's destructive capacity and because an atomic terrorist can choose where to detonate the device. Accordingly, policy in this area would sensibly focus on prevention and policing, and also perhaps on mitigation efforts, such as establishing evacuation routes to move people from contaminated areas and setting up and designating specific facilities to care for victims. Policy should also be concerned about preventing or dealing with panic.

The same generally holds for attacks with chemical, biological, and radiological weapons. The chief victims in these cases would be people, not structures, and protection measures are unlikely to be feasible. Indeed, they are nearly impossible. As with atomic attacks, policing and prevention efforts might be feasible, including, perhaps, systematic efforts to reduce a terrorist's ability to obtain or steal dangerous materials. Planning to deal with the outcome of an attack, in an effort to minimize its consequences, may also be worthwhile. It would include evacuation and other mitigation strategies and approaches. Establishing plans, procedures, and preparations to clean up after an attack might also make sense.[45]

As with many other homeland security issues, the installation of sensors to measure chemical, biological, or radiological levels and therefore to detect attacks in their early stages could save lives. This approach seems to be more of a mitigation than a protection measure. But regardless, the displacement factor looms large here. If, say, Manhattan has sensors and if the terrorists know it, there is no gain to society if the attackers simply move to Newark or Washington or Columbus.[46]

Small, Essentially Random Conventional Attacks

Far more probable than attacks with weapons of mass destruction are small, isolated attacks using such devices as conventional explosives, incendiaries, and guns. Applying the considerations laid out earlier, any efforts to protect people and structures from the effects of these attacks are unlikely to be cost-effective because of the multiplicity of targets, the ability of the terrorist to shift targets as needed, the capacity in many cases to rebuild quickly, and the inability to predict which targets are most appealing to terrorists. If the terrorists' goal is to kill people more or less at random, lucrative targets are essentially everywhere. If their goal is to destroy property, protection measures may be able to deter or inconvenience or complicate, but only to the point where the terrorists seek out something comparable among a vast—effectively infinite—array of potential unprotected targets.

An important difference here is with protection against crime. Although many efforts designed to protect people from crime may well fail to be cost effective, protection policy in this area has at least some hope of success because crime is vastly more common and, in particular, because it is comparatively easy to designate high-crime areas and to ascertain what criminals are generally after: loot. Because of these circumstances, a fair amount of prediction is possible, and protective measures can often make a potential target less vulnerable to crime, in some cases even effectively invulnerable (though there would still be a displacement problem). Specifically, if there is nothing valuable at the target, or if any valuables there cannot be lifted at acceptable cost and risk, and if criminals know this, the target becomes distinctly (and predictably) unattractive to them. For example, an entire class of targets—municipal buses—was removed from the criminal target list when exact-fare procedures were put into effect, which meant that any significant amount of money on the bus was now encased in a hardened lock box rather than in a cash drawer used by the driver to make change.

In contrast, terrorism is much more like vandalism than crimes like robbery and theft. It comes close effectively (and seemingly) to being a random occurrence, and the potential targets of the perpetrators are exceedingly difficult to predict. But ultimately, one cannot readily become invulnerable to vandalism, though displacement may be possible in some cases.[47]

Applications: Situations in Which Protection May Potentially Be Effective

For a few target sets, protection may make sense, particularly when protection is feasible for an entire class of potential targets and when the destruction of something in that target set would have quite large physical, economic, psychological, and/or political consequences.

Nuclear and Chemical Plants and Material

There are not many nuclear plants, and an adept terrorist attack on them could potentially have devastating consequences. Consequently, they seem to be prime candidates for protection. However, the big ones, nuclear reactors, already seem to be quite secure—

and, for a number of reasons, were so even before terrorism became much of an issue.

There are numerous chemical plants, although most, like nuclear plants, are placed away from population centers, a fact that may considerably reduce the urgency. It is possible to conjure damaging scenarios, but, except under the most severe circumstances, such as the 1984 chemical release, apparently by sabotage, at Bhopal, India, any dispersion is likely to have limited physical consequences. Panic, however, could enhance the effect. The same holds true for biological pathogens, although in this case, the chief fear is that terrorists will be able to make the pathogens themselves, not steal them.

Key Infrastructure Nodes

It would make sense to protect any specific infrastructure nodes whose destruction could cause widespread damage—for example, by causing a large area to lose electricity for months. It is not at all clear that any such nodes exist. However, if they do, it would probably be more efficient to expend effort to establish backup emergency redundancies rather than seek to protect the nodes themselves. At any rate, investment in this area is worthwhile, because if such nodes are susceptible to terrorist disruption, they probably are as well to more likely events such as lightning, heavy winds, and other natural hazards or human error or sabotage. A similar conclusion might hold for some dams and for concentrations of chemicals and explosives.

Various DHS documents and presidential and congressional reports and directives focus on something called "critical infrastructure." Applying commonsense English to how that phrase could be interpreted, it should be an empty category. If any element in the infrastructure is truly "critical" to the operation of the country, steps should be taken immediately to provide redundancies or backup systems so that it is no longer so.[48]

The same essentially holds true for what DHS calls "key resources," defined as those that are "essential to the minimal operations of the economy or government."[49] It is difficult to imagine what a terrorist group armed with anything less than a massive thermonuclear arsenal could do to hamper such "minimal operations." The attacks of 9/11 were by far the most damaging in history, yet even though a major commercial complex was demolished, both the economy and government continued to function at considerably above the "minimal" level.

Major Ports

There are only a few major ports in the United States, and the economy of the country depends heavily on them. Accordingly, protecting them against at least a major attack may be useful. However, since redirection of shipping is fairly easy, if costly and inconvenient, the chief problem here comes, as Stephen Flynn points out, from overreaction: policymakers could probably not restrain themselves from closing down all the ports if one were hit, thus inflicting massive costs on the economy.[50] The sensible solution in this case, obviously, would be to have people in charge who are level headed and not overburdened by such considerations. If it is true, however, that this is essentially impossible, protection of ports may be the most cost effective measure to take in this case.

Symbolic Targets

Protection measures may be justified for a small group of symbolic, even iconic, targets, like the Capitol, the White House, the Statue of Liberty, the British Parliament buildings, the Sydney Opera House, the Eiffel Tower, and the Washington Monument. In these cases, however, the main cost would be in embarrassment, because all (like the Pentagon after 9/11) could readily be repaired after an attack by a conventional explosive and because any loss of life might well be smaller than for terrorist explosions in places of congregation. Moreover, in all cases, any protective benefits should be balanced with a reasonable cost consideration: the prevention of embarrassment is not an infinite good. Given the low probability that even prime symbolic targets will be hit, limited protective measures might be all that is required. Thus, huge amounts of money have been spent in an elaborate effort to make the Washington Monument secure when the considerable bulk of that benefit might have been achieved simply by hiring a few additional security guards.

Relatedly, there may be a few potential targets that are likely to appear so lucrative to terrorists that they would have difficulty restraining themselves if the targets were inadequately protected. One might be the president of the United States, though, given assassination attempts in the past, protecting him is unfortunately wise and necessary for several reasons beyond the kind of terrorism that is of present concern. Given the proclivities of some terrorists, Israel's El Al airline would seem to be an attractive, high-visibility, rather trophy-like target, and so Israel's extraordinary efforts to screen passengers and baggage may make sense. On the other hand, countless potential Jewish targets—thousands of synagogues, for example—are highly visible and vulnerable, yet they seem to go substantially unmolested.

Application: The Case of Commercial Passenger Airliners

Finally, it may be useful to apply some of this thinking to the case of protecting commercial airlines and their passengers in the United States. Protection may be feasible, or at least may seem to be so, because, although there are many airports in the country, their number is fairly tractable. There are some 27 major airports and a few thousand smaller ones, numbers that are vastly lower than, for example, the number of highway overpasses, fast food restaurants, or places of congregation, like stadiums, theaters, churches, and assembly halls.

The Special Effect of Airliner Destruction

Unlike the destruction of other modes of transportation, the downing of an airliner (or, especially, of two or three in succession) seems to carry with it the special dangers of a widespread, lingering effect on the airline industry and on related ones, such as tourism.[51] Three years after 9/11, domestic airline flights in the United States were still 5 percent below their pre 9/11 levels, and by the end of 2004, tourism even in distant Las Vegas had still not fully recovered.[52] These shortfalls do not necessarily represent dead-weight losses to the economy because much of that money may have simply been spent elsewhere or else productively saved. However, they do suggest a very substantial disruption that unfairly affects a few industries, a disruption that was costly to all because it was felt necessary partly to mitigate the consequences by the infusion of tax money.

By contrast, if a bus or train is blown up, people still need to board them and will do so after a short period of wariness—as was found after the bombings in London and Madrid. To a considerable degree, people have a choice about whether to use commercial airliners, and many can turn to other modes of transport—or often simply not take the trip. Riders of subways, buses, and probably even ferries very often do not have the same luxury.

Similarly, if a building is destroyed, people still enter them: after 9/11, people soon returned to office buildings, even skyscrapers.

Indeed, if the 9/11 attacks had been accomplished by explosives (as was attempted in 1993 with the World Trade Center or as was accomplished with the building-demolishing bombing in Oklahoma City in 1995), there would have been a vastly lower social and economic impact because few would have systematically avoided buildings, or even urban office buildings.

The events of September 11, 2001, suggest that there can be another special cost in the case of airline terrorism. As noted above, fear of flying led many people to cancel airline trips and travel more by automobile, and studies have concluded that more than 1,000 people died in automobile accidents in 2001 alone between 9/11 and the end of that year because of such evasive behavior.[53]

It probably mattered as well on 9/11 that the airplanes were commercial passenger airliners. If they had been private or cargo planes, the effect on the airline industry (and on highway fatalities) would probably have been considerably less.

Is the Response to 9/11, Like the Event Itself, an Outlier?

Much of the concern about terrorists taking down an airliner extrapolates from the 9/11 experience, which had, as noted, a crushing, if temporary, effect on airline passenger traffic. Particularly in the few years after 2001, it was commonly said that if terrorists could now down two or three more airliners, they would destroy the airline industry.

But as the degree of destruction on 9/11 was unique in the history of terrorism, so, possibly, is the extent of the reaction. From time to time, terrorists have been able to down airliners—the Lockerbie tragedy of 1988 high among them—but the response by the flying public has not been nearly so extreme. After two Russian airliners were blown up by Chechen terrorists in 2004, that airline industry seems to have continued without massive interruption.

However tragic in its own terms, the downing of additional American airliners may not prove to be nearly as consequential as sometimes envisioned—perhaps in part because 9/11 has established such a vivid, and high, benchmark. Relevant here is the fact that the terrorist attacks on resort areas in Bali in 2002 had a far larger negative effect on tourism than did subsequent attacks in 2005.

Can the Costs Be Reduced?

Even if it is concluded that the protection of commercial passenger airliners is necessary, the process should still include sensible cost-benefit analyses in an effort to provide the best benefit at the lowest cost. Is there, in particular, any real need to have boosted expenditures and procedures beyond those already in place on September 10, 2001—or even to have continued those? There clearly has been a demand for safety from the flying public but not for specific measures such as vastly boosting the number of air marshals, forcing people to take off their shoes in security lines, or establishing a complicated no-fly list that generates an enormous number of false positives.[54]

Relaxing Some Measures. One might begin such a consideration by exploring areas in which protective measures might be relaxed with little or no likely effect either on the essential security of airline passengers or on their willingness to fly.

Actually, there have already been some modest relaxations, ones that seem to have been sensible, reduced costs, and been accepted by the flying public without, it seems, causing a decline in airline passenger traffic:

- Passengers are no longer required to undergo the unproductive, time wasting process of answering questions about whether they packed their luggage themselves and have had their bags with them at all times. This exercise, instituted after the Lockerbie bombing of 1988, generated quite possibly the greatest amount of sustained mendacity in history, particularly among people who had checked luggage at hotels for a time before going to the airport.
- Beginning in late 2005, passengers were allowed to take short scissors and knives with them on planes, as they were deemed not to pose much of a security risk. The measure was justified on the grounds that it freed screening personnel to concentrate on potentially more lethal weaponry. Perhaps that has been its consequence, although a spokesperson for the Association of Flight Attendants did alarmingly warn of another one at the time: "When weapons are allowed back on board an aircraft, the pilots will be able to land the plane safely but the aisles will be running with blood."[55]
- The inconvenient ritual of forcing passengers to remain in their seats during the last half hour of flights to Washington's Reagan National Airport has been eliminated.

- Considerations of permanently closing Washington's Reagan National Airport, potentially a very costly venture, were abandoned.
- Harassment of automobiles picking up and dropping off passengers appears to have been relaxed somewhat.
- Passengers are now usually required to show boarding passes only once to inspectors.
- Passengers no longer need to show their identification at the gate.

Further advances have been suggested. Pilots have wondered forcefully why they need to be screened for weapons since, once in the cockpit, they scarcely need weapons to crash the airplane should they decide to do so. The general requirement to screen crews at all has been questioned, particularly because ground crews and delivery personnel with equal or greater access to the plane are not screened.[56]

It is also often noted that, in something of a natural experiment, passengers boarding planes to the United States and elsewhere at foreign locales, including security-conscious Heathrow Airport in London, are not required to remove their shoes—the procedure that seems most to slow down the security line. There have been no negative consequences from this—no shoe bombs—and people do not seem to be any more reluctant to board planes.

There should also be some discussion of why American airports are still on orange alert, where they were placed after an airline bomb plot was rolled up in distant Britain in 2006. Since the additional security cost for being on orange rather than yellow alert for Los Angeles International Airport alone apparently can run to $100,000 per day, this issue would seem to deserve some reflection.[57]

Abandoning Efforts to Prevent a Replication of 9/11. Any effort designed solely to prevent a replication of the 9/11 attacks seems questionable. As pilot Patrick Smith puts it:

> Conventional wisdom says the terrorists exploited a weakness in airport security by smuggling aboard box cutters. What they actually exploited was a weakness in our mindset—a set of presumptions based on the decades long track record of hijackings. In years past, a takeover meant hostage negotiations and standoffs; crews were trained in the concept of "passive resistance." All of that changed forever the instant

American Airlines Flight 11 collided with the north tower. What weapons the 19 men possessed mattered little; the success of their plan relied fundamentally on the element of surprise. And in this respect, their scheme was all but guaranteed not to fail. For several reasons—particularly the awareness of passengers and crew—just the opposite is true today.[58]

More specifically, expensive security measures that seek to keep weapons (as opposed to explosives) out of the passenger cabin might well be reexamined. In fact, allowing passengers to bring weapons onto airplanes would have complicated the 9/11 plotters' plan, and the attacks might never have happened.

And then there are the air marshals.[59] Their chief goal, and just about their only one, is to prevent a replication of 9/11, a problem that, as indicated, doesn't seem to exist. There were fewer than 50 marshals before 9/11; there are now thousands, and the program costs hundreds of millions of dollars per year.[60] In January 2008, Australia announced a considerable cutback on the number of its sky marshals.[61] If this change is accepted by the Australians, maybe the same result could be expected in the United States.

Reconsidering the Protection of Airports. Although there may be special reasons, as suggested above, to protect airplanes, it is not at all clear that there are any special reasons to protect airports. Compared with many other places of congregation, people are more dispersed in airports (except, perhaps, in security lines), and therefore a terrorist attack is likely to kill far fewer than if, for example, a crowded stadium is targeted. In addition, airports sprawl and are only two or three stories high; therefore, a collapse of a portion of one is unlikely to be nearly as significant as the collapse of a taller or more compact structure. Moreover, if a bomb does go off at an airport, the consequences would likely be comparatively easy to deal with: passengers could readily be routed around the damaged area, for example, and the effect on the essential function of the airport would be comparatively modest.

How Much Security Theater Is Necessary?

It would be useful in such considerations to explore fully the degree to which security theater may or may not be needed. If there is a measure that makes passengers feel substantially safer, it would have to be considered a benefit even if the measure itself does not actually enhance security at all. As Cass Sunstein puts it, "The reduction of even baseless fear is a social good."[62]

However, quite a few security measures presumably carry little theatrical value: for example, air marshals are not supposed to be identifiable by passengers (or terrorists, of course), and so their absence, or presence, on a flight does nothing to affect feelings of security. Crew screening probably has a similar noneffect.

But there should be studies to determine if other measures are equally useless from this perspective. As noted, the relaxation of the ban on short pointy objects does not seem to have enhanced fear or reduced passenger traffic. Would other such changes be acceptable? What would happen to fear levels and passenger traffic if security measures were severely reduced to, say, 2000 levels—or even ended altogether?

What Are the Negative Consequences of the Security Measures?

For a full cost-benefit analysis, one would also have to consider not only the human costs, where the decline in short-haul air trips has apparently led to an increase in highway fatalities, as discussed earlier, but also the economic costs of longer waits in airports. One economist calculates that strictures effectively requiring people to spend an additional half hour in airports cost the economy $15 billion per year, whereas, in comparison, total airline profits in the prosperous 1990s never exceeded $5.5 billion per year.[63]

Included in this analysis, of course, would be a consideration of the opportunity costs. Specifically, what is being forgone in order to expend nearly $10 billion per year on airline security? Could the money be more effective—save far more lives—if it were used instead to enforce seat-belt laws or install smoke alarms?

Conclusion

"In general," concludes security expert Bruce Schneier, "the costs of counterterrorism are simply too great for the security we're getting in return, and the risks don't warrant the extreme trade offs we've been asked to make."[64] This may well be the case for the quest to make the country less vulnerable. Although there may be some areas in which the effort makes sense, much of it, on reasonably close examination, seems to have been highly questionable.

7. The Economics of Homeland Security

Veronique de Rugy

Since the attacks on the United States on September 11, 2001, policymakers have responded in two ways: by going after terrorists abroad and by trying to improve security against terrorism at home by boosting homeland security funding. Regarding the latter, Congress and the Bush administration created the Department of Homeland Security and increased total funding for homeland security activities by 259 percent between fiscal years 2002 and 2009. Total spending directed to homeland security activities was $70 billion for FY09, up from $19.5 billion in FY02, roughly $586 per American household.[1]

The key question is whether America is getting the maximum level of benefit in exchange for this increase in spending. Homeland security should be about wise choices, not just increased spending. Policymakers should focus less on how much to spend on homeland security and more on how the political process distorts spending decisions.

On that front, economists have much to contribute. This chapter takes a look at the economics of homeland security spending by asking a set of questions. How do economists think about homeland security? What does economics teach us about homeland security spending? What factors get in the way of allocating funds appropriately?

Homeland security is a legitimate function of the federal government, and it is hard to say a priori what the optimal level of spending should be. However, if homeland security spending decisions are made on a political basis rather than on sound cost-benefit analysis, that will lead to the traditional public choice failures that plague government spending more generally. As a result, homeland security funding will likely be misallocated, resulting in a less than optimal level of security in America.

Tradeoffs and Risks

Economists think about security policies in terms of tradeoffs, formally comparing the costs and the benefits, both pecuniary and nonpecuniary.[2] Tradeoffs for security can have substantial financial, social, or legal consequences that are often overlooked. Greater appreciation of these tradeoffs should lead to improved security decisions.[3]

We all make security tradeoffs. For example, when we lock the door to our house in the morning, we choose the small inconvenience of carrying a key in exchange for a modicum of security against a burglary. Also when we drive, we expect to bear what we consider an acceptable level of risk in exchange for the mobility provided by cars. People make security decision tradeoffs all the time, choosing more or less security as situations change. Optimal security decisions and policies require a good understanding of the risks and tradeoffs we face.

Another name for this exercise is risk management. Risk management is about playing the odds. When it comes to terrorism, risk management entails figuring out which attacks are worth worrying about (and spending money on) and which are better left ignored. It entails spending more resources on the serious attacks—defined as being very likely or, if successful, having devastating effects—and spending less on the trivial ones. It involves taking a finite security budget and making the best use of it. Interestingly, a recurring recommendation from the Government Accountability Office over the years has been the need to use risk management in developing a national strategy to fight terrorism.[4]

According to security expert Bruce Schneier, to think strategically about homeland security requires looking not at threats (a potential way a terrorist can attack a system) but rather at risks (a consideration of both the likelihood of the threat and the seriousness of a successful attack). Assessing and measuring risk accurately are critical to developing a strategic approach to homeland security.

The difficulty, of course, lies in the subjective nature of this assessment. Different people have different senses of what level of risk is acceptable. What's more, there is no agreed-on way in which to define threats or to evaluate risks that cross communities, societies, or industries. If you then factor in media coverage of any terrorism-related news and the emotional component it elicits, the concept of acceptable risk becomes even blurrier.

The risk of terrorism is small, especially when considered relative to the attention it commands. In 2001, for instance, terrorist attacks in the United States killed 2,978 people, with almost all deaths occurring on 9/11. During that same year, 156,005 people died from lung cancer and 44,091 from automobile accidents.[5] While nearly 3,000 deaths in one nonrepeated incident are tragic, it is considerably smaller than other mortality risks, which occur repeatedly. Of course, terrorists may hope that their future actions will result in significantly more casualties, but so far, past probabilities are a good guide to the true risk of terrorism.

Yet in practice, and in spite of the wide fatality differences, the federal government spends much less money per year to increase automobile safety—$47 million in FY08—for example, than it spends governmentwide on homeland security—$62 billion in FY08 (not counting the wars in Iraq and Afghanistan).[6]

Some argue that one reason for this spending gap stems from the involuntary nature of terrorist attacks—deaths resulting from terrorist attacks are fundamentally different from deaths resulting from either automobile accidents or cigarette smoking in that the latter risks contain a voluntary element. The benefit that drivers and tobacco users get from their choices compensates for the associated risks. Terrorism, obviously, brings no form of compensatory benefit, hence the rationale for federal involvement and subsequent spending.

If, as this rationale supposes, the federal government increases its spending and involvement where risks are imposed and do not contain a compensating benefit, then we should expect to see increased spending on protection from other risks that meet these criteria, other than terrorism. We do not. In 2008, counterterrorism spending far exceeded spending on protection from other risks with these characteristics, such as fraud or violent crime—in 2008, counterterrorism spending outpaced federal spending on the prevention of all crime by $15 billion.[7]

A more convincing explanation is that these differences in budget allocations are the product of psychology. Both social scientists and citizens struggle to assess risks of events with low probability—such as acts of terrorism.[8] Through evolution and learning, people learn to handle many of the common risks they face in life. But Americans—fortunately—do not have extensive experience with terrorism. Even sophisticated assessors of risk—such as insurance companies—have difficulty when it comes to terrorism, though they do learn from experiences of other low-probability risk events, such as major natural disasters.[9]

The economics literature suggests that the extreme levels of uncertainty inherent in terrorism may cause people to severely overestimate risks. For example, Harvard University professors W. Kip Viscusi and Richard J. Zeckhauser show that an act of terrorism creates much more uncertainty than other equally uncertain risks.[10] This uncertainty is what could greatly magnify the perception of the terrorist threat, far beyond the actual damage that any single terrorist strike has historically caused. The uncertainty that accompanies the terrorist threat, and the associated costs (e.g., the provision of security at myriad potential targets, reduced investments because of generalized uncertainty, disruption of travel, tourism, and perhaps also trade), are what allow a few terrorists, armed with relatively primitive means, to threaten powerful nations.[11]

Thus, while the risks are difficult to quantify, there is reason to suspect that individuals may ratchet up their assessments of terrorist risk and, hence, may increase their demand for homeland security spending. Such demands might induce Congress to invest in projects that would not pass a strict cost-benefit test. And, in fact, real-life experience tells us that that is what happens.

Optimal Security

While terrorism became the dominant security issue in the United States only recently, economists have long studied the optimal provision of security more generally. In the seminal paper on the economics of crime, University of Chicago professor Gary Becker used the tools of economics to think about the incentives of criminals and how to influence their behavior.[12] He explained that we could decrease unwanted behaviors by increasing their expected costs or decreasing their expected benefits. This approach also applies to terrorism.

The method most often used to discourage terrorists is to make it more difficult to carry out a successful attack. In effect, this forces terrorists to incur higher costs in time and planning as they seek alternate targets. We install Jersey barriers to keep trucks away from important buildings, screen airline passengers, and employ Internet firewalls. But such steps alone do not ensure that the resources are being used effectively. If a certain strategy reduces the threat of terrorism but has very high costs, it may not be the proper course, particularly if there is another approach that generates similar benefits at lower costs to society.

Many public policies rely on personal costs for deterrence. Incarceration is an important cost consideration for ordinary criminals and thus an efficient tool in deterring crime. It is also an effective use of resources, since imposing stiff jail sentences is cheaper than guarding every house. Unfortunately, this approach is generally ineffective against ideological extremists like terrorists, who give little weight to the personal costs of their actions. Suicide bombers, for example, will not be deterred by the prospect of jail time.[13]

Alternatively, terrorists may be deterred by decreasing their expected benefits, either by increasing the probability of thwarting an attack or by limiting the damage from a nonthwarted attack. To thwart attacks, we spend money on the Central Intelligence Agency, Federal Bureau of Investigation, and law enforcement to try to detect terrorist plots in advance. To decrease the damage from attacks, we spend money on first responders and buy gas masks. One important implication of Becker's work is that there are tradeoffs between thwarting attacks and decreasing their damage: the more effective we are at thwarting attacks, the less we presumably should spend on decreasing their damage, and vice versa.

Taking the analysis a step further, the most efficient options to combat terrorism tend to be efforts to detect terrorists themselves or to respond effectively to minimize the damage after an attack has occurred. Spending to defend particular targets is generally less efficient. Both results stem from the fact that there is an almost unlimited number of targets, and the terrorist gets to choose where to attack.[14] It is axiomatic that "a chain is only as strong as its weakest link." Likewise, elaborate security measures are only as strong as the weakest link.

For instance, in a house with two doors, the security of the entire house is equal to the security of the weakest door.[15] Whatever you do to improve the strongest door won't improve the overall security of your house. To increase the security level of your house, you need to ensure that both doors are equally strong.

This fact has important implications. First, the security measure known as target hardening is only as good as the least protected target. Also, if your main counterterrorism measure is stopping terrorists from entering the country, securing checkpoints at the borders won't do much good unless you are willing to secure the many thousands of miles around the country to the same degree. Once you are willing to do that, you must figure out whether it is the most cost-effective security measure. It's unlikely to be.

Suppose, for example, that a given city has 100 potential targets that could be perfectly defended at a cost of $20,000 each, that the damage from an undefended attack would be $500,000, and that we could mitigate half the damage from attack by spending $50,000 on first responders (mainly by saving lives and getting people to the hospital faster). If we knew where the terrorists would attack, we could spend $20,000 to prevent $500,000 worth of damage, a net savings of $480,000, which would be a prudent investment. But if we don't know the target, we would have to spend $2 million to defend all 100 targets, a net loss of $1.5 million. On the other hand, even if we did not know the target, we could spend $50,000 on first responders to reduce the damage from a successful attack on any given target by $250,000, which is an efficient tradeoff. When we don't know where terrorists will strike, it doesn't make financial sense to invest in the defense of multiple targets. This conclusion is more pronounced when the probability of an attack is low.

These figures are purely illustrative. In actuality, the numbers are even starker. There are far more than 100 potential targets. Even if we spent $20,000 or more on each, we could not perfectly defend them against attack. In addition, since the probability of an attack on any given target is infinitesimal, the costs of defending all or most of the potential targets far outweigh the benefits.

Of course, if intelligence and investigation allowed us to track down terrorists in advance successfully and to prevent attacks on *all* possible targets, that approach would have similar efficiency properties as spending on first responders. The fact that spending more money on intelligence and investigation might be far more cost-effective than spending a little on every possible target or focusing on cleaning up efficiently after an attack raises again the notion of tradeoffs. Since the number of possible attacks is effectively unlimited and the resources we can devote to the fight against terror are limited, spending should not occur without a careful cost-benefit analysis. It is perfectly reasonable to decide not to implement an anti-terrorism measure even if it has benefits if the tradeoffs are too high. For instance, locking up every Arab-looking person might be perceived as a way to reduce the potential for terrorism perpetrated by Islamic fundamentalists, but no reasonable person would suggest this approach because the costs (both pecuniary and moral) are too high.

Efficient expenditures concentrate limited resources on the most cost-effective measures rather than simply on the effective ones. For example, relative to the current air marshals program, a more cost-effective security measure would allow pilots to carry weapons. John Lott notes that "terrorists can only enter the cockpit through one narrow entrance, and armed pilots have some time to prepare themselves as hijackers penetrate the strengthened cockpit doors."[16] He adds that "the boredom and high attrition rates afflicting air marshals (who fly back and forth on long flights waiting for something to happen) does not apply to pilots." And no extra pay is needed, since many pilots have volunteered to take time off and travel to firearms training at their own expense. In addition, 70 percent of the pilots at major American airlines have a military background, which further reduces the cost of training them and increases the effectiveness of this simple measure.[17] Meanwhile, the fears of bullets damaging planes are greatly exaggerated. According to Ron Hinderberger, director of aviation safety at Boeing, "Commercial airplane structure is designed with sufficient strength, redundancy, and damage tolerance that a single or even multiple handgun holes would not result in loss of an aircraft."[18]

Simple cockpit barricades, which the airline industry has now installed at relatively low costs, have reduced the risk of another 9/11-style attack.[19] According to the Federal Aviation Administration, the purchase and installation cost of an enhanced cockpit door is estimated at between $30,000 and $50,000. The total cost to airlines is estimated at between $300 million and $500 million over a 10-year period, including increased fuel consumption costs resulting from heavier doors.[20] Congress originally appropriated $100 million for the FAA to distribute to U.S. airlines for aircraft security enhancements, $97 million of which was given to the airlines to help defray the costs of cockpit doors (approximately $13,000 per door). This means that the total government cost was estimated at between $92.3 million and $120.7 million over a 10-year period.[21]

In contrast, the burgeoning U.S. system for screening every bag of every airline passenger has already cost taxpayers $34 billion in the last seven years and will cost an additional $7.8 billion in FY10.[22] This system does little to prevent 9/11-style hijacking, which is empirically the largest airline-related risk.[23] Furthermore, this checked-bag screening does not necessarily reduce the probability of the destruction of airplanes, since neither carryon bags nor airfreight are systematically checked for explosives, and terrorists have revealed a propensity to engage in suicidal behavior. Whether this $7.8 billion is an efficient allocation of resources depends on whether alternative, less costly measures have been crowded out by this spending.

Federal expenditures are not the only costs associated with homeland security. Even though successful terrorist attacks can impose significant economic costs, defense and homeland security spending displaces resources from the private sector toward security measures that, even where necessary, are not economically productive.[24] The Joint Economic Committee observes that "increased spending on security will likely be associated with lower economic growth since more capital and labor are diverted toward security production and away from the production of final demand."[25]

For example, the true cost to taxpayers of the Transportation Security Administration goes far beyond its expected $7.8 billion budget in FY10. A back-of-the-envelope calculation suggests that if 624 million passengers each spend one hour waiting in line, the aggregate opportunity cost incurred by these passengers is at least $16 billion per year.[26] That is an enormous cost imposed on citizens by an agency whose main measure of success is to have "intercepted seven million prohibited items at airport checkpoints, including just over 600 firearms."[27] Read differently, that means that roughly 0.008 percent of items intercepted are firearms and 99.992 percent of intercepted items are harmless: for example, tweezers, breath fresheners, and lighters. Further, TSA's statistics do not account for the intent of the owners of the 600 firearms seized.

In short, because security always involves tradeoffs, more security spending does not always mean more security, and more security does not always make us better off.

Who Should Pay for Homeland Security?

An important related question, one rarely asked, is what is the economic reasoning behind the emphasis on *federal* provision of homeland security? Cost-benefit analysis and risk management can help us decide who is best suited to address a given risk.

National defense is often cited as the archetypal public good. One person's consumption of a public good does not prevent another person from consuming the same good, meaning that the good is nonrivalrous.[28] Another characteristic of public goods is that they are nonexcludable; in other words, it is hard or impossible to prevent anybody from getting access to and enjoying the public good once it is produced. Private goods have opposite characteristics: they are rivalrous and excludable.

Economic theory suggests that it is efficient to have governments provide public goods but to rely on private markets for the provision of nonpublic goods. By this logic, for example, governments should provide national defense, but markets should produce washing machines.

As already mentioned, a key feature of terrorism is that the threat is generalized (it can happen anywhere, at any time), and yet any particular attack is local. By implication, then, homeland security is a mix of public and private goods. Accordingly, governments should provide some types of homeland security, while other types are best left to private actors. For example, governments should invest in intelligence gathering to track down terrorists because that is a public good that benefits all citizens. Police can deter attacks on public places, such as restaurants and cafes. But the protection of private property, such as personal residences, should be largely left to individuals.[29]

A similar logic applies to which aspects of homeland security are public goods at the national versus state level (see Table 7.1). Espionage, intelligence, and immigration control benefit all the states, so the federal government should make these investments. But the benefits of protecting public infrastructure, such as bridges and water treatment plants, are enjoyed by the residents of a particular state or locality rather than many states, so these investments should be made at the local level. There might be adverse effects throughout the economy if a specific bridge were to be destroyed, but the principal economic impact of such an unfortunate event would be felt locally.

Federal security measures should benefit the entire nation. In that sense, federal homeland security grants—grants distributed by the

Table 7.1
WHO SHOULD BE RESPONSIBLE FOR HOMELAND SECURITY?

Federal Government	State and Local Government	Private Sector
Espionage Intelligence Immigration Electric grid	Protection of public infrastructure, such as bridges, water reservoirs, and ports First responders	Protection of privately owned structures, including businesses, skyscrapers, and individual houses

federal government to the states to build up their response capacities—are not making us more secure. The billions going to state and local governments would be best spent on bolstering the core functions of federal law enforcement and the intelligence services (or not spent at all) instead of subsidizing local fire and police departments throughout the country.

Alternatively, instead of wasting money on building response capacity, federal funding could be spent to create a truly national prevention system with a robust capacity for independent state and local intelligence operations, early warning, exchange and exploitation of information, and domestic counterterrorism. The fact that grant programs have proved far more effective when federal money has been used to fund vulnerability assessments and to encourage public-private partnerships does not mean that investing money on first responders is not important.[30] However, states and local communities should be in charge of most of their preparedness efforts. If police officers feel they need more equipment to do their jobs, or firefighters need training or gym memberships they are not getting right now, they should turn to their state and local officials for funding.

A less clear-cut case involves mixed goods, or goods that are in essence private but that, if successfully attacked, would have serious public consequences. Chemical plants, nuclear facilities, physical infrastructures, or the Internet all fall in that category.

For instance, counterterrorism experts have long predicted that numerous deaths could result from an intentional release of a toxic chemical from one of the nation's 15,000 chemical-processing facilities—including chemical-manufacturing plants, petroleum tank farms, and pesticide companies—that contain large quantities of potentially deadly chemicals. They point to an accidental chlorine gas leak at a Honeywell refrigeration plant in Baton Rouge, Louisiana, on July 20, 2003, that sent four workers to the hospital and forced 600 residents to stay indoors. As a result, some experts have asked that the government (state, local, or federal) require chemical facilities to use safer technologies. Other experts have claimed that there should be a single national standard for the chemical industry that preempts state and local government authority.[31]

Thankfully, most of those suggestions never materialized. For one thing, if a disaster were to occur, the consequences would be mainly localized, undermining the rationale for the federal action. More importantly, it is inappropriate for the federal government to dictate specific industrial processes. Chemical plants face a constantly changing technical environment due to competition. Homeland security regulations in this area should be flexible and should allow managers to find solutions to security problems.

Another common mixed-good example is cyberwarfare. The scenario most frequently discussed is the one of terrorists' attacking a computer network, wreaking havoc and paralyzing the nation. Obviously, the interconnection of information networks and critical infrastructures, all of which are private, could, if successfully shut down by terrorists, have a dramatic effect on the economy.

James A. Lewis of the Center for Strategic and International Studies, explains that cyberterrorism entails "the use of computer network tools to shut down critical national infrastructures (such as energy, transportation, government operations) or to coerce or intimidate a government or civilian population." The premise of cyberterrorism is that, as a nation's critical infrastructure systems become more dependent on computer networks for their operation, new vulnerabilities are created—"a massive electronic Achilles' heel."[32] The question then is who should be responsible for protecting these networks, and indirectly for protecting the nation's critical infrastructure?

Ultimately, it boils down to the probability of such a successful attack. Can terrorists really attack cybernetworks in a way that would take down the nation's infrastructure? If the probability of such an attack were very high, considering the tremendous costs involved, there would probably be a justification for government involvement in cybersecurity. If it weren't, then the private sector should be responsible for its security.

So which is it? According to Schneier, contrary to the current perception, cyberterrorism's threat to national security is largely overstated. He explains: "These attacks are very difficult to execute. The software systems controlling our nation's infrastructure are filled with vulnerabilities, but they're generally not the kinds of vulnerabilities that cause catastrophic disruptions. The systems are designed to limit the damage that occurs from errors and accidents."

Concerns that a terrorist attack "would cause a problem more serious than a natural disaster," are misplaced, Schneier explains, because it "is surprisingly hard" to cause widespread harm. For example,

> in January 2003, the SQL Slammer worm disrupted 13,000 ATMs on the Bank of America's network. But before it happened, you couldn't have found a security expert who understood that those systems were dependent on that vulnerability. We simply don't understand the interactions well enough to predict which kinds of attacks could cause catastrophic results, and terrorist organizations don't have that sort of knowledge either—even if they tried to hire experts.[33]

While there is no doubt that computer network vulnerabilities are an increasingly serious problem for businesses, the risk of cyberterrorism to our national security is still low. Hence, mitigating this risk should remain a private matter rather than a government one.

Aside from the low probability of a successful attack, there remains the question of the feasibility of government cyberterrorism protection. Technologies and terrorist vulnerabilities within these cybernetworks are constantly changing, and no one has better knowledge of these changes and the probability of a successful attack than the people who manipulate and operate this environment daily in order to create a profit. Strategic homeland security measures in this arena require that the technical and local knowledge be allowed to locate its own best solutions to potential security threats. Instead of sweeping mandates at the federal or state levels, government officials can implement performance-based standards to a given level of safety while allowing private-sector innovation.

A Public Choice Approach to Homeland Security Spending

Most decisions governing homeland security spending are filtered through the political process. Each participant in this process has an incentive to maximize the benefits for him- or herself, and, as such, decisions are not always based on an assessment of the common good. This is one of the key insights from public choice economics.

Bruce Schneier poses an interesting hypothetical to illustrate that point.[34] Imagine that after 9/11, all the players involved in airline security were in a room trying to figure out what to do. Some members of the public are scared to fly, others aren't. The airlines are desperate to get more people flying but are wary of security systems that are too expensive. They are also worried that increased security might impose great organizational costs on them. The elected officials in the room, thinking about reelection, are concerned that they might be blamed for the attacks. And they need to be seen by voters as doing something to improve security. The FAA is torn between its friends in the airline industry and its other friends in government.

Because everyone in this example is hypothetically looking at the security problem from his or her own perspective, very few individuals are really trying to figure out the right security tradeoffs. As a consequence, the airline industry is happy to let the government take over the job of airport screening because it won't cost the industry as much and it won't be its fault if there is another attack. The politicians want to be perceived as actively addressing the concerns of the voters and are glad to expand the federal government's role in airport screening. The FAA enjoys its increased powers in a context that pleases the government and the airlines, and the public likes the feeling that something is being done. While the various interest groups might be satisfied by the resulting policy, this does not mean that the measures adopted will end up increasing security.

For some time now, the White House and the Office of Management and Budget have been, at least theoretically, trying to think about risks and tradeoffs from a more than purely parochial perspective. But their efforts have not yet translated into visible changes in practice. For instance, if they were thinking about risks and security tradeoffs, we would see budget allocations that expand high-priority activities and eliminate or defer the less important or redundant ones. However, "a look at budgets since the department [of home-land security] was established reflects little in the way of realign-ment," explains Cindy Williams, a principal research scientist of the Security Studies Program at the Massachusetts Institute of Technol-ogy. Williams continues:

> Department funding rose by more than 40 percent between 2003 and 2007, but there has been only minimal reallocation of budgets from areas of lower risk or priority to functions the department says are more important. With the exception of added spending to support the Secure Border Initiative announced by President Bush in November 2005, the depart-ment's main operating components each enjoy about the same share of the DHS budget today as they did when the department was created.[35]

Also, while security tradeoffs should be considered when allocat-ing resources among the three categories related to national defense (i.e., defense, homeland security, and international affairs), Williams finds that "much of the post-9/11 real increase in national security budgets goes not to make the United States safer from the threat of catastrophic terrorism, but [has gone instead] to operations in Iraq and business as usual in the Department of Defense."[36]

Public choice theory underlines the different incentives and pro-cesses that operate when goods are sought through political means rather than through economic means.[37] For instance, if you have to use your own money to buy the lock on the door to protect your house, you will make sure that the increased security from the lock is worth the price of the lock. An individual spending his or her own money makes sure that anticipated benefits exceed the costs.[38] In the political process, though, the people buying the lock are rarely the ones paying for it. As such, they have less incentive to balance costs and benefits.

The political appropriation and distribution of a good concentrate its benefits and disperse its costs. Many people can be taxed at a low rate so a few people can be given large sums. Special-interest groups have an incentive to lobby the government to see that wealth is transferred to them. The term economists use to describe such lobbying is "rent seeking."[39] These pressure groups have a clear advantage in a political process where politicians frequently hear nothing from the many payers and much from the few beneficiaries.[40]

Members of Congress have a strong incentive to steer federal money to their districts or to reward particular industries; by contrast, they have little incentive to reduce wasteful federal spending.[41] Witness the increasing number of low-priority and wasteful spending items—also called pork-barrel spending—introduced by Congress at the last moment into federal spending bills and directed to a particular state locality or even a specific facility.[42] That dynamic plagues DHS allocations as well. And "homeland security" pressure groups—for example, first responders, state officials, and/or specific industries (e.g., the airlines)—have an incentive to lobby lawmakers to try to grab a bigger share of the funding allocated to homeland security programs and/or to transfer their responsibilities to the federal government. The Cato Institute's Chris Edwards gives a good example of this type of behavior in his book *Downsizing the Federal Government*: "On March 4, 2004, 3,000 state officials flew into Washington to lobby Congress for larger first responder grants; they were followed on March 16 by firefighters from across the country coming to lobby Congress."[43]

When programs are funded at the federal level in the form of grants to the states, a U.S. representative from Wyoming has no incentive to admit that his state is not a likely terrorist target or that if it ever were a target, damages would be limited, probably less costly than the grants distributed to prevent an attack or to respond to it. This representative has no incentive to turn down federal money or request that the federal dollars be allocated based on risks and that other states get more funds than his. He has even less incentive to volunteer sending his state taxpayers' dollars to benefit other states. By contrast, when responsibility for first-responder programs is retained by the states, then the governor of Wyoming and the state officials should be able to assess risk and potential damages to the state more accurately. Since, in theory, states can't run deficits, state officials have a more direct incentive to decide whether to spend more on homeland security or on other accounts.

Economics and public choice theory suggest a commonsensical approach to counterterrorism that lawmakers have little incentive to embrace. Not every jurisdiction requires a bomb squad. The probability of a bomb-related incident occurring in a given American town is low, while the cost of maintaining a bomb squad is high. Given the choice, some local jurisdictions are unlikely to choose bomb protection over protection from higher-probability threats, like fire and flood; others may prefer to maintain bomb protection. Local financial incentives can solve the federal risk assessment quandary; as local lawmakers allocate their budgets, they are forced to take risk management into account.

Unfortunately, many lawmakers at all levels—local, state, and federal—see things differently. They insist that the federal government should pay for their respective state response capacities and that federal grants to state and local governments be allocated based on a formula that guarantees every state an equal minimum amount of funds, regardless of risk or need. As a result, rural, less populated areas often receive a disproportionate amount of money relative to the threat. That everyone gets a piece of the pie has been made more important than security itself.

Conclusion

Since the number of possible attacks is unlimited, while the resources we can devote to preventing them are very limited, spending decisions should involve careful cost-benefit analysis. Members of Congress are unlikely to embrace this principle. Recall, for instance, their reaction when DHS Secretary Michael Chertoff explained why he wouldn't change his transit-security policy in the wake of the July 2005 London terrorist bombings that killed 56 people and injured 700. He explained that this dramatic event was just that: a single event. He told a reporter: "The truth of the matter is that a fully loaded airplane with jet fuel, a commercial airliner, has the capacity to kill 3,000 people. A bomb in a subway car may kill 30 people. When you start to think about priorities, you are going to think about making sure you don't have a catastrophic thing first."[44]

His comments drew sharp criticism, mainly from senators representing metropolitan areas with mass transit systems. They argued that such systems are vulnerable to terrorists, as demonstrated by the London and earlier Madrid bombings. According to them, these vulnerabilities needed to be addressed with more funding. However, all transportation systems have inherent weaknesses; if the justification for federal intervention were vulnerability, every mode of transportation would qualify, and we would quickly run out of funds.

The truth that most people ignore is that not all terrorist attacks have the same consequences. The 9/11 attacks claimed close to 3,000 lives. In comparison, a successful backpack bomb attack on the Washington, D.C., subway might kill 30 people; and at the other end of the spectrum, the detonation of a less-than-perfect one-kiloton nuclear bomb in lower Manhattan would—in the estimation of the Federation of American Scientists—kill at least 200,000 people.[45]
These statistics should help clarify where our priorities should be, especially if probabilities as well as harms are taken into account. But as we know, federal budget allocations do not reflect actuarial probabilities. In the last four years, DHS has spent $700 million on transit security and $34 billion on aviation security. During the same period, however, total spending on nuclear-threat reduction by the Departments of Homeland Security, Energy, State, and Defense was just $6 billion, with just $1 billion of that going to protect vulnerable stockpiles of fissile material abroad. The reality of the counterterrorism budget allocation process is that it has more to do with knee-jerk reaction to the terrorist news of the day than with security priorities and tradeoffs.
So what is the solution? First, we must remember that the attacker always has the advantage of choosing where to attack, and terrorists will look for weaknesses in our defenses. For instance, if we seal our ports to prevent terrorists from bringing dangerous material inside the country on a ship, they can alternatively go through the thousands of miles of the country's unprotected and unprotectable borders. What's more, there is no way to protect everything from every possible mode of attack.
As John Mueller explains, one cost-effective option might be that instead of trying to protect hundreds of targets, we should save the money, and then if something happens, use the money to repair the damage.[46] Then we could go after the people who actually did the crime. As for airline security, instead of spending massive amounts of money to keep harmful objects off planes, a more effective measure would be to try to keep harmful people off planes. Again, intelligence is the solution, not prohibiting everyone from carrying toothpaste and nail polish onto planes. Unfortunately, it is doubtful that such policies could see daylight in our current political climate.
In the end, the lack of understanding of risk and tradeoffs often results in a poor allocation of our homeland security budget. Our

counterterrorism strategy should be altered to reflect the true dimensions of the different types of risks (not threats) we face. Furthermore, we should assign the responsibility for addressing a particular threat to the entity most able to reduce it and most likely to benefit from its reduction.

Yet we should go even further. Bad security is often worse than no security at all. By trying, and failing, to make ourselves more secure, we make ourselves less secure. We make poor tradeoffs, and we are asked to give up much in terms of money and freedom in exchange for little or no real benefit. Surely, the misplaced perception of security isn't worth that.

8. The Atomic Terrorist?[1]

John Mueller

Alarm about the possibility that small groups could set off nuclear weapons has been repeatedly raised at least since 1946 when atomic bomb maker J. Robert Oppenheimer contended that if three or four people could smuggle in units for an atomic bomb, they could "destroy New York." Thirty years later, nuclear physicist Theodore Taylor proclaimed the problem to be "immediate" and explained at length "how comparatively easy it would be to steal nuclear material and step by step make it into a bomb." At the time, he thought it variously already too late to "prevent the making of a few bombs, here and there, now and then," or "in another ten or fifteen years, it will be too late."[2] Three decades after Taylor, we continue to wait for terrorists to carry out their "easy" task.

In the wake of 9/11, concern about the atomic terrorist surged even though the attacks of that day used no special weapons. By 2003, United Nations Ambassador John Negroponte judged there to be "a high probability" that within two years al Qaeda would attempt an attack using a nuclear or other weapon of mass destruction. And it was in that spirit that in 2004, Graham Allison produced a thoughtful, influential, and well-argued book, *Nuclear Terrorism: The Ultimate Preventable Catastrophe*, relaying his "considered judgment" that "on the current path, a nuclear terrorist attack on America in the decade ahead is more likely than not." He had presumably relied on the same inspirational mechanism in 1995 to predict that "in the absence of a determined program of action, we have every reason to anticipate acts of nuclear terrorism against American targets before this decade is out."[3] He has quite a bit of company in his perpetually alarming conclusions.

However, thus far terrorist groups seem to have exhibited only limited desire and even less progress in going atomic. This may be because, after brief exploration of the possible routes, they, unlike generations of alarmists, have discovered that the tremendous effort required is scarcely likely to be successful.

Obtaining a Finished Bomb: Assistance by a State

One route a would be atomic terrorist might take would be to receive or buy a bomb from a generous like-minded nuclear state for delivery abroad. This is highly improbable, however, because there would be too much risk, even for a country led by extremists, that the ultimate source of the weapon would be discovered. As one prominent analyst, Matthew Bunn, puts it, "A dictator or oligarch bent on maintaining power is highly unlikely to take the immense risk of transferring such a devastating capability to terrorists they cannot control, given the ever present possibility that the material would be traced back to its origin." Important in this last consideration are deterrent safeguards afforded by "nuclear forensics," the rapidly developing science (and art) of connecting nuclear materials to their sources even after a bomb has been exploded.[4]

Moreover, there is a very considerable danger to the donor that the bomb (and its source) would be discovered before delivery or that it would be exploded in a manner and on a target the donor would not approve—including on the donor itself. Another concern would be that foreign intelligence might infiltrate the terrorist group.[5]

There could be some danger that terrorists would be aided by private (or semi private) profiteers, like the network established by Pakistani scientist A. Q. Khan. However, Khan's activities were easily penetrated by intelligence agencies (the Central Intelligence Agency, it is very likely, had agents within the network), and the operation was abruptly closed down when it seemed to be the right time.[6] Moreover, the aid he tendered was entirely to states with return addresses whose chief aim in possessing nuclear weapons would be to deter or to gain prestige—he did not aid stateless terrorist groups whose goal presumably would be actually to set off the weapons.

In addition, almost no one would trust al Qaeda. As one observer has pointed out, the terrorist group's explicit enemies list includes not only Christians and Jews, but all Middle Eastern regimes; Muslims who don't share its views; most Western countries; the governments of India, Pakistan, Afghanistan, and Russia; most news organizations; the United Nations; and international nongovernmental organizations. Most of the time, it didn't get along all that well even with its host in Afghanistan, the Taliban government.[7]

Stealing or Illicitly Purchasing a Bomb: Loose Nukes

There has also been great worry about "loose nukes," especially in post Communist Russia—weapons, "suitcase bombs" in particular, that can be stolen or bought illicitly. However, both Russian nuclear officials and experts on the Russian nuclear programs have adamantly denied that al Qaeda or any other terrorist group could have bought such weapons. They further point out that the bombs, all built before 1991, are difficult to maintain and have a lifespan of one to three years, after which they become "radioactive scrap metal." Similarly, a careful assessment conducted by the Center for Nonproliferation Studies has concluded that it is unlikely that any of these devices have actually been lost and that, regardless, their effectiveness would be very low or even nonexistent because they (like all nuclear weapons) require continual maintenance.[8] Even some of those most alarmed by the prospect of atomic terrorism have concluded, "It is probably true that there are no 'loose nukes,' transportable nuclear weapons missing from their proper storage locations and available for purchase in some way."[9]

It might be added that Russia has an intense interest in controlling any weapons in its territory since it is likely to be a prime target of any illicit use by terrorist groups, particularly Chechen ones, of course, with whom it has been waging a vicious on-and-off war for well over a decade. The government of Pakistan, which has been repeatedly threatened by terrorists, has a similar interest in controlling its nuclear weapons and material—and scientists. Notes Stephen Younger, former head of nuclear weapons research and development at Los Alamos National Laboratory, "Regardless of what is reported in the news, all nuclear nations take the security of their weapons very seriously."[10] Even if a finished bomb were somehow lifted somewhere, the loss would soon be noted and a worldwide pursuit launched.

Moreover, as technology has developed, finished bombs have been outfitted with devices that will trigger a nonnuclear explosion that will destroy the bomb if it is tampered with. And there are other security techniques: bombs can be kept disassembled with their component parts stored in separate high security vaults, and things can be organized so that two people and multiple codes are required not only to use the bomb but to store, maintain, and deploy it. If the terrorists seek to enlist (or force) the services of someone who already knows how to detonate the bomb, they would find, as Younger stresses, that "only a few people in the world have the knowledge to cause an unauthorized detonation of a nuclear weapon." Weapons designers know *how* a weapon works, he explains, but not the multiple types of signals necessary to set it off, and maintenance personnel are trained only in a limited set of functions.[11]

There could be dangers in the chaos that would emerge if a nuclear state were utterly to fail, collapsing in full disarray—Pakistan is frequently brought up in this context and sometimes North Korea as well. However, even under those conditions, nuclear weapons would likely remain under heavy guard by people who know that a purloined bomb would most likely end up going off in their own territory, would still have locks (and in the case of Pakistan, would be disassembled), and could probably be followed, located, and hunted down by an alarmed international community. The worst-case scenario in this instance requires not only a failed state but a considerable series of additional permissive conditions, including consistent (and perfect) insider complicity and a sequence of hasty, opportunistic decisions or developments that click flawlessly in a manner far more familiar to Hollywood scriptwriters than to people experienced with reality.[12]

Building a Bomb of One's Own

Since they are unlikely to be able to buy or steal a usable bomb and since they are further unlikely to have one handed off to them by an established nuclear state, the most plausible route for terrorists would be to manufacture the device themselves from purloined materials. This is the course identified by a majority of leading experts as the most likely scenario to lead to nuclear terrorism.[13]

Because of the dangers and difficulties of transporting and working with plutonium, a dedicated terrorist group, it is generally further agreed, would choose to try to use highly enriched uranium.[14] The idea would be to obtain as much as necessary and then to fashion it into an explosive. To cut corners, the group would presumably be, to the degree possible, comparatively cavalier about safety issues, such as radiation exposure.

The likely product of this effort would not be a bomb that could be dropped or hurled since this would massively complicate the delivery problem. Rather, the terrorists would seek to come up with an "improvised nuclear device" (IND) of the simplest design, one that could be set off at the target by a suicidal detonation crew. The simplest design is a gunlike device in which masses of highly enriched uranium are hurled at each other within a tube. At best, such a device would be, as the deeply concerned Graham Allison acknowledges, "large, cumbersome, unsafe, unreliable, unpredictable, and inefficient."[15]

The process is a daunting one even in this minimal case. In particular, the task requires conquering a considerable series of difficult hurdles, and in sequence. The following discussion attempts to lay out these hurdles in a systematic manner.

Procuring Fissile Material

To begin with, today and likely for the foreseeable future, stateless groups are simply incapable of manufacturing the required fissile material for a bomb because the process requires an effort on an industrial scale. Moreover, a state is unlikely to supply them with the material for the same reasons a state is unlikely to give them a workable bomb.[16] Thus, they would need to steal or illicitly purchase this crucial material.

Although there is legitimate concern that some fissile material, particularly in Russia, may be somewhat inadequately secured, circumstances have improved considerably on this score, and Pakistan keeps exceedingly careful watch over its bomb-grade uranium. Moreover, even sleepy, drunken guards will react hostilely (and noisily) to a raiding party. Thieves also need to know exactly what they want and where it is, which presumably means trusting bribed, but not necessarily dependable, insiders. And to even begin to pull off such a heist, the terrorists would need to develop a highly nuanced street sense in foreign areas often filled with people who are congenitally suspicious of strangers.[17]

But outright armed theft is exceedingly unlikely, not only because of the resistance of guards but also because chase would be immediate. A more plausible route would be to corrupt insiders to smuggle out the required fissile material. However, this approach requires the terrorists to pay off a host of greedy confederates, including brokers and money transmitters, any one of whom could turn on them or, either out of guile or incompetence, furnish them with useless stuff.[18]

Because of improved safeguards and accounting practices, it is increasingly unlikely that the theft would remain undetected.[19] This factor is an important development, because once someone notices that some uranium is missing, the authorities would investigate the few people who might have been able to assist the thieves, and anyone who seems suddenly to have become prosperous will likely arrest their attention right from the start. Even one initially tempted by, seduced by, or sympathetic to, the blandishments of the smooth-talking foreign terrorists might well soon develop sobering second thoughts and go to the authorities.

Insiders might also come to ruminate over the fact that, once the heist was accomplished, the terrorists would, as analyst Brian Jenkins puts it none too delicately, "have every incentive to cover their trail, beginning with eliminating their confederates." He also points out that no case of a rogue Russian scientist working for terrorists or foreign states has ever been documented.[20]

It is also relevant to note that over the years, known thefts of highly enriched uranium have totaled fewer than 16 pounds or so. That amount is far less than that required for an atomic explosion: for a crude bomb, over 100 pounds are necessary to produce a likely yield of one kiloton.[21] Moreover, none of these thieves was connected to al Qaeda, and most arrestingly, none had buyers lined up—nearly all were caught while trying to peddle their wares. Indeed, concludes analyst Robin Frost, "there appears to be no true demand, except where the buyers were government agents running a sting." Since there appears to be no real commercial market for fissile material, each sale would be a one-time affair, not a continuing source of profit like drugs, and there is no evidence of established underworld commercial trade in this illicit commodity.[22] Consequently, sellers need to make all their money on the single transaction.

Of course, there may also have been additional thefts that went undiscovered.[23] However, the difficulty of peddling such a special substance suggests that any theft would have to be done on consignment—the thief is unlikely to come across likely purchasers while wandering provocatively down the street like a purveyor of drugs or French postcards. Even a "theft on spec" requires that the sellers advertise or that they know where and how to contact their terrorist buyer—presumably through intermediaries trusted by both sides, all of whom must be paid off. Moreover, it is likely that no single seller would have enough purloined material, requiring multiple clandestine buys.

If terrorists were somehow successful at obtaining a sufficient mass of relevant material, they would then have to transport it hundreds of miles out of the country over unfamiliar terrain and probably while being pursued by security forces.[24]

Crossing international borders would be facilitated by following established smuggling routes and for a considerable fee, opium traders (for example) might provide expert, and possibly even reliable, assistance. But the routes are not as chaotic as they appear and are often under the watch of suspicious and careful criminal regulators.[25] If they became suspicious of the commodity being smuggled, some of them might find it in their interest to disrupt passage, perhaps to collect the bounteous reward likely to be offered by alarmed governments if the uranium theft had been discovered. It is not at all clear, moreover, that people engaged in the routine, if illegal, business of smuggling would necessarily be so debased that, even for considerable remuneration, they would willingly join a plot that might kill tens of thousands of innocent people.

To reduce dangers, the atomic terrorists might split up their booty and smuggle it out in multiple small amounts. In this, however, they would have to rely on the hope that every single container would escape notice and suspicion.

Constructing an Atomic Device

Once outside the country with their precious booty, terrorists would need to set up a large and well-equipped machine shop to manufacture a bomb and then to populate it with a select team of highly skilled scientists, technicians, and machinists. The process would also require good managers and organizers.

The group would have to be assembled and retained for the monumental task without generating consequential suspicions among friends, family, and police about their curious and sudden absence from normal pursuits back home. Pakistan, for example, maintains a strict watch on many of its nuclear scientists even after retirement.[26]

Members of the bomb-building team would also need to be utterly devoted to the cause, of course. And they would need to be willing to put their lives, and certainly their careers, at high risk, because after their bomb was discovered, or exploded, they would likely become the targets of an intense worldwide dragnet facilitated by the fact that their skills would be uncommon ones.

Some observers have insisted that it would be "easy" for terrorists to assemble a crude bomb if they could get enough fissile material. However, Christoph Wirz and Emmanuel Egger, two senior physicists in charge of nuclear issues at Switzerland's Spiez Laboratory, bluntly conclude that the task "could hardly be accomplished by a subnational group." They point out that precise blueprints are required, not just sketches and general ideas, and that even with a good blueprint, the terrorist group "would most certainly be forced to redesign." They also stress that the work is difficult, dangerous, and extremely exacting, and that the technical requirements "in several fields verge on the unfeasible."[27]

Los Alamos research director Younger has made a similar argument, expressing his amazement at "self declared 'nuclear weapons experts,' many of whom have never seen a real nuclear weapon," who "hold forth on how easy it is to make a functioning nuclear explosive." Information is readily available for getting the general idea behind a rudimentary nuclear explosive, but none of it is detailed enough for "the confident assembly of a real nuclear explosive." Although he remains concerned that a terrorist group could buy or steal a nuclear device or be given one by an established nuclear country, Younger is quick to enumerate the difficulties the group would confront when attempting to fabricate one on their own. He stresses that uranium is "exceptionally difficult to machine," while "plutonium is one of the most complex metals ever discovered, a material whose basic properties are sensitive to exactly how it is processed," and both require special machining technology. Younger concludes, "To think that a terrorist group, working in isolation with an unreliable supply of electricity and little access to tools and supplies [could fabricate a bomb or IND] is far fetched at best."[28] Under the best of circumstances, the process could take months or even a year or more, and it would all, of course, have to be carried out in utter secrecy even while local and international security police are likely to be on the intense prowl. In addition, people or criminal gangs in the area may observe with increasing curiosity and puzzlement the constant coming and going of technicians unlikely to be locals. Unless they live constantly in the shop (itself a noticeable event), the conspirators would eat, sleep, drink, and recreate elsewhere, bumping into curious, and potentially inquiring, people. It would obviously be vital to keep from inadvertently divulging any information about their project that might incite suspicion—a wariness that could itself inspire suspicion—and to maintain a plausible and consistent cover story. Through all this, they would have to remain loyal to the cause, avoiding disillusionment as well as consequential homesickness and interpersonal frictions.

The process of fabricating an IND requires, then, the effective recruitment of people who at once have great technical skills and will remain completely devoted to the cause. In addition, a host of corrupted coconspirators, many of them foreign, must remain utterly reliable; international and local security services must be kept perpetually in the dark; and no curious outsider must get wind of the project over the months or even years it takes to pull it off.

Transporting and Detonating the Device

The finished product could weigh a ton or more.[29] Encased in lead shielding to mask radioactive emissions, it would then have to be transported to, and smuggled into, the relevant target country.

The conspirators could take one of two approaches. Under one approach, they would trust their precious and laboriously fabricated product to the tender mercies of the commercial transportation system, supplying something of a return address in the process and hoping that transportation and policing agencies, alerted to the dangers by news of the purloined uranium, would remain oblivious.

Perhaps more plausibly, the atomic terrorists would hire an aircraft or try to use established smuggling routes, an approach that, again, would require the completely reliable complicity of a considerable number of criminals, none of whom develops cold feet or becomes attracted by reward money. And even if enough reliable coconspirators can be assembled and corrupted, there is still no guarantee their efforts will be successful. There is a key difference between smuggling drugs and smuggling an atomic weapon. Those in the drug trade assume that, although authorities will intercept a fair portion of their material , the amount that does get through will be enough to supply them with a tidy profit. That may be tolerable for drug smugglers, but it is distinctly unsettling for terrorists seeking to smuggle in a single, large, and very expensively obtained weapon.[30]

However transported, the enormous package would have to be received within the target country by a group of collaborators who are at once totally dedicated and technically proficient at handling, maintaining, detonating, and perhaps assembling the weapon after it arrives.

This crew would then have to move the IND over local roads to the target site without arousing suspicion. And finally, at the target site, the crew, presumably suicidal, would have to detonate its improvised and untested nuclear device, one that, to repeat Allison's description, would be "large, cumbersome, unsafe, unreliable, unpredictable, and inefficient." While doing this, they would have to hope, and fervently pray, that the machine shop work was proficient, that there were no significant shakeups in the treacherous process of transportation, and that the thing, after all this effort, isn't a dud.

The Financial Costs

The financial costs of the extended operation in all its cumulating, or cascading, entirety could become monumental. There would be expensive equipment to buy, smuggle, and set up, and people to pay—or pay off. Some operatives might work for free out of dedication, but the vast conspiracy also requires the subversion of an array of criminals and opportunists, each of whom has every incentive to push the price for cooperation as high as possible. Any criminals who are competent and capable enough to be effective allies in the project are likely to be both smart enough to see opportunities for extortion and psychologically equipped by their profession to be willing to exploit them.

Assessing the Likelihood of Terrorist Success

In an article on the prospects for atomic terrorism, Bill Keller of the *New York Times* suggests that "the best reason for thinking it won't happen is that it hasn't happened yet," and that, he worries, "is terrible logic."[31] However, "logic" aside, there is another quite good reason for thinking it won't happen: the task is incredibly *difficult.*

I have arrayed a lengthy set of obstacles confronting the would be atomic terrorist. Those who warn about the likelihood of a terrorist bomb contend that a terrorist group could, if often with great difficulty, surmount each obstacle—that doing so in each case is "not impossible."[32] But it is vital to point out that, while it may be "not impossible" to surmount each step, the likelihood that a group could surmount a series of steps quickly becomes vanishingly small.

Even the alarmed Matthew Bunn and Anthony Wier contend that the atomic terrorists' task "would clearly be among the most difficult types of attack to carry out" or "one of the most difficult missions a terrorist group could hope to try." But, stresses the CIA's George Tenet, a terrorist atomic bomb is "possible" or "not beyond the realm of possibility."[33] Accordingly, it might be useful to take a stab at estimating just how "difficult" the atomic terrorists' task, in aggregate, is—that is, how far from the fringe of the "realm of possibility" it might be.

Most discussions of atomic terrorism deal in a rather piecemeal fashion with the subject—focusing separately on individual tasks, such as procuring highly enriched uranium or assembling a device or transporting it. However, as the Gilmore Commission, a special advisory panel to the president and Congress, stresses, setting off a nuclear device capable of producing mass destruction presents not only "Herculean challenges" but also requires that a whole series of steps be accomplished. If each is not fully met, the result is not simply a less powerful weapon but one that can't produce any significant nuclear yield at all or can't be delivered.[34]

Following this perspective, an appropriate approach is to catalog the barriers that a terrorist group must overcome to carry out the task of producing, transporting, and then successfully detonating an improvised nuclear device. Table 8.1 attempts to do this, and it arrays some 20 of these barriers—*all* of which must be surmounted by the atomic aspirant. Actually, it would be quite possible to come up with a longer list: in the interests of keeping the catalog of hurdles to a reasonable number, some of the entries are actually collections of tasks and could be divided into two or three or more. For example, number 5 on the list requires that purloined highly enriched uranium be neither a scam nor part of a sting nor of inadequate quality due to insider incompetence. This hurdle could as readily be rendered as three separate ones.

Table 8.1
THE ATOMIC TERRORIST'S TASKS IN THE MOST LIKELY SCENARIO

---

1. An inadequately secured source of adequate quantities of highly enriched uranium (HEU) must be found.
2. The area must be entered while avoiding detection by local police and locals wary of strangers.
3. Several insiders who seem to know what they are doing must be corrupted.
4. All the insiders must remain loyal throughout the long process of planning and executing the heist, and there must be no consequential leaks.
5. The insiders must successfully seize and transfer the HEU, the transferred HEU must not be a scam or part of a sting, and it must not be of inadequate quality due to insider incompetence.
6. The HEU must be transported across the country over unfamiliar territory while its possessors are being pursued.
7. To get the HEU across one or more international borders, smugglers must be employed, and they must remain loyal despite, potentially, the temptations of a massive reward even as no consequential suspicion is generated in other smugglers using the same routes who may be interested in the same money.
8. A machine shop must be set up in an obscure area with imported, sophisticated equipment without anyone becoming suspicious.
9. A team of highly skilled scientists and technicians must be assembled, and during production, all members of the team must remain absolutely loyal to the cause and develop no misgivings or severe interpersonal or financial conflicts.
10. The complete team must be transported to the machine shop, probably from several countries, without suspicion and without consequential leaks from relatives, friends, and colleagues about the missing.
11. The team must have precise technical blueprints to work from (not general sketches) and must be able to modify them appropriately for the precise purpose at hand over months (or even years) of labor, without being able to test.

12. Nothing significant must go wrong during the long process of manufacture and assembly of the (IND).
13. There must be no inadvertent leaks from the team.
14. Local and international police, on high (even desperate) alert, must not be able to detect the project using traditional policing methods, as well as the most advanced technical detection equipment.
15. No locals must sense that something out of the ordinary is going on in the machine shop with the constant coming and going of nonlocal people.
16. The IND, weighing a ton or more, must be smuggled without detection out of the machine shop to an international border.
17. The IND must be transported to the target country either by trusting the commercial process filled with people on the alert for cargo of this sort or by clandestine means, which requires trusting corrupt coconspirators who may also know about any reward money.
18. A team of completely loyal and technically accomplished coconspirators must be assembled within, or infiltrated into, the target country.
19. The IND must successfully enter the target country and be received by the in country coconspirators.
20. A detonation team must transport the IND to the target place and set it off without anybody noticing and interfering, and the untested and much traveled IND must prove not to be a dud.

In contemplating the task before them, would be atomic terrorists effectively *must* go through an exercise that looks much like this. If and when they do so, they are likely to find their prospects daunting and accordingly uninspiring or even terminally dispiriting.

Assigning and Calculating Probabilities

The discussion thus far has followed a qualitative approach: synthesizing a considerable amount of material to lay out the route a terrorist group must take to acquire and detonate an atomic bomb in the most likely scenario. This exercise alone suggests the almost breathtaking enormity of the difficulties facing the would be atomic terrorist. A quantitative assessment reinforces this conclusion.

Assigning a probability to the terrorists' being able to overcome each barrier is, of course, a tricky business. Any such exercise should be regarded as rather tentative and exploratory, or perhaps simply as illustrative—though it is done all the time in cost-benefit analysis.

One might begin a quantitative approach by adopting probability estimates that purposely, and heavily, bias the case in the terrorists' favor. In my view, this would take place if it is assumed that the terrorists have a fighting chance of 50 percent of overcoming each of the 20 obstacles displayed in Table 8.1, though for many barriers, probably almost all, the odds against them are surely much worse than that. Even with that generous bias, the chances that a concerted effort would be successful are less than one in a million, specifically 1,048,576. If one assumes, somewhat more realistically, that their chances at each barrier are one in three, the cumulative odds of their being able to pull off the deed drop to one in well over three billion—specifically 3,486,784,401. Moreover, all this focuses on the effort to deliver a single bomb. If the requirement were to deliver several, the odds become, of course, even more prohibitive.

Multiple Attempts

The odds considered so far are for a single attempt by a single group, and there could be multiple attempts by multiple groups, of course. But the odds would remain long even with multiple concerted attempts. If there were 100 such efforts over a period of time, using the one-chance-in-two assumption for each obstacle, the chance that at least one of them would be successful comes in at less than 1 in over 10,000. At the far more realistic assumption of one chance in three for each obstacle, it would be about 1 in nearly 35 million.[35]

Additionally, if there were a large number of concerted efforts, policing and protecting would presumably become easier because the aspirants would be exposing themselves repeatedly and would likely be stepping all over one another in their quest to access the right stuff. Furthermore, each foiled attempt would likely expose flaws in the defense system, holes the defenders would then plug, making subsequent efforts more difficult.

Also, the difficulties for the atomic terrorists are likely to *increase* over time because of much-enhanced protective and policing efforts by self-interested governments. Already, for example, by all accounts Russian nuclear materials are much more adequately secured than they were 10 or 15 years ago.[36] In addition, the science of nuclear forensics will advance, heightening pressure on states to secure their weapons material.

Other Acquisition Scenarios

These odds are for the most plausible scenario in which a terrorist group might gain a bomb: constructing one from highly enriched uranium obtained through illicit means. As noted, there are other routes to a bomb: stealing a fully constructed one or receiving one as a gift by a nuclear state. However, as also noted, those routes are generally conceded, even by most of the most alarmed, to be considerably *less* likely to result in a terrorist success than the one outlined in Table 8.1.

Assistance by a state would shorten the terrorist group's list of hurdles considerably, of course, but they would be replaced by the big one: the exceedingly low likelihood that a nuclear state would trust it with one of its precious bombs.

The theft of a finished bomb would also shorten the list of hurdles. However, it would generate new ones as well, such as the necessity to defeat locks and the difficulty of finding purloinable nuclear weapons in an age in which these weapons are increasingly under lock and key and in which insiders who could productively help with the theft are few and ever more likely to be found out after the deed was accomplished.

Comparisons

Improbable events, even highly improbable ones, do sometimes occur, of course. But although any event that is improbable is, at the same time and by definition, possible, it is obviously a fundamental fallacy to conclude that the fact that improbable events do occasionally transpire means that an improbable event should somehow be taken to be likely.

Huge numbers of people buy public lottery tickets despite the fact that the odds can easily be worse than a million to one against them, and a (very) few of these gamblers do, of course, cash in. However, a lottery loser forfeits only a limited amount of money

153

in each million to one fling, while losers in the atomic terrorism enterprise could easily end up sacrificing not only all their financial resources in a single concerted attempt but their lives as well.

Another comparison might be made with the 9/11 events. The difficulties confronting the hijackers were considerable, and the conspirators certainly were extremely clever and lucky. But there has never been a terrorist attack that has been remotely as destructive and, despite innumerable predictions that 9/11 was a harbinger, it has thus far remained an aberration.[37]

Moreover, whatever the hijackers' difficulties, they were nothing like those confronting the would be atomic terrorist. The size of the conspiracy was very small, technical requirements were minimal, obtaining flight training only took the money to pay for it, the weapons they used could legally be brought on planes, and, most importantly, they were exploiting an environment in which the policy was to cooperate with hijackers rather than fight and risk the entire plane.[38] Even in that enormously advantageous policy environment, the 9/11 hijackers failed to accomplish their mission with the last of the four planes.

In addition, the personnel requirements are far higher in the atomic case. The conspiracy—or actually the sequential sets of conspiracies—mandate the enlistment of a much larger number of people, and most of them must be not only absolutely loyal but also extremely skilled at an elaborate series of technical, organizational, and conspiratorial tasks. Moreover, the 9/11 plotters did not have to rely on strangers or criminals, while the steadfast cooperation of such people would be central to an atomic conspiracy. And carrying out the 9/11 operation itself required a few hours of concentrated work and dedication, not the months or even years that would be required of atomic terrorists.

Progress and Interest

The degree to which al Qaeda has pursued, or even has much interest in, a nuclear weapons program may have been exaggerated. There is some occasional evidence to indicate that the group might have some interest in atomic weapons, but it is limited and often ambiguous. The same can be said about evidence that al Qaeda has actively sought to achieve an atomic capacity.

154

The 9/11 Commission insists that "al Qaeda has tried to acquire or make nuclear weapons for at least ten years," but the only substantial evidence it supplies comes from an episode that supposedly took place around 1993 in Sudan when al Qaeda apparently sought to purchase some uranium, which turned out to be bogus.[39] Information about this supposed venture apparently comes entirely from Jamal Ahmed al-Fadl, who defected from al Qaeda in 1996 after he had been caught stealing $110,000 from the organization. Interestingly, Lawrence Wright relays the testimony of the man who allegedly actually purchased the substance for Osama bin Laden as well as that of a Sudanese intelligence agent. Both assert that, although there were various other scams going around at the time that may have served as grist for al-Fadl, the uranium episode never happened.[40]

As a key indication of al Qaeda's desire to obtain atomic weapons, many have focused on a set of conversations in Afghanistan in August 2001 that two Pakistani nuclear scientists reportedly had with Osama bin Laden and three other al Qaeda officials. Pakistani intelligence officers characterize the discussions as "academic," and they also maintain that to be the descriptor the scientists "insisted" on using. The officers do report, however, that the scientists "described bin Laden as intensely interested in nuclear, chemical and biological weapons." But the questions do not seem to be very sophisticated, and as the scientists themselves have reportedly insisted, it seems that the discussion was wide ranging and academic (even rather basic) and that they provided no material or specific plans. Moreover, the scientists likely were incapable of providing truly helpful information because their expertise was not in bomb design, which might be useful to terrorists, but rather in the processing of fissile material, which is almost certainly beyond the capacities of a nonstate group, as discussed earlier.[41]

Khalid Shaikh Mohammed, the apparent mastermind behind the 9/11 attacks, reportedly says that al Qaeda's atom bomb efforts never went beyond searching the Internet. After the fall of the Taliban in 2001, technical experts from the CIA and the Department of Energy examined documents and other information uncovered by intelligence agencies and the media in Afghanistan. According to an official American report, they "judged that there remained no credible information that al Qa'ida had obtained fissile material or acquired a nuclear weapon." Moreover, they found no evidence of "any radioactive material suitable for weapons." They did uncover, however, a "nuclear-related" document discussing "openly available concepts about the nuclear fuel cycle and some weapons related issues." Physicist and weapons expert David Albright has also examined this evidence and is more impressed, but even he concludes that any al Qaeda atomic efforts were "seriously disrupted"—indeed, "nipped in the bud"—by the invasion of Afghanistan in 2001. Whatever his evaluation of the situation before the event, Albright concludes that after the invasion, "the overall chance of al Qaeda detonating a nuclear explosive appears on reflection to be low."[42]

Rumors and reports that al Qaeda has managed to purchase an atomic bomb, or several, have been around now for over a decade, beginning around 1998. Louise Richardson catalogs a number of the loose nuke stories, and Brian Jenkins has also sifted through them. Richardson concludes, "There can be little doubt that most of these reports are as reliable as the reports that Saddam Hussein was developing and stockpiling weapons of mass destruction." And in his assessment of these "vague rumors and reports," Jenkins points out that, "although the facts of these reported contacts, deals, and deliveries were shrouded in mystery, the 'shocking revelations' were often shorn of uncertainty and offered as 'empirical proof,' presented as fact and accepted on faith."[43] If any of the several reports suggesting al Qaeda had acquired an atomic arsenal over a decade ago were true, one might think the terrorist group (or in the case of the most spectacular of the reports, their Chechen suppliers) would have tried to set one off by now. Or one might be led to suspect that al Qaeda would have left some trace of the weapons behind in Afghanistan after it made its very hasty exit in 2001. But, as noted earlier, none was found.

Pakistani journalist Hamid Mir was brought in to interview bin Laden just a day or two before al Qaeda fled Afghanistan in 2001, and bin Laden supposedly asserted: "If the United States uses chemical or nuclear weapons against us, we might respond with chemical and nuclear weapons. We possess these weapons as a deterrent."[44] Given the military pressure they were under at the time, and taking into account the evidence of the primitive nature of al Qaeda's nuclear program (if it could be said to have had one at all), the reported assertions, while unsettling, appear to be best interpreted as a desperate bluff.

Bin Laden has pronounced on the nuclear weapons issue a few other times. Some of those pronouncements can be viewed as threatening, but they are rather coy and indirect, indicating perhaps something of an interest, but not acknowledging a capability. And as Richardson concludes: "Statements claiming a right to possess nuclear weapons have been misinterpreted as expressing a determination to use them. This in turn has fed the exaggeration of the threat we face."[45]

After an exhaustive study of available materials, Anne Stenersen of the Norwegian Defence Research Establishment concludes that although "it is likely that al Qaeda central has considered the option of using non conventional weapons," there "is little evidence that such ideas ever developed into actual plans, or that they were given any kind of priority at the expense of more traditional types of terrorist attacks."[46]

When examined, then, the evidence of al Qaeda's desire to go atomic and its progress in accomplishing this exceedingly difficult task is remarkably skimpy, if not completely negligible. The scariest stuff—a decade's worth of loose nuke rumor, chatter, and hype— seems to have no substance whatever.

Capacity

However, assuming the group, or one like it, would actually like to be able to make or steal an atomic bomb or two, how capable is it of accomplishing a task that, as suggested earlier, is enormously difficult?

The key portions of al Qaeda central may well actually total only a few hundred people. They also assist with the Taliban's distinctly separate, far larger, and very troublesome insurgency in Afghanistan. Beyond this tiny band, there are thousands of sympathizers and would be jihadists spread around the globe who mainly connect in Internet chat rooms, engage in radicalizing conversations, and variously dare one another to actually do something.[47]

Any "threat," particularly to the West, appears, then, principally to derive from self-selected people, often isolated from one another, who fantasize about performing dire deeds. From time to time, some of them, or others closer to al Qaeda central, may actually manage to do some harm. And occasionally, they may even be able to pull off something large, like 9/11. But in most cases, their capacities and schemes—or alleged schemes—seem to be far less dangerous than initial press reports vividly, even hysterically, suggest.

Most important for present purposes, however, any notion that the actual al Qaeda enemy has the capacity to come up with nuclear weapons, even if it wanted to, looks far-fetched in the extreme. Although there have been plenty of terrorist attacks in the world since 2001, all (thus far, at least) have relied on conventional destructive methods.

For the most part, terrorists seem to be heeding the advice found in a memo on an al Qaeda laptop seized in Pakistan in 2004: "Make use of that which is available . . . rather than waste valuable time becoming despondent over that which is not within your reach." That is, keep it simple, stupid. And in fact, it seems to be a general historical regularity that terrorists tend to prefer weapons that they know and understand, not new, exotic ones.[48]

In an appearance before a Senate committee on January 11, 2007, Robert Mueller, director of the Federal Bureau of Investigation, testified that, although he remained concerned that things could change in the future, "few if any terrorist groups" were likely to possess the required expertise to produce nuclear weapons—or, for that matter, biological or chemical ones.[49] Moreover, as two analysts independently suggest, the terrorist use of unconventional weapons can be especially counterproductive by turning off financial supporters, dividing the movement, and eliciting major crackdowns.[50]

Acceptable Risk

The purpose here has not been to argue that policies designed to inconvenience the atomic terrorist are necessarily unneeded or unwise. Rather, in contrast with the many who insist that atomic terrorism under current conditions is rather—indeed, *exceedingly*— likely to come about, I have contended that it is hugely unlikely. In part because of the current policy environment—but also because of a wealth of other technical and organizational difficulties inherent in the deed—the atomic terrorists' task under present conditions is already monumental, and their likelihood of success is vanishingly small. Efforts to further enhance this monumentality, if cost effective and accompanied with only tolerable side effects, are generally desirable—although to me they scarcely seem as urgent as their proponents repeatedly proclaim.

As Allison appropriately points out, it is important in all this to consider not only the likelihood an event will take place but also its consequences. Therefore, one must be concerned about catastrophic events even if their likelihood is small.

At some point, however, probabilities become so low that, even for catastrophic events, it begins to make sense to ignore, or at least to back burner, them: the risk becomes "acceptable." Consider the odds that a wheel on a speeding automobile will suddenly shear off. That horror is surely "not impossible," yet legions of motorists effectively find it so improbable that they are routinely willing to risk their lives that it will not happen—it is, in short, an acceptable risk.

The British could at any time attack the United States with their submarine-launched missiles and kill millions of Americans—far more than even the most monumentally gifted and lucky terrorist group. Yet the risk that this potential (and fully possible) calamity might take place evokes little concern; essentially it is "accepted." Meanwhile, Russia, with whom the United States enjoys a rather strained relationship, could at any time do vastly more damage still with its nuclear weapons, a fully imaginable calamity that goes substantially ignored.

In constructing what he calls "a case for fear," Cass Sunstein notes that if there is a yearly probability of 1 in 100,000 that terrorists could launch a nuclear or massive biological attack, the risk would cumulate to 1 in 10,000 over 10 years and to 1 in 5,000 over 20 years. These odds, he suggests, are "not the most comforting."[51] Comfort, of course, lies in the viscera of those to be comforted, and, as he suggests, many would probably have difficulty settling down with odds like that. But there must be *some* point at which even these people's concerns would ease. Just perhaps it is at some of the levels suggested here: 1 in 1 million or 1 in 3 billion per attempt.

The same consideration holds for Vice President Dick Cheney's "one percent doctrine." A top CIA analyst told him late in 2001 that al Qaeda probably did not have a nuclear weapon but that he couldn't "assure you that they don't." To this, Cheney replied, "If there's a one percent chance that they do, you have to pursue it as if it were true."[52] Cheney's observation is a somewhat confused, but effective, way of saying that one should take low-probability events that could have an exceedingly high impact very seriously indeed. And a 1 percent chance of a terrorist atomic attack would clearly fit into that category. It's just that the chances, while perhaps not zero, do not seem to be anywhere remotely near 1 percent. It's not that they are necessarily 1 in 3.5 billion, but they aren't anything like 1 in 10, 1 in 100, or 1 in 1,000. Perhaps, in fact, they are comparable to, or even lower than, those for a thermonuclear attack from Russia.

The potential for atomic terrorism may indeed be the single most serious threat to the national security of the United States. Assessed in the appropriate context, however, that could actually be seen to be a comparatively cheering conclusion. Sensible cost-effective policies designed to make that probability even lower may be justified, given the damage that can be inflicted by an atomic explosion. But unjustified alarmism about the likelihood and imminence of atomic terrorism has had policy consequences that have been costly and unnecessary.

9. Assessing the Threat of Bioterrorism

Milton Leitenberg[1]

Various forms of cancer kill roughly 565,000 Americans per year, tobacco kills around 440,000, and obesity causes perhaps 400,000 or more deaths.[2] Approximately 1.7 million patients develop infections annually while undergoing treatment in U.S. hospitals, resulting in an estimated 99,000 deaths.[3] These four causes account for roughly 1.5 million U.S. deaths per year, every year. A single organism, *Clostridium difficile*, causes some 350,000 infections and 15,000–20,000 deaths per year.[4] In 1990, the Institute of Medicine at the U.S. National Academy of Sciences estimated that microbial resistance, largely caused by the use of antibiotics in food supplements for cattle and chickens, cost the U.S. health care system approximately $5 billion per year.[5] In 2008, that cost was estimated at $20 billion per year.[6] Bioterrorism killed no U.S. citizens in the 20th century and five to date in the 21st century.

Since the anthrax scare of October and November 2001—in which 22 people were sickened, of whom 5 died—the U.S. government has appropriated $64 billion for biological weapons prevention and defense. The proposed current rate of annual appropriation for this purpose is $7 billion, which will likely continue in the future.[7]

Placing the two brief paragraphs above alongside each other presents the crux of the issues examined in this chapter. Can we present a reasonable estimate of the threat of bioterrorism to the United States? How has the subject been treated in the political domain? What are the consequences of some of the U.S. government's responses to the problem since 2001? Five policy questions will be reviewed. The first and most basic is the assessment of the bioterrorist threat to the United States. Under this rubric, the nature of the political discussion surrounding the issue of bioterrorism in the United States in recent years is examined. The second issue is how the U.S. government's response since 2001 has increased the proliferation potential of biological weapons (BWs) and damaged national

161

security. The third is the diversion of resources within the U.S. public health sector. The fourth issue is the misdirection of public health efforts in developing nations. The final policy issue to be examined is that of oversight and regulation of the burgeoning U.S. biodefense program.

Assessment of the Current Threat of Bioterrorism to the United States

The problem of assessing the threat of bioterrorism can be separated into four considerations: the status of state offensive biological weapons programs, evidence of proliferation from state BW programs, evidence of state assistance to nonstate actors to develop or produce biological agents or weapons, and efforts to develop biological agents or weapons by nonstate actors that are true international terrorist groups.

Official U.S. government statements in the late 1980s claimed that four nations possessed offensive BW programs when the Biological Weapons Convention was signed in 1972 and that this number increased to 10 by 1989.[8] In November 1997, U.S. government officials raised the estimate to 12, 9 of which the United States identified by name in the intervening years. In 2001, the estimate was 13. Since then, the U.S. government has removed Libya, Iraq, and Cuba from the list (it had removed South Africa in 1995 without public notice when that government terminated both its biological and chemical weapons programs)—a reduction of essentially one-third. But strikingly, as early as 2003, official U.S. intelligence assessments became markedly more qualified about which countries were definitively developing BWs.[9] Defense Intelligence Agency Director Michael Maples's threat assessment presentation on January 11, 2007, accentuated the lack of specifics on the number and status of offensive state BW programs:

- "North Korea's resources include a biotechnical infrastructure that could support the production of various biological warfare agents."
- "Iran has a growing biotechnology industry, significant pharmaceutical experience and the overall infrastructure that could be used to support a biological warfare program. DIA believes Iran is pursuing development of biological weapons."

- "China possesses a sufficiently advanced biotechnology infra-structure to allow it to develop and produce biological agents."
- "We judge Russia also continues research and development that could support its chemical and biological warfare programs."
- "India and Pakistan . . . both . . . have the infrastructure to sup-port biological and some aspects of the chemical warfare programs."
- "Syria's biotechnical infrastructure is capable of supporting lim-ited biological agent development. DIA assesses Syria has a program to develop select biological agents."[10]

Only the statements on Iran and Syria refer explicitly to offensive BW programs; the other statements fail to support the suggestion that these particular countries possess an offensive BW program. These latter statements could apply to the United States and most European countries. These more muted and limited descriptions suggest that not as many countries possessed offensive BW programs as previously believed. In fact, these evolving assessments—and the Maples testimony in particular—raise serious questions about what basis in reality existed for the estimates of national BW programs in the 1970s and 1980s, excluding the Soviet Union, South Africa, Iraq, and perhaps Iran.

Because these recent estimates are so uncertain but have the benefit of accumulated intelligence, past estimates are likely to have been more questionable, as they were presumably generated on less intel-ligence. It now seems likely that the number of countries thought to have offensive BW programs in the early 1970s through 1989 might more accurately be estimated at four or five. In recent years, then, official U.S. estimates of the number of such programs have declined by at least one-third, leaving roughly a half dozen at most.[11] And the U.S. intelligence community has qualified its assessments of those remaining programs to such a significant degree that it is difficult to judge what degree of an "offensive" nature—the develop-ment, testing, production, or stockpiling of biological agents or weapons—exists in those programs.

Statements by innumerable U.S. government officials, academic analysts, and journalists between 1989 and 2003 nearly uniformly described the proliferation of state-run BW programs as a constantly increasing trend.[12] It now seems clear that was not the case. In fact, the number of state BW programs was probably more or less flat.

Available evidence indicates that proliferation from state-run offensive BW programs has been minimal. The former South African and Iraqi BW programs resulted in no known proliferation. As for the Soviet Union, only about 10 scientists are known to have immigrated to any country of BW proliferation concern in the post-Soviet period. Some were recruited by Iran, but most of this group worked in institutes belonging to the former Soviet Academy of Sciences, not in research institutes primarily serving the former Soviet BW program. Several immigrated to Israel.[13] The United States never included Israel on its lists of BW-proliferated states, although Israel almost certainly maintained an offensive BW program for many years and may still do so.

One can be even more definitive regarding assistance from state-run BW programs to terrorist organizations seeking to develop or to produce biological agents or weapons: there is no evidence whatsoever of any such activity. U.S. intelligence agencies have always considered the likelihood of such assistance to be extremely low, and they expect the same to remain the case in the future.[14]

Finally, the history of attempts by nonstate actors to develop or use biological agents has been remarkably limited. The significant episodes are all well known. The first was the use of salmonella, bacteria that cause diarrhea, in 1984 by the Rajneesh cult, in a failed attempt to influence a local election in Oregon. The second was Aum Shinrikyo's 1990–1993 failed effort to obtain and culture strains of *Clostridium botulinum* and *Bacillus anthracis* and disperse the resulting products. The group never succeeded in obtaining a pathogenic strain of either organism. Its culturing and dispersal efforts also came to naught. A third case was al Qaeda's effort in Afghanistan between 1997 and 2001 to obtain a pathogenic culture of *B. anthracis* and to initiate work with the organism. Once again, the effort failed, as the organization was unable to obtain a pathogenic strain of *B. anthracis*. Al Qaeda's work was extremely incompetent. It had barely begun preparations when a joint allied military team raided and occupied its facilities in December 2001.[15] The most recent significant episode took place in the United States in September and October 2001—the so-called Amerithrax incidents.[16] These were the dispersal of a purified, dry-powder preparation of *B. anthracis* sent through the U.S. postal system to multiple addressees, killing five people.

The al Qaeda and the Amerithrax events are the most significant but for opposite reasons. The barely initiated, rudimentary, and failed attempt by al Qaeda is important because of the nature of the group—an international terrorist organization with a wide organizational structure, demonstrated initiative, and a record of successful, albeit conventional, attacks. The Amerithrax attacks are significant because of the nature of the material prepared and the perpetrator; the mailings demonstrate what a professional is capable of, but identifying the perpetrator was essential to explaining who could make such a product and under what conditions. In other words, identification would provide critical insight into both the likelihood of international terrorist organizations' developing similar capabilities and how quickly such a threat could emerge. Since the interruption of the al Qaeda BW project in December 2001, there are no indications that the group has resumed those efforts. Accounts of al Qaeda offshoot groups in the United Kingdom, France, or Iraq producing ricin, a far simpler task, are all spurious. There have also been no publicly identified indications that any other international terrorist group has initiated the development of BW agents in the intervening years.[17]

Although al Qaeda's efforts to develop a biological weapon failed, the group's efforts were provoked by the severely overheated discussion in the United States about the imminent dangers of bioterrorism. A message from al Qaeda's second-in-command, Ayman al-Zawahri, to his deputy, Muhammad Atef, on April 15, 1999, noted, "We only became aware of them [BWs] when the enemy drew our attention to them by repeatedly expressing concerns that they can be produced simply with easily available materials."[18] In a similar vein, terrorism expert Brian Jenkins of the RAND Corporation has been at pains to point out, "We invented nuclear terror."[19] If in the coming decades we do see a successful attempt by a terrorist organization to use BWs, blame for it can be in large part pinned on the incessant scaremongering about bioterrorism in the United States, which has emphasized and reinforced its desirability to terrorist organizations.

In terms of bioterrorism perpetrated by a terrorist organization, the Amerithrax events are an outlier. They were almost certainly carried out by a U.S. scientist, fully trained, with access to pathogenic strains and optimum working conditions, as discussed later in this chapter. A terrorist group has never carried out a mass-casualty bioterrorist event. Yet thanks to the steady stream of prognostications that essentially explain to terrorists why BWs would be of

165

great utility to them, such an event may well happen. Unfortunately, those interested in keeping the level of government funding for biodefense high will likely continue to make remarks of the same sort.

In the late 1990s and early 2000s, several General Accounting Office reports noted that the government had not performed a comprehensive bioterrorism threat assessment. Even after the initiation of greatly increased biodefense expenditures beginning in fiscal year 2002, such a threat assessment was not performed. Homeland Security Presidential Directive 10 states, "The United States requires a continuous, formal process for conducting routine capabilities assessments to guide prioritization of our on-going investments in biodefense-related research, development, planning, and preparedness."[20] A DHS bioterrorism risk assessment model was used to generate the DHS threat assessment in 2006. A critique of the DHS model written by Alan Pearson, director of the Biological and Chemical Weapons Program at the Center for Arms Control and Non-Proliferation, notes:

> The first "Bioterrorism Risk Assessment," prepared by the DHS National Biodefense Analysis and Countermeasures Center (NBACC) using a methodology developed by Battelle Memorial Institute, was completed on January 31, 2006, and a report on the assessment was published on October 1, 2006. The assessment used threat scenarios and consequence modeling to rank 28 biological agents . . . according to their relative risk. For this purpose, the estimated likelihood of agent use in a range of different scenarios ("the probability that an adversary acquires, produces, and disseminates a biological weapon," based on intelligence community input and the judgment of subject matter experts) was multiplied by the projected consequences resulting from each scenario (using data vetted by the Department of Health and Human Services). The risk calculation was weighted towards high-consequence events.[21]

The computer model produced a massive compilation of more than one million different combinations of variables, many of which were run in hundreds of iterations. In September 2008, a review committee established by the U.S. National Academy of Sciences released an extensive critique of the Battelle/DHS assessment model.

The NAS review group noted that the DHS model ranks each pathogen according to its level of risk, based on subjective event probabilities and their consequences. The subjective event probabilities were elicited from dozens of biological weapons experts.[22]

The DHS model claimed that frequency of initiation and "estimated likelihood of agent use" were at least in part "based on intelligence community input." However, it seems likely that there was little or no information of that nature available to the intelligence community, particularly if there were very few or no terrorist groups in the field actively operating BW development programs. The "intelligence input" was to include expression of interest, which are commonly jihadist rhetorical exhortations, and these almost never include reference to particular pathogens. The statement that the model depended on "subjective event probabilities . . . elicited from . . . experts" again suggests a lack of actual intelligence concerning all 27 agents.[23] It follows that the model was a theoretical exercise not based on actual intelligence; it is vulnerability assessment, not threat assessment.

Ostensibly to compensate for the lack of verified intelligence input, the NAS committee urged that the model should evaluate the choices of an "intelligent," or "adaptive," adversary. This would only further compound the abstract quality of the model. The actual record of known terrorist groups indicates that not one has yet mastered the most elementary aspects of microbiology. (Ricin extraction from crushed seed pulp is a chemical process that requires no culturing of organisms.) To suggest that for purposes of "research, development, planning and preparedness" the U.S. government should now assume an "intelligent" and "adaptive" enemy posits capabilities that no terrorist group currently has or is likely to have for years to come. The "intelligent" and "adaptive" adversary was the perpetrator of the Amerithrax events.

Discourse on Bioterrorism in Washington

The history of exaggerating the bioterrorist threat is a long one. It began in 1986 with an attack on the validity of the Biological Weapons Convention by Douglas Feith, then an assistant to Richard Perle in President Ronald Reagan's Defense Department and until August 2005 undersecretary of defense for policy. Feith introduced the idea, now widely adopted, that advances in the microbiological sciences and the global diffusion of the relevant technology heighten the threat of BW use. Though molecular genetics and globalization have advanced drastically since 1986, it does not necessarily follow that the BW threat has grown. As noted, the number of states that maintain offensive BW programs has decreased. And despite the global diffusion of knowledge and technology, the incidence of terrorist networks' creating BWs has remained very low over the entire period.

But alarmism continues. In 2005, Tara O'Toole, then chief executive officer and director of the Center for Biosecurity at the University of Pittsburgh Medical Center, said: "This is not science fiction. The age of Bioterror is now."[24] The office of Vice President Cheney was the driving force behind the Bush administration's emphasis on bioterrorism.[25] Cheney was influenced by the highly unrealistic "Dark Winter" scenario developed by Dr. O'Toole, which one author has noted was "intended to put a real scare into government policy makers and members of Congress."[26] Cheney was apparently greatly alarmed about the potential use of BWs by terrorists and reportedly believed he might soon become a victim.[27]

Homeland Security Presidential Directive 10, "Biodefense for the 21st Century," states, "Biological weapons in the possession of hostile states or terrorists pose unique and grave threats to the safety and security of the United States and our allies." A recent panel established by the National Academy of Sciences went further: "The threat posed by biological agents employed in a terrorist attack on the United States is arguably the most important homeland security challenge of our era."[28] In 2005, then Senator William Frist (R-TN), who coauthored the legislation that initiated these expenditures, said, "The greatest existential threat we have in the world today is biological . . . an inevitable bio-terror attack [would come] at some time in the next 10 years."[29] In 2008, an academic author based a book on "the realization that no other problem facing humanity is so potentially cataclysmic and has been so inadequately addressed."[30] According to many U.S. political figures and experts, the $64 billion is therefore money well spent fighting a dangerous threat.

For two decades, we have been told that bioterrorism would be perpetrated by terrorist groups with an international presence and international political objectives. As noted, however, these groups have little or no scientific competence, little or no knowledge of microbiology, and no known access to pathogen strains or laboratory facilities. The most recent U.S. National Intelligence Council terrorist assessment makes no reference to any such capabilities.[31] The report of the Commission on the Prevention of Weapons of Mass Destruction Proliferation and Terrorism, released in December 2008, stated, "We accept the validity of intelligence estimates about the current rudimentary nature of terrorist capabilities in the area of biological weapons."[32]

Nevertheless, during congressional testimony in July 2008, Jeffrey Runge, an assistant secretary of the Department of Homeland Security, claimed: "The risk of a large-scale biological attack on the nation is significant. We know that our terrorist enemies have sought to use biological agents as instruments of warfare, and we believe that capability is within their reach."[33] Runge said that what keeps him up at night "is a possibility of a large-scale biological attack on our homeland" and that he would describe "the current biological threat environment as illustrated by the effect a biological attack might have in a city like Providence," Rhode Island. But such a scenario of BW use created by modelers does not at all represent "the current biological threat environment." It is instead a classic vulnerability assessment, without any reference to a specific validated threat. Even with a validated threat, one cannot know in advance what the outcome of any particular attempted attack would be. This fact is illustrated by two prominent events: the use of the chemical agent sarin by the Japanese cult Aum Shinrikyo in Tokyo in 1995 and the anthrax dispersion in the United States in 2001. These attacks (for different reasons) resulted in only a small fraction of the casualties that might have occurred.

Joint testimony by a triumvirate of Runge's DHS colleagues echoed the idea that a serious BW threat to the United States exists:

> The Nation continues to face the risk of a major biological event that could cause catastrophic loss of human life, severe economic damages and significant harm to our Nation's critical infrastructures and key resources. . . . The threat of bioterrorism has not subsided, and the impact of a large-scale bioterrorism event, such as the widespread dissemination of an aerosolized form of anthrax or other deadly biological pathogen, would have a serious effect on the health and security of the Nation.[34]

These lines, intermingled with some others containing a fair amount of distorted and misleading information regarding the simplicity of preparation and even weaponization of pathogens, are typical. Pages could be filled with examples of ignorance or disinformation on the subject. Numerous authors beat a tocsin of the bioterrorist threat, though not the U.S. intelligence community, as indicated in testimony in 2006 and 2009 in addition to the WMD Commission quote noted earlier.

Other examples of the general tenor include reports and special commissions emphasizing the supposed threat of bioterrorism that were released during the fall of 2008. In September 2008, the congressionally mandated Commission on the Prevention of Weapons of Mass Destruction Proliferation and Terrorism previewed its report that was designed to "deepen both our assessment of the threat today and what we can do about it."[35] The commission's cochair, former senator Robert Graham (D-FL), stated, "My own assessment at this point is the more likely form of attack is going to be in a biological weapon."[36]

In contrast to this alarmist attitude, a proposed presidential platform statement submitted in August 2008 by the Federation of American Societies for Experimental Biology, an organization composed of 21 biomedical research societies and the largest life sciences group in the United States, did not refer to "bioterrorism" at all.[37]

That same month, the Federal Bureau of Investigation announced that Bruce E. Ivins, a staff scientist at the U.S. Army Medical Research Institute for Infectious Diseases, was responsible for the 2001 anthrax attacks. Ivins had worked at USAMRIID for 27 years, including 20 years of work with anthrax. This disclosure that a longtime insider, not a nonstate terrorist group, was responsible for a deadly BW attack on U.S. soil changed the entire construct of where the primary risks of bioterrorism lay and of what degree of competence a serious perpetrator would have. In 2002, Steven Block of Stanford University commented:

> The fundamental question here is are we victims of our own anthrax, or our own expertise, or is this a further fallout from Al Qaeda? It's a critical question. This is the first biological warfare of the 21st century, and our proper response to it—morally, politically and in every other way—depends on our understanding which it is.[38]

Dr. O'Toole, however, had quickly been convinced on the most tenuous of suppositions that the anthrax attacks had been carried out by al Qaeda. She prepared a memorandum making that argument, which was sent to the FBI and to CIA Director George Tenet and was "circulated among top government officials."[39]

In October 2009, the blue-ribbon Graham-Talent Commission produced a "Progress Report," a clear effort to further boost government spending. The report's executive summary stated:

> In recent years, the United States has received strategic warnings of biological weapons use from dozens of government reports and expert panels. The consequences of ignoring these warnings could be dire. For example, one recent study from the intelligence community projected that a one- to two-kilogram release of anthrax spores from a crop duster plane could kill more Americans than died in World War II. [40]

As already noted, the "strategic warnings" are the highly exaggerated generic claims. As for the scenario suggested, no matter who conceived it, the outcome claimed is inconceivable. Over 450,000 Americans died in World War II. Modeling scenarios depends on a wide variety of variables: strain selection, culturing and growth conditions, harvesting and preservation, and another set of environmental variables on release. Mortality might vary from zero to some calculated number. One to two kilograms (2.2 to 4.4 pounds) of anthrax spores would more likely produce mortality in the hundreds in an open-air release, not over 450,000.[41] Moreover, no known terrorist group has the ability to produce a dry-powder preparation of anthrax, making the entire scenario implausible.

In a recent book written by former national security advisers Brent Scowcroft and Zbigniew Brzezinski, Scowcroft refers to the propagation of an "environment of fear" in the United States, which Brzezinski adds has made us "more susceptible to demagogy" that "distorts your sense of reality" and "channels your resources into areas which perhaps are not of first importance." Brzezinski continues:

> We have succumbed to a fearful paranoia that the outside world is conspiring through its massive terrorist forces to destroy us. Is that a real picture of the world, or is it a classic

paranoia that's become rampant and has been officially abetted? If I fault our high officials for anything, it is for the deliberate propagation of fear.[42]

Warnings regarding the bioterrorist threat are one of the major components in producing that "environment of fear." A few very determined and very vocal nongovernment purveyors of the bioterrorism threat, backed by one or two private foundations, have significantly contributed to producing that atmosphere. The Sloan Foundation funded at least 14 conferences in the United States and overseas, four of which were held by Interpol and three by the Department of Homeland Security.[43] Building on the fear emerging from the 9/11 and the Amerithrax attacks, this movement helped generate the $64 billion to date in federal expenditure, a large federal bureaucracy, strong congressional advocates, multiple research institutes and journals, and a thriving contractor industry—the same "stakeholders" who now call for the continuation of efforts to fight and prevent bioterrorism.

Bruce Hoffman, a terrorism expert, explained the situation after 2001 in a scathing comment:

> [Bioterrorism] was where the funding was, and people were sticking their hands in the pot. It was the sexiest of all the terrorism threats and it was becoming a cash cow. So the threat of bioterrorism became a kind of self-fulfilling prophecy. It was archetypical Washington politics in the sense that you generate an issue and it takes on a life of its own.[44]

This depiction is valid. What is needed, however, is more substantive detail regarding "the politics of bioterrorism," for example, the instrumental role of Vice President Dick Cheney noted earlier.

In October 2008, David Koplow, professor of law at Georgetown University Law Center and a former deputy legal counsel in the Department of Defense, wrote:

> Bioterrorism is a serious, important danger, one that deserves serious, focused attention. But empowering a bioterrorism-industrial complex, and fostering a needless climate of fear, paranoia, and helplessness cannot lead to fashioning reliable, long-term solutions. Rational policy requires a genuine, level-headed risk assessment, and a sustained, balanced approach, not a knee-jerk public relations drama.[45]

Reduction of U.S. Security by Increasing BW Proliferation Potential

The hyping of the bioterrorism threat has been accompanied by various policies that actually heighten the odds that the United States will experience another biological weapons attack. Ironically, most of these policies are part of U.S. biodefense efforts. The subject will be dealt with only cursorily here. It can be seen as a composite of several elements, some of which are extensively described in other publications and others of which are touched on in other sections of this chapter. Seven examples are provided here.

As indicated earlier, the role of exaggerated threat pronouncements can *stimulate* interest in BWs among nonstate actors. If for 10 to 15 years terrorist groups are told that a biological weapon is fantastically powerful, easy to acquire and produce, and will kill millions of people, they are going to become curious about it, even if they are ignorant about microbiology. And once it has been trumpeted worldwide for years, the false message is difficult to withdraw.

Disinformation and misinformation about the biological weapons threat encourage disastrous and costly policy decisions.[46] The leading example, of course, is the spurious "determination" that Iraq had produced mobile vehicles to make BW agents. This charge, presented to the entire world, was used as one of the major public justifications by the Bush administration for invading Iraq in 2003.[47] The concocted "Dark Winter" scenario did much to influence Vice President Cheney and the subsequent drive by the Bush administration for a national smallpox vaccination program.[48]

Another problem is the way government officials communicate about the aftermath of a BW attack or any attack. If officials constantly tell the public that the greatest damage following the use of a BW agent will be *panic* (contradicting to a large degree the claim of mass-casualty effects), there *will* be panic if and when such an event occurs. This message too is difficult to withdraw after officials and experts have mistakenly propagated it for decades. If instead officials drop inflated predictions and the public is told that the government is doing the best it can to prepare protections and defenses, that the nation will survive and recover, and that there is *no* need for panic, panic can be avoided. That is the lesson from every civil defense experience worldwide to date, in wartime and in peacetime.

The massive increase in the number of scientists and laboratories working with select agents—those pathogens of interest to biodefense programs—heightens the risk of a deadly accident. Before 2001, there were perhaps several hundred scientists working on what are now select agents, in approximately several dozen laboratories at most. As of August 2008, there were 399 institutions and 14,797 scientists authorized to work with select agents.[49] As of October 2007, there were no fewer than 4,000–5,000 BSL-3-level laboratories in the United States, of which 1,356 were authorized to work with select agents.[50] As is universally the case for both infrastructure and humans, accidents occur more or less in direct proportion to the number of individuals involved and the number of transactions or events that take place. The more dangerous laboratories there are, the greater will be the incidence of accidents. Together with the release of a Government Accountability Office report in September 2009, a GAO official testified to Congress that the "increase in the number of researchers working with hazardous pathogens would 'inevitably' lead to an amplified risk of bioterrorist attack perpetrated by a scientist working at a biocontainment facility."[51]

The dramatic increase in the size and the nature of biodefense experimentation will likely stimulate biodefense programs in other states. That increase elsewhere is already manifest. In 1993, there were reportedly 13 national biodefense programs. In 2007, that number had doubled to 25 national programs.[52] There is no way to predict how these programs will develop in the coming decades.

The publication of biodefense-related research may prove useful to those developing bioweapons. To see what information might be used for "biological weapons development utility," presumably by unauthorized entities, the Department of Defense commissioned a study in 2003 to investigate journals such as *Scientific American*, *Science*, and *Molecular Microbiology*.[53] Five years later, a team from the Centers for Disease Control and the U.S. Army's Dugway Proving Ground published a peer-reviewed paper describing the methodology for production and aerosol dispersion of weaponized, dry-powder *B. anthracis*.[54] This information was almost certainly not previously publicly available, and its publication makes a mockery of the oft-repeated claim that "recipes" for BWs are readily available on jihadi websites, where the information is practically useless. More importantly, the research and publication also violate the spirit and possibly the words of Article I of the Biological Weapons Convention. Had such a document been unearthed in Iraq before 2002, it probably would have been considered proof of an offensive Iraqi BW program.

Another danger is the export of "dual-purpose" equipment used in the production of biological agents. Between 1999 and 2003, the U.S. Department of Defense was responsible for the massive export to purchasers in Gulf States of such equipment.[55] It is extremely likely that the great majority of this equipment was resold to Iran at the same time that the U.S. government was for years attempting to curtail shipments of such equipment to Iran.

Diversion of Resources from Other U.S. Public Health Needs

A faulty threat assessment will lead to faulty national priorities and misallocated resources by successive administrations and Congress. If avoiding deaths in the order of medical magnitude were the criterion used to guide the national allocation of resources, they would go overwhelmingly toward fighting smoking, obesity, antibiotic-resistant infections, and the other leading sources of mortality

Figure 9.1
CDC FUNDING FOR CHRONIC DISEASE AND BIOTERRORISM
(FY 2000–2008)*

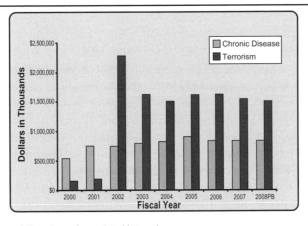

* Terrorism refers *only* to bioterrorism.

enumerated in the opening paragraph of this chapter rather than toward preparing to counter the "select agents" of interest to biodefense.[56]

Even as the United States appropriated $64 billion to defend against select agents since 2001, U.S. life expectancy stood at 42nd in the world, and child mortality ranked 29th—despite the fact that the United States spends more on health care per person than any other country.[57]

However, if we look at the Centers for Disease Control's budget over the past eight years, we see something strikingly different: essentially flat funding for chronic disease and a large increase in spending on select agents and bioterrorism (see Figure 9.1).[58] Certainly, an expenditure of $57 billion has served to increase U.S. preparedness against the use of biological agents, but a very large portion of that sum does not serve dual-purpose utilities, that is, benefiting general U.S. public health needs as well.[59] The distribution of grants from the *National Institute of Allergy and Infectious Diseases* follows a similar pattern. Far more grants went to research on *B. anthracis* than to research dealing with organisms that kill thousands of people annually.[60] In addition, the National Institutes of Health has on average distributed only around $220 million per year since FY07 for research on antibiotic resistance, with a substantial portion of that going to antibiotic resistance in select agents, and therefore oriented primarily toward biodefense rather than general public health.[61]

Misdirection of Public Health Efforts in Low-Income Countries

The problem of misdirecting public health efforts in low-income countries, which is clearly akin to the diversion of public health resources in the United States, is a recent one. It is the consequence of proselytizing efforts by U.S. officials and private analysts active in propagating the conception of a bioterrorism threat. Early in the post-2001 U.S. biodefense buildup, U.S. government representatives tried to convince their European counterparts, particularly in member states of the North Atlantic Treaty Organization, to follow suit. The government officials in those countries who composed the audience for the U.S. urgings most often did not share the alarmed U.S. view of the imminence of a bioterrorist attack. The same held for the scientific cohort in those countries. Nevertheless, with time, U.S. efforts have had some success.

In addition, a series of international conferences sponsored by Interpol and funded by the Sloan Foundation in different geographic regions sought to convince law enforcement agencies that they should turn increased attention and resources toward measures and programs related to bioterrorism. That was followed by a conference for senior-level public health authorities in African countries also funded by the Sloan Foundation. The conference urged the relevant officials in those countries to provide more resources and consideration to issues that relate to bioterrorism, in fact, to make the subject one of their primary concerns.[62] Of greater importance was a March 2009 report produced by the U.S. National Academy of Sciences, which again urged public health officials in these countries to take up the problem of bioterrorism.[63] Experts from the U.S. Centers for Disease Control testifying to the NAS study group offered the following recommendations:

- Ensure the program is consistent with local priorities.
- Avoid taking personnel from other important local programs.
- Ensure local buy-in of activity.
- Ensure program compatibility and integration with existing local activities, structures, methods and equipment.[64]

Though the NAS report ultimately repeated the last admonition, it would be impossible to induce the recommendations basic to the report without subverting public health programs in the selected developing nations based on their own needs, that is, the pattern of disease incidence in those countries that causes major mortality.

Nearly all these countries have drastically underfunded their public health sectors and have been faced with enormous disease burdens for decades. The number of trained public health professionals in these countries is always a small fraction of those needed to deal with existing public health problems, which in many of these countries, due to HIV infection, is nothing short of catastrophic. As a single example, at a minimum, between 700,000 and 2.7 million people die yearly of malaria. Over 75 percent of them are African children.[65]

Global priorities are clear. Global mortalities per year are poverty, 7.3 million; HIV/tuberculosis/malaria, 6 million; diarrheal disease,

3.5 million; smoking, 5 million; measles, 0.5–1 million; warfare, 1 million: a total of approximately 24 million people, year in-year out.[66] Bioterrorism mortality is zero. A World Health Organization report noted, "Disproportionate investment in a limited number of disease programmes considered as global priorities in countries that are dependent on external support has diverted the limited energies of ministries of health away from their primary role."[67] Attempting to convince ministries of health in African countries to make bioterrorism a primary concern can only divert them further from their primary role.[68]

Regulation of a Dramatically Increased National Biodefense Program

A few weeks after the events of September 11, 2001, a professionally prepared dry-powder anthrax preparation was distributed through the U.S. postal system. Two envelopes that were sent to the U.S. Senate offices of Patrick Leahy and Tom Daschle were of particular importance due to the technical quality of the preparation. The response of the Congress and the administration was twofold. One was the massive increase in funding for biodefense, which comprised enhancing preparedness; purchase of drugs, vaccines, and detectors; and research, including the construction of a sizable number of new dedicated research facilities.[69] The other was the passage of the Public Health Security and Bioterrorism Preparedness and Response Act of 2002, the so-called select agent legislation. Under its provisions, the CDC and the Department of Agriculture specified a list of "select agents" of particular biodefense concern, and new requirements were established concerning the facilities and scientists that worked with such agents. Research institutions that possessed any of the select agents were required to register with the CDC, the exchange and transfer of samples of the agents between scientists had to be approved by the CDC, a requirement for security and inventory management was established, and some personal reliability oversight was established for those working with the agents.

The regulations were needed. In his catalog of illicit uses of biological agents in the 20th century, Seth Carus found that laboratories and culture collections were the preferred source of pathogens and toxins for terrorists and criminals and that thefts were primarily conducted by insiders. There is no evidence that any terrorist or criminal group has ever successfully acquired a pathogenic microorganism from nature.[70] In addition, laboratory accidents inevitably happen. In the past few years, several have occurred in the most specialized and supposedly highly controlled facilities in Boston and Texas, built with post-2002 funding.

Other dangers arise via routine operations, neither accidents nor intended malice, that turn up problems of an unforeseen nature. For example, an effort to catalog select agent culture collections in Department of Defense facilities in 2008 led to unanticipated and astonishing problems. After months of investigation, USAMRIID reported in June 2009 that no fewer than 9,202 uncataloged microbial culture vials had been found in 335 freezers and refrigerators at the laboratory.[71] Since the official database had listed 66,000 items, the "missing" increment represented about 13 percent of the total. There were two lessons from this incident. First, a CDC investigation of USAMRIID in September 2008 did not discover the problem of unlisted samples. Second, neither USAMRIID nor other U.S. Army biodefense laboratories had previously made complete inventories despite legislation in force since 2002 requiring them to do so.[72] A U.S. Government Accountability Office report released in August 2009 indicated that several major high-containment facilities had been slow to upgrade their facilities in the preceding 12 months.[73]

Another danger requiring regulation is the production and dissemination of knowledge by the U.S. biodefense program that could benefit both potential BW proliferators and nonstate actors. A report prepared by a committee of the U.S. National Academy of Sciences in 2004 identified seven classes of experiments, which illustrated the types of research that should require review and discussion by informed members of the scientific and medical community before they are undertaken or, if carried out, before they are published in full detail.[74] As a result of a recommendation in that report, a year later the president established the National Science Advisory Board for Biosecurity, with the mandate "to provide advice, guidance and leadership regarding biosecurity oversight of dual-use research." In 2007, after two years of deliberations, the NSABB arrived at an ineffective recommendation that the oversight task be assigned to individual institutional biosafety committees (IBCs) at laboratories in universities, government contractor facilities, and other facilities

179

across the country. The IBCs were established in the late 1970s because of concerns about molecular genetic (recombinant DNA) research. Their assigned function was to review proposed research projects in their own institutions. A report published in 2004 had demonstrated that the IBCs were, in most locations, nonfunctional in carrying out their existing, far simpler task.[75] In many institutions, the IBCs did not even exist, and where they did exist on paper, they did not follow supposedly mandatory guidelines for all institutions receiving federal funding. It was inconceivable that they could also perform the role that the NAS report suggested.

The greatest danger is deliberate misuse of research facilities to do harm. On August 1, 2008, the FBI identified a highly qualified researcher who had worked at USAMRIID for three decades as the individual whom they considered responsible for preparing and distributing the anthrax preparation used in the Amerithrax events. In response, various authorities began to recommend additional biosecurity measures. For example, a two-person workplace rule and other measures were recommended to increase security in U.S. laboratories working with select agents. The congressionally mandated report, *World at Risk: The Report of the Commission on the Prevention of WMD Proliferation and Terrorism*, released in December 2008, recommended a review of domestic pathogen security and increased government oversight of high-containment laboratories. Nothing in those suggestions would seem to be particularly striking. As another author has noted:

> In the United States, airplane and river barge pilots, physicians, nurses, clinical laboratory technicians and even cosmetologists must receive specialized education and training and pass federal or state licensing examinations in order to practice their respective professions. Licensure ... allows the government to keep records of who these professionals are and where they practice.[76]

Suggestions of possible new restrictions beyond those already legislated in 2002 produced a dramatic response. The first published expression was authored, ironically, by five members of the NSABB. They warned in an editorial that

> the damage to the future of America will be infinitely greater if one incident, no matter its extent, devastates our scientific endeavors because of precipitous regulatory responses so

onerous as to cripple research in this country to our detriment and to the advantage of other countries. Our nation's strength has been in its willingness to accept risk as a necessary component of scientific development in diverse areas from vaccines and other therapeutic measures to space exploration. It is imperative that our political leadership remembers this also and acts in a commensurate manner.[77]

These claims appear dubious at best. First, added regulation would apply to a minute fraction of researchers in molecular biology, not to biological and medical sciences as a whole. Second, classification and segregation of important portions of nuclear physics after 1945 certainly did little to impede the mass of Nobel Prizes in Physics earned by U.S. physicists since then. Increased oversight and/or regulation would be unlikely to have any negative effect on U.S. science, health, or economic competitiveness.

Other "stakeholders" quickly lined up to oppose further regulation. At a meeting organized by the American Association for the Advancement of Science, Dr. Gronvall of the UPMC Center for Biosecurity claimed that the post-2001 regulations "hindered public health," and that "she and her colleagues would like to see a more nuanced approach to countering the bioterrorism threat that includes increased security through robust research."[78] The NSABB released a report titled *Enhancing Personnel Reliability among Individuals with Access to Select Agents*, which opposed any increase in personnel reliability programs, urged a reduction in the list of select agents, and suggested that working scientists observe their coworkers and report infractions of regulations.[79] A joint letter from the Federation of American Societies for Experimental Biology and the Association of American Medical Colleges endorsed the views of the earlier NSABB report and requested a regulatory system that allowed "the flexibility of developing site-specific performance based standards."[80] Finally, administrators at the AAAS prefigured their own report due in July 2009 by an editorial in *Science* that repeated the NSABB warning of "unintended negative consequences, including over-restricted access to vital resources and a constrained ability to collaborate internationally on a broad range of topics."[81] One of the authors of the *Science* editorial argued that "we are basically cutting ourselves out of the game for global health as well as the global research enterprise, and that's not good."[82] The comment was based on the fact that several swine flu samples were sent from Mexico to a laboratory in Canada instead of to the CDC in the United States—hardly evidence of a collapse of the U.S. role in "global health as well as the global research enterprise."

Members of the NSABB have explained that the group feared a "chill" to the biodefense research community. History suggests that these reactions are unfounded. In 1988, a Senate committee held extensive hearings on the Biological Defense Research Program existing at that time, including safety management in the U.S. Army's biodefense research facilities. In response, the Army wrote new safety regulations that formalized compliance with directives and standards of a dozen U.S. regulatory agencies. USAMRIID, its scientists, and its research are not known to have suffered in any way from those regulations 20 years ago.[83] It is important to recall that the current regulations and all the debate surrounding them concern *only* scientists working with select agents in high-containment facilities. Those opposing any further federal regulation and hoping for reversal of some of the existing regulations have been well organized, and they are virtually the only voice heard in the public arena. Nevertheless, a study by Victoria Sutton published in 2009 indicated that 93 percent of responding scientists who were funded to do biodefense agreed that work on select agents should be regulated.[84]

On November 4, 2009, the Senate Homeland Security and Governmental Affairs Committee approved a bill "intended to improve security at the nation's biological research facilities."[85] It was sent to the Senate floor after months of preparation. One of its provisions was that the secretaries of health and human services and agriculture should "stratify" the select agent list. That meant, in effect, *reduce* the number of agents being held under more rigid guidelines.

A Final Word

The White House should institute oversight of all relevant biodefense research and development programs carried out by all departments, agencies, and subagencies to ensure that they comply with U.S. obligations under Article I of the Biological Weapons Convention, which prohibits the development (as well as production, stockpiling, acquisition, and retention) of biological weapons. Preferably, such oversight of all biodefense research carried out by federal agencies or private contractors should be reviewed at the level of the

National Security Council. All oversight should include classified research.[86]

Policymakers should also end the fearmongering and huckstering of the bioterrorism threat, which has been divorced from reality for years.[87] Unfortunately, such overheated rhetoric appears to be spreading to several other countries, notably India and Russia. Gross exaggeration, propaganda, and alarmism about BWs are counterproductive, inducing interest by nonstate actors in precisely the kinds of activities that the United States would like to prevent and generating a dangerous set of overreactions at home.

10. Managing Fear: The Politics of Homeland Security

Benjamin H. Friedman

Americans want more homeland security than they need. That is the politics of homeland security in a nutshell. It results from two things. First, cognitive biases cause people to worry more about terrorists than they should and to demand more protection from them than cost-benefit analysis recommends. Second, U.S. citizens' information about terrorism comes largely from politicians and government organizations with an interest in reinforcing excessive fears.

These tendencies create political demand for ill-conceived counterterrorism policies. Few policymakers will buck that demand and fight overreaction to terrorism. But for those willing to look, the history of health and safety regulation and defense policy reveals strategies to limit overreaction. Policymakers can improve communication strategies by promoting a stiff-upper-lip attitude toward terrorism that emphasizes strength, not vulnerability. They can use cost-benefit analysis to justify decisions that limit the provision of defenses. They can design resource-allocating institutions to compare different kinds of risks and remedies against them—making the cost of homeland security measures more transparent. A more cynical approach is to embrace security theater, answering demands for counterterrorism with policies that serve other purposes while holding down spending. All these strategies are used today, but not enough.

This chapter explains why Americans demand too much homeland security and offers ways to manage the problem. That focus requires limiting discussion of the idea that the terrorism is less of a threat one generally hears.[1] Still the reader should take away the point that fear of terrorism is a bigger problem than terrorism. Terrorism, after all, takes its name not from violence but from the emotion it provokes. But homeland security policy considers mostly the former. That is a shame, especially because the defenses we mount against terrorists often heighten our fears of them.

Here, the term "overreaction" refers to policies that fail cost-benefit analysis and thus do more harm than good or to advocacy of those policies. This is not to say that all goods and harms easily reduce to economic value. But when we consider the wisdom of policies, including their contribution to values like our sense of right, we have a kind of cost-benefit ledger in our minds. We are prepared to call some actions excessive to their purpose and therefore overreactions. Certainly, this judgment is subjective, and some readers will question mine.

Homeland security means domestic efforts to stop terrorism or mitigate its consequences. In that sense, the name of the Department of Homeland Security misleads. Much of what DHS does is not homeland security, and much of its budget does not count as homeland security spending, according to the Office of Management of Budget.[2] I use the "odiously Teutono/Soviet" phrase "homeland security" with regret, only because it is so common.[3] Only a nation that defines its security excessively needs to modify the word "security" to describe defense of its territory. In most nations, "security" or "defense" would suffice.

Vulnerability, Risk, and Fear

Vulnerability to terrorism is inevitable. We can focus our defenses on high-value targets like crowded football stadiums, jumbo jets, nuclear power plants, the White House, and the Capitol, but there remain countless malls, festivals, and trains to bomb. We can make it harder for malfeasants to enter the United States, costing ourselves via lost travel, immigration, and business. But border control can only be an aspiration in a country that has 12,883 miles of coast, legally admits 177 million foreigners each year, and shares 5,500 miles of border with its top trading partner.[4] If invulnerability is the goal, there is no limit on homeland security spending.

Vulnerability is not risk, however. Vulnerability considers the possibility of harm, risk its probability. The United States has several attributes that reduce the risk of terrorism at home. First, democratic ideology and mature liberal institutions undermine motivation for U.S. residents to embrace political violence, including terrorism. Oppressive societies have no monopoly on terrorist creation, but they produce more than their share.[5] Because terrorism tends to be local, this is good news for Americans. Long before anyone used the phrase "homegrown terrorism," the United States had an effective policy to prevent it, which is to be itself: a liberal, prosperous society. That policy, along with immigration patterns, helps explain why there is not a large militant Islamic population in the United States, as there is in Spain or England, nor much evidence of terrorist cells.[6] Despite extensive hunting, just a handful of true terrorists have been arrested in the United States in recent years.[7]

Second, our economy and government limit the consequences of terrorist attacks. Homeland security experts often claim that U.S. society is brittle, that even a cyberattack could cripple our economy.[8] They say we need to transform ourselves into a resilient society that can withstand attacks and disasters. This view overlooks our existing resilience. Health care facilities, emergency response organizations, and capital to rebuild limit terrorism's potential damage here. Poor, misgoverned societies are the brittle ones. In the United States, most storms and attacks are nuisances that do little lasting harm. Even catastrophic events, like Hurricane Katrina or the 9/11 attacks, barely affect the national economy (the reaction to 9/11 is another matter).[9]

The argument that we are brittle is similar to strategic airpower theory, which claims that the destruction of critical economic nodes can halt a nation's industrial output and force its surrender. History shows that the theory severely underestimates the amount of violence needed to cripple most states. Modern societies have repeatedly maintained economic output and their will to fight under attacks far more destructive than what today's terrorists can muster.[10]

Economic trends heighten our safety. The transition to a more service-based economy means relying less on physical infrastructure and more on information, which is hard to destroy, as it exists in dispersed networks and brains. Lowered communication and transportation costs, meanwhile, leave us less dependent on any particular supplier or region, making recovery from supply disruptions easier. Think of it this way: the closure of a supermarket in a town with only one is more disruptive than the closure of one in a city with many.

These characteristics of the United States limit the risk that terrorism poses here. The nature of our enemy limits it further. Many

187

analysts depict the 9/11 attacks as evidence that we are in a new era of megaterrorism perpetrated by highly professional organizations employing unconventional weapons.[11] Conventional wisdom says that two trends made history useless in studying modern terrorism. First, the spread of jihadist ideology replaced the more limited aims and violence of past terrorism with apocalyptic goals and unlimited carnage.[12] Second, the proliferation of destructive technology democratized killing power.

Eight years and counting later, with plenty of conventional terrorism abroad and almost none in the United States, evidence is mounting that these trends are overstated or wrong—that 9/11 was more aberration than a harbinger of an age of deadlier terrorism.[13] Terrorism using biological or nuclear weapons should still worry us, but the common claim that these sorts of attacks are virtually inevitable is overstatement.

Al Qaeda was never a global conspiratorial organization strategically dispatching well-trained operatives. Even in its late 1990s heyday, al Qaeda was instead a small vicious group, based in Afghanistan, vying for control of a larger and far-flung collection of jihadist groups and cliques of varying competence and aims (jihadists themselves are a tiny minority of the Islamist movement).[14] The U.S. invasion of Afghanistan degraded al Qaeda's already limited cohesion and its managerial ability. Today, al Qaeda consists mostly of "groups of guys," as Marc Sageman puts it, united mainly by common ideology, not organization.[15] Even al Qaeda's "core" group in Pakistan no longer looks like a coherent organization.

The claim that jihadism is spreading appears to be wrong, probably backward; the outgrowth of looking only at recent history. Today, jihadism's popularity seems to be waning.[16] This is not surprising given that the ideology considers the vast majority of people on the planet, including most Muslims, enemies deserving murder. If this decline is real, it comes in spite of the United States' decision to declare a global war on terrorism and fight indefinitely in two Muslim countries, steps that strengthened the jidahist claim that the West is attacking Islam. What's more, most jihadists do not attack the United States. Even in the 1990s, few of these groups embraced al Qaeda's goal of attacking us, "the far enemy." Now that number seems to be shrinking.[17]

The democratization of killing power has more validity. Weapons technology has certainly improved with time, and it does proliferate.

Yet the proliferation has not occurred as fast or as thoroughly as feared. Predictions that nuclear weapons technology would quickly spread to dozens of states—made regularly since the dawn of the nuclear age—have proved false.[18] The number of states maintaining or developing biological weapons has declined in recent years, contrary to many predictions.[19] The failure of these forecasts probably stems from technological determinism—a focus on technical feasibility rather than the political ends that arms serve.

The same error confounds predictions about the proliferation of unconventional weapons to terrorists. Most groups are uninterested, probably because conventional attacks reliably produce the results they seek and because they remain rooted in local political struggles. This parochialism makes them more like past terrorists, who sought few dead and many watching, than the apocalyptic warriors we are told to expect. This is true even of some jihadist groups, which generally have not attempted to develop these weapons, whatever their rhetoric.

Of course, al Qaeda did attempt to develop biological weapons in Afghanistan before the U.S. invasion, and there are credible stories that it considered developing nuclear weapons and even sought fissile materials.[20] But these attempts failed. They help demonstrate why al Qaeda is unlikely to succeed in mass destruction.

Mass violence has historically been the product of bureaucratic, hierarchical organizations that belong to states or insurgencies that approximate them. Bureaucratic organizations reliably store and dispense knowledge. They divide labor to allow efficiency and coordinated activity. States provide them with plentiful capital, manpower, and technical expertise. Historically, only armies had the manpower to carry out mass violence with small arms. More advanced weapons that allow a few people to kill many, such as artillery, strike aircraft, and especially nuclear weapons, required industrial capability that states controlled.

Because they are generally clandestine, terrorist groups usually lack these attributes. Policing or military attacks prevent clandestine networks from gathering. That makes it difficult to gain and transfer deadly knowledge, amass wealth, and build the physical plants needed to make sophisticated weapons. Failure characterizes the short history of nonstate organizations' building unconventional weapons for mass-casualty attacks.[21]

The claim that the Internet can replace training camps is at best partially true.[22] Social factors—probably the volume and speed of interactions that happen in person—make on-site training more effective than the remote kind. Most organizations that effectively coordinate activity, whether it is the Marines or the New England Patriots, still avoid virtual training.

Terrorist groups that are most like states and relatively unmolested, like Hezbollah, are most capable of producing more sophisticated weapons. But because they are like states and attached to territory and local political ends, they are subject to deterrence. They are therefore less likely to want or use such weapons. In any case, no such group now targets the United States.

The near future of terrorism in the United States should then resemble the recent past. There will be a few conventional attacks, mostly abroad, that will kill a handful of Americans in an average year. Mohammed Atta has no better claim to the future of terrorism than Ayman Farris, who hoped to down the Brooklyn Bridge with a blowtorch, or various other terrorist incompetents arrested in the United States in recent years.[23] In its ability to do harm, al Qaeda is more like the anarchist movement in its heyday, transnational troublemakers, than the Nazis. In most of the United States, the danger of terrorism is statistically nonexistent, or near it. The right amount of homeland security spending in those areas is none.

The American public does not share this view. A July 2007 Gallup poll found that 47 percent were very or somewhat worried that they or someone in their family would become a physical victim of terrorism.[24] Although lower than the almost 60 percent of Americans who felt this way in late 2001, the total was similar to the numbers in 2002 and the average finding since. That poll also found that 47 percent of Americans thought a terrorist attack was very or somewhat likely in the United States in the next several weeks.[25] The number of Americans answering this way had declined significantly since late 2001, when almost three-fourths of those polled felt this way, but had held roughly steady since 2002.

These polls demonstrate several things. First, Americans are overly afraid of terrorists. Even in 2000, when 24 percent were very or somewhat worried that terrorism would harm them or their family, Americans overestimated the low probability of harm. Second, 9/11 seems to have caused a spike in fear that eased after a few months but stayed higher than reality merited. Third, most Americans do not use the evidence of terrorist weakness, the years without serious attack, to update their beliefs.

Inflated fear creates a permissive environment for overreaction to terrorism. Security politics becomes a seller's market where the public will overpay for counterterrorism policies. The most important effect of this fear has been heightened U.S. militarism: the indefinite extension of the war in Afghanistan, the war in Iraq, and the near doubling of the U.S. defense budget (excluding war spending), in real terms. Beyond their stated rationale, the latter two have little relevance to counterterrorism.

More relevant here is the country's mounting homeland security bill. While it remains tiny compared to defense spending—roughly one-tenth—government-wide homeland security spending has grown fast, from about $12 billion in fiscal year 2000 to around $66 billion for FY09.[26] DHS's budget grew from $31 billion in FY03 to $55 billion in FY10. Adjusting for inflation, that is over 45 percent growth.[27] Most of the spending goes to the operational cost of its agencies—the biggest are Borders and Customs, the Coast Guard, the Federal Emergency Management Agency, the Secret Service, the Transportation Security Administration, and Immigration and Customs Enforcement. These agencies, hurriedly pulled together into DHS in 2002, are not primarily concerned with counterterrorism.[28] The Border Patrol prevents illegal immigration; the Secret Service guards the president; the Coast Guard rescues ships; FEMA cleans up after storms; and so on. Their contribution to counterterrorism is secondary. Still, they have all won massive funding boosts since 9/11. The agency that probably contributes most to domestic security is the Federal Bureau of Investigation, in the Department of Justice.

In addition, homeland security regulations hinder commerce. One OMB estimate says that major (meaning more than $100 million in annual cost) homeland security regulations cost the U.S. economy $3.4 billion to $6.9 billion every year.[29] Additional homeland security costs are state and local security spending and some private security purchases.

Are these costs worth it? The uncertainty of the benefit provided by homeland security policies makes it hard to say. Attacks are so rare and affected by so many factors that it is impossible to determine what lives particular security efforts save. Still, historical fatality statistics give rough estimates.

The average number of Americans killed annually by terrorists between 1971 and 2001 was 104. The total would be far lower, just a handful, if 9/11 were not included. Using this figure and several other scenarios that estimate possible lives saved by homeland security spending, Mark Stewart and John Mueller analyze the cost-effectiveness of the post-9/11 increase in homeland security spending (what is spent annually above what was being spent annually before the attacks, plus inflation). They find that with the added spending, the United States spends between $63 million and $630 million per life saved.[30] That is exponentially more than what experts consider to be cost-effective, using market measures of the value of a statistical life.[31] Most health and safety regulations cost far less per life saved, usually a few million.[32]

It seems that overall homeland security spending is not worthwhile, although particular programs might be. The point here is not to engage in extended cost-benefit analysis of homeland security spending but to suggest that homeland security policymakers should. To date, little of this analysis occurs in government, as discussed below.

There is not room here to respond to the many objections to this approach to homeland security and to the broader idea that we are overreacting to terrorism. I respond only to the two objections that have the most merit. One claim is that government should spend heavily to avoid the small risk of terrorism because our inevitable overreaction to the attacks we would otherwise fail to prevent will cost far more.[33] In other words, if an expensive overreaction is bound to occur, it is a cost of terrorism, which might justify the seemingly excessive up-front cost of defense. A problem with this argument is that overreaction might happen only following rare, shocking occasions like 9/11. Future attacks might be accepted without strong demand for more expensive defenses. Another problem is that the defenses might not significantly contribute to preventing attacks and overreaction. The argument's main failure is its implicit claim that all overreaction is alike. Not all countries react to terrorism the same way. Overreaction can be better or worse.

A more interesting claim is that the utilitarian premises of cost-benefit analysis are inappropriate because terrorism is not just a source of mortality or economic harm, like carcinogens or storms, but political coercion that offends our values. Defenses against human, political dangers provide deterrence and a sense of good. Those benefits may be impossible to quantify.[34] Another way to put it is that both terrorism and counterterrorism are concerned with something more than safety. They deal with fear and the political effects of attacks. What seems excessive from a cost-benefit standpoint is appropriate given these considerations.

This argument is right except for the last sentence. That is, as a justification for our counterterrorism policies, this argument proves too much. Its logic serves any policy said to combat terrorism, no matter how expansive and misguided. Cost-benefit analysis is just one tool for considering policy's worth, but it is a necessary one. Because resources are always constrained, we always need to assess how useful policies are in producing safety. It appears that homeland security policies are inefficient in that sense. Were it the case that these policies greatly reduced public fear and blunted terrorists' political strategy, they would nonetheless be worthwhile. But something closer to the opposite appears to be true. Al Qaeda wants overreaction—bin Laden brags of bankrupting the United States— and the policies seem as likely to cause alarm as to prevent it.[35]

The Origins of Overreaction

This chapter offers two kinds of explanations for exaggerated fear. The first concerns psychological biases that cause people to overestimate terrorism's danger.[36] The second explanation is the biased information that Americans get about terrorism—a result of the incentives that pressure those who provide this information and its socialization.[37]

Cognitive Errors

In economic terms, the public lacks incentive to acquire accurate risk information.[38] The world is complex. Time is short. No one can be an expert in everything. So people make risk assessments via heuristics, mental shortcuts based on impressions, and received wisdom.

These heuristics reliably cause errors in assessing danger. For example, we tend to ignore the high probability of small gains or losses and focus on big payoffs or disaster despite their remote odds.[39] In other words, people rarely think in terms of expected utility, which is why lotteries thrive. People also generally value losses more than equal gains.[40] This effect, loss aversion, creates status quo bias, a tendency to protect what we have rather than seek what we can gain. A related idea is that people value the elimination of a risk more than its reduction by an equal amount.[41] Thus, people will pay more to reduce a risk from 10 percent likelihood to zero likelihood than from 20 percent to 10 percent, even though they get the same increment of safety.

These tendencies help explain why both leaders and the public invest heavily against disasters like terrorist attacks even where their likelihood is remote. Hoping to eliminate an already small risk, they pay opportunity costs far bigger than the added increment of safety merits. In that sense, the voting public cannot get enough of a good thing.[42]

Cognitive psychology tells us that people rely too heavily on initial impressions of risk and discount later information, an effect called anchoring.[43] Sticking to initial assessments allows us to avoid the mental effort of recalculation. We prematurely assume that a few pieces of data represent a trend and avoid reevaluating, fitting new data to a theory rather than vice versa.[44] Even experts overinterpret a small number of findings.[45]

The assessment of terrorism after an event like 9/11, powerful enough to sweep away previously anchored ideas about the threat, may cause us to exclude subsequent evidence of terrorist weakness. People fail to reconsider their view that 9/11 demonstrated the arrival of a new era of catastrophic terrorism even as evidence against the proposition mounts.

Another heuristic is representativeness; people use previously understood events to estimate the probability of a new one, rather than considering its past frequency.[46] Representativeness causes the conjunction fallacy, where people fail to realize that an outcome that requires several conditions to hold has a lower probability than each condition.[47] The conjunction fallacy helps explain why people overestimate the odds of unconventional weapons attacks and other complex terrorist plots. Such attacks require success in a series of tasks. Failure at one can prevent success.[48] People likely fail to consider each hurdle's detrimental effect on the odds of success. They use some prior event to estimate the probability of the new one.

A related misperception is the tendency to see intentionality, centralization, or agency where there is none. We imagine patterns, failing to appreciate randomness.[49] This tendency, and perhaps old, representative ideas of how enemy organizations function, help explain why Americans see al Qaeda as a worldwide conspiratorial organization with a strategy rather than a loose movement with many strategies. Unrelated attacks, videos, and travel seem coordinated because we imagine a hierarchical organization, much as Communism seemed monolithic.[50]

Also important in considering the perception of terrorism is the availability heuristic, where people overestimate the odds of events or scenarios that they can picture. Events become cognitively available when they are recent, when they create memorable images, and when they receive great publicity.[51] Shark attacks are an example. Because terrorism creates strong images and attracts media attention, it is a quintessentially available risk. Images of the collapsing World Trade Center remain unforgettable for most Americans. Politicians' and the media's tendency to talk about foreign attacks keeps the risk cognitively available for most Americans. Therefore, they see it as more likely than probability merits.

People also tend to overestimate the danger of risks that provoke dread, which are those that are novel or perceived as involuntary.[52] Though terrorism's novelty may be fading for most Americans, it is involuntary. Victims knowingly assume no risk.

Because of how we are wired, terrorism is almost a perfect storm for provoking fear and overreaction, which is its point. Cognition alone, however, cannot explain public demand for protection from danger. We also need to understand the incentives that motivate the experts that teach us about danger.[53] In the national security realm, that means the government, which dominates both the creation and interpretation of information about threats.[54] This information originates in intelligence collection and analysis, congressional hearings, government-funded studies, and agency reports. The loudest voices in national security debates are executive branch officials, candidates for office, agency heads, and nominally independent experts relying on government information and beholden to political interests due to inclination, ambition, and funding.

Political Motives

This section outlines elites' political incentives to exaggerate terrorist capability. A caveat is needed first. What follows is not an

195

argument that people are simply products of their organizational or electoral interests. On the contrary, people throughout the government often serve the national interest at the expense of their own. Their presence in the government can be an example. The point is that competing interests mask and damage the national interest. The arguments below are not laws of politics but pressures that create a general tendency, even though people often resist them.

One source of bias in the information Americans get about the terrorist threat is the need to justify American foreign policy commitments. U.S. foreign policy is largely unrestrained. Wealth allows us to distribute troops and promises hither and yon, and liberal ideology encourages it. We rarely need to worry that these actions will trigger a large war with a rival power, unlike during the cold war. At home, the cost of militarism is diffuse. For citizens of continental European powers in the early 20th century or the Athenians that Thucydides chronicled, war often meant participating in fighting, and foreign policy failures brought disaster: conquest, plundered cities, and the like. For most Americans, the only clear and present danger from our defense policies is marginally higher taxes or economic harm from national debt. The dead are confined to the volunteer military.

Still, these policies and the military spending that supports them have to be sold to voters, particularly when the policies begin. The justification need not match the motivation. Whether our policies aim to promote liberty, serve bureaucratic interests, or occur out of inertia, policymakers justify them with arguments about security. Ideological arguments are made too, but danger is a better pitch. People see threats as more legitimate justifications for policies than ideological ends. The search for enemies is constant.[55]

The structure of American government heightens this tendency to repackage policies, especially new ones, as security projects. Even in foreign policy, power in the U.S. government is uniquely diffuse. Both in the executive branch bureaucracy and Congress, there are a variety of actors (veto players, political scientists call them) whose approval may be needed to make new policy. One way to enact change is alarm, a sense of crisis that either alarms other veto players into supporting change or convinces them that because the public thinks so, compliance is necessary.[56] Policymakers, including the president, both generate and employ fear to make policy.

Because of these two factors—the need to sell commitments and the diffusion of power in American government—almost every recent U.S. foreign policy strategy or proposal has been said, by someone in power, to combat terrorism. Even before 9/11, the tendency existed. The Clinton administration portrayed its defense budgets as a means to spread global order, which would combat numerous ills, including terrorism.[57] The Bush administration fashioned its Wilsonian impulse to spread democracy by force as counterterrorism. The invasion of Iraq is just the most prominent example.[58] Different officials in the administration had different reasons for war, but President Bush's main goal seems to have been to spread liberalism in the Middle East.[59]

Other examples of repackaging policies as counterterrorism, albeit less disciplined and effective than the selling of the war in Iraq, abound. Policies that the Bush administration sold as counterterrorism include foreign aid, trade agreements, anti-drug efforts, and the president's energy plan, including the proposal to drill for oil in the Arctic National Wildlife Refuge.[60] As a presidential candidate, Barack Obama justified U.S. intervention in Sudan on counterterrorism grounds.[61] His administration now uses similar arguments to champion foreign aid and other programs that promote good government abroad.[62]

It might seem that the tendency of leaders to use public fears of terrorism to sell policies reflects fear rather than causes it. Actually, both occur. As an echo increases noise by reflecting it, elite efforts to employ public fear increase it.

The two-party system also encourages U.S. politicians to inflate the terrorist threat. A multiparty system might include dovish or isolationist parties with an interest in downplaying the danger to appeal to supporters' anti-war positions. In the United States, the parties engage in competitive threat inflation. Neither sees advantage in helping Americans perceive their safety.[63] Both parties are generally hawkish, the Republicans more so due to their determination to stay to the Democrats' right on security issues. They do not always agree on counterterrorism policy, but the argument generally concerns the best way to combat the threat, not its size. For example, in recent years Democrats framed their opposition to continuing the war in Iraq as evidence of their dedication to counterterrorism. They said that Iraq was taking resources from the more important counterterrorism mission in Afghanistan, not that terrorism is too small a threat to justify indefinite participation in foreign civil wars. Democrats deflected Republicans' claims that they are soft on terrorism by urging more homeland security spending.[64]

This competition in alarmism created the Department of Homeland Security. In 2002, Democrats, led by presidential candidate Senator Joseph Lieberman, advocated creating the department, taking up a recommendation made by the blue-ribbon Hart-Rudman Commission.[65] The Bush administration did not believe that the government deficiencies revealed by the 9/11 attacks required a new cabinet department or security grants to states and localities. It preferred more limited reforms, including the creation of a Homeland Security Council in the White House. But there was no political benefit in making its case, and it capitulated.[66]

Creating the department meant increasing the incentives to herald our insecurity in the face of terrorism. William Clark, writing about the history of risk assessment, notes that medieval Europeans did not much fear witches until they created an inquisition to find them.[67] The inquisition provided its members work, which they justified by promoting the witch threat. Institutionalizing the hunt heightened fear of the danger hunted.

Modern national security organizations do not burn heretics, but they too promote fear. Threats fade, but the organizations that combat them remain, making today's fear tomorrow's.[68] Public organizations are reliable servants of their purpose or mission for three reasons. First, the mission serves the organization's power structure. The division of labor within the organization requires a hierarchy, which a new mission would threaten. The beneficiaries of the current arrangement rarely embrace changes that upset it.[69] Second, successful public organizations tend to infuse their members with its values, making them servants of the organization's mission. Members tend to see their organization's interest as the public's.[70] Third, current ways of doing business have reliably brought outside support, especially funding.[71] In the national security realm, preserving the mission means preserving the sense of threat that justified it. Organizations can promote threats via congressional testimony, reports, leaks, press conferences and releases, sponsored research, and congressional allies whose districts benefit from the provision of defenses against the threat.

The tendency to promote threats to protect missions is strongest in large and highly focused organizations like the Air Force, which mostly hypes threats requiring strategic airpower, its preferred mission. The tendency is weaker in more fractious and smaller organizations, like those that compose DHS. Reduced sense of mission means less incentive to sell a particular threat. Fewer resources mean less ability to do so.

Like the Defense Department, which was its model, DHS is a management apparatus uniting several mostly independent organizations. Its critical functions are carried out by these subsidiary agencies. Where the counterterrorism mission complements their legacy missions, the agencies have an incentive to promote the terrorist threat. The mission of the Bureau of Customs and Border Protection, for example, is basically to guard borders against illegal immigrants and search entrants for contraband. Protecting borders against terrorists requires few doctrinal changes but arguably more manpower and budget. Counterterrorism is good for the agency, consistent with its mission, but not essential to its survival. Similar dynamics exist in other DHS agencies, like the Secret Service, where guarding the president against terrorists complements the legacy mission. In some cases, however, counterterrorism may compete with traditional missions for resources, diluting incentives to inflate the threat. Small budgets—less than one-tenth the size of U.S. military services'—limit these agencies' ability to influence public opinion. Collectively, DHS agencies contribute to the public's fear of terrorism, but not much.

The department's managers perform two functions that encourage them to promote the terrorist threat. First, they promote the department's budget, which means harping on vulnerability to terrorism. Second, the secretary has become a public advocate for safety, somewhat like the U.S. surgeon general. Though DHS leaders no longer talk about or change the much-mocked national color-coded threat system, the department still preaches vigilance and preparation for disaster.[72] Despite vagueness about the type of disaster, these exhortations remind people of terrorism's danger.[73]

The department also promotes threat inflation by distributing grants for preparedness—mainly via the Office of Domestic Preparedness and the Federal Emergency Management Agency.[74] The Science and Technology Directorate also makes research grants. These grants amount to less than $5 billion annually, small money in the U.S. federal budget, but they encourage rent seeking among nearly everyone who has a large hand in commerce or a small hand in public safety: ports, police, firefighters, mayors, governors, college deans, nurses, hospitals administrators, and even schools. Along with funds, the grants distribute claims of vulnerability.

Despite all this, homeland security institutions are not the main promoters of the terrorist threat. That distinction belongs to the military-industrial complex, or iron triangle. This is a not conspiracy but a set of actors in the Pentagon, Congress, think tanks, academia, and the defense industry with a common interest in high military spending and thus in public fear of enemies that justify it, which have been lacking since the cold war.[75] The elements of the complex do not always agree, of course. The Army has a different ideal enemy than the Navy. Members of Congress with shipyards in their districts worry about China more than those with Army bases. Missile defense boosters warn of North Korean missiles, not insurgents.

One can imagine a counterterrorism strategy that relies only on organizations that most directly combat terrorism: the FBI, the Special Operations Command and the organizations that compose it, the intelligence agencies, and military units like the National Guard and Northern Command that participate in homeland defense. After 9/11, we might have reduced the funding for conventional military forces to increase funding for these entities. In that case, these relatively small agencies would have heralded the terrorist threat, while the military services, whose missions are largely unrelated to terrorism, would have ignored or even denigrated the danger to protect their budgets.

Instead, the United States, at least during the Bush administration, defined counterterrorism as a military struggle, requiring global effort, two indefinite counterinsurgency campaigns, and conventional wars against states said to be aligned with terrorists. As a result, the whole military-industrial complex benefited from our national fixation on al Qaeda. Fear of terrorism helped the defense budget grow by over 40 percent, adjusting for inflation, from 2001 until the present. That increase does not include direct spending on wars. That rising tide lifted all Pentagon boats, though not equally. Even the elements of the services least connected to counterterrorism, like the Navy's surface fleet and the Air Force's fighter community, shared in the counterterrorism spoils.[76]

Today, the idea that attacks on states can serve counterterrorism has fallen from official favor, thanks to Iraq and the end of the Bush administration. But the military remains linked to counterterrorism by the idea that the United States must plan on a series of unconventional wars to prevent unruly states from becoming terrorist havens.[77] Though the ground forces still prefer conventional missions, they increasingly embrace counterinsurgency and sell it as counterterrorism. The argument for the relevance of the Air Force and Navy to the threat is more tenuous, but both services make it, largely by focusing on their platforms' ability to strike land-based targets.[78] The services' willingness to promote the threat, while diminished, remains. Contractors and congressional allies reflect these views.

Experts in think tanks and academia also fuel Americans' overwrought fear of terrorists. After 9/11, a new set of academic institutions and think tanks appeared to absorb federal homeland security funds, overlapping partially with the entities that already existed to aid the military establishment.[79] Homeland security degree programs emerged to provide manpower to federal and state agencies that participate in homeland security.[80]

Ideological inclination, careerism, and funding cause think tanks and academic security experts to write about how to control danger, not its probability. Relative to their peers, people who study war tend to support defense measures, just as people who study development tend to support foreign aid. The hope for political appointments encourages some experts to reflect one party's perspective. Because neither party is reliably honest about the limited terrorist threat, neither are ambitious experts. Many receive funding from a part of the national security bureaucracy and reflect its biases.

The problem is not lying, although that occurs. The problem is the imbalance of perspectives and its effect on public threat perception. When everyone in the counterterrorism business simply does his or her job and conveys information about how to limit vulnerability, they focus public attention on the danger rather than its low probability.

The media, famously called a free marketplace of ideas, is a failed market when a strong interest faces no like interest to generate competing ideas.[81] On matters of national security, unlike environmental issues, for example, there is rarely a strong interest that gains from correcting overestimation of danger. Reporters lack the time and incentive to challenge conventional ideas. In part because of the cognitive biases discussed above, alarmism sells.

These various incentives to promote the terrorist threat are more than the sum of their parts. Socialization heightens their power. People adapt their opinions to their peers' because they learn from them and because conformity is socially easier than dissent. Agreement tends to make people's views more extreme.[82] The result is blowback, where self-interested threat inflation is believed not only by the public but also by the organizations that purvey it.[83]

Fighting Overreaction

Cognitive bias and the variety of interests that bias the information that Americans get about terrorism nearly guarantee that Americans will excessively fear terrorism and demand overwrought policy responses to it. Democratic government encourages politicians to act on these demands. Overreaction is then highly probable for the foreseeable future. Experience in dealing with other dangers, however, suggests strategies to control overreaction. The rest of this chapter discusses these strategies.

Communication

The obvious response to threat inflation is to point out that it is wrong and demand that policymakers be honest. This tactic is not wholly ineffective. If analysts demonstrate that terrorists are not all they are cracked up to be, parts of the public will get the message. That message may encourage people who hesitated to express similar views to be more open, creating a ripple effect. Moreover, if analysts attack overwrought statements, their authors might think twice about fearmongering. Politicians are not immune to embarrassment. The prominence of the word "fearmongering" in American political discourse is evidence that a social norm may restrain egregious threat inflation. Yet among the incentives that govern the way our leaders talk about threats, this new norm, if it exists, is a small force.

Other communications strategies depend on the willingness of policymakers to articulate more restrained views of terrorist capability. As noted above, while doing so is unlikely to serve leaders' personal interests, some may still try it. One method is to emphasize our strength and al Qaeda's weakness. We mythologize the British for keeping calm and carrying on amid the blitz. We call our country the home of the brave. Action heroes in our movies are steely amid danger. And yet we insist that terrorists can easily wreck our society, an enemy so menacing that every American must discuss escape plans from their attacks with their children and maintain vigilance on highways and trains.

Leaders should point out that terrorists are in the fear business, so we can defeat them by not fearing them.[84] Instead of treating our enemies like supermen, leaders could call them what they are: desperate, weak people who nonetheless occasionally cause tragedy. Some politicians have talked this way without being ejected from office. New York Mayor Michael Bloomberg, for example, when asked about an unfeasible plan by would-be terrorists to blow up fuel tanks at JFK airport, said:

> There are lots of threats to you in the world. There's the threat of a heart attack for genetic reasons. You can't sit there and worry about everything. Get a life. . . . You have a much greater danger of being hit by lightning than being struck by a terrorist.[85]

Another strategy is to adopt communications policies mindful of the cognitive biases discussed above. This strategy should occur as part of a cultural change in DHS; it ought to think of itself as not just a risk manager but also as a fear manager. In this volume, Priscilla Lewis outlines some ways in which official communication about terrorism can improve. DHS should institutionalize these methods. Still, it must be noted that scholars know more about cognitive biases than about how to fix them. And the department's interests limit its willingness to downplay the terrorist threat.

Science

A more promising strategy to fight overreaction to terrorism is to expand the use of risk management as a justification for avoiding wasteful counterterrorism policies. Risk management means using processes employing cost-benefit estimates to make policies. This sort of analysis helps policymakers figure out whether policy proposals make sense, but it is more useful as a justification for decisions already made. It enhances the power of central decisionmakers that must consider the opportunity costs of chasing after particular dangers. It takes power from agencies whose more parochial perspectives encourage them to overspend against those dangers.

Government ultimately belongs to interests, not science, but science has more legitimacy. One reason people obey authority, as Max

Weber explained, is because they agree that rationality ought to triumph. Science is powerful in a society dominated by enlightenment values. A formal process of employing technical expertise helps convince people that policy is wise. Cost-benefit analysis may not be especially scientific—it's more like common sense dressed up with footnotes and formulas—but what matters is that it seems scientific. If DHS tells the people of New Hampshire, for example, that the federal government will not fund port security in Portsmouth, it is useful to have a lengthy report full of charts and graphs making that case.

The regulatory review system managed by the Office of Information and Regulatory Analysis in OMB serves this function. As the regulatory state grew in the mid-20th century, so did the idea of creating institutions in the executive branch to determine whether the new health and safety regulations were worth their cost. Business interests that bore much of that cost naturally favored this approach.[86] Behind the process lies the idea that the public's alarmist view of particular risks creates a demand for overreaction, which Congress translates into agencies with a tendency to overregulate.[87] OIRA is a countervailing force, albeit a weak one, given its limited influence on public opinion and Congress. Indeed in many cases, Congress mandates rules via legislation, so OIRA cannot stop them.

The regulatory review process took on much of its current form with the Reagan administration's Executive Order 12291. The process, which subsequent administrations have left mostly intact, requires most regulatory agencies to prepare regulatory impact statements before issuing major new regulations. The statements are supposed to demonstrate that the regulation is cost-effective and that no better alternative exists. OIRA's civil servants then review these statements and reject those regulations found lacking, preventing them from taking effect. In practice, there is ongoing give and take between OIRA and the agencies.[88]

Regulatory review is far from perfect. Attempts to evaluate alternatives to regulation are generally perfunctory. Insufficient scientific knowledge obviates accurate estimates of regulatory impact. Scholars who study regulation debate how much the process has done to avoid overly onerous regulations.[89] What they do agree on, however, is that regulatory review is a tool of executive branch officials willing to use it.[90] Rejected regulations tend to have two characteristics: they fail cost-benefit analysis and White House officials opposed them.[91] Employing a scientific decisionmaking process does not make decisions scientific, but it has political value.

Systems analysis in the Pentagon performs a similar role. When he became secretary of defense at the start of the Kennedy administration, Robert McNamara created the Systems Analysis Office (later the Office of Program Analysis and Evaluation) to employ quantitative methods of comparing weapons systems. He also created a new budgeting system to empower the office's analysis.[92] The new system doubtless produced many useful insights, but its true value, intentional or not, was in overcoming opposition to those decisions from the military services and their allies on Capitol Hill. Eventually, the services learned the new lingo and developed their own cadres of technical analysts, lessening the civilian advantage. This arms race in analytical expertise demonstrates the power of the tool.

Though risk management has become a mantra in DHS, it remains underused. The second secretary of homeland security, Michael Chertoff, habitually expounded on risk management to resist congressional efforts to use homeland security grants as pork, even as he exaggerated the terrorist danger.[93] The department now has several offices dedicated to risk management.[94] It has adopted formulas to determine what regions are vulnerable enough to terrorism to deserve preparedness grants. Much of Congress has fought these reforms, preferring to keep set-asides for all states.[95] But grants, as noted, are a small portion of the department's budget.

DHS and its OMB overseers should expand its use of risk management in two ways. First, they should better use the regulatory review process. Because the relevant executive orders cover DHS, its regulations require regulatory impact statements and OIRA review. Thus far, however, the impact statements have not made an honest effort to evaluate regulatory benefits, and OIRA has never rejected them.[96] DHS either asserts that benefits are unknowable, estimates what the regulations would have to accomplish to make sense, or claims that a regulation prevents an annual 9/11, exaggerating benefits.[97] As discussed above, benefits cannot be assessed precisely, but rough estimates, using history rather than imagination, show far less danger averted and thus very high cost per life saved. Impact statements should be made even for regulations that Congress mandated, such as the requirement that people crossing into the United States from Canada provide a passport or the requirement that U.S. inspectors ultimately inspect every shipping container entering U.S. ports. The exercise will give ammunition to those arguing against these laws. OIRA should start rejecting DHS regulations that fail cost-benefit tests.

More importantly, DHS should use risk management in the rest of its budget—in allocating funds within and across its agencies. DHS has an Office of Program Analysis and Evaluation. This office should produce analysis that shows where DHS can most efficiently deploy its dollars. It might show that the Coast Guard's new cutters are unlikely to contribute to counterterrorism, for example, or that attempting to defend trains against terrorism is not cost-effective. DHS's leaders have not truly made this office part of the budget-making process, despite its official role, and have not shifted money across agencies from year to year.[98] There seems to be no evaluation of efficacy of past spending. Future secretaries should take a more active role in guiding the budget and should use the program analysis office to do so. They should try to place analysts fluent in cost-benefit analysis throughout the organization, particularly in the program analysis office. That means more people with economics training as opposed to military experience. The downside of this approach is that it may upset Congress (just as the House Armed Services Committee threatened to defund the Pentagon's Office of Systems Analysis under McNamara).[99] But that is a fight worth institutionalizing.

Because of its reliance on unelected technocrats to resist overreaction, this strategy is somewhat undemocratic. In another sense, though, it is simply a way of strengthening the national interest by better balancing parochial concerns. This brings us to the next strategy, which is to structure decisions about homeland security spending so that more risks compete—to make tradeoffs more explicit.

Institutional Design

In their famous study of defense decisionmaking, *How Much Is Enough*, Alain Enthoven and K. Wayne Smith write that the secretary of defense should make decisions about defense spending, not because he has the most expertise but because he is in the best position to do so.[100] The military services focus on the dangers that they best defend against. The secretary's job is to balance their concerns. The president uses the Office of Management and Budget to balance resource allocation among national security dangers and other sorts of dangers.

This observation is consistent with the view of government expressed in the Federalist Papers and by scholars called pluralists.[101] Pluralists say that government is the arena for the competition of interests, manifest in particular congressional agencies and executive agencies. Federalism is supervised competition among them to produce a national interest. A similar way to think about government is a competition of risk preferences. One person frets about Iran's missiles. Someone else fears environmental degradation. A third worries about the tax burden on wealth creation. Agencies and members of Congress serve some of these preferences. They clash in the formation of the federal budget.

Theoretically, the job of OMB and other central agents in the government is to distribute resources among cabinet departments and the agencies within them to maximize spending efficiency across risk categories. In reality, things rarely work like that. Resource competition intensifies with bureaucratic proximity. Missions and the threats they confront compete mostly within agencies, and to a lesser extent within cabinet departments. The location of missions within agencies and departments determines who fights whom and thus affects the resources they receive. Institutional design is the arrangement of tradeoffs among competing risk preferences.

If you want to constrain spending against a particular danger, put it in an agency dominated by other concerns. Missile defense skeptics, for example, should push for missile defense to be the business of the Air Force, not the Missile Defense Agency. The Air Force's preference for new fighters would constrain spending on missile interceptor technology. Something similar occurs today with the Navy's mine warfare community, which is kept down by more powerful Navy communities that worry about other things. Subcomponents of every federal agency, including DHS, compete.

As discussed above, the Bush administration populated DHS with agencies that have missions unrelated to terrorism. It attempted, ultimately unsuccessfully, to make DHS "revenue neutral," meaning that it would not add to federal spending. That created competition between the legacy missions of DHS agencies and their new counterterrorism mission, likely restraining spending on both.[102] But public alarm about terrorism increased spending on DHS, loosening that restraint.

A better way to limit spending on homeland security would have been to avoid creating the department in the first place. Domestic counterterrorism would then have been performed by agencies without that as their primary mission, limiting enthusiasm for it. This resistance occurs today in homeland security agencies left out of DHS. The Defense Department, for example, is not eager to assign troops needed for foreign wars to Northern Command, which wants them for homeland security missions. Because the FBI got responsibility for domestic intelligence, as opposed to a new agency, the tendency to overinvest in that function is muted. The FBI leadership remains attached to its primary, crime-fighting function.

We are likely stuck with the department, however, so other solutions are needed. The most obvious has been discussed: heighten the power of central decisionmaking in DHS to balance the various harms—storms, illegal immigration, terrorists—that the department confronts. Another approach is to beef up the staffs of those in OMB and congressional budget committees who oversee various agencies and encourage overseers to look at security spending as a zero-sum endeavor. That is, a dollar on homeland security should be a dollar less for defense or intelligence. Make the al Qaeda hawks compete with the China hawks or even the environmentalists.

A counterterrorism strategy that gave budgetary priority to nonmilitary tools would enhance this competition of risks. As discussed above, if the White House tells the military—in strategy documents, decisions, and speeches—that it is no longer an agent of counterterrorism, except on rare occasions, it will discourage services from hyping the threat. If they lost budget to the agencies that fight terrorism, the services might even publicly downplay the danger and encourage their agents to do so.[103] Similar risk competition could occur across the entire government if the White House frames budget decisions as competitive and deficits mount. If federal health care expenses grow without overall spending increases, that spending may come at the expense of security spending. That fight might create a more functional marketplace of ideas about security dangers, improving public threat perception.

A related tactic is to devolve decisionmaking about spending on homeland security to states or localities. That means stopping federal homeland security grant making.[104] Because of their organizational perspectives and the ability to run deficits, federal homeland security officials need not much consider the grants' opportunity costs. States and cities, however, do not share these characteristics. If they pay for homeland security, they appreciate the cost in terms of less traditional policing, fewer new roads, and so on. They have a better perspective on relative priorities.

Security Theater

A final strategy to contain overreaction to terrorism is to deflect it. Security theater describes measures that provide not security but a sense of it.[105] People tend to dismiss this strategy as dishonest and useless. Only the former is true. The reduction of exaggerated fears is useful, particularly if it prevents more costly responses.

The downside of this approach is that the spectacle of security might simply remind people of dangers and heighten fear. You then get the worst of both worlds: increased fear without increased security. For that reason, this strategy is a last resort, a political necessity used only after other methods fail to contain fears. But if public fears cannot be dispelled, the response might be to put on a cheap show to answer fear without breaking the bank. Cass Sunstein, the current head of the Office of Information and Regulatory Affairs, and Richard Zeckhauser advocate this approach:

> The government should not swiftly capitulate if the public is demonstrating action bias and showing an excessive response to a risk whose expected value is quite modest. A critical component of government response should be information and education. But if public fear remains high, the government should determine which measures can reduce [fear] most cost effectively, almost in the spirit of looking for the best "fear placebo." Valued attributes for such measures will be high visibility, low cost, and perceived effectiveness.[106]

The quintessential example of this strategy in homeland security is putting National Guard troops in airports in the panicked days after 9/11. The troops did little to stop hijackings, but they may have made people feel safer and more willing to fly.

A related approach is to channel fear of a danger into measures that accomplish other useful ends. An example is the Eisenhower administration's reaction to Sputnik, which is recounted by historian Robert Divine.[107] The Soviet satellite launch in 1957 alarmed the

U.S. public. They feared that the Soviets had bested Americans in technological prowess and would soon have the ability to attack the continental United States with an intercontinental ballistic missile carrying a nuclear warhead. Eisenhower knew that these fears were overwrought. U.S. ballistic missiles programs were ahead of their Soviet rivals in targeting and reentry, which space shots do not require. Secret U-2 flights revealed limited Soviet progress in deploying intercontinental ballistic missiles. Eisenhower worried that alarm would cause ruinous increases in defense spending. He tried to calm the public in press conferences and in his "chin-up" speeches, but he mostly failed. Hawks in both parties echoed public fears and called for higher defense spending. The public remained worried.

Eisenhower decided that "this alarm could be turned into a constructive result," as Edward Land, founder of Polaroid and member of a key White House advisory committee, put it.[108] The White House harnessed alarm to several ends. The first was science education. Despite Eisenhower's general opposition to federal education spending, those in his administration encouraged legislation that created scholarships for college and increased National Science Foundation grant spending. They created a White House science adviser. They used concern about U.S. missile programs to push Congress to strengthen the power of the defense secretary over the services. To manage civilian space programs, they backed creation of the National Aeronautics and Space Administration. These changes were cheap, at least in the short term. They helped Eisenhower resist calls for higher defense spending, a massive civil defense program, and other measures he thought harmful. Even so, he could not prevent hawks from harping on a phony missile gap and forcing through some spending increases.

U.S. homeland security policy might be thought of as security theater. The Bush administration arguably saw homeland security as politically necessary but ineffective counterterrorism. It collected a set of agencies tangentially related to domestic counterterrorism in DHS, made a fuss about it, and tried to hold down the bill.[109] The department bought fancier Coast Guard ships, hired more border guards, and declared that vulnerability to terrorism had been lowered. The administration used fear of terrorism to justify policies, like war in Iraq and higher defense spending, that it supported for reasons largely unrelated to terrorism.

Although it does not seem inclined to do it, the current administration might stem demand for excessive homeland security, especially if additional attacks occur, by holding down spending and declaring that other priorities, like increased hospital capacity or more police, serve homeland security. This solution resembles the prior one, in that where you put government functions affects how people perceive their use. If you call activities homeland security, especially by sticking them into the department with that name, they appear to serve that end.

Conclusion

Our first line of defense against our tendency to overreact to terrorism is to be truthful about the threat and push for the same from politicians and security officials. But people's psychological tendency to overrate remote dangers like terrorism, and leaders' interest in exploiting those fears, make these tools insufficient. Lessening threat inflation requires addressing its causes.

Better communication methods may reduce psychological errors, but political incentives limit the number of elites eager to communicate better. One strategy to alter these incentives is to enhance the use of cost-benefit analysis in DHS—institutionalizing rationality in a more technocratic DHS. We can further limit overreaction by cutting the number of organizations engaged in counterterrorism. Declaring that terrorism is not a military problem diminishes the military-industrial complex's incentive to hype its danger. It would be better still if counterterrorism and military spending are considered zero-sum. That might encourage the military and its agents to publicly deflate the terrorist threat as a way to protect their budgets. Enhancing the executive branch's ability, via OMB, to compare dangers across government agencies might have a similar effect, particularly as deficits strain spending. A last resort for limiting fear's damage is to embrace the spectacle of homeland security, answering exaggerated fears of terrorism with cheap displays of security that do little harm. If you cannot quiet nightmares with truth, use myth. A less cynical relative of this strategy is to declare other priorities to be homeland security, so that fear of terrorism funds them. This strategy is wise if those priorities are.

11. The Impact of Fear on Public Thinking about Counterterrorism Policy: Implications for Communicators

Priscilla Lewis[1]

We have all heard admonitions about the need to manage strong emotions in order to make sound decisions. Children are urged to "count to 10" before acting or speaking out of anger. Adults who have lost a loved one or who have been diagnosed with a serious illness are counseled to "take some time" before making any major life choices. People nod in agreement when reminded that "the only thing we have to fear is fear itself."

The actual relationship between emotion and reason is complex. But commonsense cautions about the power of fear and other strong emotions are both common and sensible. Almost everyone can remember acting rashly or in a shortsighted, counterproductive way when faced with some frightening or traumatic situation.

Terrorism is exquisitely calibrated to exploit this tendency in individuals and societies. While public concerns about terrorism have been displaced somewhat by economic anxieties—Americans are not living in a constant state of fearfulness about terrorism—research and observation alike show that the thought patterns laid down by the trauma of 9/11 are easily reactivated. Fear and the worldview created by fear have played a significant role in shaping the national discussion about counterterrorism policy and approaches to the terrorism threat. Eight years after the events of 9/11, terrorism-related anxieties retain their power to enhance the appeal of some policies and diminish others. Fearmongering remains a tempting political ploy that can derail debate and narrow policy options. Events (such as recent attacks and attempts) continue to stimulate new public fears and provide new opportunities for the manipulation of those fears. And countering fear-based arguments has proved extremely difficult for even the most skilled communicators.

Eliminating fear as a response to danger is neither feasible nor desirable. But concerned policy experts, advocates, elected officials, and community leaders can do a better job of *managing* the fear factor. By understanding how fear affects public thinking and by learning how to counter some of fear's negative effects, influential communicators may be able to help prevent strong public emotions from being channeled in unconstructive directions.

As described below, the fear factor has important psychological and cognitive dimensions as well as cultural dimensions, all of which have implications for communicators. Also described below are the results of messaging research conducted in 2009 by the Topos Partnership for the U.S. in the World Initiative. Influential communicators are already deploying a variety of themes and narratives intended to promote a different kind of public conversation about terrorism. Topos's research explored how some of those explanatory narratives actually fare when fear shapes public reasoning. The research asked which themes and messages, if reinforced both before and after the next crisis, might help us build and sustain support for farsighted, effective, and principled security policies—even under the adverse psychological and cognitive conditions created by fear.

Fear's Effects on Individual Psychology and Cognition

Many different academic disciplines and research methodologies have shed light on how people reason and how they see the world when they feel their safety is threatened. Such insights help to define the unique challenges that face communicators who are trying to build mainstream support for strategic, farsighted security policies in fearful times.

Mortality Salience: The Political Psychology of Fear

Since the late 1980s, academic psychologists in a growing area of study called "terror management theory" have looked at what happens to people's emotions and thought processes when they are confronted with reminders of their own eventual death.[2] In hundreds of published experiments, researchers have demonstrated that induced "mortality salience"—awareness of the inevitability of death—leads people to cling more strongly to their cultural world-views. The hypothesis is that since cultural worldviews function as symbolic protectors against psychological terror (by providing meaning, continuity, and self-respect), then reminding people of the underlying source of their fear increases their need to value their own worldview.[3]

To put this in more specific terms, mortality reminders seem to trigger disdain for other races, religions, and nations; a preference for strong, traditional leaders and for authoritarian rather than prag-matic leadership; a heightened fidelity to one's own group; and increased stereotyping and suspicion of other groups.[4] It seems that mortal fear—fear of the sort that is triggered by threats to personal safety and the safety of loved ones—inclines people to favor a certain kind of leadership and an "us vs. them" approach to defining and meeting threats. During the Bush administration, political psycholo-gists drew on terror management theory and the mortality salience hypothesis to explain the president's widespread popularity and the relative imperviousness to criticism of his administration's counter-terrorism policies, even as some of those policies foundered or ran afoul of core democratic values.[5] Indeed, in repeated experiments, asking research subjects to think about death or just reminding them of the attacks on 9/11 led to significantly increased support for President Bush and his security policies, regardless of the subjects' political affiliations.[6]

Serious fears of a more general nature (e.g., concerns about the "cultural disruptions" caused by economic insecurity or demo-graphic change) may have similar effects, predisposing people to accept the authority of strong leaders, to exaggerate specific threats, and to believe that desperate measures are necessary and warranted.[7]

Implications for Communicators: These findings suggest that even sympathetic audiences will follow unhelpful paths of reasoning when they are under the influence of fear. Communicators need to be aware that some arguments and messages that ordinarily are effective may not have the desired result—and may even backfire—in the context of perceived threats to safety and security.

The Fear System in the Brain: Consciousness Commandeered

Mortality salience experiments yield important clues about the psychology of fear. But what is it about the *physiological* state of fearfulness that makes people gravitate toward one course of action rather than another? Neuroscientific research offers insights about the "fear system" in the brain and what happens when that system is aroused.

In broad strokes, there is an "ancient" part of the brain, called the amygdala. It is the part of the brain we share with all mammals—and it produces near-instantaneous reactions to danger. Developed during the period of human evolutionary history when instinctive responses to attack made the difference between life and death, this part of the brain acts outside of consciousness, taking in stimuli, putting out stress hormones, raising blood pressure, accelerating the pulse. It mobilizes the familiar "fight or flight" response, but it can also trigger a freezing and numbing response, or submission.[8] This ancient fear system coexists with the uniquely human part of the brain—the prefrontal cortex—that is the site of reason and judgment (i.e., conscious thought) and plays an essential role in generating such "social emotions" as compassion and empathy.[9]

The brain's fear system produces terror when precipitously aroused and chronic anxiety during milder, sustained arousal. When hyperaroused, the brain's fear system literally commandeers consciousness, as Topos puts it—guiding and influencing our thinking and in some instances determining whether we are able to "think" at all.

Neurologist Joseph LeDoux argues that the two parts of the brain are actually reciprocally related.[10] In order for the fear system to respond to a perceived threat, the cortex has to be shut down—and along with it, presumably, some ability to think critically (such as about policy choices), to reference abstract concepts (such as justice or fairness), and to feel compassion for fellow beings. LeDoux suggests that the converse could also be true: activation of the prefrontal region might inhibit the fear system (although achieving this kind of reciprocity is likely to be difficult once the fear system has become hyperaroused).[11]

Implications for Communicators: Fearful people are unlikely to be persuaded by arguments based on abstract concepts (even familiar ones like fairness) or fine cognitive distinctions (like the difference between a suspected terrorist who might be innocent and a proven terrorist). At the same time, if communicators can get people to "think" by offering a fresh, credible idea—a new insight—it may help check the activity of the fear system and enable people to take in new information.

Fear's Worldview: It's a Jungle Out There

How does the world appear to people when they are operating in threat mode—when the fear system has been aroused or when mortality salience has been activated? Exploratory research conducted in 2008 for U.S. in the World and the National Security Network sheds light on how people think about threats to security in the current, post-9/11 environment.[12]

This research confirmed and extended findings about fear that have also emerged from the work of other investigators. The interviews showed how threats to personal safety or the safety of loved ones cause people's lens on the world to narrow to the most immediate factors in the environment. People go on heightened alert for possible dangerous intentions on the part of others, and they become inclined to assume the worst about others' intentions.

As the same team of researchers also found in an earlier project commissioned by the FrameWorks Institute,[13] Topos found that people who are not experts on foreign policy tend to interpret security threats in personal terms, ascribing human motivations and mindsets to other countries. They think of other countries and world actors as friendly or malevolent, motivated by anger, kindness, or some psychological state like "hating" or "liking." When people understand international relations in these interpersonal terms, factors like treaties, institutions, political dynamics, systemic conditions, and so on—the explanations and solutions that international relations and security experts emphasize—are "cognitively invisible."

Similarly, nonexperts rely on analogies to familiar scenarios as ways of making sense of security threats. The most frequently cited scenario, in interviews and focus groups, is the schoolyard—the first place many of us experience conflict and confrontation with our peers (without the presence of adults), and where "standing up to bullies" is one of the lessons to be learned. Other analogies cited include "the Wild West" and "the jungle." It is notable that these are all scenarios where self-reliance is key, where "appeasement" is a dangerous temptation, where the normal rules don't apply, and where following the rules is perceived as a disadvantage, since no one else is constrained by such niceties.

In short, when serious national security threats loom, nonexperts start to see the entire world as a scary place, full of enemies whose behavior cannot be modified or controlled except by force. Immediate concerns take precedence—after all, this is an "emergency"— and laws and values may have to be set aside in favor of doing "whatever it takes" to stay safe.

Implications for Communicators: The Topos Partnership's analysis shows that when people are operating in threat mode, they will reject any policy prescription that seems to put principles before safety; anyone seen as making such a suggestion will be viewed as at best unrealistic and at worst dangerously irresponsible or deluded. Concerns about the long-range consequences of policy decisions (such as losing the trust of allies, breeding more terrorists, and so on) may be acknowledged as valid, but ultimately are likely to be dismissed as irrelevant to the current (emergency) situation. In general, people will reject solutions that cannot be connected intuitively to their personal safety ("How does this protect me and my family?"), which means that communicators have to do more than just assert a relationship between national security and (for example) respect for human rights. They must connect the dots for people in a simple, commonsense way.

Misjudging Risk: Stone-Age Brains in the 21st Century

Compounding fear's problematic psychological and cognitive effects is the reality that humans are not particularly good assessors of risk—at least, not the kinds of risks they face in the 21st century.

There is a large and fascinating body of research on this topic.[14] For example, it appears that people judge highly memorable events that have been broadcast everywhere through the media as more likely to recur, even if they are actually quite rare or remote (school shootings, child abductions, and, of course, terrorist attacks). People regard as more dangerous the things they have negative feelings about (foreigners, Islam), whereas they underrate as risks statistically more dangerous things about which they feel positive or neutral (cars, cigarettes). The perception that harm is intended by some

218

person or persons increases the sense of risk; the "scary other" (terrorist) produces a level and kind of fear that the "scary phenomenon" does not.

There are other relevant glitches in people's ability to calculate risk. Even the most unlikely scenarios seem more probable if they contain one familiar, stereotypical element. This suggests that since people already know that terrorists "hate us" and "want to harm us," any scenario involving a terrorist attack, no matter how complex or unlikely, becomes at least somewhat plausible. To complicate matters further, highly complex scenarios feel much more plausible to people than they actually are. People's judgments also tend to conform with those of their peers, especially (surprisingly enough) when the issue is very important. If people think others are frightened—including the experts—this may exacerbate their own fearfulness, with all the consequences for reasoning suggested above.

Implications for Communicators: It will not be easy to change the public conversation about terrorism by citing data that compare the risk of dying in a terrorist attack to other risks or by putting terrorism "in perspective" as one among many important challenges that the United States must address. In fact, messages that seem to be aimed at minimizing the terrorist threat are likely to be rejected as "out of touch with reality."

Coping with Fear: Responses to Psychological Trauma

The study of psychological trauma and recovery provides important clues about how, and under what conditions, people can move past unreasoning fear. These clues may help opinion leaders and communicators understand what is likely to exacerbate or reduce public fears.[15]

For traumatized individuals as well as communities, it seems that passivity and disempowerment are likely to feed fearfulness, while active coping and affiliation with others tend to calm fears. Sitting alone in front of a television watching endless repetitions of bad news is one of the worst things an individual can do in the aftermath of a crisis. At the community level, this means that crisis response strategies that are disempowering—like sending in teams of outside experts after the fact—are far less effective than building on existing community resources and leadership to prepare for and cope with crisis.

Some psychologists and psychiatrists believe that the impulse to care for others—a "tend-and-befriend" response—is as ancient and hard-wired a response to stress as the fight/flight or freezing/numbing responses; it is certainly more conducive to recovery.[16] Taking problem-solving action that is related to the current situation, especially in partnership with others (what psychologists call "affiliative coping"), aids healing.[17] And while compulsive remembering is an inevitable aspect of trauma, collaboration to memorialize trauma can be an important step toward moving on. In Madrid, after the attacks of March 11, 2004, large public demonstrations of shared sorrow and sober determination probably helped to meet such a need.[18]

Implications for Communicators: Given the importance of positive and affiliative action for building individual and community resilience, it is clear that opinion leaders and elected officials who want to help the public manage fear must do more than offer a new explanatory narrative about terrorism and policy responses to it. They also need to encourage citizen action that strengthens the social fabric and is related to the emotions and concerns people are having (neither "go shopping" nor "here is my 10-point policy agenda" will fit the bill). Many policy experts are unaccustomed to connecting with their audiences in this way, and they may be especially uncomfortable with the notion of inviting citizens to help shape local or national responses to crisis. But overall, constructing opportunities for positive communal action may be one of the most important things leaders can do to reduce public fearfulness and, perhaps, to reduce the appeal of precipitous reactions that are based on fear.

Cultural Dimensions of the Fear Factor

In addition to its psychological and cognitive dimensions, the fear factor has important cultural dimensions that have implications for communicators.

Many observers have pointed, appropriately, to the fear-amplifying role played by a sensationalistic media and by a political climate in which ideologues feel free to manipulate public fears.[19] These dynamics are so troubling that it is easy to overlook the pressures and even the positive intentions that drive some journalists and politicians to amplify public fears. But an appreciation of these nuances can help communicators think more strategically about how to cultivate allies in the media and government who might be willing to play a more constructive role in managing public fears.

For example, the principle of "if it bleeds, it leads" is deeply entrenched in the media. The news and entertainment media bear significant responsibility for the pervasiveness of certain familiar, unhelpful narratives related to terrorism (like the "ticking time bomb" scenario that the majority of Americans now connects with the issue of torture or the images of fanaticism and violence that dominate depictions of Muslim and Arab societies). But most individual journalists are simply motivated to tell a good story.[20] After all, journalists are storytellers, not professional risk assessors, and the best stories are vivid, dramatic, emotionally compelling, and unusual—unfortunately, the very features that lead readers to overestimate the consequences and the probability of an event's recurrence. While a journalist may be personally skeptical of a given prediction or claim about some impending danger, the daily pressures of reporting offer few opportunities and little encouragement for pursuing those doubts.

As for political leaders, some undoubtedly have used fear to advance their agendas (and to frame their agendas in ways the media will cover). But elected leaders in general are driven by a dread of being wrong; they have every reason to overwarn and very little reason to reassure the public about threats that might materialize despite their best efforts. In addition, elected officials are inevitably preoccupied with putting out fires, not with educating the public about the "big picture." And for many elected leaders and their staffs, there is a significant knowledge and confidence gap when it comes to terrorism and counterterrorism issues.[21] Meanwhile, policymakers are being bombarded with threat analyses that typically start by assessing our vulnerabilities rather than our adversaries' capabilities and intentions, with the result that the "consequences" part of the analysis trumps the "probability" part every time.[22]

There is also reason to believe that Americans as a people may be less resilient when it comes to fear than they were in the past or than citizens of other developed nations. Peter Stearns, a historian of emotions, argues that Americans have tried so hard to eliminate fear from their lives and their children's lives that they have come to believe they should never have to experience fear. When they do, they are outraged as well as frightened and are desperate to blame or punish someone for making them afraid. In their efforts to avoid the experience of fear, Americans may have lost some confidence in their ability to handle fear; it also seems possible that highly individualistic Americans may be less inclined to organize collective responses and support systems for coping with fear-inducing events. In short, this analysis suggests that some of the negative effects of fear are amplified for Americans by the very nature of their "relationship" with the emotion of fear.[23]

Implications for Communicators: In light of these cultural dynamics, communicators should avoid implying that people are simply weak or ignorant if they feel more afraid of terrorism than experts think they ought to be. By the same token, communicators should not imply that people are immoral if they have concluded, based on the "ticking time bomb" scenarios so common in the media, that torture may be necessary in exceptional cases. Furthermore, understanding the needs that shape the decisions of politicians and journalists could help communicators craft their "asks and offers" more strategically. Opinion leaders might work to make it politically safer for elected officials to model a more pragmatic and disciplined kind of leadership on terrorism issues by providing validation and backup for efforts to calm public fears. To help potential allies in the media play a constructive role in managing public fears, opinion leaders might share their concerns and point to credible research findings about the negative effects of fear on public reasoning, while also working to ensure that their own communications to the media tell a compelling story without stoking unnecessary fearfulness.

Talking about Terrorism and Responses to Terrorism

Given the power of the fear factor to influence thinking, promoting a more constructive public conversation about terrorism and responses to terrorism is one of the toughest communications challenges facing responsible opinion leaders today. In recent years, as the extent of this challenge became more evident, communicators have worked hard to develop messages about terrorism that might help listeners avoid some of the cognitive and psychological traps set by fear, opening the door to public consideration of alternative policy approaches. Which strategies for talking about terrorism with the mainstream American public are most likely to achieve this goal? Summarized below is a unique qualitative research effort that was commissioned by U.S. in the World and carried out by the Topos Partnership.[24]

Testing Themes and Frames

In the spring and summer of 2009, U.S. in the World and members of its network of issue experts and advocates collected and cataloged some of the core ideas that opinion leaders have been using to try to calm public fears and introduce arguments about the need for more farsighted approaches to security and counterterrorism. These were among the ideas in circulation:

• Terrorism is not really the existential threat it has been made out to be.
• Responses to terrorism should be consistent with America's values.
• Our counterterrorism policies have to be smarter and more effective.
• We should consider the long-range consequences of our decisions.
• We must not let ourselves be guided by fear.
• We need to beware of politicians who manipulate our fears for their own purposes.
• Our national history proves we are strong enough to withstand the terrorist threat.

The Topos Partnership then designed a qualitative test of these and other core ideas, seeking to gauge their effect on people's thinking about terrorism-related policy choices. The core ideas were embodied in paragraph-length "narratives," all of which were presented to the research subjects as statements made by public officials on the seventh anniversary of the 9/11 attacks. Participants were also instructed to think back to that frightening day in order to create an even more challenging context for the messages. After hearing or reading the statement, participants were asked questions about their understanding of the main point, what they could remember about it, whether they agreed, who they thought would make such a statement, and why.[25]

The purpose of the testing was not to develop specific messaging recommendations or talking points but rather to determine which big themes and ideas—which cognitive frames (a frame is a central organizing idea for making sense of events or information)—might help reduce public fear, stimulate different thinking about security options, and be memorable and repeatable enough to hold up under the stress of a fear-inducing event.

The findings were sobering, though there were also some promising results.

Overall Observations The research confirmed many of the communications challenges identified in the first section of this chapter. Findings showed that safety concerns consistently trumped moral principles, even among respondents who agreed about the importance of America's values. The "emergency" frame consistently trumped efforts to encourage attention to the long-term consequences of our decisions. With 9/11 as the explicit context, messages that seemed to minimize the danger of terrorism or that focused on the relatively small risk of dying in a terrorist attack were dismissed by many as off-target and unrealistic. And as would be expected, fear and safety concerns made it difficult for people to hold on to fine conceptual distinctions, such as between terrorists and suspected terrorists. Instead, simple contrasts between good/bad and us/them prevailed.

The testing also highlighted some additional and important challenges for communicators:

- People desire *action* against threats. Narratives that seemed to take options off the table without offering clear alternatives that address people's security concerns were heard—and rejected—as counseling inaction. Communicators must provide clear signals about ways in which we can and should act.
- Appeals to history and tradition ran up against the belief that the current moment is unique and urgent. People questioned the relevance of lessons from the past, especially if that was the primary thrust of the message. Messages should sound immediately relevant and should not rely too heavily on appeals to history or tradition.
- Narratives about being smart and effective were appealing, but they did little to change people's thinking. Being "smart" was

taken to mean whatever people already believed about how to fight terrorism. Many interpreted the message as support for being tough and aggressive, for example. Or they heard the message as support for "smarter bombing," "smarter use of torture," or "smarter use of surveillance technology"—not as an argument for rethinking the overall approach to counterterrorism. The researchers concluded that communicators must be wary of messages that contain the slightest ambiguity about what kind of approach to counterterrorism is best.

False Leads This last observation points to a cross-cutting challenge affecting many of the messages about terrorism: Apparent agreement with a message does not mean that all its inferences are taken to heart. People can accept and even repeat many propositions, but the effects on thinking may not be significant.

For example, respondents greeted messages about the importance of America's values with enthusiasm and could easily repeat them, but most would immediately assert that we do not have the luxury of respecting our values in the current emergency situation. People responded well to messages that tried to redirect fear into anger or scorn for terrorists (such as, "Let's tell the terrorists to go to hell by living as we've always lived and preserving our values"), but the anger was easily channeled away from its basis in "not forgetting who we are" to support for "tougher" treatment of terrorist suspects (including treatment that is not consistent with our values). Messages about not letting ourselves be manipulated by fearmongering politicians also engaged respondents, but they tended to default to the belief that all politicians are manipulative and that nobody in government can be trusted.

Messages about "being stronger than the terrorists are" were heard as efforts to "buck people up"—an appropriate thing for leaders to try to do but not relevant to the problem of taking action against terrorism. Told that "we shouldn't give terrorists what they want—they want us to be fearful and to abandon our values," people agreed that Americans should not be fearful, but this formulation did not prevent listeners from suspecting that they were being asked to put principles over their safety, a tradeoff they consistently rejected.

Finally, because the public is already familiar with the broad outlines of the debate about "rights" and "security," many relevant ideas no longer have much power to change how people think about terrorism and counterterrorism. Familiarity leads many people to stop paying attention to the substance of arguments—concluding, "Oh, I know what this is about"—especially because people have also become very attuned to the ideological orientation of narratives. People are quick to identify certain narratives as "Democratic" or "Republican" and to dismiss such messages as partisan.

Emotional Management Is Not Enough

Another important observation to emerge from this qualitative research is that managing fear is not enough, by itself, to promote a more constructive conversation about terrorism. Messages that calmed or seemed to have the potential to calm fears did not automatically change thinking about policy choices. The gap between the individual/personal perspective on this issue and the collective/national perspective seems to be very difficult to bridge.

Fear, by its nature, is experienced at the level of individual feelings and decisions, and people were inclined to stay at that level. Messages about not falling prey to fear were typically taken to refer to individuals' own feelings, not to collective policy decisions. Reduced to a "Churchillian exhortation" (as the researchers put it) about mastering our own personal fears, such a message ends up being quite compatible with all sorts of policy approaches. Calming fear is probably a necessary but insufficient precondition for constructive public conversation about counterterrorism policy.

Green Shoots?

Two narratives showed some promise for doing both—calming fears and promoting new thinking about policy directions.

Overreaction Hurts Us The most helpful frame tested was the idea that "when we overreact to terrorism, we hurt ourselves." The idea that overreaction hurts us is simple and user-friendly. It works at both the individual and collective levels. As suggested at the beginning of this chapter, almost everyone understands the risk of overreacting to stress in a counterproductive way—yet people also had little difficulty applying the idea to policy reactions, such as abuses of government power, excessive use of military force, not working closely with allies, or losing our identity/values.

The message seems to calm fears without sounding as if it counsels inaction (though we will return shortly to the question of which actions this message does support). It is fresh enough to stimulate people intellectually (i.e., it is not the typical framework for talking about responses to terrorism), and it connects the dots clearly (i.e., it does not just warn against overreacting but explains that "we mustn't overreact because then we make mistakes in judgment that harm us").

Respondents did not tend to default immediately to existing beliefs but rather engaged with the message at some length. In other words, one might argue, this narrative seems to have the power to activate a listener's critical faculties—the cognitive part of the brain whose activation may help suppress the fear system—in ways that other narratives did not. Respondents' reactions suggested that this narrative might even help inoculate people against efforts at fearmongering.

Self-Aggrandizing Terrorist. One weakness of the very promising "overreaction" narrative is that it may not be emotionally engaging enough to satisfy in a crisis since it is about dampening emotions and actions. Another tested narrative seemed to have an effect on thinking but also seemed to be emotionally engaging. This narrative asserted that terrorists are common criminals who want to be treated as something more—as supervillains or martyrs—and we should not accommodate them (by creating special rules or courts for them, by putting aside our values, by reorienting our foreign policies, etc.).

The notion here is not just that terrorism should be treated as a law enforcement matter (a now-familiar concept that has little effect) but that we should treat terrorism as a law enforcement matter because self-aggrandizing terrorists want us to treat it otherwise. This new element appears to be emotionally and intellectually engaging; it does not downplay the idea of maintaining security, and it even provides for retribution of a sort.

The "self-aggrandizing terrorists" frame has some real weaknesses, though, including the fact that the anger it attempts to channel turns out to be compatible with support for policies that may be counterproductive. Also, the concept may not hold up in the aftermath of a major terrorist act that feels more like an act of "war" than a "crime."

Finally, this frame fails to take account of the probable need in some instances for counterterrorism activities that fall outside the domain of law enforcement. On balance, the weaknesses of this narrative are problematic enough that Topos urges caution about using it on its own or without careful attention to context.

Developing a Successful Message

A better understanding of how fear affects public thinking and a hard look at the limitations of some messages are making clearer the kinds of messages that can manage the fear factor effectively.

A successful message will be "easy to think," in the words of the Topos Partnership; it will allow for consideration of action against terrorism; it will be concrete rather than abstract; it will connect the dots and suggest a bigger picture in some simple, accessible way. More specifically, it will perform both at the level of "emotional management" (calming fear, dampening the tendency to precipitate action, reducing submissiveness to authority) *and* at the level of reasoning about policy (encouraging people to think about the bigger picture/longer-term consequences, promoting clearer thinking). Finally, an effective message will point to a *better* response to terrorism, not simply negate unhelpful responses that are nonetheless consistent with people's instinctive reactions and perceptions.

Additional research to refine promising messages should certainly be done. But advocates, issue experts, scholars, and policy advisers who want to promote new thinking about counterterrorism also need to do some work of their own, informed by messaging research. While policy analysts have written extensively about the nature of the terrorism threat and appropriate responses to it, there is not yet a simple, positive narrative that can compete effectively with the logic of prevailing narratives like "doing whatever is necessary to capture or kill terrorists." Until concerned opinion leaders have developed and built consensus around a clear, commonsense message about what exactly Americans and their government *should* do, think, and feel about terrorism, even the most effective explanations of why some responses to terrorism are counterproductive will not significantly change public thinking in times of fear.

During the weeks and months immediately after 9/11, opinion surveys showed that the American public—despite its sorrow, fear, and anger—wanted the government to take time before reacting in order to build international support and make the right strategic choice.[26] It seems that the popular wisdom about strong emotions mentioned at the beginning of this chapter actually guided public thinking in those early days.

Yet in the years since then, public fears have often been channeled in harmful directions, and today the public remains divided and uncertain about some of the most important issues related to counter-terrorism policy. Focus group research suggests that even citizens who question aspects of America's response to terrorism find it difficult to articulate their logic or defend their point of view when confronted with fear-based arguments.[27]

Communicating strategically about terrorism, like any effort to change the public conversation about a major policy issue, is both a messaging challenge and a substantive challenge, and the two are interconnected. There are important lessons to be learned and built on from the messaging research described in this chapter. But if influential communicators are to reframe the debate about terrorism, they must also do a more compelling and accessible job of describing what an alternative counterterrorism agenda looks like and how it works to keep us safe. In other words, they must provide their own clear answer to a critical question: What do we do after we "count to 10"?

12. Communicating about Threat: Toward a Resilient Response to Terrorism[1]

William J. Burns

The threat of terrorism has loomed large in our public discourse since the events of September 11, 2001. These events, and particularly the conclusions we have drawn from them, have profoundly influenced the way we think about the risks our nation and communities face. We have added to our vernacular terms like "anthrax," "suitcase nukes," "dirty bombs," and "homeland security." Threats in the Middle East, perceived by a fearful and angry public, took us to war with far-reaching consequences few could have imagined.

Arguably, terrorism is not our largest challenge, but it is a threat likely to bring out the best and worst in our nature. Following our present course, we will continue to allow fear and anger to permeate our national debates and unduly influence our judgment. We will amplify some risks at the expense of doing little about others. Along the way, we may squander adversity, allowing it to teach us precious little of what could make us stronger as individuals and as a country.

Fortunately, our nation can embrace another course, one in which we accept the lessons adversity teaches with calm, compassionate deliberation. By understanding fear, we can temper it, and, ideally, overcome it. Research shows that perception of fear is affected by several factors, including the characteristics of the fear-inspiring event, cultural influences, and the diffusion of information in society. Fear causes individuals and society as a whole to ignore probabilities and to indulge costs going beyond what is appropriate or necessary.

This information points to a number of responses. Effective risk communication and other methods can foster resilience and confidence. Public discourse about terrorism should better reflect the known facts, and political leaders should engage citizens in a sustained, factual dialogue about terrorism in which they are participants rather than objects of protection. Effective communications about terrorism will provide the kind of information that empowers individuals, institutions, and communities to make better risk decisions. Research on risk communications has begun to reveal how this can be done. More research is needed to discover what communications to what communities will elicit resilience, fend off fear, and equip society to resist terrorism.

Terrorism: A "New Species of Trouble"?

Terrorism is designed to make a community feel afraid and uncertain; it is about heightened vulnerability. It seeks to disrupt society with fear and dispel any sense of safety.[2] Long term, terrorism seeks to exact costs that go far beyond immediate victims or damaged property and into the social and political fabric. The danger people perceive may far exceed any reasonable statistical risk of being harmed, but feeling vulnerable, people may consider high expenditures and important personal freedoms a fair trade for the perception of personal security.

Terrorism differs from other types of disasters in two fundamental ways. First, terrorism is a product of intentionality and malevolence. Second, terrorism allows no natural closure, no way to sound the all clear. The sense of alarm persists much longer than in other types of disasters regardless of their scale.

These differences have prompted some authors to refer to terrorism as a "new species of trouble."[3] Responding to this challenge will require insight, resolve, and cooperation among diverse groups with unique perspectives. Learning to communicate about the risk of terrorism requires that we first examine its currency, fear.

Fear: Event Characteristics

Terrorism inspires fear because of its unique ability to evoke uncertainty and highlight people's perception that they lack control over their own safety.[4] The characteristics of a terror event contribute to this uncertainty and lack of perceived control.

In 2004 and 2006, my colleague Paul Slovic and I (psychologist and decision analyst, respectively, at Decision Research, an academic research institute focusing on judgment and decisionmaking) sought to understand the relative importance people placed on event characteristics in determining their perceptions of risk and their response.[5] We created hypothetical scenarios that systematically varied a number of factors past research had identified as salient. Specifically, we focused on the presence of terrorism, mechanism of harm, intent or motive behind the event, negligence in managing risk, and type of victim. Students from a university in southern California were recruited to evaluate 16 paragraph-long vignettes. These students were business majors, many had families, almost all had jobs, and were on average about 23 years old. The setting for these events was a local theme park to increase the relevance for participants. After reading all 16 scenarios, we asked the students questions pertaining to their perceived risk and risk-related behaviors for each vignette. These rating-style questions were followed by open-ended questions that attempted to understand what might be driving their ratings of the scenarios.

The vignettes varied in the following way. Half the scenarios involved acts of terrorism depicting either an anthrax release or a bomb blast. The other half portrayed the spread of a virulent flu outbreak or a propane tank explosion. Statements such as "to instill fear in the hearts of Americans" versus "to negotiate the release of prisoners" were included to contrast terrorists' motives. Nonterrorist events were described as either criminal or accidental. Criminal motive was depicted by the suggestion that "foul play could not be ruled out" followed by a very brief description of suspicious activities. We were also interested in the potential threat of terrorist suicide missions, and so four of the terrorist vignettes involved acts of suicide. To examine negligence, four of the nonterrorist vignettes involved a possible failure to take precautions (security or otherwise) to prevent the spread of the flu or the explosion of a propane tank. In addition, half the scenarios depicted tourists as the victims, while the other half portrayed government officials as the victims. We also varied the number of victims killed (0, 15, 495).

We examined the relationship between each of the factors with perceived risk and a number of risk-related behaviors (e.g., following media coverage of the event, avoiding public places, leaving the city). We found that terrorism loomed large in people's perceptions and was easily the most important predictor of perceived risk. This finding was based on a statistical investigation of the data and on the open-ended comments people gave about the characteristics of the events that caused them particular concern. Using these two criteria, we also found that concern with the mechanism involved (infectious disease more than explosions), intentionality (criminal motive in the case of nonterrorism), and possible failure to take precautions to prevent an intentional or accidental mishap were important predictors. We have found in prior work that perceived negligence sets the stage for blame and even outrage.[6] The victim was also important. Harm to civilians appeared more threatening than harm to government officials. These scenarios took place in a local theme park, and so for some respondents, the realization that children could also have been at risk greatly heightened their sense of concern. Acts of suicide and promises "to instill fear in the hearts of Americans" heightened the perceived risk of terrorism as well. What did not loom large in people's minds was the death toll. Surprisingly, the number of fatalities contributed little to people's perception of risk.

We extended these studies in 2007 and 2008 to include scenarios involving earthquakes and cyberattacks. We depicted earthquakes as harming twice as many people as the anthrax attacks. The cyberattacks physically harmed no one. As before, casualties were not the deciding difference in response. The earthquakes inspired far less perceived risk and fear than the anthrax attacks. Likewise, the cyberattacks caused significantly more perceived risk than the earthquakes (equal to the anthrax scenarios) though less fear.

When asked what factors contributed to their perceptions of risk, respondents pointed to malicious intent, effects that were difficult to understand or control, and lack of competence by those in charge. We concluded that terrorism presents a particular policy challenge because the public finds it difficult to know what to do to obtain closure following these kinds of threats.

Fear: Cultural Influences

Cultural factors also influence public response. These factors shape behaviors toward hazards and emotionally charged issues. Cultural influences predispose people to interpret risk communication messages differently as well.

Mary Douglas, an anthropologist, and Aaron Wildavsky, a political scientist, were major contributors to the cultural theory of risk.[7] They postulated that people's behaviors toward different threats could be explained largely by where individuals were positioned on two cultural dimensions. The first dimension they termed "group" to describe the degree to which people feel affinity with, and bound by their association with, meaningful social groups. The second dimension they termed "grid" to describe the tendency for individuals to value rules, laws, and traditions.

The intersection of these core beliefs produced four cultural types. Hierarchists (high group, high grid) value both the welfare of the group and lines of authority and social stability. They tend to trust experts and the technologies experts sanction. Egalitarians (high group, low grid) also value the welfare of the group, but they prize equality and fear the concentration of power. They tend to distrust experts and desire the management of technologies to be open to public scrutiny. Individualists (low group, low grid), on the other hand, do not necessarily gravitate toward social groups and prefer as few rules and regulations as necessary. These are the libertarians. They distrust regulatory constraints on their ability to chart their own way and, like egalitarians, prefer the management of technologies to be open to public debate. Fatalists (low group, high grid) feel little affinity with any group but acknowledge the presence of a well-defined social and political hierarchy. Unlike the other three groups they feel disempowered and are unlikely to have their voice heard.

Using this cultural typology, Kerry Herron and Hank Jenkins-Smith, both professors in public policy at Texas A&M University, conducted surveys in 1993 and 1995 that investigated public perceptions of U. S. policies surrounding nuclear weapons.[8] They found that hierarchists and individualists rated the benefits of possessing nuclear weapons significantly higher and rated the risks significantly lower than did egalitarians. Likewise, egalitarians had a significantly higher belief that it was feasible to ban all nuclear weapons in the next 25 years than did either hierarchists or individualists.

Dan Kahan, a law professor at Yale University, and his associates conducted field experiments to better understand these cultural differences and how they might influence the way people receive risk communication messages.[9] Unlike Herron and Jenkins-Smith, they examined the influence of the group and grid dimensions individually. They found that people scoring higher on the grid dimension (valuing rules and regulations) or scoring lower on the group dimension (preferring autonomy) had lower perceived risk with respect to global warming and gun ownership. Regarding national security, higher-grid respondents tended to reject the notion that the Iraq War had increased the threat of terrorism and also showed higher support for the war. Lower-group respondents showed equal concern for terrorism but did not support policies that might afford greater power to government or allow infringement on privacy.

Perhaps most striking were their findings that people gave markedly more credit to the risk information provided them if they either agreed with the proposed solution or felt a cultural affinity with the source. Current differences over the seriousness of the terrorist threat may have more to do with the proposed solutions offered by different camps than by expert assessments of probabilities. Those findings suggest that it may be possible to frame risk dialogue in a way that does not trigger cultural resistance to the message. For example, discussing international terrorism as a worldwide police action rather than a "war on terrorism" may be more attractive to egalitarians and individualists. Understanding cultural differences is central to guiding public response to crises, and it suggests using different communications strategies for dealing with different groups.

Fear: Amplification vs. Resilience

When a disaster occurs, communities react immediately, and news flows rapidly through the media and by word of mouth. Social scientists have observed that certain institutions (e.g., media) and groups (e.g., political action) amplify certain types of risks. Seeking to explain this phenomenon, Roger Kasperson, a geographer who has extensively studied how people respond to hazards, worked with colleagues at Clark University and Decision Research to postulate the concept of the social amplification of risk. This conceptual framework predicts that adverse events like terrorism will interact with psychological, social, institutional, and cultural processes in ways that may amplify community response to the mishap.[10] This amplification may cause the impact of the event to extend far beyond the direct damage to victims, property, or environment and may result in immense indirect consequences.[11]

Figure 12.1 depicts both the process of amplification and the process of coping with a disaster. A terrorist attack is likely to inflict immediate costs to a community in the form of casualties, property damage, and first response. The media, the public, and institutions will respond to these immediate consequences, and the public will in turn assess the level of threat. For most people, uncertainty and perceived lack of control will be high, and many will experience emotions like fear.

Figure 12.1
THE SOCIAL AMPLIFICATION OF RISK AND POLICY RESILIENCE

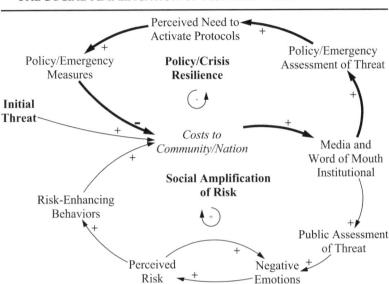

Fear increases perceived risk, which may lead to risk-enhancing behaviors (e.g., failing to shelter in place, refusing to get vaccinated, choosing to drive rather than fly, withdrawing large amounts of cash from the bank). Often people engage in risk-enhancing behaviors to increase their sense of control during a crisis.[12] Maintaining or restoring the perception of control is an important way to head off risk-enhancing behaviors.

In crisis situations, people may have limited information, preventing them from appreciating how they may be placing themselves and others at increased risk. For example, if a dirty bomb were to explode in a large city, under most circumstances, everyone would be better protected by staying indoors. It is not hard to imagine, though, that many people would disobey instructions to shelter in place. Some would leave to find their children or other family members, others to escape from what they believe is significant exposure to radiation. The increased traffic congestion caused by people

237

declining to shelter in place could pose a life-threatening risk to trauma victims needing emergency care. In the aftermath, people might not return to areas they thought were exposed to radioactive materials despite assurances from experts that these areas were safe. Avoiding these areas would magnify economic losses and inflict further damage on the community.

Fortunately, casualties, heightened fear, and economic hardship also prompt communities to respond in ways that offset this amplifying cycle. Communities that are well prepared have policies and protocols in place to activate emergency measures. Local authorities and first responders address the immediate needs for medical attention, food, and shelter. Equally important, social agencies, faith-based organizations, and friends offer emotional support and reassurance. These measures begin to restore control, both actual and perceived, among community members, which facilitates recovery. The speed with which a community returns to normal depends on the relative strength of each loop. Communities can affect this balance through preparation and risk communication.

Paul Slovic and I have simulated the diffusion of fear in a community following different types of disasters, including terrorist attacks.[13] Based on surveys and simulations, we predict that fear will be much more pronounced following a terrorist attack than for technological accidents and natural disasters. These simulations indicate that fear escalates rapidly, while anxiety, perceptions of risk, and stress decrease much more slowly. Our findings suggest that once generated, fear and other disquieting emotions take time to abate, possessing their own form of psychological inertia. Surveys following the 9/11 attacks support these findings.

Three other sources corroborate our modeling conclusions. First, Fynnwin Prager, a policy studies graduate student at the University of Southern California, and his colleagues at CREATE, the Center for Risk and Economic Analysis of Terrorism Events, investigated public response to the July 2005 London subway bombings.[14] They compared actual subway ridership with econometric predictions of ridership had there not been a terrorist attack. Consistent with our simulations, they also found a rapid decline in ridership followed by a slow return to the subway after several months, even though all stations were fully operational within a few weeks. This reluctance to take the subway is particularly interesting in that other modes of transportation in London are either very expensive or inconvenient. According to Prager, ridership decreased by 47 million from what it should have been during the months from July to December 2005.

Second, from June 2008 until November 2009, the VIX index, often referred to as a measure of investor fear, showed that the same pattern of emotional response played out among the investment community following the dire warnings of a potential financial meltdown in September 2008.[15] Beginning with the collapse of Lehman Brothers, investor fears rose rapidly to unprecedented heights. In fact, index levels were almost double what they were the week following the 9/11 attacks. It would take almost nine months for the index to return to pre-crisis levels.

Third, Paul Slovic, Ellen Peters (also a psychologist at Decision Research), and I launched an online study of the public's response to the financial crisis on September 29, 2008—coincidently, the day on which the Dow would experience its largest point drop in history.[16] We surveyed a national panel of several hundred people seven times over the following year. Questions covered perceived risk (job, savings, investments, retirement, Wall Street, global warming, terrorism), emotions (fear, anger, worry, anxiety, sadness), trust (president, Congress, treasury secretary, business leaders), and behaviors (changes in investments, reduction in spending, postponement of doctor or dental appointments, acts of community service, and so forth). What we have found so far is that perceived financial risk (e.g., retirement) on average was very high in fall 2008. It dropped momentarily after the election and then rebounded to pre-election levels. There were also large differences across individuals indicating that not everyone was reacting to the crisis in the same way. The same was true of people's negative emotions. Anger was especially high and directed toward those they believed responsible, Wall Street and the nation's political leaders. As expected, perceived risk was positively correlated with people's fear. Trust for the president was moderate and remained so (with a small decline in later months). Trust for Congress and especially business leaders continues to be extremely low. Further, trust was negatively correlated with perceived risk, fear, and anger.

The results echo points just raised regarding the important role of trust and policy. Our findings regarding the relationships among anger, fear, and trust in the midst of this crisis underscore how important it is to appear competent and trustworthy. For the first several months of our study, there was little encouraging economic news. Even so, people's perceived risk (except job risk) and negative emotions have declined steadily, indicating that many Americans are adjusting. This finding suggests a form of resilience in the face of ongoing challenges that may prove important during other types of crises. Well into our study, our national panel was still not inclined to spend. Those with the highest perceived risk continued to postpone larger purchases and even to put off going to see their doctor. Throughout, concerns about finances completely trumped worries about terrorism. These studies regarding the London bombings, investors' fears, and most recently public response to the financial crisis lend support to our contention that perceived risk and fear rise very quickly but decline much more slowly.

In addition to tracking fear, we used our simulation model to vary the speed with which a community was able to reduce fear to targeted levels (e.g., not more than 10 percent of community members in a state of fear) following different crisis scenarios. We found that rapid intervention to quell fear (within three days in our model) reduced the level of adverse reaction in a community and hastened a return to normalcy. A swift intervention naturally requires immediate and effective restoration of safety and basic services. First responders are well positioned to do this. However, the American Red Cross and other emergency organizations have warned, and experience has shown, that for many large-scale disasters, citizens may be on their own for several days. Delays of this kind serve to heighten uncertainty and perceptions of lack of control. Community leaders who have established trust and who are skilled in the use of social media (e.g., Internet networking channels, cell phones), crisis communications that have been pretested, and well-informed citizens throughout neighborhoods of every demographic can speed such intervention. We believe that efforts made by well-coordinated community groups to reduce uncertainty and restore a sense of perceived control may help mitigate negative reactions. Effective intervention is pivotal because, while media coverage and casual conversation may turn to other issues, residual feelings linger and may influence risk perceptions and behaviors far into the future. These observations should give pause to politicians who would use fear to further their own agenda to the long-term detriment of the public good.

Fear: Ignoring Probabilities

Terrorist attacks are, of course, staged to gain widespread media attention. Following an attack, vivid and memorable images produce very negative emotions, causing people to overreact to events posing vanishingly small probabilities of future harm.[17] Public attention is largely riveted on the consequences of potential attacks and not on the likelihood of their ability to inflict future injury. This phenomenon is so pronounced that researchers have come to refer to it as "probability neglect."[18]

Ignoring probabilities does not lead to better decisionmaking. Risk analysts and policymakers who pay attention to probabilities find that public demand for protection does not match up with informed and careful assessments of risk. John Mueller, a political scientist at Ohio State University, colorfully and comprehensively describes the nation's tendency to exaggerate the risk of low-probability, high-consequence events in his book *Overblown*.[19] He examines a number of threats posed by terrorism and discusses their associated security costs. He concludes that these investments in security have not been well placed.

Mueller acknowledges that the public is genuinely concerned about terrorism. He cites national polls that indicate that even five years after the events of 9/11, more than 40 percent of the public worry that a member of their family will be a victim of a terrorist attack. Of course, this level of concern is not even remotely close to expert assessment of the likelihood of such an occurrence.

Why does the public neglect probabilities and instead worry about dire events that almost certainly will not happen? People do so because such threats command attention, and because it is much easier to imagine vivid consequences than to think hard about likelihoods. According to Mueller, the salience of threat information is fueled by politicians, bureaucrats, media, and risk entrepreneurs who stand to benefit from public alarm. Cass Sunstein, a law professor at Harvard University and now head of the Office of Information and Regulatory Affairs in the White House, suggests that the most practical solution might be to encourage the public to focus on other matters rather than to convince it that the probabilities of these threats are exceedingly small.[20]

Fear: Costs

Fear does serve a useful function when it causes us to flee from danger or exercise caution in our actions—nature has its own wisdom here. However, President Franklin D. Roosevelt understood fear's darker side, and he noted it famously in his first inaugural address:

> This is preeminently the time to speak the truth, the whole truth, frankly and boldly. Nor need we shrink from honestly facing conditions in our country today. This great nation will endure as it has endured, will revive and will prosper. So, first of all, let me assert my firm belief that the only thing we have to fear is fear itself—nameless, unreasoning, unjustified terror which paralyzes needed efforts to convert retreat into advance.[21]

The phrase "unreasoning, unjustified terror which paralyzes needed efforts" is key. Unreasoning fear may exact a high cost to our state of mind, civil liberties, and economy.

Surveys at the time indicated that many continued to be fearful and highly stressed for months following the events of 9/11.[22] Researchers also found a connection between heightened sense of threat and willingness to restrict civil liberties in the aftermath of these tragic events.[23] In 2001, Kerry Herron and Hank Jenkins-Smith found that almost 50 percent of Americans they polled strongly agreed that government must stop terrorism even if it intruded on some people's rights and privacy; in 2003, this number was still substantial at 30 percent.[24] Ben Sheppard, a policy analyst at the Institute for Alternative Futures, cataloged a number of political outcomes following the 9/11 attacks (e.g., new powers of detention and surveillance given to the executive branch and law enforcement agencies, decreased distinction between collecting intelligence and gathering evidence for a criminal proceeding, and tripling of the number of Border Patrol agents).[25]

And there are economic costs associated with being afraid. Consider what happened to the airline industry. One econometric study concluded that fear accounted for as much as a 30 percent demand shock to the industry.[26] Peter Gordon, an economist at the University of Southern California, and his associates, using input-output modeling, found similar impacts to the airline industry attributable to the 9/11 attacks.[27] Adam Rose, at the University of Southern California and also an economist at CREATE, has developed a computable general equilibrium modeling framework for estimating the total economic impacts for both natural disasters and terrorist attacks. He has concluded that, in addition to estimating the direct damages from these kinds of events, assessing the additional impact from emotional and behavioral factors was also very important.[28]

James Giesecke, an economist at Monash University, colleagues of mine at CREATE, and I used computable general equilibrium modeling to compute the economic impact of a dirty-bomb detonation in the financial district of Los Angeles.[29] The scenario was patterned after a dirty-bomb scenario depicted among the U. S. Department of Homeland Security's National Planning Scenarios in which 180 people die and 270 are seriously injured.[30] Property damage was assumed to be negligible. The area was a six-by-six-block section of the downtown sector. Our simulation separated economic impacts due to direct resource losses (i.e., casualties, property damage, and business interruption) from those that were primarily behavioral in nature (i.e., reduced consumption due to perceived contamination, demands for increased wages to work near the financial district, and increased investor premiums to do business in the downtown area). In the short run (less than a year), the largest economic losses resulted from a potential 30-day business shutdown of the financial district. This shutdown amounted to a reduction of $1.87 billion economic output for the city of Los Angeles. In the long run, risk-related behaviors dominated and represented a $3.01 billion loss for a typical year thereafter. Investigating a seven-year time horizon and assuming a linear decay of perceived risk and fear, we concluded that such an event would cost the city of Los Angeles approximately $10.67 billion. Recall that we assumed the attack produced little property damage and that the downtown reopened after 30 days. To understand the contribution of risk perception to economic losses, we compared direct resource and behavioral impacts. The ratio of behavioral impacts to direct resource impacts turned out to be 5.71. That is, for every dollar likely to be lost due to casualties or initial forgone business, almost six dollars would be lost because of investor and public reaction.

Business interruption costs can be mitigated to some extent by rapid intervention and coordinated efforts among community agencies. The short-run challenge is balancing the need to get businesses open again (or relocated) against safety concerns. These tradeoffs can and should be thought about in advance. We calculated that shutting down the financial district would cost the city of Los Angeles $62 million per day. The next immediate challenge is restoring investor and consumer confidence as quickly as possible. Decreasing perceived risk and fear is best accomplished by building trust and by developing risk communication before such a crisis.

Fear: Implications for Policy

The goal of risk communication is to help foster good risk decisions, especially in the face of extreme threat. Natural disasters, technological accidents, terrorism, and economic crises vie for public attention. What these threats have in common is that they all make people feel vulnerable. When faced with crisis, people frequently feel uncertain about what the event signals for the future and how they might cope with its consequences.

Terrorism, of course, seeks to exploit this tendency, hoping to cause governments to overreact in response to public fear or anger. The problem is not that the public will panic or emotionally fall apart after an event like a terrorist strike.[31] Rather, prolonged focus on the consequences of a potential threat such as a terrorist attack produces three behaviors. First, people tend to ignore the probability of the calamity occurring and as a result overweight the event's importance.[32] Second, they often fail to consider the costs of responses to this threat.[33] Third, they tend to become so distracted by their concerns with emotionally charged threats that they ignore other important matters.[34]

As an illustration, consider public support for the U. S. invasion of Iraq. Following the events of 9/11, fear, anger, and the public's focus on terrorism and weapons of mass destruction made it much easier for the Bush administration to sell the war.[35] Paying little regard to plausibility, many Americans saw the prospect that terrorists could detonate a nuke in an American city as almost inevitable without immediate and drastic action. They gave short shrift to what the nation would pay to go to war. Saying that ignoring these tradeoffs and critical uncertainties proved costly is an understatement.[36]

One of al Qaeda's primary objectives has been to severely damage the U. S. economy. Even with the economic ripple effects following the 9/11 attacks, al Qaeda was unable to achieve this goal. Yet by fall 2008, America was at the brink of economic collapse, not because of a terrorist attack but because of the nation's neglect and inability to regulate crucial financial markets. America spent the years following 9/11 focused almost exclusively on the emotionally charged threat of global terrorism. In retrospect, it is clear that much more attention should have been given to the less dramatic but more consequential mortgage and security markets.

As the example illustrates, neglecting probabilities and tradeoffs fosters policies that may not be in the long-term best interests of the country. It is crucial to understand the science behind the public response to threats like terrorism and to outline, then implement, effective risk communication at both the national and community levels.

Communicating about Threat

Americans can choose a different and more resilient way of responding to protracted threats like terrorism. Shifting public response will require better-articulated policy tradeoffs and a deeper understanding of the connection between policy choices and their long-term consequences; better-calibrated risk communications; and particularly more focus on attitudes and behaviors that foster a meaningful sense of control. Talking about risks in a way that promotes understanding and that dispels fear is critical to resilient response.

Dialogue about Policy Tradeoffs

Paul Slovic, colleagues of ours from CREATE, and I have attempted to understand why perceptions of terrorism are so resistant to change. Our ongoing discussions often return to the following questions: Where on the national stage has there been a discussion of the larger patterns of terrorism worldwide that would help us put events in perspective? It has been several years; do most people now have a good understanding of the deeper causes behind international terrorism? Are Americans positioned to make informed choices as to which policies they might support to increase their security now and long term? Most importantly, have these tragic events caused people to look carefully at prevailing beliefs, values, and assumptions and consider their effect on world affairs? From our perspective, the answer continues to be largely no to all four queries. This observation should be cause for concern. John Sterman and Peter Senge, both experts in system dynamics at the Massachusetts Institute of Technology, observe that it is extremely difficult to anticipate the long-term outcomes of policy without careful research that particularly examines prevailing mental models (beliefs, values, and decision rules).[37] Without meaningful public discourse and scientific investigation, important policy decisions are likely to have unintended consequences such as have been experienced in the Middle East.

There are no easy technological, economic, or military fixes for the challenges that face the United States and Western society; the years ahead will require substantial insight and fortitude and may involve significant turmoil. If we want to fear less, the explanations we entertain about world events should be grounded in science and squared with our highest values.

How individuals understand and explain the underlying causes of terrorism may dictate their responses to terrorist threats. In his pioneering work on learned helplessness and learned optimism, Martin Seligman, a psychologist at the University of Pennsylvania, has studied how people explain the causes of adversity to themselves.[38] He finds that people who see the causes behind present difficulties as temporary and the effects of such difficulties as not catastrophic are more hopeful, less anxious, and more likely to persevere. They are, simply put, more resilient.

To foster this resilience, terrorism policy and dialogue should focus more on sound information and less on perpetuating the notion that we can prevent all or most forms of risk, including terrorism. The public can be trusted with the truth. A useful model is the way a skillful physician communicates about a potential medical problem with a patient. The doctor neither hides nor hypes the risks involved. Instead, he or she first discusses the problem with the patient, seeking to identify areas of concern and gaps in understanding (decreasing uncertainty). This is typically followed by a discussion of possible options and corresponding tradeoffs (increasing actual and perceived control). Coming to grips with decision tradeoffs is important because seeking to feel unduly safe in one area may materially restrict our opportunity to pursue goals we value individually and as a nation. Bruce Schneier, a leading systems analyst, reminds us that we need to be very mindful of the tradeoffs we make in our security decisions.[39] Risk and policy analysts, working closely with behavioral scientists, have much to contribute to this dialogue.

Unreasonable expectations about safety may serve to stifle dialogue about important tradeoffs across the many security, health, and environmental risks that exist. No nation or community has unlimited funds with which to drive these risks to near zero. Instead, these threats must be studied and prioritized. Policymakers should allocate resources in a judicious manner that best reflects national and community values. Whatever risk that remains must be faced with understanding and calm. Identifying gaps in public knowledge about certain risks will help, and factual information should be used to guide risk messaging. Scientists and policymakers must work together toward this end.

Better-Calibrated Risk Communications

Gaining a broad perspective on terrorism would reassure and calm the public, but resilience would also benefit greatly from targeted and well-crafted risk communications. For this we need a careful and fine-tuned discussion of the different aspects of terrorist threats. This discussion must involve a collaborative dialogue with both experts and the public.

Baruch Fischhoff, a psychologist at Carnegie Mellon University, and his colleagues have sought to facilitate such collaboration with an approach that is both applied and grounded in risk and behavioral science.[40] When communicating about a certain risk, they suggest that experts be consulted first to develop a representation that captures all important aspects of the particular risk. Using this model as a guide, researchers should interview and survey the public to determine their understanding of the risk. Risk communication would then go toward filling gaps in public understanding. Messages should be subjected to careful testing before being distributed to a wide audience.

They have applied this approach to a number of case studies, including climate change, power-frequency fields, radon in homes, and HIV/AIDS. For example, in the case of radon, these researchers conducted extensive interviews and surveys to determine laypeople's understanding of what radon is, where it comes from, what its dangers are, and how it is removed from a home. They then compared interview and survey results with expert representations of the primary issues associated with radon to identify gaps in understanding. They crafted risk messages and developed and tested different risk brochures aimed at improvements in public understanding.

This approach appears especially promising in communicating about various terrorist threats. Consider the difficulty of communicating about different types of biological and radiological attacks.[41] These hazards are complex, poorly understood, and likely to be very emotionally charged.[42] Thorough study of the public's knowledge deficits and acute attention to the development of messages will be required to build trust in risk managers' recommendations.[43]

Political leaders should also attend to how they present likelihoods of threat. Many in the public are not skilled with numerical information, for example. Poorly presented statistical information may heighten their perceptions of risk, especially emotionally charged risks.[44]

Best practices have also emerged that may be applied to communicating about terrorism itself.[45] Tim Sellnow, a professor of communication at the University of Kentucky, and his colleagues emphasize that risk messages should be policy relevant, culturally sensitive, and transparent with respect to what is currently known or uncertain.

As for crisis communications, Rose McDermott, a political scientist at the University of California, Santa Barbara, and Phillip Zimbardo, a psychologist at Stanford University, advise that, wherever possible, warnings should be specific (e.g., region of the country at increased risk, how the investigation is unfolding, what citizens are to do, if anything).[46] The idea is to alert as few people as necessary and for as brief a period as essential. Debriefings should be forthright, indicating what went right or wrong in terms of detection or response.

Consider how to plan for communicating with the public following a dirty-bomb attack. It would be important to have developed and tested risk messages surrounding policy recommendations (a city mayor would have to order people to shelter in place or evacuate within minutes of the explosion). Such messages would have to be sensitive to different constituencies (parents of school-age children would need to know their children are safe from radioactive debris). How should city officials advise citizens about known radiation levels throughout the city?

Plans would have to address uncertainties as well. For example, officials may not know how the perpetrators obtained the radioactive materials or if they are capable of striking again. Involving the public early would be key. Issues surrounding radiation are very difficult to explain, and it would be crucial to identify concerns and gaps in public understanding (a dirty bomb is different from a nuclear bomb). It is critical to design and test these types of communications in advance of any crisis. It is unlikely that they can be designed properly in the midst of a terrorist attack.

Risk analysts have made considerable progress in both the assessment (e.g., identification, quantification) and the management (e.g., communication, mitigation) of risk.[47] Behavioral scientists have learned a great deal about risk communication and people's response to different threats.[48] However, Paul Slovic and Elke Weber, a psychologist at Columbia University, caution that there are likely to be meaningful differences between technical risk estimates and public perceptions of risk.[49] They emphasize that risk managers need to be sensitive to these differences, especially to the level of trust the public places in mechanisms used to address particular risks.

Our expectations and public discourse about terrorism—and safety and economic stability more generally—should better reflect scientific and expert consensus. Risk communication strategies should be devised in advance. And public officials should discuss potential threats in a way that gives every American a sense of role in the solution. This latter point is especially important.

Attitudes and Behaviors That Foster Control

Communicating effectively about terrorism should provide the kind of information that empowers individuals, institutions, and communities to make better risk decisions. It should be based on sound science and a deep respect for public understandings and concerns. Ideally, it should foster resilience and not fear, as skills and self-efficacy improve. Admittedly, communicating about events that were "unthinkable" a decade ago is very difficult.[50] Since 9/11, we have made mistakes, but we can boast notable successes as well.

Consider first the weakness of the color-coded warning system that admonishes the public to be vigilant and aware of all things suspicious. What risk or behavioral science is this system based on? Normal people habituate to this type of message—these alerts have become little more than background noise. In fact, journalists have noted the uncanny timing of threat alerts during political downturns.[51] True or spurious, these suggestions of manipulation have eroded trust.

In other areas, significant progress has been made. For example, the Department of Homeland Security has taken steps to incorporate concepts from the risk analysis community into policy and official communications.[52] Probabilities and consequences are now explicitly discussed in risk policy. Additionally, DHS has created national planning scenarios that characterize many of the threats the nation faces.[53] These scenarios have proved useful guides to regional training exercises. All these things begin the process of empowering people, localities, and local institutions to understand and manage risks.

In 2004, DHS launched the first of its many university centers to enlist the help of the academic community. Collaborative research across many disciplines continues to contribute to our understanding of risk communication as it relates to national security. However, the pool of research talent has hardly been tapped in the area of behavioral science, and much important work remains to be done. DHS has also sponsored the Community Emergency Response Team program. This program trains neighborhood volunteers to work closely with first responders and local officials in times of disaster. CERT provides excellent training in risks associated with natural disasters and most technological accidents. Importantly, CERT fosters resilience by encouraging community members to be involved with protecting themselves and their neighbors.

Fostering resilience in the face of future threats depends in part on scientists' ability to identify critical gaps in public knowledge and risk managers' skill to address these deficiencies with the right risk messages. Risk communication and policies that promote resilient response to disasters will require a commitment to research in a number of important areas.

If we are to effectively address the uncertainty and perceived lack of control that follow acts of terrorism, we need to identify gaps in public understanding well before such events. Risk domain experts should be queried about probabilities, consequences, causal mechanisms, and possible mitigation strategies. Significant progress has already been made along these lines.

For example, Louise Comfort, a professor of public and international affairs at the University of Pittsburgh, has looked at how communities worldwide have responded to major earthquakes to better understand the dynamics of crisis and effective policy and communication.[54] She makes a number of insightful observations, based on a survey of the literature and her own empirical work, that are relevant to the threat of terrorism. First, a community's ability to effectively mobilize its citizens depends critically on the level of awareness, skill, access to resources, and commitment to action before the event's occurrence. Preparation matters. Second, communities appear to have a collective memory of the tragic event, which continues to influence the later choices of organizations and individuals. Experience matters. Third, important communication feedback loops transmit information that allows members in a community to adjust to altered conditions and provide the mechanisms to learn and adapt. Relevant and timely information matters. Fourth, over time, relationships among group members may be enhanced in a way that significantly improves a community's performance in the face of threat. Group dynamics matter.

People rarely react to mishaps as experts would have them do. Rather, public response to a crisis typically follows a path defined by education and preparation, experience, information, community cohesiveness, and intergroup collaboration during the event. Cultural influences and characteristics of the event also matter. Responses may not be proportional to the probabilities or consequences associated with the threat. Collective reactions depend critically on initial conditions of preparation and group interactions as the crisis unfurls.

Communities, like organizations, respond best to crisis when key players have already established deep lines of communication and know one another's responsibilities, priorities, and capacities. For example, in the Los Angeles dirty-bomb study mentioned earlier, we had an opportunity to meet in City Hall with key emergency response and business managers. It was instructive to see how well each of these professionals from diverse agencies (e.g., fire, police, health, environment, chamber of commerce) knew not only his or her own mission but his or her counterparts' missions. This knowledge is particularly important because, in the event of a disaster, tradeoffs must be made that address competing interests. Capacity to respond and recover needs to be nurtured at the neighborhood level as well. Resilience has its roots in local skills and relationships. Developing these skills and relationships is the motivation behind DHS's CERT training.

Fortunately, social scientists and mathematical modelers have developed simulation approaches that address nonlinear response to crisis (i.e., response not proportional to outcome probabilities and consequences). This research may provide additional insight into these matters.[55] These simulations may also allow us to generalize our findings to a wide variety of contexts.

There are three key policy and risk communication challenges that will be important to consider. First, how does the collective reaction of a community before and during a crisis emerge from the interaction of individual behaviors? As individuals we operate on imperfect information, but as communities we often exhibit insight and rationality. Second, how in turn do the emergent characteristics of response (e.g., community goals, norms) influence individual behaviors? Social norms often bring out the best or worst in individuals, especially during times of crisis. Third, how, through nuanced risk communication and policy influences, can we facilitate these reciprocal influences to the collective good for communities, nations, and the world?

Researchers will continue, through interviews and surveys, to investigate the public's understanding of risk and will carefully catalog and profile gaps in knowledge. These findings should lead to significant improvements in risk and crisis communication. However, progress in the understanding of how groups interact within communities while preparing for and responding to crises may prove to be the most important scientific contribution. Advances in mathematical modeling now permit researchers to test their theories and policy recommendations in a virtual environment. A time has arrived in which community leaders and first responders may learn to manage risk not only in the field through personal and sometimes costly experience but in the lab through their participation in risk management simulations.

Conclusion

International terrorism and volatility in global markets have given us good reason to examine our readiness to respond. Terrorism continues to loom large in the public mind with far-reaching effects on the nation's economy and policies. Terrorists use fear and anger to encourage the public to feel powerless and to provoke the nation to overreact. Fear is rooted in perceptions of uncertainty and lack of control regarding salient threats. It is difficult to sound the all clear following actual or threatened terrorist strikes.

People often ignore the low probability that dire events will occur. They take actions that are frequently not reasonable based on the facts. These are understandable but costly mistakes.

Resilience in the face of terrorism demands that the public be encouraged to participate in its own protection. Expectations concerning safety must be made reasonable and balanced with the risks posed by other hazards. Restoring perceived control and involving citizens in community preparedness efforts should be a major focus of communications efforts. Facing the threat of terrorism requires identifying gaps in public understanding and targeting risk communication at these deficiencies. Risk perception research is making progress toward these ends. Lagging, however, is the translation of this research into risk management practice.

In recent years, we have seen the power of events to shape people's thoughts and behaviors, and to capture public discourse. On occasion, we have forsaken reason and empathy, forgetting the larger consequences of our policies and their boomerang effects. Despite our missteps, America may yet offer the voice of calm and deliberative action to a world as shaken as we are. And through these travails, we must lead by example, inspired by our constitutional freedoms and drawing from the best of our science and culture. Resilience and compassion should infuse our policies so that they offer security at a price we will not regret later.

Notes

Chapter 1

1. Professor Audrey Kurth Cronin is the author of *Ending Terrorism: Lessons for Defeating al-Qaeda* (London: Routledge, 2008), and *How Terrorism Ends: Understanding the Decline and Demise of Terrorist Campaigns* (Princeton, NJ: Princeton University Press, 2009). The ideas in this chapter are drawn from research and work done for these two publications. She is a professor of strategy at the National War College in Washington, D.C., as well as a senior research associate in Oxford University's Changing Character of War Programme in Oxford, England. This chapter contains only the author's personal views and should not be construed as representing any official government position.

2. Robert Pape is the most prominent scholar to assert this view with respect to suicide attacks. See for example, Robert A. Pape, *Dying to Win: The Strategic Logic of Suicide Terrorism* (New York: Random House, 2005).

3. This discussion builds on Martha Crenshaw's excellent "Terrorism and Global Security," in *Leashing the Dogs of War: Conflict Management in a Divided World*, ed. Chester A. Crocker, Fen Osler Hampson, and Pamela Aall (Washington: U.S. Institute of Peace, 2007), pp. 73–75.

4. See Audrey Kurth Cronin, "Cybermobilization: The New *Levee en Masse*," *Parameters* 36, no. 2 (Summer 2006): 77–87.

5. On Chechnya, see Audrey Kurth Cronin, "Russia and Chechnya," in *Democracy and Counterterrorism: Lessons from the Past*, ed. Robert J. Art and Louise Richardson (Washington: U.S. Institute of Peace, 2007), pp. 383–424.

6. For a strident condemnation, see Stephen Blank, "Russia's Ulster: The Chechen War and Its Consequences," *Demokratizatsiya* 9, no. 1 (Winter 2001): 5–25. More generally, see Rachel Denber, "'Glad to Be Deceived': The International Community and Chechnya," in *Human Rights Watch World Report 2004*, accessed at http://www.hrw.org/legacy/wr2k4/7.htm on 2 March 2010.

7. To avoid endless debates over the meanings of the terms "tactical" and "strategic," we are borrowing "process" and "outcome" from economist Herbert Simon's "From Substantive to Procedural Rationality," in *Method and Appraisal in Economics*, ed. Spiro J. Latsis (Cambridge: Cambridge University Press, 1976), pp. 129–48.

8. See, for example, Brigitte L. Nacos, "Revisiting the Contagion Hypothesis: Terrorism, News Coverage, and Copycat Attacks," *Perspectives on Terrorism* 3, no. 3, September 2009, http://www.terrorismanalysts.com/pt/index.php?option=com_content&view=article&id=120:revisiting-the-contagion-hypothesis-terrorism-news-coverage-and-copycat-attacks.

9. See, for example, Bruce Hoffman, "Al Qaeda Isn't Dead Yet," CNN.com, September 9, 2008, http://www.cnn.com/2008/POLITICS/09/09/hoffman.alqaeda/index.html.

10. See, for example, Alan Dershowitz, *Why Terrorism Works: Understanding the Threat, Responding to the Challenge* (New Haven, CT: Yale University Press, 2002); Ehud Sprinzak, "Rational Fanatics," *Foreign Policy*, September–October 2000, p. 66; and Robert A. Pape, "The Strategic Logic of Suicide Terrorism," *American Political Science Review* 97, no. 3 (August 2003): 343–61.

11. A full explanation of this statistical work is set forth in the appendix of Cronin, *How Terrorism Ends*, pp. 207–22.

12. The RAND/MIPT database has been incorporated into the START (Study of Terrorism and Responses to Terrorism) database at the University of Maryland, which can be accessed at http://www.start.umd.edu/data/.

13. See David C. Rapoport, "Terrorism," in *Routledge Encyclopedia of Government and Politics*, vol. 2, ed. Mary Hawkesworth and Maurice Kogan (London: Routledge, 1992), p. 1067.

14. See Audrey Kurth Cronin, "How al-Qaeda Ends: The Decline and Demise of Terrorist Groups," *International Security* 31, no. 1 (Summer 2006): 7–48.

15. For an excellent discussion of efforts to confront Islamic fundamentalism locally in Southeast Asia, for example, see Christopher S. Bond and Lewis M. Simons, "The Forgotten Front," *Foreign Affairs* 88, no. 6 (November–December 2009): 52–64.

16. The best advocate for considering al Qaeda a global insurgency is David Kilcullen. See "Countering Global Insurgency," *Strategic Studies* 28, no. 4 (August 2005): 597–618.

Chapter 2

1. Some of my own publications have contributed to the area of inquiry, although my thoughts on these matters are continually evolving and (hopefully) becoming more refined. For example, see *The Making of a Terrorist: Recruitment, Training and Root Causes* (Westport, CT: Praeger, 2005); *Teaching Terror* (Lanham, MD: Rowman & Littlefield, 2006); and *Countering Terrorism and Insurgency in the 21st Century* (Westport, CT: Praeger, 2007).

2. For more on this, see James Forest, ed., *Influence Warfare: How Terrorists and Governments Fight to Shape Perceptions in a War of Ideas* (Westport, CT: Praeger, 2009).

3. For example, please see Mohammed Hafez, "Political Repression and Violent Rebellion in the Muslim World," in *The Making of a Terrorist: Recruitment, Training and Root Causes*, ed. James J. F. Forest (Westport, CT: Praeger, 2005), pp. 74–91; Lydia Khalil, "Authoritarian and Corrupt Governments," in *Countering Terrorism and Insurgency in the 21st Century*, vol. 2, *Combating the Sources and Facilitators*, ed. James J. F. Forest (Westport, CT: Praeger, 2007), pp. 76–92; Ted Robert Gurr, *Why Men Rebel* (Princeton, NJ: Princeton University Press, 1970); and Alan B. Krueger and Jitka Maleckova, "Education, Poverty and Terrorism: Is There a Causal Connection?" *Journal of Economic Perspectives* 17, no. 4 (Fall 2003): 119–44.

4. Martha Crenshaw, "The Causes of Terrorism," *Comparative Politics* 14, no. 4 (July 1981): 379–99; Jeffrey Ian Ross, "Structural Causes of Oppositional Political Terrorism," *Journal of Peace Research* 30, no. 3 (1993): 317–29; and Assaf Moghadam, *The Roots of Terrorism* (New York: Chelsea House, 2006).

5. This of course does not account for the relatively few cases where an individual was used unwillingly (through ignorance or coercion) to conduct terrorist activity.

6. The recent trend of popular moderate Muslim preachers on Saudi satellite TV is an especially promising development in this regard.

7. Even when armed groups such as animal rights activists or anti-abortionists attack laboratories and clinics, their overall target is human behavior.

8. Maxwell Taylor, *The Terrorist* (London: Brassey's, 1988).

9. Jerrold M. Post, "Terrorist Psycho-Logic: Terrorist Behavior as a Product of Psychological Forces," in *Origins of Terrorism: Psychologies, Ideologies, Theologies, States of Mind*, ed. Walter Reich (Baltimore: Woodrow Wilson Center Press, 1998), pp. 25–40.

10. Robert Robins and Jerrold Post, *Political Paranoia: The Psychopolitics of Hatred* (New Haven, CT: Yale University Press, 1997).

11. See, for example, Raymond H. Hamden, "Unresolved Trauma and the Thirst for Revenge: The Retributional Terrorist," in Forest, *The Making of a Terrorist*, vol. 1, *Recruitment*, pp. 165–78; Albert Bandura, "Mechanisms of Moral Disengagement," in Forest, *The Making of a Terrorist*, vol. 2, *Training*, pp. 34–50; and Chris Stout, "Introduction," in *Psychology of Terrorism: Coping with the Continuing Threat*, condensed ed., ed. Chris Stout (Westport, CT: Praeger, 2004), pp. xv–xix.

12. Walter Lacquer, "Left, Right and Beyond: The Changing Face of Terror," in *How Did This Happen? Terrorism and the New War*, ed. James Hoge and Gideon Rose (Oxford: Public Affairs, 2001), pp. 71–82.

13. Michael E. Leiter, director, National Counterterrorism Center, Testimony (Statement for the Record) before the Senate Committee on Homeland Security and Governmental Affairs, Hearing on Roots of Violent Islamist Extremism and Efforts to Counter It, July 10, 2008.

14. John Horgan, "The Social and Psychological Characteristics of Terrorism and Terrorists," in *Root Causes of Terrorism: Myths, Realities and Ways Forward*, ed. Tore Bjørgo (London: Routledge, 2005), p. 45.

15. For example, Andrew Silke found that they are rarely mad, and very few suffer from personality disorders. Andrew Silke, "An Introduction to Terrorism Research," in *Research on Terrorism: Trends, Achievements and Failures*, ed. Andrew Silke (London: Frank Cass, 2004), p. 20.

16. Clark McCauley, "Psychological Issues in Understanding Terrorism and Response to Terrorism," in Stout, *Psychology of Terrorism*, p. 35.

17. Marc Sageman, *Understanding Terror Networks* (Philadelphia: University of Pennsylvania Press, 2004), p. 91.

18. Martha Crenshaw, "The Logic of Terrorism: Terrorist Behavior as a Product of Strategic Choice," in Reich, *Origins of Terrorism*, pp. 7–24.

19. Stout, "Introduction," p. xiv. See also, Rex A. Hudson, *Who Becomes a Terrorist and Why: The 1999 Government Report on Profiling Terrorists* (Guilford, CT: Lyons Press, 2001); and Robert A. Pape, "The Strategic Logic of Suicide Terrorism," *American Political Science Review* 97, no. 3 (August 2003): 343–61.

20. For more on this, please see John Horgan, "The Search for the Terrorist Personality," in *Terrorists, Victims and Society: Psychological Perspectives on Terrorism and Its Consequences*, ed. Andrew Silke (New York: John Wiley, 2003); and Andrew Silke, "Cheshire-Cat Logic: The Recurring Theme of Terrorist Abnormality in Psychological Research," *Psychology, Crime and Law* 4 (1998): 51–69.

21. For example, see Leiter, Testimony, July 10, 2008; Fathali M. Moghaddam, "The Staircase to Terrorism: A Psychological Exploration," *American Psychologist* 60, no. 2 (2005): 161–69; and Clark McCauley, "Pathways towards Radicalization," START Research Brief, National Consortium for the Study of Terrorism and Responses to Terrorism, College Park, MD, October 2008.

22. Max Taylor and John Horgan, "A Conceptual Framework for Addressing Psychological Process in the Development of the Terrorist," *Terrorism and Political Violence* 18, no. 4 (2006): 2.

23. Leiter, Testimony, July 10, 2008.

24. Sageman, *Understanding Terror Networks*, p. 178.

25. Martha Crenshaw, *Terrorism in Context* (College Station, PA: Pennsylvania State University Press, 1995); Bruce Hoffman, *Inside Terrorism*, 2nd ed. (New York: Columbia University Press, 2006); Louise Richardson, *What Terrorists Want* (New York: Random House, 2006); and Daniel Benjamin and Steve Simon, *The Age of Sacred Terror* (New York: Random House, 2002).

26. See Ehud Sprinzak, "Fundamentalism, Terrorism, and Democracy: The Case of the Gush Emunim Underground," paper presented at the Woodrow Wilson International Center for Scholars, Washington, September 1986; Ehud Sprinzak, "The Psychopolitical Formation of Extreme Left Terrorism in a Democracy: The Case of the Weathermen," in Reich, *Origins of Terrorism*, pp. 65–85; and Ariel Merari, "The Readiness to Kill and Die: Suicidal Terrorism in the Middle East," in Reich, *Origins of Terrorism*, pp. 192–210.

27. Bandura, "Mechanisms of Moral Disengagement," pp. 42–47.

28. See James J. F. Forest, "The Final Act: Ideologies of Catastrophic Terror," Fund for Peace Expert Series, n.d., http://www.fundforpeace.org/web/images/pdf/forest.pdf.

29. Assaf Moghadam, "The Salafi-Jihad as a Religious Ideology," *CTC Sentinel* 1, no. 3 (February 2008): 14–16.

30. According to Andrew Kydd and Barbara Walter, "Of the forty-two groups currently designated as foreign terrorist organizations by the U.S. state department, thirty-one seek regime change, nineteen seek territorial change, four seek policy change, and one seeks to maintain the status quo." Andrew Kydd and Barbara Walter, "The Strategies of Terrorism," *International Security* 31, no. 1 (Summer 2006): 52.

31. The Islamic Movement of Uzbekistan, also known as the Islamic Party of Turkestan, is made up of militant Islamist extremists mostly from Uzbekistan but includes other central Asian nationalities and ethnic groups as well. The group has mainly conducted small-scale armed attacks, including car bombings and hostage takings in Kyrgyzstan, Uzbekistan, and Tajikistan.

32. Jerrold M. Post, "When Hatred Is Bred in the Bone: The Socio-Cultural Underpinnings of Terrorist Psychology," in Forest, *The Making of a Terrorist*, vol. 2, *Training*, pp. 18–19.

33. Bard O'Neil and Donald J. Alberts, "Responding to Psychological, Social, Economic and Political Roots of Terrorism," in Forest, *Countering Terrorism and Insurgency in the 21st Century*, vol. 2, *Combating the Sources and Facilitators*, pp. 306–13.

34. Mia Bloom, *Dying to Kill: The Allure of Suicide Terrorism* (New York: Columbia University Press, 2005).

35. This discussion builds on Martha Crenshaw's enormously useful typology from the early 1980s. See Crenshaw, "The Causes of Terrorism," pp. 379–99.

36. For example, Jeffrey Ian Ross identified seven kinds of "structural" grievances that are the most important contributors to political violence—ethnic, racial, legal, political, religious, social, and economic (including poverty, exploitation, expropriation, indebtedness, and unemployment). See Ross, "Structural Causes of Oppositional Political Terrorism," p. 325. According to Michael Leiter, the most common catalysts that lead to terrorist radicalization include blocked social mobility, political repression,

and relative socioeconomic deprivation. Leiter, Testimony, July 10, 2008. Shawn Flanigan has suggested that a great deal of political violence originates from a sense of social and political exclusion and in situations where the minority grievances are not sufficiently met. Shawn Teresa Flanigan, "Charity as Resistance: Connections between Charity, Contentious Politics, and Terror," *Studies in Conflict and Terrorism* 29, no. 7 (2006): 644. Also see Khalil, "Authoritarian and Corrupt Governments," pp. 76–92.

37. Recent examples of triggering events include the films of Theo Van Gogh, which precipitated a violent response among Islamist radicals and eventually led to his murder; the publication of cartoons portraying the Prophet Mohammed, which produced a wave of violent protests and actions worldwide; and Israel's military actions against Lebanese and Palestinian militants, which have mobilized protests among Muslims as far away as Indonesia.

38. Increased birth rates and the age composition of populations in developing countries affect resource consumption, prices, government revenues and expenditures, demand for jobs, and labor wages. Demographic and socioeconomic conditions could lead to the emergence of more terrorism and terrorists for many decades to come. Paul R. Ehrlich and Jianguo Liu, "Socioeconomic and Demographic Roots of Terrorism," in Forest, *The Making of a Terrorist*, vol. 3, *Root Causes*, pp. 160–71.

39. National Intelligence Council, *Global Trends 2025: A Transformed World* (Washington: Government Printing Office, November 2008), p. 43, http://www.dni.gov/nic/NIC_2025_project.html. Also see Colleen McCue and Kathryn Haahr, "The Impact of Global Youth Bulges on Islamist Radicalization and Violence," *CTC Sentinel* 1, no. 1 (October 2008): 12–14.

40. Shahdad Naghshpour, Joseph J. St. Marie, and Samuel S. Stanton Jr., "The Shadow Economy and Terrorist Infrastructure," in Forest, *Countering Terrorism and Insurgency in the 21st Century*, vol. 2, *Combating the Sources and Facilitators*, pp. 219–35.

41. James Forest, "Influence Warfare and Modern Terrorism," *Georgetown Journal of International Affairs* 10, no. 1 (Spring 2009): 81–89. Also see Bruce Hoffman, "The Use of the Internet by Islamic Extremists," Testimony before the House Permanent Select Committee on Intelligence, May 4, 2006, p. 18, http://rand.org/pubs/testimonies/CT262-1.

42. Gabriel Weimann, "Terrorist Dot Com: Using the Internet for Terrorist Recruitment and Mobilization," in Forest, *The Making of a Terrorist*, vol. 1, *Recruitment*, pp. 53–65.

43. Abu Yahya al-Libi, "To the Army of Difficulty in Somalia," al Sahab Media, http://www.tawhed.net/dl.php?i=1309092i (accessed December 27, 2009); English translation is available at http://www.archive.org/details/Army-of-Difficulty-in-Somalia (accessed December 27, 2009).

44. P. H. Liotta and James F. Miskel, "Digging Deep: Environment and Geography as Root Influences for Terrorism," in Forest, *The Making of a Terrorist*, vol. 3, *Root Causes*, pp. 254–65.

45. For more on this, please see Erica Chenoweth, "Instability and Opportunity: The Origins of Terrorism in Weak and Failed States," in Forest, *The Making of a Terrorist*, vol. 3, *Root Causes*, pp. 17–30. Also, Kydd and Walter speculate that "democracies may be more constrained in their ability to retaliate than authoritarian regimes." Kydd and Walter, "The Strategies of Terrorism," p. 61.

46. Peter W. Singer, "Corporate Warriors: The Rise of the Privatized Military Industry and Its Ramifications for International Security," *International Security* 26, no. 3

(Winter 2001/2002): 196. Also, an excellent example is found in *Jane's Intelligence Review*, "African Struggle over Smuggled Weapons," November 23, 1999.

47. Christopher Carr, "Combating the International Proliferation of Small Arms and Light Weapons," in Forest, *Countering Terrorism and Insurgency in the 21st Century*, vol. 2, *Combating the Sources and Facilitators*, pp. 127–41.

48. See, for example, Benjamin R. Barber, "Terrorism, Interdependence and Democracy," in Forest, *The Making of a Terrorist*, vol. 3, *Root Causes*, pp. 207–19; and Michael Mousseau, "Terrorism and Export Economies: The Dark Side of Free Trade," in Forest, *The Making of a Terrorist*, vol. 3, *Root Causes*, pp. 189–203.

49. Paul Pillar, "The Democratic Deficit: The Need for Liberal Democratization," in Forest, *Countering Terrorism and Insurgency in the 21st Century*, vol. 2, *Combating the Sources and Facilitators*, pp. 42–55; and Paul Pillar, "Superpower Foreign Policies: A Source for Global Resentment," in Forest, *The Making of a Terrorist*, vol. 3, *Root Causes*, pp. 31–44.

50. For example, Christopher Jasparro recently argued that countering an ideology requires determining a message's origin, the paths along which it has diffused, and how the conditions by which it resonates vary from place to place. See Christopher Jasparro, "Sociocultural, Economic and Demographic Aspects of Counterterrorism," in Forest, *Countering Terrorism and Insurgency in the 21st Century*, vol. 2, *Combating the Sources and Facilitators*, pp. 421–22.

51. Kim Cragin and Scott Gerwehr, *Dissuading Terror: Strategic Influence and the Struggle against Terrorism* (Santa Monica, CA: RAND Corporation, 2005); and Kim Cragin and Peter Chalk, *Terrorism and Development: Using Social and Economic Development to Inhibit a Resurgence of Terrorism* (Santa Monica, CA: RAND Corporation, 2003).

52. For example, Anthony Cordesman recently argued that Saudi security is best protected through social, religious, and economic reforms, not by their current security-only approach. Anthony H. Cordesman, "Saudi Security and the War on Terrorism: International Security Operations, Law Enforcement, Internal Threats, and the Need for Change," Center for Strategic and International Studies, Washington, March 3, 2002, http://www.csis.org/media/csis/pubs/saudiwarterr030302.pdf. Sherifa Zuhur recommends that the United States encourage the Saudi government to increase political participation, improve the intelligence services, urge responsiveness to human rights, and increase multilateral discussions relating to anti-terrorism. Zuhur, "Saudi Arabia: Islamic Threat, Political Reform, and the Global War on Terror," Strategic Studies Institute, U.S. Army War College, March 2005, http://www.strategicstudiesinstitute.army.mil/Pubs/display.cfm?pubID=598.

53. According to Paul Pillar, the most fundamental point in favor of democracy is that when rulers are answerable to the ruled and must compete for the people's favor to gain or retain office, they are more likely than in autocracies to govern in the people's interests and not exclusively in their own. Pillar, "The Democratic Deficit," in Forest, *Countering Terrorism and Insurgency in the 21st Century*, vol. 2, *Combating the Sources and Facilitators*, pp. 43–45.

54. Francesco Cavatorta, "The Role of Democratization in Reducing the Appeal of Extremist Groups in the Middle East and North Africa," pp. 56–75; and Khalil, "Authoritarian and Corrupt Governments," pp. 76–92, both in Forest, *Countering Terrorism and Insurgency in the 21st Century*, vol. 2, *Combating the Sources and Facilitators*.

55. Joseph Nye, *The Paradox of American Power: Why the World's Superpower Can't Go It Alone* (New York: Oxford University Press, 2002).

56. For example, see Gabriel Weimann, "When Fatwas Clash Online: Terrorist Debates on the Internet," in Forest, *Influence Warfare*, pp. 49–74.

57. Moghadam, "The Salafi-Jihad as a Religious Ideology," pp. 14–16.

58. See Forest, "Influence Warfare and Modern Terrorism," pp. 81–89; and Hoffman, "The Use of the Internet by Islamic Extremists," p. 18.

59. For more on this, see Gabriel Weimann, "Virtual Training Camps: Terrorist Use of the Internet," in *Teaching Terror*, ed. James J. F. Forest (Lanham, MD: Rowman & Littlefield, 2006); Jarret Brachman and James J. F. Forest, "Terrorist Sanctuaries in the Age of Information: Exploring the Role of Virtual Training Camps," in *Denial of Sanctuary: Understanding Terrorist Safe Havens*, ed. Michael Innes (London: Praeger Security International, 2007), pp. 124–38; and Hoffman, "The Use of the Internet by Islamic Extremists," p. 18.

60. See its website at http://www.radicalmiddleway.co.uk.

61. Kyai Haji Abdurrahman Wahid and C. Holland Taylor, "In Indonesia, Songs against Terrorism," *Washington Post*, October 7, 2005.

62. Asra Q. Nomani, "Heroes and Pioneers: Amr Khaled," *Time*, May 14, 2007, p. 99.

63. Robert F. Worth, "Preaching Moderate Islam and Becoming a TV Star," *New York Times*, January 3, 2009.

64. For more on this, please see Forest, *Influence Warfare*.

Chapter 3

1. Portions of this chapter are derived from Cale D. Horne and Mia Bloom, "Is Terrorism the Poor Man's Patent?: Evaluating the Connection between Poverty, Education and Political Violence," manuscript prepared for the annual meeting of the International Studies Association, New York, February 2009.

2. Ekmeleddin Ihsanoglu, "An Invitation to a New Partnership from the Organization of the Islamic Conference (OIC) to President Barack Obama," reprinted in the *New York Times International*, January 20, 2009, http://www.oic-oci.org/nyt/nyt_20_1_2009.pdf.

3. John Horgan, *Walking Away from Terrorism* (London: Routledge, 2009), p. 40.

4. Lindy Kerin, "Understanding Terrorism: The Psychology of Suicide Bombers," *The World Today*, September 14, 2006, http://www.abc.net.au/worldtoday/content/2006/s1741219.htm.

5. Jeff Victoroff, "The Mind of the Terrorist: A Review and Critique of Psychological Approaches," *Journal of Conflict Resolution* 49, no. 1 (2005): 3

6. Marc Sageman, "A Review of Michael Kenney, *From Pablo to Osama*," *Terrorism and Political Violence* 19, no. 4 (2007): 623–24.

7. Michael Hogg and Graham Vaughan, *Social Psychology* (Harlow, UK: Pearson Education Limited, 2005).

8. Paul Gill, "A Political Psychology Analysis of Suicide Bomber Radicalization," paper presented at the 31st Annual Scientific Meeting of the International Society of Political Psychology, Sciences Po, Paris, France, July 9, 2008, p. 3

9. Tore Bjørgo, ed., *Root Causes of Terrorism: Myths, Reality, and Ways Forward* (London: Routledge, 2005), pp. 225–27 *passim*.

10. See, Ariel Merari, "The Psychology of Extremism," paper presented to Institute for Social Research seminar series, University of Michigan, Ann Arbor, February 11, 2002.

11. Quoted in Claude Berrebi, "Evidence about the Link between Education, Poverty and Terrorism among Palestinians," Princeton University Industrial Relations Section Working Paper no. 477, September 2003.

12. Quoted in ibid., p. 6.

13. George W. Bush, "Remarks to the United Nations Financing for Development Conference," Monterrey, Mexico, March 22, 2002, http://www.gpo.gov/fdsys/pkg/WCPD-2002-03-25/pdf/WCPD-2002-03-25-Pg483.pdf.

14. Quoted in Vincent Ferraro, "Globalizing Weakness: Is Global Poverty a National Security Threat?" undated working paper, p. 6, http://www.wilsoncenter.org/news/docs/ACF59B0.doc.

15. Michael Radu, "The Futile Search for Root Causes of Terrorism," Foreign Policy Research Institute, April 23, 2002, http://www.fpri.org/enotes/americawar.20020423.radu.futilesearchforrootcauses.html.

16. On this point, see the chapter by Paul R. Pillar and Christopher Preble in this volume.

17. Quoted in Berrebi, "Evidence," 2003. p. 38.

18. Alan B. Krueger, *What Makes a Terrorist: Economics and the Roots of Terrorism* (Princeton, NJ: Princeton University Press, 2007). See also, Alan B. Krueger and Jitka Maleckova, "Education, Poverty and Terrorism: Is There a Causal Connection?" National Bureau of Economic Research Working Paper no. 9074, 2002; and Alan B. Krueger, "Education, Poverty and Terrorism: Is There a Causal Connection?" *Journal of Economic Perspectives* 17, no. 4 (2003): 119–44.

19. Walter Reich, "The Poverty Myth," *Wilson Quarterly* 32, no. 1 (Winter 2008): 104.

20. See Horne and Bloom, "Is Terrorism the Poor Man's Patent?"

21. Ethan Bueno de Mesquita, "The Quality of Terror," *American Journal of Political Science* 49, no. 3 (2005): 515–30.

22. See, for example, Krueger and Maleckova, "Education, Poverty and Terrorism"; and Claude Berrebi, "Evidence about the Link between Education, Poverty and Terrorism among Palestinians," *Peace Economics, Peace Science and Public Policy* 13, no. 1 (2007): 1–36. David A. Jaeger and colleagues similarly conclude that no relationship exists between a range of demographic variables and Palestinian support for the Second Intifada. However, this study focuses on the effect of Israeli and Palestinian casualties generally (and not military and civilian casualties separately), as it pertains to support for the intifada. Because the effects of military and civilian casualties are not examined separately, Palestinian support for terrorism as the term is normally understood cannot be assessed. See David A. Jaeger, Esteban F. Klor, Sami Miaari, and M. Daniele Paserman, "The Struggle for Palestinian Hearts and Minds: Violence and Public Opinion in the Second Intifada," Centre for Economic Policy Research, April 2008, http://www.cepr.org/pubs/dps/DP6793.asp.

23. Diego Gambetta and Steffen Hertog, "Engineers of Jihad," Sociology Working Paper no. 2007-10, University of Oxford, 2007, http://www.nuff.ox.ac.uk/users/gambetta/Engineers%20of%20Jihad.pdf; Krueger, *What Makes a Terrorist*; Krueger and Maleckova, "Education, Poverty and Terrorism"; and Berrebi, "Evidence," 2007.

24. Other studies of terrorism have come under fire recently over the issue of sampling on the dependent variable. See critique of Robert Pape, "The Strategic Logic of Suicide Terrorism," *American Political Science Review* 97, no. 3 (2003): 343–61, in Scott Ashworth, Joshua D. Clinton, Adam Meirowitz, and Kristopher W. Ramsay, "Design, Inference, and the Strategic Logic of Suicide Terrorism," *American Political Science Review* 102, no. 2 (April 2008): 269–73; and Pape's response in "Methods and

Findings in the Study of Suicide Terrorism," *American Political Science Review* 102, no. 2 (2008): 275–77.

25. Charles Russell and Bowman Miller, "Profile of a Terrorist," in *Perspectives on Terrorism*, ed. Lawrence Zelic Freedman and Yonah Alexander (Wilmington, DE: Scholarly Resources Inc., 1977), pp. 45–60.

26. Gambetta and Hertog, "Engineers of Jihad."

27. Alan B. Krueger and David Laitin, "Kto Kogo?: A Cross-Country Study of the Origins and Targets of Terrorism," unpublished paper, 2003, http://www.krueger.princeton.edu/terrorism3.pdf; and James A. Piazza, "Rooted in Poverty?: Terrorism, Poor Economic Development, and Social Cleavages," *Terrorism and Political Violence* 18, no. 1 (March 2006): 159–77

28. Alberto Abadie, "Poverty, Political Freedom, and the Roots of Terrorism," *American Economic Review* (Papers and Proceedings) 96, no. 2 (2006): 50–56.

29. S. Brock Blomberg, Gregory D. Hess, and Akila Weerapana, "Economic Conditions and Terrorism," *European Journal of Political Economy* 20, no. 2 (2004): 463–78. Other forms of organized violence show a more consistent relationship to socioeconomic conditions in a society at large. For example, recent studies point to a causal connection between general socioeconomic conditions and genocide, Manus I. Midlarsky, "The Demographics of Genocide: Refugees and Territorial Loss in the Mass Murder of European Jewry," *Journal of Peace Research* 42, no. 4 (2005): 375–91; revolution and ethnic conflict, Marie L. Besançon, "Relative Resources: Inequality in Ethnic Wars, Revolutions, and Genocides," *Journal of Peace Research* 42, no. 4 (2005): 393–415; and "everyday" social violence, Mohammad Zulfan Tadjoeddin and Syed Mansoob Murshed, "Socio-Economic Determinants of Everyday Violence in Indonesia: An Empirical Investigation of Javanese Districts, 1994–2003," *Journal of Peace Research* 44, no. 6 (2007): 689–709.

30. See Krueger, *What Makes a Terrorist*; Krueger and Maleckova, "Education, Poverty, and Terrorism"; Gambetta and Hertog, "Engineers of Jihad"; and Berrebi, "Evidence," 2007.

31. Robert Winnett and David Leppard, "Leaked No. 10 Dossier Reveals al Qaeda's British Recruits," *Sunday Times*, July 10, 2005, http://www.timesonline.co.uk/tol/news/uk/article542420.ece.

32. John Horgan, "Disengaging from Terrorism," in *The Faces of Terrorism: Cross Disciplinary Explorations*, ed. David Canter (London: Wiley–Blackwell, 2009), pp. 257–76.

33. *Terrorist Lives* (London: Brassey's, 1994), p. 24.

34. Max Taylor, "Rational Choice, Behaviour Analysis and Political Violence," in *Routine Activity and Rational Choice: Advances in Criminological Theory*, ed. R. V. Clarke and M. Felson (Rutgers, NJ: Transaction Press, 1992).

35. Swati Parashar, "Terrorism: Root Causes," South Asia Analysis Group Paper no. 1521, November 29, 2005, http://www.saag.org/common/uploaded_files/paper1521.html.

36. Horgan, "Disengaging from Terrorism." p. 264.

37. John Horgan, *Psychology of Terrorism* (London: Routledge, 2005), p. 158.

38. Radu, "The Futile Search for Root Causes of Terrorism."

39. Bjørgo, *Root Causes of Terrorism*.

40. Audrey Kurth Cronin, *How Terrorism Ends: Understanding the Decline and Demise of Terrorist Campaigns* (Princeton, NJ: Princeton University Press, 2009).

41. Horgan, *Walking Away from Terrorism*.
42. Bjørgo, *Root Causes of Terrorism*.

Chapter 4

1. Transcript of President Bush's Address to Congress, September 20, 2001, CNN.com, http://archives.cnn.com/2001/US/09/20/gen.bush.transcript/.
2. For a critical review of the erosion of these protections after 9/11, see Gene Healy, "Deployed in the U.S.A: The Creeping Militarization of the Home Front," Cato Institute Policy Analysis no. 503, December 17, 2003.
3. Fred Weir, "In Moscow, a Test Case for Government Accountability," *Christian Science Monitor*, January 22, 2003; and "Moscow Theatre Siege Claims Rejected," BBC News, January 23, 2003, http://news.bbc.co.uk/2/hi/europe/2688419.stm.
4. Mike Eckel, "Russians Mark 5 Years Since Beslan School Tragedy," Associated Press, September 1, 2009.
5. Descriptions of several of Israel's failed operations are in Paul R. Pillar, *Terrorism and U.S. Foreign Policy* (Washington: Brookings Institution Press, 2001), p. 99.
6. Paul K. Davis and Brian Michael Jenkins, *Deterrence and Influence in Counterterrorism: A Component in the War on al Qaeda* (Santa Monica, CA: RAND Corporation, 2002).
7. Raymond Tanter, *Rogue Regimes: Terrorism and Proliferation* (New York: St. Martin's Press, 1998), pp. 164–65.
8. Jeffrey Gettleman and Eric Schmitt, "U.S. Kills Top Qaeda Militant in Southern Somalia," *New York Times*, September 14, 2009. See also "Suspected Terrorist Killed in U.S. Raid in Somalia," Associated Press, September 15, 2009.
9. Thomas Lum and Larry Niksch, "The Republic of the Philippines: Background and U.S. Relations," RL 33233, Congressional Research Service, January 15, 2009, pp. 16–18. See also Raymond Bonner and Carlos H. Conde, "U.S. and Philippines Join Forces to Pursue Terrorist Leader," *New York Times*, July 23, 2005; Peter Brookes, "Flashpoint: No Bungle in the Jungle," *Armed Forces Journal*, September 2007; and Max Boot, "Treading Softly in the Philippines," *Weekly Standard*, January 5, 2009.
10. David Hirst, "Obituary: Sheikh Ahmed Yassin," *Guardian* (UK), March 23, 2004, http://www.guardian.co.uk/news/2004/mar/23/guardianobituaries.israel.
11. A discussion of the effects of Israel's assassination operations is in Daniel Byman, *The Five Front War: The Better Way to Fight Global Jihad* (New York: John Wiley, 2008), pp. 113–24.
12. Timothy Noah, "Al-Qaida's Rule of Threes," *Slate*, December 5, 2005, http://www.slate.com/id/2131627/.
13. Paul McGeough, *Kill Khalid: The Failed Mossad Assassination of Khalid Mishal and the Rise of Hamas* (New York: New Press, 2008).
14. Ben Farmer, "Afghanistan President Hamid Karzai Hopes Barack Obama Will Bring 'Peace,'" *Telegraph* (UK), November 5, 2008, http://www.telegraph.co.uk/news/newstopics/uselection2008/barackobama/3385388/Afghanistan-President-Hamid-Karzai-hopes-Barack-Obama-will-bring-peace.html.
15. David Kilcullen and Andrew McDonald Exum, "Death from Above, Outrage Down Below," *New York Times*, May 17, 2009.
16. The United States also backed Ethiopia's military intervention, which further undermined U.S. standing and emboldened the extremists. See David Axe, "Somalia, Redux: A More Hands-Off Approach," Cato Institute Policy Analysis no. 649, October 12, 2009.

17. See especially Stephen Biddle, "Afghanistan and the Future of Warfare," *Foreign Affairs* 82, no. 2 (March–April 2003): 31–46.

18. On this point, see also Marc Lynch, "Afghanistan Strategy Debate," *Foreign Policy.com*, August 10, 2009, http://lynch.foreignpolicy.com/posts/2009/08/10/afghanistan_strategy_debate.

19. Paul R. Pillar, "Who's Afraid of a Terrorist Haven?" *Washington Post*, September 16, 2009.

20. Michael Howard, "A Long War?" *Survival* 48, no. 4 (Winter 2006–07): 7–14.

21. "Terminology to Define the Terrorists: Recommendations from American Muslims," Office for Civil Rights and Civil Liberties, Department of Homeland Security, January 2008, p. 1.

22. Peter Ford, "Europe Cringes at Bush 'Crusade' against Terrorists," *Christian Science Monitor*, September 19, 2001, http://www.csmonitor.com/2001/0919/p12s2-woeu.html.

23. Jeffrey Record, *Bounding the Global War on Terrorism* (Carlisle, PA: Strategic Studies Institute, 2003), p. v, http://www.strategicstudiesinstitute.army.mil/Pubs/Display.Cfm?pubID=207.

24. "Report of the Defense Science Board Task Force on Strategic Communication," Office of the Under Secretary of Defense for Acquisition, Technology, and Logistics, January 2008, pp. 19, 43.

25. See, for example, Norman Podhoretz, *World War IV: The Long Struggle against Islamofascism* (New York: Doubleday, 2007).

26. Dick Cheney, interview with Chris Wallace, recorded August 28, 2009, FoxNews.com.

27. Newt Gingrich, "President Obama Should Fire Attorney General Eric Holder," *Washington Examiner*, August 28, 2009.

28. Chicago Council on Global Affairs, *Global Views, 2008: Anxious Americans Seek a New Direction in United States Foreign Policy: Results of a 2008 Survey of Public Opinion* (Chicago: Chicago Council on Global Affairs, 2009), pp. 11–12.

29. Jennifer Agiesta and Jon Cohen, "Public Opinion in U.S. Turns against Afghan War," *Washington Post*, August 20, 2009.

Chapter 5

1. The prior attacks were the 1993 World Trade Center bombing and the 1995 Bojinka plot.

2. For more on this, see Chapter 4 in this volume.

3. The Obama administration has expressed a similar logic. See, for example, "A New Approach for Safeguarding Americans," speech by John Brennan, assistant to the president for homeland security and counterterrorism, Center for Strategic and International Studies, Washington, August 6, 2009, http://csis.org/files/attachments/090806_brennan_transcript.pdf.

4. In addition to the Hart-Rudman Commission's Phase 1 report, they include the 1994 "Redefining Security: A Report to the Secretary of Defense and the Director of Central Intelligence," from the Joint Security Commission, established by the Secretary of Defense in 1993; the 1996 Defense Science Board, "Report of the Defense Science Board Task Force on Information Warfare—Defense (IW-D)"; the 1997 report of a specially convened "National Defense Panel," created as part of the first congressionally mandated Quadrennial Defense Review; and the October 1997 Report of the

Presidential Commission on Critical Infrastructure Protection, chaired by retired General Robert Marsh.

5. On the controversy surrounding legislation requiring that DHS eventually screen all containers entering the United States, see Chris Strom, "Officials Criticize Plan to Scan All Cargo," *National Journal's Technology Daily*, July 11, 2007, http://www.govexec.com/story_page.cfm?articleid = 37437&dcn = e_hsw.

6. U.S. Government Accountability Office, "Homeland Security Grant Program Risk-Based Distribution Methods: Presentation to Congressional Committees," November 14, 2008, and December 15, 2008, p. 2, http://www.gao.gov/new.items/d09168r.pdf.

7. For more on this point, see Cass Sunstein, *Risk and Reason: Safety, Law and the Environment* (New York: Cambridge University Press, 2002); and Aaron Wildavsky, *Searching for Safety* (New Brunswick, NJ: Transaction Books, 1988).

8. U.S. Government Accountability Office, "Homeland Security Grant Program Risk-Based Distribution Methods," p. 15.

9. On the inclusion of the Amish Country Popcorn Company and many other obscure locations on the DHS's National Asset Database, see Eric Lipton, "Come One, Come All, Join the Terror Target List," *New York Times*, July 12, 2006, http://www.nytimes.com/2006/07/12/washington/12assets.html. On Weeki Wachee Springs, see Mary Spicuzza,"Weeki Wachee Mermaids in Terrorists' Cross Hairs?" *St. Petersburg Times*, April 22, 2005, http://www.sptimes.com/2005/04/22/news_pf/Hernando/Weeki_Wachee_mermaids.shtml. On Kentucky bingo, see Jessica Shoemaker, "Bingo Terrorism," Waste Watcher, Citizens Against Government Waste, February 21, 2006, http://www.cagw.org/site/News2?page = NewsArticle&id = 9712.

10. Federal Bureau of Investigation, U.S. Department of Justice, "Uniform Crime Report: Crime in the United States, 2007," http://www.fbi.gov/ucr/cius2007/documents/murdermain.pdf.

11. Warren Rudman, Stephen Flynn, Leslie Gelb, and Gary Hart, "Our Hair Is on Fire," *Wall Street Journal*, December 16, 2004. See also the related report *America Still Unprepared—America Still in Danger: Report of an Independent Task Force Sponsored by the Council on Foreign Relations* (New York: Council on Foreign Relations, 2002), http://www.cfr.org/publication.html?id = 5099.

12. After retracting its initial estimate of 150 million casualties.

13. World Health Organization, "Cumulative Number of Confirmed Human Cases of Avian Influenza A/(H5N1)Reported to WHO," December 30, 2009, http://www.who.int/csr/disease/avian_influenza/country/cases_table_2009_12_30/en/index.html.

14. On some issues surrounding quarantines for avian flu, see Brian Friel, "Bird Flu Fears Raise Quarantine Questions," *National Journal*, October 25, 2005, http://www.govexec.com/dailyfed/1005/102505nj1.htm.

15. On terrorism and biological weapons, see Milton Leitenberg, *Assessing the Biological Weapons and Bioterrorism Threat* (Carlisle, PA: Strategic Studies Institute, 2005), http://www.strategicstudiesinstitute.army.mil/pubs/display.cfm?pubID = 639. For a summary, see his chapter in this volume. See also Audrey Kurth Cronin, "Terrorist Motivations for Chemical and Biological Weapons Use: Placing the Threat in Context," Order Code RL31831, Congressional Research Service, Washington, 2003, http://www.fas.org/irp/crs/RL31831.pdf; John Parachini, "Putting WMD Terrorism into Perspective," *Washington Quarterly* 26, no. 4 (Autumn 2003): 37–50, http://

www.twq.com/03autumn/docs/03autumn_parachini.pdf; and W. Seth Carus, "The Rajneeshees (1984)," in *Toxic Terror: Assessing Terrorist Use of Chemical and Biological Weapons*, ed. Jonathan B. Tucker (Cambridge, MA: MIT Press, 2000), pp. 55–70.

16. U.S. Strategic Bombing Survey, Summary Report (European War), 1945, http://www.anesi.com/ussbs02.htm. See also, Stephen T. Hosmer, *Psychological Effects of U.S. Air Operations in Four Wars, 1941–1991* (Santa Monica, CA: RAND Corporation, 1996).

17. U.S. Department of Homeland Security, "Budget-in-Brief: Fiscal Year 2010," p. 3, http://www.dhs.gov/xlibrary/assets/budget_bib_fy2010.pdf.

Chapter 6

1. I would like to thank Mark Stewart for valuable comments, and the Centre for Infrastructure Performance and Reliability at the University of Newcastle, Australia, for support.

2. Bart Hobijn and Erick Sager, "What Has Homeland Security Cost? An Assessment: 2001–2005," *Current Issues in Economics and Finance* 13, no. 2 (2007): 2.

3. "National Infrastructure Protection Plan: Partnering to Enhance Protection and Resiliency," U.S. Department of Homeland Security, 2009, p. 7.

4. Jeremy Shapiro, "Managing Homeland Security: Develop a Threat Based Strategy," Opportunity 08 Paper, Brookings Institution, 2007, p. 6; and Stephen Flynn, *The Edge of Disaster: Rebuilding a Resilient Nation* (New York: Random House, 2007).

5. For a discussion of their low success rate at achieving their goals, see Max Abrahms, "Why Terrorism Does Not Work," *International Security* 31, no. 2 (Fall 2006): 42–78.

6. Mark G. Stewart, "Cost Effectiveness of Risk Mitigation Strategies for Protection of Buildings against Terrorist Attack," *Journal of Performance of Constructed Facilities* 22, no. 2 (2008): 115–20.

7. Bill Gertz, "5,000 in U.S. Suspected of Ties to al Qaeda; Groups Nationwide under Surveillance," *Washington Times*, July 11, 2002.

8. Testimony by Mueller can be found at http://www.fbi.gov/congress/congress.htm.

9. Brian Ross, "Secret FBI Report Questions Al Qaeda Capabilities: No 'True' Al Qaeda Sleeper Agents Have Been Found in U.S.," ABC News, March 9, 2005, http://abcnews.go.com/WNT/Investigation/story?id=566425&page=1.

10. Michael Isikoff and Mark Hosenball, "The Flip Side of the NIE," *Newsweek*, August 15, 2007, http://www.newsweek.com/id/32962.

11. Glenn L. Carle, "Overstating Our Fears," *Washington Post*, July 13, 2008.

12. Independent tallies of such attacks are supplied in Anthony H. Cordesman, *The Challenge of Biological Weapons* (Washington: Center for Strategic and International Studies, 2005), pp. 29–31; Brian Michael Jenkins, *Unconquerable Nation: Knowing Our Enemy and Strengthening Ourselves* (Santa Monica, CA: RAND Corporation, 2006.), pp. 179–84; and "Jihadi Attack Kill Statistics," IntelCenter, August 17, 2007, p. 11, http://www.intelcenter.com/JAKS-PUB-v1-8.pdf.

13. Andrew Mack, "Dying to Lose: Explaining the Decline in Global Terrorism," in *Human Security Brief 2007* (Vancouver: Simon Fraser University, 2008), pp. 8–21.

14. Carle, "Overstating Our Fears"; Marc Sageman, *Leaderless Jihad: Terror Networks in the Twenty-First Century* (Philadelphia: University of Pennsylvania Press, 2008); and Fawaz Gerges, "Taking on Al Qaeda," *Washington Post*, June 17, 2008.

15. Randall Monger and Macreadie Barr, "Nonimmigrant Admissions to the United States: 2008," Annual Flow Report, Office of Immigration Statistics, U.S. Department of Homeland Security, April 2009.

16. Guy Lawson, "The Fear Factory," *Rolling Stone*, February 7, 2008, pp. 60–65.

17. Michael Kenney, "Organizational Learning and Islamic Militancy," National Institute of Justice, U.S. Department of Justice, 2009, http://www.ncjrs.gov/pdf files1/nij/grants/226808.pdf.

18. Mette Eilstrup Sangiovanni and Calvert Jones, "Assessing the Dangers of Illicit Networks: Why al Qaida May Be Less Dangerous than Many Think," *International Security* 33, no. 2 (Fall 2009): 7–44.

19. "National Infrastructure Protection Plan," p. 11.

20. See Max Abrahms, "What Terrorists Really Want: Terrorist Motives and Counterterrorism Strategy," *International Security* 32, no. 4 (Spring 2008): 78–105.

21. In contrast, see "National Infrastructure Protection Plan," pp. 33, 37.

22. John Mueller, *Overblown: How Politicians and the Terrorism Industry Inflate National Security Threats, and Why We Believe Them* (New York: Free Press, 2006), p. 2.

23. For an analysis of this likelihood, see Brian Michael Jenkins, *Will Terrorists Go Nuclear?* (Amherst, NY: Prometheus Books, 2008); John Mueller, *Atomic Obsession: Nuclear Alarmism from Hiroshima to Al Qaeda* (New York: Oxford University Press, 2010); and, in contrast, Graham T. Allison, *Nuclear Terrorism: The Ultimate Preventable Catastrophe* (New York: Times Books, 2004). As is discussed a bit more fully later, weapons of mass destruction are not particularly relevant to a discussion of protection measures because they cannot be protected against for the most part. Policing, mitigation, and resilience measures may, however, be useful, but, as indicated at the outset, those are not the policies of concern here.

24. For a study concluding that, because of the low probability of a terrorist attack, it is not worth spending more than a few thousand dollars per year (far less than hiring a single security guard) to protect even the 2 percent of the commercial buildings in the United States that can be considered "large," see Stewart, "Cost Effectiveness of Risk Mitigation Strategies."

25. Howard Kunreuther, "Risk Analysis and Risk Management in an Uncertain World," *Risk Analysis* 22, no. 4 (August 2002): 662–63.

26. Jerry Ellig, Amos Guiora, and Kyle McKenzie, *A Framework for Evaluating Counterterrorism Regulations* (Washington: Mercatus Center, George Mason University, 2006), p. 7.

27. "U.S. Shopping Malls: Unlikely al Qaeda Targets," Stratfor, Austin, TX, November 9, 2007.

28. On this issue, see also Robert Powell, "Defending against Terrorist Attacks with Limited Resources," *American Political Science Review* 101, no. 3 (August 2007): 527–41; and Clark Kent Ervin, *Open Target: Where America Is Vulnerable to Attack* (New York: Palgrave Macmillan, 2006), pp. 156–58. A DHS report acknowledges this problem but does not really explore its implications, instead simply suggesting that it "underscores the necessity for a balanced, comparative approach that focuses on managing risk commensurately across all sectors and scenarios of concern." "National Infrastructure Protection Plan," p. 11.

29. Mark G. Stewart, "Risk and Cost Benefit Assessment of Counter Terrorism Protective Measures to Infrastructure," Research Report no. 272.01.2009, Centre for Infrastructure Performance and Reliability, University of Newcastle, Australia, 2009.

30. Mimi Hall, "Terror Security List Way Behind," *USA Today*, December 9, 2004.

31. Veronique de Rugy, personal conversation, February 2007.

32. See Veronique de Rugy, "The Case for Doing Nothing," *Cato Unbound*, September 28, 2006, http://www.cato-unbound.org/2006/09/28/veronique-de-rugy/the-case-for-doing-nothing/; and Mueller, *Overblown*, p. 74. For an otherwise impressive study where this is not done, see Tom LaTourrette and others, *Reducing Terrorism Risk at Shopping Centers: An Analysis of Potential Security Options* (Santa Monica, CA: RAND Corporation, 2006).

33. "Progress in Developing the National Asset Database," OIG 06 40, Office of Inspector General, U.S. Department of Homeland Security, June 2006; and John D. Moteff, "Critical Infrastructures: Background, Policy, and Implementation," RL30153, Congressional Research Service, 2007.

34. Frank Furedi, "Fear and Security: A Vulnerability Led Policy Response," *Social Policy and Administration* 42, no. 6 (December 2008): 651.

35. Amanda Ripley, "How Safe Are We? The Fortification of Wyoming, and Other Strange Tales from the New Front Line," *Time*, March 29, 2004, http://www.time.com/time/magazine/article/0,9171,993684,00.html. On this issue, see also Ian S. Lustick, *Trapped in the War on Terror* (Philadelphia: University of Pennsylvania Press, 2006); and, in contrast, Tyler Prante and Alok K. Bohara, "What Determines Homeland Security Spending? An Econometric Analysis of the Homeland Security Grant Program," *Policy Studies Journal* 36, no. 2 (2008): 243–56.

36. Steve Emerson, *Jihad Incorporated: A Guide to Islam in the US* (Amherst, NY: Prometheus Books, 2006), p. 120; and Lawson, "The Fear Factory."

37. "National Infrastructure Protection Plan," p. 34.

38. Cass R. Sunstein, "Terrorism and Probability Neglect," *Journal of Risk and Uncertainty* 26, no. 2–3 (March–May 2003): 121–36.

39. Mueller, *Overblown*, p. 31.

40. LaTourrette and others, *Reducing Terrorism Risk at Shopping Centers*.

41. Ellig, Guiora, and McKenzie, *A Framework for Evaluating Counterterrorism Regulations*; and Garrick Blalock, Vrinda Kadiyali, and Daniel H. Simon, "The Impact of Post 9/11 Airport Security Measures on the Demand for Air Travel," *Journal of Law and Economics* 50, no. 4 (November 2007): 731–55.

42. Kevin R. Grosskopf, "Evaluating the Societal Response to Antiterrorism Measures," *Journal of Homeland Security and Emergency Management* 3, no. 2 (2006): 1–9.

43. Bruce Schneier, *Beyond Fear: Thinking Sensibly about Security in an Uncertain World* (New York: Copernicus Books, 2003).

44. Mark G. Stewart and John Mueller, "Cost Benefit Assessment of United States Homeland Security Spending," Research Report no. 273.01.2009, Centre for Infrastructure Performance and Reliability, University of Newcastle, Australia, 2009.

45. For an excellent discussion of this issue, see Elizabeth Eraker, "Cleanup after a Radiological Attack: U.S. Prepares Guidance," *Nonproliferation Review* 11, no. 3 (Fall–Winter 2004): 167–85. There should also be discussions about applying the very conservative standards now in place for determining when an area has become "contaminated," especially with respect to radiological releases. Even to discuss this problem, however, presents considerable political problems. See Mueller, *Atomic Obsession*, pp. 195–97. See also Ripley, "How Safe Are We?"

46. Such an elemental consideration does not appear to be part of the decision process, judging from a *Washington Post* discussion of the issue. Spencer S. Hsu, "New York Presses to Deploy More Bioweapons Sensors," *Washington Post*, January 9, 2008.

47. New York seems to have been able to get graffiti under control on the subways. However, that was accomplished not by making the subways invulnerable but rather by continually cleaning up the graffiti, thus reducing the vandals' incentive to decorate.

48. Stewart, "Risk and Cost Benefit Assessment."

49. "National Infrastructure Protection Plan," p. 15n.

50. Flynn, *The Edge of Disaster*, pp. 35–36, 93.

51. Schneier, *Beyond Fear*, pp. 235–36.

52. On domestic flights, see Roger Bray, "Flights Recover to Level before 9/11," *Financial Times*, September 14, 2004. On Las Vegas, see Richard A. Clarke, "Ten Years Later," *Atlantic Monthly*, January–February 2005, p. 63. Some Las Vegas casinos report that their fourth quarter earnings in 2001 were about one-third of the previous year's.

53. Michael Sivak and Michael J. Flannagan, "Consequences for Road Traffic Fatalities of the Reduction in Flying Following September 11, 2001," *Transportation Research Part F: Traffic Psychology and Behaviour* 7, no. 4–5 (July–September 2004): 301–5; and Garrick Blalock, Vrinda Kadiyali, and Daniel Simon, "Driving Fatalities after 9/11: A Hidden Cost of Terrorism," *Applied Economics* 41, no. 14 (2009): 1717–29.

54. Marcus Holmes, "Just How Much Does That Cost, Anyway? An Analysis of the Financial Costs and Benefits of the 'No Fly' List," *Homeland Security Affairs* 5, no. 1 (January 2009): 1–22.

55. Sara Kehaulani Goo, "TSA Would Allow Sharp Objects on Airliners," *Washington Post*, November 30, 2005.

56. Patrick Smith, "The Airport Security Follies," *New York Times*, December 28, 2007, http://jetlagged.blogs.nytimes.com/2007/12/28/the-airport-security-follies/.

57. Sara Kehaulani Goo, "Going the Extra Mile," *Washington Post*, April 9, 2004.

58. Smith, "Airport Security Follies"; Schneier, *Beyond Fear*, pp. 123–24, 247–48; and Mueller *Overblown*, p. 4.

59. Mark G. Stewart and John Mueller, "A Risk and Cost Benefit Assessment of United States Aviation Security Measures," *Journal of Transportation Security* 1 (2008): 143–59; and Mark G. Stewart and John Mueller, "A Risk and Cost Benefit Assessment of Australian Aviation Security Measures," *Security Challenges* 4, no. 3 (Spring 2008): 45–61.

60. De Rugy, "The Case for Doing Nothing," p. 4.

61. Paul Maley, "Overhaul Cuts Sky Marshals by a Third," *Australian*, January 23, 2008, http://www.theaustralian.news.com.au/story/0,25197,23094399-601,00.html.

62. Sunstein, "Terrorism and Probability Neglect," p. 132.

63. Roger D. Congleton, "Terrorism, Interest Group Politics, and Public Policy," *Independent Review* 7, no. 1 (Summer 2002): 62.

64. Schneier, *Beyond Fear*, p. 249.

Chapter 7

1. Author's calculation based on U.S. Department of Homeland Security, *Budget-in-Brief Fiscal Year 2010*, 2009, http://www.iaem.com/committees/GovernmentAffairs/documents/DHSBudgetinBriefFY2010.pdf; George W. Bush, "Securing the Homeland, Strengthening the Nation," February 2002, http://www.dhs.gov/xlibrary/assets/homeland_security_book.pdf; and Department of Labor, Bureau of Labor Statistics, Current Population Survey, March 2009.

2. For a good discussion about the concept of tradeoffs, see James Buchanan, *Cost and Choice: An Inquiry in Economic Theory* (Indianapolis: Liberty Fund, 1999).

3. Bruce Schneier, *Beyond Fear: Thinking Sensibly about Security in an Uncertain World* (New York: Copernicus Books, 2003), p. 3.

4. "Homeland Security: A Risk Management Approach Can Guide Preparedness Efforts," GAO-02-208T, General Accounting Office, Washington, October 31, 2001, p. 2. Also see "Combating Terrorism: Selected Challenges and Related Recommendations," GAO-01-822, General Accounting Office, Washington, September 20, 2001.

5. "Mortality Tables," Centers for Disease Control and Prevention, U.S. Department of Health and Human Services, http://www.cdc.gov/nchs/nvss/mortality_tables.htm.

6. Office of Management and Budget, *Budget of the United States Government, FY2009, Summary Tables* (Washington: Government Printing Office, 2008), p. 142.

7. Office of Management and Budget, *Budget of the United States Government, FY2010, Historical Tables* (Washington: Government Printing Office, 2009), p. 55.

8. The difficulty of estimating low-probability risks is stressed by Howard Kunreuther, *Disaster Insurance Protection: Public Policy Lessons* (New York: John Wiley, 1978).

9. There is recent and substantial literature on insurance and terrorism risk in the wake of 9/11. See, for instance, Jeffrey R. Brown, Randall S. Kroszner, and Brian H. Jenn, "Federal Terrorism Risk Insurance," working paper, National Bureau of Economic Research, Cambridge, MA, 2002; Gordon Woo, "Insuring against Al Qaeda: Risk Management Solutions," paper presented at a meeting of the National Bureau of Economic Research, Cambridge, MA, January 31, 2003; and Howard Kunreuther, Erwan Michael-Kerjan, and Beverly Porter, "Assessing, Managing and Financing Extreme Events: Dealing with Terrorism," working paper, National Bureau of Economic Research, Cambridge, MA, 2003.

10. W. Kip Viscusi and Richard J. Zeckhauser, "Sacrificing Civil Liberty to Reduce Terrorism Risks," working paper, John F. Kennedy School of Government, Harvard University, Cambridge, MA, 2003.

11. Manuel Trajtenberg, "Defense R&D in the Anti-Terrorist Era," working paper, National Bureau of Economic Research, Cambridge, MA, 2003.

12. Gary Becker, "Crime and Punishment: An Economic Approach," *Journal of Political Economy* 76, no. 2 (1968): 169–217.

13. See John R. Lott Jr., *The Bias against Guns: Why Almost Everything You Have Heard about Gun Control Is Wrong* (Washington: Regnery, 2001), chap. 6. Lott tests the economic model (that if you make something more difficult or increase the cost of being caught for doing something, people do less of it) on perpetrators of multiple-victim public killings. He finds that in this case, although legal sanctions such as higher death penalty execution rates should imply both fewer attacks and fewer people harmed, it is less of a significant factor in deterring multiple-victim killings than it is in deterring normal murders. Also see Bruno S. Frey and Simon Luechinger, "How to Fight Terrorism: Alternatives to Deterrence," working paper, Institut für Empirische Wirtschaftsforschung, Zurich, 2003.

14. For more on this point, see John Mueller, "Assessing Measures Designed to Protect the Homeland," in this volume.

15. Schneier, *Beyond Fear*, p. 103.

16. John R. Lott Jr., "Pilots Still Unarmed," *New York Post*, January 6, 2004.

17. Ibid.

18. Quoted in John R. Lott Jr., "Marshals Are Good but Armed Pilots Are Better," *Wall Street Journal Europe*, January 2, 2004.

19. For a complete explanation of the cost-effectiveness of reinforced cockpit doors in airplanes, see Schneier, *Beyond Fear*, p. 46. Other experts have raised the fact that some engineering constraints in the wall and the hinges where the doors are hung might reduce the effectiveness of these doors. See Lott, "Pilots Still Unarmed." Yet it still seems to be a very cost-effective measure.

20. "Airlines Meet FAA's Hardened Cockpit Door Deadline," press release, Federal Aviation Administration, April 4, 2003.

21. Ibid.

22. Office of Management and Budget, *Budget in Brief FY2010*.

23. Bruce Schneier makes this point using the data compiled by Wm. Robert Johnston and published in the "Worst Terrorist Strikes U.S. and Worldwide." Twelve out of 25 of the deadliest terrorist strikes of the last 80 years are airline related. Ten out of these 12 involve the crash of a hijacked plane. Schneier, *Beyond Fear*, p. 240.

24. For a good discussion on the economic costs of terrorism, see S. Brock Bloomberg, Gregory D. Hess, and Athanasios Orphanides, "The Macroeconomic Consequences of Terrorism," working paper, CESifo, Munich, 2004.

25. Joint Economic Committee, "The Economic Costs of Terrorism," special report prepared at the request of the United States Congress, May 2002, p. 7.

26. "Median Weekly Earnings of Full-Time Wage and Salary Workers by Detailed Occupation and Sex," Bureau of Labor Statistics, U.S. Department of Labor, 2008.

27. David M. Stone, assistant secretary of the Transportation Security Administration, Testimony before the Senate Committee on Commerce, Science, and Transportation, February 15, 2005, http://bulk.resource.org/gpo.gov/hearings/109s/22942.txt.

28. For a good review of the literature and a discussion of defense as a public good, see D. Gold, "Does Military R&D Generate International Public Goods?" paper presented at the annual meeting of the American Economic Association, New York, January 3, 1999.

29. Of course, saying that some areas of homeland security have public features and should probably be provided by the government does not exclude the possibility of inefficient and wasteful provision of that good. Even when the federal government is best suited to deliver a given security measure, that doesn't necessarily mean that it will be efficient. For instance, we know that one of the biggest failures before the 9/11 attacks was the lack of information sharing between the different levels of government. An important counterterrorism goal should have been to set in place an efficient system to ensure that such an oversight never happens again. Eight years later, scant progress has been made in this area, in spite of dramatic spending increases.

30. James Carafano, "Homeland Security Dollars and Sense #2: Misplaced Maritime Priorities," Webmemo no. 648, Heritage Foundation, Washington, February 2, 2005.

31. Margaret Kriz, "Security Leak," *National Journal*, August 2, 2003, p. 2476.

32. James A. Lewis, "Assessing the Risks of Cyber Terrorism, Cyber War and Other Cyber Threats," Center for Strategic and International Studies, December 2002, http://csis.org/files/media/csis/pubs/021101_risks_of_cyberterror.pdf.

33. Bruce Schneier, "The Risk of Cyber-Terrorism," *Crypto-Gram Newsletter*, June 2003, http://www.schneier.com/crypto-gram-0306.html#1. See also Evgeny Morozov, "Cyber-Scare: The Exaggerated Fears over Digital Warfare," *Boston Review*, July–August 2009, http://bostonreview.net/BR34.4/morozov.php.

34. Schneier, *Beyond Fear*, p. 33.

35. Cindy Williams, "Paying for Homeland Security: Show Me the Money," MIT Center for International Studies Audit of the Conventional Wisdom, 07-08, May 2007, http://web.mit.edu/cis/pdf/Audit_05_07_Williams.pdf.

36. Cindy Williams, "Budgets to Make America Safer," MIT Center for International Studies Audit of the Conventional Wisdom, 06-10, June 2006, http://web.mit.edu/cis/pdf/audit_williams_6_06.pdf.

37. See James Buchanan and Gordon Tullock, *The Calculus of Consent* (Ann Arbor: University of Michigan Press, 1962).

38. Buchanan, *Cost and Choice*.

39. For a discussion about the economics of interest groups, see Mancur Olson, "The Logic," in *The Rise and Decline of Nations: Economic Growth, Stagflation, and Social Rigidities* (New Haven, CT: Yale University Press, 1982), pp. 17–35. Also see George J. Stigler, "Free Riders and Collective Action: An Appendix to Theories of Economic Regulation," *Bell Journal of Economics and Management Science* 5, no. 2 (1974): 359–65; and Gary S. Becker, "A Theory of Competition among Pressure Groups for Political Influence," *Quarterly Journal of Economics* 98, no. 3 (1983): 371–400. For a good description of the theory of rent seeking, see Gordon Tullock, "The Welfare Costs of Tariffs, Monopolies, and Theft," *Western Economics Journal* 5 (1967): 224–32; and Robert Tollison, "Rent Thinking: A Survey," *Kylos* 35, no. 4 (1982): 575–601.

40. For discussion about the dynamic of pressure groups, see Becker, "A Theory of Competition," pp. 371–400; and Gary Becker and Casey Mulligan, "Deadweight Costs and the Size of Government," working paper, National Bureau of Economic Research, Cambridge, MA, 1998.

41. For a discussion on pork-barrel spending, see, for example, Daron Acemoglu and James Robinson, "Inefficient Redistribution," *American Political Science Review* 95 (2001): 649–61; and David Baron, "Majoritarian Incentives, Pork Barrel Programs, and Procedural Control," *American Journal of Political Science* 35 (1991): 57–90. See also Stephen Coate and Stephen Morris, "On the Form of Transfers to Special Interests," *Journal of Political Economy* 103 (1995): 1210–35; and Kenneth Shepsle and Barry Weingast, "Political Preferences for the Pork Barrel: A Generalization," *American Journal of Political Science* 25 (1981): 96–112.

42. G. M. Grossman and E. Helpman, "Protection for Sale," *American Economic Review* 84 (1994): 833–50.

43. Chris Edwards, *Downsizing the Federal Government* (Washington: Cato Institute, 2005), p. 32. Economists Timothy Besley and Stephen Coate have looked at the tradeoffs in the provision of local public and private goods and conclude that politics is an important factor in the move toward more centralization of local responsibilities and the inefficient allocation of resources. Federalization of airline screeners and the trend toward the federalization of law enforcement and first-responder programs are recent examples consistent with their theory. Timothy Besley and Stephen Coate, "Centralized Versus Decentralized Provision of Local Public Goods: A Political Economy Analysis," working paper, National Bureau of Economic Research, Cambridge, MA, 1999. See also Stephen Coate, "Distributive Policy Making as a Source of Inefficiency in Representative Democracies," working paper, Penn Institute of Economic Research, Philadelphia, 1997.

44. Nicole Gaouette, "$31.8 Billion Homeland Security Bill Passes," *Los Angeles Times*, July 15, 2005.

45. "Responding to Nuclear Attacks," Backgrounder, Council on Foreign Relations, January 13, 2006, http://cfrterrorism.org/security/nuclear.html.

46. Nick Gillespie and Jesse Walker, "State of War: Interview of John Mueller," *Reason*, October 2006, http://www.reason.com/news/show/36868.html. Also see John Mueller, *Overblown: How Politicians and the Terrorism Industry Inflate the National Security Threat and Why We Believe Them* (New York: Free Press, 2006).

Chapter 8

1. This chapter draws on John Mueller, *Atomic Obsession: Nuclear Alarmism from Hiroshima to Al Qaeda* (New York: Oxford University Press, 2009). The book argues that, whatever their effect on activist rhetoric, strategic theorizing, defense budgets, and political posturing, nuclear weapons have had at best a quite limited effect on history, have been a substantial waste of money and effort, do not seem to have been terribly appealing to most states that do not have them, are out of reach for terrorists, and are unlikely materially to shape much of our future, even as nuclear proliferation, while not necessarily desirable, is unlikely to prove to be a major danger or to accelerate.

2. On Oppenheimer, see Kai Bird and Martin Sherwin, *American Prometheus: The Triumph and Tragedy of J. Robert Oppenheimer* (New York: Knopf, 2005), p. 349. On Theodore Taylor, see John Mcphee, *The Curve of Binding Energy* (New York: Farrar, Straus & Giroux, 1974), p. 7 (immediate, easy), pp. 195–97 (probabilities).

3. For Negroponte's prediction, see letter from the Permanent Representative of the United States of America to the United Nations to the Chairman of the Committee, April 17, 2003, http://www.globalsecurity.org/security/library/report/2003/n0335167.pdf. See also Graham. T. Allison, *Nuclear Terrorism: The Ultimate Preventable Catastrophe* (New York: Times Books, 2004), p. 15; and Graham T. Allison, "Must We Wait for the Nuclear Morning After?" *Washington Post*, April 30, 1995.

4. Matthew Bunn, *Securing the Bomb 2007* (Cambridge, MA: Harvard University Press, 2007), p. vi. See also William Langewiesche, *The Atomic Bazaar: The Rise of the Nuclear Poor* (New York: Farrar, Straus & Giroux, 2007), p. 20; Matthew Bunn, "A Mathematical Model of the Risk of Nuclear Terrorism," *Annals of the American Academy of Political and Social Science* 607, no. 1 (September 2006): 115; Matthew Bunn and Anthony Wier, "Terrorist Nuclear Weapon Construction: How Difficult?" *Annals of the American Academy of Political and Social Science* 607, no. 1 (September 2006): 137; and Brian Michael Jenkins, *Will Terrorists Go Nuclear?* (Amherst, NY: Prometheus Books, 2008), p. 198. For an excellent discussion of nuclear forensics, see Michael A. Levi, *On Nuclear Terrorism* (Cambridge, MA: Harvard University Press, 2007), pp. 127–33.

5. Robin M. Frost, *Nuclear Terrorism after 9/11* (London: International Institute for Strategic Studies, 2005), p. 64; and Jenkins, *Will Terrorists Go Nuclear?* p. 143.

6. Langewiesche, *The Atomic Bazaar*, pp. 169–72.

7. On al Qaeda's enemies, see Peter Bergen, "Where You Bin? The Return of Al Qaeda," *New Republic*, January 29, 2007, p. 19. On the Taliban government, see Lawrence Wright, *The Looming Tower: Al-Qaeda and the Road to 9/11* (New York: Knopf, 2006), pp. 230–31, 287–88.

8. For the low effectiveness of stolen nukes, see Anna Badkhen, "Al Qaeda Bluffing about Having Suitcase Nukes, Experts Say," *San Francisco Chronicle*, March 23, 2004; "'Suitcase Nukes': A Reassessment," Center for Nonproliferation Studies, Monterey

Institute of International Studies, Monterey, CA, 2002, pp. 4, 12; Langewiesche, *The Atomic Bazaar*, p. 19; Jenkins, *Will Terrorists Go Nuclear?* pp. 149–50; and McPhee, *The Curve of Binding Energy*, pp. 145–46.

9. Anna M. Pluta and Peter D. Zimmerman, "Nuclear Terrorism: A Disheartening Dissent," *Survival* 48, no. 2 (Summer 2006): 56. See also Frost, *Nuclear Terrorism after 9/11*, pp. 17–23; and Stephen M. Younger, *The Bomb: A New History* (New York: Ecco, 2009), p. 152.

10. Stephen M. Younger, *Endangered Species* (New York: Ecco, 2007), p. 93. See also Younger, *The Bomb*, pp. 152–53.

11. On triggers, see Jenkins, *Will Terrorists Go Nuclear?* p. 141. On disassembled parts, see Mitchell Reiss, *Bridled Ambition: Why Countries Constrain Their Nuclear Capabilities* (Washington: Woodrow Wilson Center Press, 1995), pp. 11, 13; Joby Warrick, "Pakistan Nuclear Security Questioned: Lack of Knowledge about Arsenal May Limit U.S. Options," *Washington Post*, November 11, 2007; and Younger, *The Bomb*, pp. 153–54. See also Christoph Wirz and Emmanuel Egger, "Use of Nuclear and Radiological Weapons by Terrorists?" *International Review of the Red Cross* 87, no. 859 (September 2005): 502, http://www.icrc.org/Web/eng/siteeng0.nsf/htmlall/review 859 p497/$File/irrc_859_Egger_Wirz.pdf; Langewiesche, *The Atomic Bazaar*, p. 19; and Levi, *On Nuclear Terrorism*, p. 125.

12. On Pakistan's disassembled nukes, see Warrick, "Pakistan Nuclear Security Questioned." For a discussion of the failed state scenario, including useful suggestions for making it even less likely, see Levi, *On Nuclear Terrorism*, pp. 133–38. On the unlikelihood of a Pakistani collapse, see Juan Cole, "Obama's Domino Theory," *salon.com*, March 30, 2009, http://www.salon.com/opinion/feature/2009/03/30/afghanistan/.

13. Levi, *On Nuclear Terrorism*, p. 26. See also Charles D. Ferguson and William C. Potter, *The Four Faces of Nuclear Terrorism: Threats and Responses* (New York: Routledge, 2005), chaps. 3–4.

14. Richard L. Garwin and Georges Charpak, *Megawatts and Megatons* (New York: Knopf, 2001), p. 314; Bill Keller, "Nuclear Nightmares," *New York Times Magazine*, May 26, 2002; http://www.nytimes.com/2002/05/26/magazine/nuclear-nightmares.html; Dafna Linzer, "Nuclear Capabilities May Elude Terrorists, Experts Say," *Washington Post*, December 29, 2004; Allison, *Nuclear Terrorism*, pp. 96–97; Wirz and Egger, "Use of Nuclear and Radiological Weapons," p. 500; Frost, *Nuclear Terrorism after 9/11*, pp. 27–28; Bunn and Wier, "Terrorist Nuclear Weapon Construction," p. 135; Langewiesche, *The Atomic Bazaar*, pp. 21–23; Levi, *On Nuclear Terrorism*, pp. 73–81; and Younger, *The Bomb*, pp. 142–43.

15. On gun type, see Garwin and Charpak, *Megawatts and Megatons*, p. 350; and Allison, *Nuclear Terrorism*, pp. 95–97.

16. On the industrial scale of production, see Allison, *Nuclear Terrorism*; Bunn and Wier, "Terrorist Nuclear Weapon Construction," pp. 136–37; Langewiesche, *The Atomic Bazaar*, p. 20; and Levi, *On Nuclear Terrorism*, p. 15. For likelihood supplied by state, see Bunn, *Securing the Bomb 2007*, pp. 17–18; Jenkins, *Will Terrorists Go Nuclear?* p. 142.

17. Langewiesche, *The Atomic Bazaar*, pp. 33–48.

18. See also Levi, *On Nuclear Terrorism*, pp. 29, 32–33.

19. Ibid., chap. 5.

20. Jenkins, *Will Terrorists Go Nuclear?* p. 140 (incentive), pp. 152–53 (no case).

21. For known thefts, see Linzer, "Nuclear Capabilities May Elude Terrorists." For 100 pounds per kiloton, see Garwin and Charpak, *Megawatts and Megatons,* pp. 314, 350.

22. On buyers lined up, see Linzer, "Nuclear Capabilities May Elude Terrorists." See also Frost, *Nuclear Terrorism after 9/11,* pp. 9, 11–17; Pluta and Zimmerman, "Nuclear Terrorism," p. 60; Younger *Endangered Species,* p. 87; Levi, *On Nuclear Terrorism,* pp. 25, 66, 140; and Jenkins, *Will Terrorists Go Nuclear?* pp. 150–51.

23. Bunn and Wier, "Terrorist Nuclear Weapon Construction," p. 137; George Tenet and Bill Harlow, *At the Center of the Storm: My Years at the CIA* (New York: HarperCollins, 2007), pp. 276–77; and Bunn, *Securing the Bomb 2007,* p. 24.

24. Langewiesche, *The Atomic Bazaar,* pp. 48–50.

25. Ibid., pp. 54–65.

26. Daniel Pearl and Steve LeVine, "Pakistan Has Ties to Group It Vowed to Curb— Military State's Elite Is Linked to Activities of Nuclear Scientist," *Wall Street Journal,* December 24, 2001.

27. On the easy assembly of bombs, see Graham T. Allison and others, *Avoiding Nuclear Anarchy: Containing the Threat of Loose Russian Nuclear Weapons and Fissile Material* (Cambridge, MA: MIT Press, 1996), p. 12; and Wirz and Egger, "Use of Nuclear and Radiological Weapons," pp. 499–502.

28. Younger, *Endangered Species,* p. 86 (wrong), p. 93 (concerned), p. 88 (exceptionally difficult). On "far fetched at best," see Younger, *The Bomb,* p. 146.

29. Carson J. Mark and others, "Can Terrorists Build Nuclear Weapons?" in *Preventing Nuclear Terrorism: The Report and Papers of the International Task Force on the Prevention of Nuclear Terrorism,* ed. Paul Leventhal and Yonah Alexander (Lexington, MA: Heath, 1987), pp. 55, 60; and Bunn and Wier, "Terrorist Nuclear Weapon Construction," p. 142.

30. On this issue, see Levi, *On Nuclear Terrorism,* pp. 88, 95.

31. Keller, "Nuclear Nightmares."

32. For example, Bunn and Wier, "Terrorist Nuclear Weapon Construction," pp. 10–30.

33. Ibid., pp. 133–34, 147; and Tenet and Harlow, *My Years at the CIA,* pp. 266, 279.

34. Gilmore Commission, "First Annual Report to the President and the Congress, Part I: Assessing the Threat," December 15, 1999, p. 31.

35. Matthew Bunn has gone through a somewhat similar exercise and assigns probabilities that I consider to be wildly favorable to the terrorists. In his model, for example, he assumes terrorists stand a 40 percent chance of overcoming *everything* arrayed in barriers 8 through 15 of Table 8.1 and a monumental 70 percent chance of overcoming everything in barriers 16 through 20. This is comparable to assuming a nearly 90 percent chance of overcoming each barrier in the first instance and a chance of well over 90 percent for each in the second. With parameters like that and with some additional considerations, he is able to conclude that there is a 29 percent chance of a terrorist atomic bomb being successfully detonated in the next decade. Bunn, "A Mathematical Model of the Risk of Nuclear Terrorism."

36. Frost, *Nuclear Terrorism after 9/11,* pp. 17–23; Pluta and Zimmerman, "Nuclear Terrorism," p. 57; Bunn, *Securing the Bomb 2007,* pp. 13–14, 25–26, 36–37; Ferguson and Potter, *The Four Faces of Nuclear Terrorism,* p. 145; and Langewiesche, *The Atomic Bazaar,* pp. 27–33.

37. On this issue, see John Mueller, "False Alarms," *Washington Post,* September 29, 2002; and Russell Seitz, "Weaker Than We Think," *American Conservative,* December 6, 2004.

38. Patrick Smith, "The Airport Security Follies," *New York Times*, December 28, 2007, http://jetlagged.blogs.nytimes.com/2007/12/28/the-airport-security-follies/. See also Bruce Schneier, *Beyond Fear: Thinking Sensibly about Security in an Uncertain World* (New York: Copernicus Books, 2003), pp. 123–24, 247–48; and John Mueller, *Overblown: How Politicians and the Terrorism Industry Inflate the National Security Threat and Why We Believe Them* (New York: Free Press, 2006), p. 4.

39. *The 9/11 Commission Report: Final Report of the National Commission on Terrorist Attacks upon the United States* (Washington: Government Printing Office, 2004), pp. 60, 380. See also Tenet and Harlow, *My Years at the CIA*, p. 261.

40. Wright, *The Looming Tower*, pp. 5, 411–12.

41. Kamran Khan and Molly Moore, "Nuclear Experts Briefed bin Laden, Pakistanis Say," *Washington Post*, December 11, 2001.

42. On al Qaeda's Internet research, see Jenkins, *Will Terrorists Go Nuclear?* p. 27. On the official American report, see *Report to the President of the United States of the Commission on the Intelligence Capabilities of the United States Regarding Weapons of Mass Destruction* (Washington: Government Printing Office, March 31, 2005), p. 272; David Albright, "Al Qaeda's Nuclear Program: Through the Window of Seized Documents," paper presented at the Nautilus Institute Special Forum 47, 2002, http://www.nautilus. org/archives/fora/Special-Policy-Forum/47_Albright.html.

43. Louise Richardson, *What Terrorists Want: Understanding the Enemy, Containing the Threat* (New York: Random House, 2006), p. 162; and Jenkins, *Will Terrorists Go Nuclear?* p. 274.

44. Bruce Lawrence, ed., *Messages to the World: The Statements of Osama bin Laden* (London: Verso, 2005), p. 142n.

45. Richardson, *What Terrorists Want*, p. 162. See also Susan B. Martin, "The Threat Is Overblown," in *Debating Terrorism and Counterterrorism*, ed. Stuart Gottlieb (Washington: Congressional Quarterly Press, 2010), p. 187; and Anne Stenersen, *Al-Qaida's Quest for Weapons of Mass Destruction: The History behind the Hype* (Saarbrücken, Germany: VDM Verlag, 2008), p. 31.

46. Stenersen, *Al-Qaida's Quest*, p. 39.

47. Wright, *The Looming Tower*. See also Marc Sageman, *Leaderless Jihad* (Philadelphia: University of Pennsylvania Press, 2008); and Andrew Mack, "Dying to Lose: Explaining the Decline in Global Terrorism," in *Human Security Brief 2007* (Vancouver: Simon Fraser University, 2008), pp. 8–21.

48. On the laptop memo, see Craig Whitlock, "Homemade, Cheap and Dangerous: Terror Cells Favor Simple Ingredients in Building Bombs," *Washington Post*, July 5, 2007. See also John Parachini, "Putting WMD Terrorism into Perspective," *Washington Quarterly* 26, no. 4 (Autumn 2003): pp. 44–46; and Stenersen, *Al-Qaida's Quest*. On historical terrorism, see David C. Rapoport, "Terrorists and Weapons of the Apocalypse," *National Security Studies Quarterly* 5, no. 1 (Summer 1999): 51; Gilmore Commission, "First Annual Report," p. 37; and Schneier, *Beyond Fear*, p. 236.

49. Testimony available at http://www.fbi.gov/congress/congress.html.

50. For two independent analysts on terrorist acquisition of weapons of mass destruction, see Parachini, "Putting WMD Terrorism into Perspective," pp. 43–46; and Martin, "The Threat Is Overblown," p. 189. See also Glenn L. Carle, "Overstating Our Fears," *Washington Post*, July 13, 2008.

51. Cass R. Sunstein, "The Case for Fear," *New Republic*, December 11, 2006, p. 32.

52. Tenet and Harlow, *My Years at the CIA*, p. 264.

Chapter 9

1. Portions of this chapter appeared in "The Self-Fulfilling Prophecy of Bioterrorism," *Nonproliferation Review* 16, no. 1 (March 2009): 95–109. The author thanks the publishers for permission to use that material.

2. For U.S. annual cancer mortality statistics, see "Cancer Statistics 2008 Presentation," American Cancer Society, http://www.cancer.org/docroot/PRO/content/PRO_1_1_Cancer_Statistics_2008_Presentation.asp. For statistics on mortality due to smoking, see Centers for Disease Control and Prevention, "Cigarette Smoking among Adults—United States, 2006," *Morbidity and Mortality Weekly Report* 56, no. 44, November 9, 2007, pp. 1157–61. Because smoking is estimated to contribute roughly 160,000 of the cancer deaths per year, that amount was subtracted from the total to avoid double-counting. For statistics on mortality due to obesity, see Ali H. Mokdad, James S. Marks, Donna Stroup, and Julie L. Gerberding, "Actual Causes of Death in the United States, 2000," *Journal of the American Medical Association* 291 (2004): 1238–45; David B. Allison, Kevin R. Fontaine, JoAnn E. Manson, June Stevens, and Theodore B. VanItallie, "Annual Deaths Attributable to Obesity in the United States," *Journal of the American Medical Association* 282, no. 16 (1999): 1530–38; JoAnn E. Manson, Patrick J. Skerrett, Philip Greenland, and Theodore B. VanItallie, "The Escalating Pandemics of Obesity and Sedentary Life," *Archives of Internal Medicine* 164, no. 3 (February 9, 2004): 249–58; and Katherine M. Flegal, Barry I. Graubard, David F Williamson, and Mitchell H. Gale, "Cause-Specific Excess Deaths Associated with Underweight, Overweight, and Obesity," *Journal of the American Medical Association* 298, no. 17 (2007): 2028–37. Mortality due to obesity costs the United States $90 billion in direct health costs per year. The obesity mortality figure of 365,000 was based on U.S. data for 2000 and has certainly been surpassed by now.

3. Kevin Sack, "Guidelines Set for Preventing Hospital Infections," *New York Times*, October 9, 2008; and Centers for Disease Control, *Public Health Report*, March–April 2007.

4. Tara Parker-Pope, "Stomach Bug Crystallizes a Threat from Antibiotics," *New York Times*, April 14, 2009.

5. P. Harrison and J. Lederberg, eds., "Antibiotic Resistance: Issues and Options," a workshop report of the Forum on Emerging Infections, National Academy of Sciences, Washington, 1990.

6. Infectious Disease Society of America, "Facts about Antibiotic Resistance," Arlington, VA, revised May 21, 2009. This organization estimated that the sum reached as high as $50 billion per year in 2009, although this is likely to be an overestimate given the figure for 2008.

7. Center for Arms Control and Non-Proliferation, "Federal Funding for Biological Weapons Prevention and Defense, Fiscal Years 2001 to 2009," Washington, April 14, 2008, http://www.armscontrolcenter.org/media/_fy2009_bw_budgetv2.pdf. An additional $1 billion was added in August 2008, but the fiscal year 2009 figure includes a one-time allocation of $2.5 billion, possibly leaving expected future annual levels at $7.5 billion.

8. Milton Leitenberg, *Assessing the Biological Weapons and Bioterrorism Threat* (Carlisle, PA: Strategic Studies Institute, December 2005), pp. 11–20, http://www.strategic studiesinstitute.army.mil/pubs/download.cfm?q=639.

9. U.S. Central Intelligence Agency, "Unclassified Report to Congress on the Acquisition of Technology Relating to Weapons of Mass Destruction and Advanced Conventional Munitions, 1 July through 31 December 2003," http://www.fas.org/irp/threat/july_dec2003.htm.

10. Lt. Gen. Michael Maples, "Current and Projected National Security Threats to the United States," Statement for the Record before the U.S. Senate Select Committee on Intelligence, January 11, 2007, http://intelligence.senate.gov/070111/maples.pdf.
11. Senior U.S. intelligence official, conversation with author, June 2008.
12. I have picked one significant example from many. It appears in a chapter by the deputy director of the U.S. Air Force Counterproliferation Center that sets out to dispel "important myths" suggesting that the BW threat was less than imminent. "The likelihood that biological weapons will be used against our nation continues to rise. . . . Additionally, more countries today have active BW programs than at any other time." Col. Jim Davis, "A Biological Wake-Up Call: Prevalent Myths and Likely Scenarios," in *The Gathering Biological Warfare Storm*, by Jim Davis and Barry Schneider (Maxwell Air Force Base, AL: USAF Counterproliferation Center, April 2002), pp. 289–91.
13. Milton Leitenberg, *The Problem of Biological Weapons* (Stockholm: Swedish National Defence College, 2004), p. 18.
14. Senior U.S. intelligence official, conversations with author, 1997–1999.
15. The 2005 Silberman-Robb Commission report claims that al Qaeda in Afghanistan did obtain "Agent X," which is understood to have meant a *B. anthracis* pathogenic strain and not a vaccine strain. The claim appears to be incorrect. See Leitenberg, *Assessing the Biological Weapons and Bioterrorism Threat*, pp. 36–38.
16. Amerithrax is the code name of the FBI investigation of the 2001 anthrax attacks.
17. Cross-topical comparisons can often provide useful insights. Although not a biological pathogen, the chemical contamination of a wide variety of food products in China with the chemical compound melamine demonstrated that the motive of financial profit and not "terrorism" led to the use of the compound as an adulterant in a wide array of processed foods.
18. Alan Cullison, "Inside al-Qaida's Hard Drive," *Atlantic Monthly*, September 2004, http://www.theatlantic.com/doc/200409/cullison; Alan Cullison and Andrew Higgins, "Forgotten Computer Reveals Thinking behind Four Years of Al-Qaida Doings," *Wall Street Journal*, December 31, 2001; and Andrew Higgins and Alan Cullison, "Terrorist's Odyssey: Saga of Dr. Zawahiri Illuminates Roots of Al-Qaida Terror," *Wall Street Journal*, July 2, 2002.
19. Brian Jenkins, *Will Terrorists Go Nuclear?* (Amherst, NY: Prometheus Books, 2008); and RAND Corporation Capitol Hill briefing, September 9, 2008. The success of the ideas of Graham Allison, a major proponent of the imminence of nuclear terrorism, and like-minded others are indicated by public opinion polls that show that 40 percent of Americans reportedly believe that terrorists will detonate a nuclear weapon within 5 years. When American nuclear scientists were asked what that likelihood was within 10 years, the median answer was 10–20 percent likely; the reply from European nuclear scientists was 1 percent likely. This is described by Jenkins in his Capitol Hill briefing.
20. White House, "Homeland Security Presidential Directive 10: Biodefense for the 21st Century," April 2004, http://www.fas.org/irp/offdocs/nspd/hspd-10.html.
21. Alan Pearson, "Documents on the Department of Homeland Security 2006 Bioterrorism Risk Assessment," Center for Arms Control and Non-Proliferation, Washington, January 9, 2008, p. 1.
22. Gregory S. Parnell, Luciana L. Borio, Gerald G. Brown, David Banks, and Alyson G. Wilson, "Scientists Urge DHS to Improve Bioterrorism Risk Assessment,"

Biosecurity and Bioterrorism: Biodefense Strategy, Practice, and Science 6, no. 4 (October 2008): 353–56.

23. Ibid., p. 354.

24. Anne Applebaum, "Only a Game," *Washington Post*, January 19, 2005. O'Toole is now a senior official in the Department of Homeland Security.

25. Former senior official in the Department of Homeland Security, conversation with author, March 8, 2007.

26. William Clark, *Bracing for Armageddon? The Science and Politics of Bioterrorism in America* (New York: Oxford University Press, 2005), p. 19. Three other 2008 books of related interest are David P. Fidler and Larry Gostin, *Biosecurity in the Global Age* (Stanford, CA: Stanford University Press, 2008); Jacqueline Langwith, ed., *Bioterrorism, Opposing Viewpoints Series* (Detroit: Gale/Cengage Learning, 2008), a book designed for students, pairing essentially opposite viewpoints on 12 individual issues within the overall subject; and Anne L. Clunan, ed., *Terrorism, War, or Disease* (Stanford, CA: Stanford University Press, 2008), a more scholarly examination of case studies to determine whether an outbreak of disease is a deliberate use of biological weapons, a deliberate false allegation, or a natural disease outbreak.

27. Elisabeth Bumiller and Eric Schmitt, "Threats and Responses: The Vice President; Cheney, Little Seen by Public, Plays a Visible Role for Bush," *New York Times*, January 31, 2003; and Jane Mayer, "Excerpt: 'The Dark Side,'" National Public Radio, July 15, 2008, http://www.npr.org/templates/story/story.php?storyid= 92528583. Clark erroneously refers to Dark Winter as "a government exercise." It was not. It was staged by a collaboration of several private groups.

28. White House, "Homeland Security Presidential Directive 10"; and National Research Council, "Department of Homeland Security's Threat Risk Assessment: A Call for Change," Washington, 2008. See also Parnell and others, "Scientists Urge DHS to Improve Bioterrorism Risk Assessment."

29. "U.S. Senate Leader Urges 'Manhattan Project' against Bio-Terror Threat," *Agence France Presse*, January 27, 2005.

30. Barry Kellman, *Bioviolence: Preventing Biological Terror and Crime* (Cambridge: Cambridge University Press, 2008), p. 1.

31. National Intelligence Council, "The Terrorist Threat to the Homeland," National Intelligence Estimate, July 2007.

32. Bob Graham and others, *World At Risk: The Report of the Commission on the Prevention of WMD Proliferation and Terrorism* (New York: Vintage Books, 2008), p. 11, or at http://www.preventwmd.gov/report.

33. Jeffrey W. Runge, Testimony before the U.S. House of Representatives, Committee on Homeland Security, Subcommittee on Emerging Threats, Cybersecurity, and Science and Technology, July 22, 2008, p. 2, http://homeland.house.gov/SiteDocuments/20080723153005-80109.pdf.

34. "Joint Statement of Mr. Robert Hooks, Mr. Eric Myers and Dr. Jeffrey Stiefel, U.S. Department of Homeland Security, regarding 'One Year Later—Implementing the Biosurveillance Requirements of the 9/11 Act,'" before the House Committee on Homeland Security, Subcommittee on Emerging Threats, Cybersecurity, and Science and Technology, July 16, 2008, p. 2, http://homeland.house.gov/SiteDocuments/20080716143618-13187.pdf.

35. Siobhan Gorman and David Crawford, "WMD Panel Urges Focus on Biological Threats," *Wall Street Journal*, September 9, 2008.

36. Ibid.

37. Letter to Kevin McCarthy, chair of the Platform Committee, Republican National Committee, from the Federation of American Societies for Experimental Biology, August 1, 2008.

38. Johann Neuman, "Scientists Weigh In with Deductions on Anthrax Killer," *Los Angeles Times*, April 21, 2002, http://articles.latimes.com/2002/apr/21/news/mn-39193.

39. William J. Broad and David Johnston, "A Nation Challenged: Bioterrorism Report Linking Anthrax and Hijackers Is Investigated," *New York Times*, March 23, 2002; and Steve Fainaru and Ceci Connolly, "Memo on Florida Case Roils Anthrax Probe; Experts Debate Theory Hijacker Was Exposed," *Washington Post*, March 29, 2002.

40. The commission's final report was published in January 2010. Commission on the Prevention of Weapons of Mass Destruction Proliferation and Terrorism, "Prevention of WMD Proliferation and Terrorism Report Card: An Assessment of the U.S. Government's Progress in Protecting the United States from Weapons of Mass Destruction Proliferation and Terrorism," Washington, D.C., January 2010, http://www.preventwmd.gov/prevention_of_wmd_proliferation_and_terrorism_report_card/.

41. A model developed by the World Health Organization produced, under optimum conditions for all variables, a *maximum* of 100,000 deaths using 50 kilograms (112 pounds) of dry-powder anthrax delivered over a city of 5 million people in an economically developed country, 35,000 deaths in a city of 1 million, and 24,000 deaths in a city of 500,000. Fewer than totally optimum conditions would produce proportionately lower mortalities. *Health Aspects of Chemical and Biological Weapons* (Geneva: World Health Organization, 1970), Table 10, pp. 98–99. The same estimate was used in Frederick R. Sidell, Ernest T. Takauji, and David R. Franz, eds., *Medical Aspects of Chemical and Biological Warfare* (Washington: Office of the Surgeon General, U.S. Army Medical Department, 1997).

42. Zbigniew Brzezinski and Brent Scowcroft, *America and the World: Conversations on the Future of American Foreign Policy* (New York: Basic Books, 2008), pp. 239–40.

43. Richard Danzig, "Preparing for Catastrophic Bioterrorism: Toward a Long-Term Strategy for Limiting Risk," Center for Technology and National Security Policy, National Defense University, Washington, May 2008, p. 47.

44. Clark, *Bracing for Armageddon?*, p. 158. Clark does not provide the original source but relies on the quotation in a secondary source. Quoted in Susan Wright, "Terrorists and Biological Weapons: Forging the Linkage in the Clinton Administration," *Politics and the Life Sciences* 25, no. 1–2 (2007): 100.

45. David Koplow, "Losing the War on Bioterrorism," *Security Law Commentary*, Georgetown Law Center on National Security and the Law, October 6, 2008, http://www.securitylawbrief.com/commentary/2008/10/losing-the-war.html.

46. Bioterrorism seems peculiarly vulnerable to this problem. Pages could be filled with examples of false information on bioterrorism from publications in the professional literature authored by "experts." There are also periodic outbursts of stories in the press and blogs that are totally fictitious. There were three examples early in 2009. In January 2009, there was a rash of stories about an Algerian terrorist group's alleging that they had produced plague organisms, which caused their own death. The story was a fantasy. In June 2009, the *Washington Times* reported that al Qaeda was seeking to penetrate the Mexican-U.S. border so that one of its members could disperse anthrax on the White House lawn. The story was based on the ridiculous

exhortation by an al Qaeda sympathizer in Kuwait aired on Al Jazeera television earlier in the year. See Sara A. Carter, "Al-Qaida Eyes Anthrax Attack on U.S. from Mexico," *Washington Times*, June 3, 2009. The story was then picked up by the Pakistani press, *Stars and Stripes*, Fox News, "and across conservative talk radio and the blogosphere" ("Alarming Report of Attacks," thespectrum.com, June 11, 2009). And in April and May 2009, there was another kind of disinformation: deliberate and opportunistic. When the recent swine flu outbreak began in Mexico and the United States, stories appeared in Israel (April 25, 2009), Iran (May 6 and 12, 2009), Syria (May 4–5, 2009), and Russia (May 14, 2009) accusing one or the other of having produced the swine flu virus in a laboratory and releasing it. The Russian article, which appeared in the newspaper *Argumenty I Fakti* and on a *Pravda* website, both of which are closely associated with the Russian government, accused the United States of being responsible for the swine flu outbreak.

47. U.S. Central Intelligence Agency, "Iraq's Weapons of Mass Destruction Programs," 2002, unclassified, http://www.gwu.edu/~nsarchiv/NSAEBB/NSAEBB80/wmd14.pdf; and Kathleen M. Vogel, "'Iraqi Winnebagos™ of Death': Imagined and Realized Futures of U.S. Bioweapons Threat Assessment," *Science and Public Policy* 35, no. 8 (October 2008): 561–73. An equally spurious claim, raised by Vice President Cheney as late as September 14, 2003, long after U.S. inspection teams were searching Iraq, was that Iraq had been working with smallpox in the period before the U.S. invasion. "Smallpox fears were part of the case the Bush administration used to build support for invading Iraq—and they were raised again as recently as last weekend by Vice President Dick Cheney." Dafna Linzer, "No Evidence Iraq Stockpiled Smallpox," Associated Press, September 18, 2003. In addition, "Shortly after the first anthrax victim died in October, the Bush administration began an intense effort to explore any possible link between Iraq and the attacks and continued to do so even after scientists determined that the lethal germ was an American strain, sciences and government officials said. . . . 'We looked for any shred of evidence that would bear on this, or any foreign source,' a senior intelligence official said of an Iraq connection. 'It's just not there.' . . . 'I know there are a number of people who would love an excuse to get after Iraq,' said a top federal scientist involved in the investigation." William J. Broad and David Johnston, "U.S. Inquiry Tried, but Failed, to Link Iraq to Anthrax Attack," *New York Times*, December 22, 2001.

48. Other cases are comparatively more trivial, such as a University of Texas researcher's defending her research to produce a vaccine against ricin by stating, "Large stockpiles of ricin have been found in several countries in the Middle East." The statement is a complete fiction: "Large stockpiles of ricin" have never "been found" in any country, in the Middle East or anywhere else. University of Texas Southwestern, "UT Southwestern Researchers Develop Effective, Safe Vaccine against Deadly Bioterrorism Toxin Ricin," press release, September 4, 2002, http://www.sciencedaily.com/releases/2002/09/020909065008.htm.

49. Data courtesy of Dr. Richard Ebright in a letter to author, June 8, 2009.

50. U.S. Government Accountability Office, "High-Containment Biosafety Laboratories: Preliminary Observations on the Oversight of the Proliferation of BSL-3 and BSL-4 Laboratories in the United States," GAO-08-108T, Washington, October 4, 2007, http://www.gao.gov/new.items/d08108t.pdf. Widely disparate numbers have appeared in the literature despite seemingly authoritative sources. In September 2005, a contractor study prepared for the National Institute of Allergy and Infectious Diseases identified 277 domestic BSL-3 labs, clearly an extremely incomplete survey,

while in January 2007, the Department of Health and Human Services and the Department of Homeland Security estimated that there were 630 BSL-3 and BSL-4 labs, still only a fraction of the total number. Frank Gottron and Dana A. Shea, "Oversight of High-Containment Laboratories: Issues for Congress," R-40418, Congressional Research Service, Washington, March 5, 2009.

51. Yudhijit Bhattachargee, "Lawmakers Signal Tougher Controls on Pathogenic Research," *Science* 326, no. 5949 (October 2, 2009): 28–29; U.S. Government Accountability Office, "High Containment Laboratories: National Strategy for Oversight is Needed," GAO-09-574, September 21, 2009; Editorial, "Containing Risk: The Ad-Hoc Proliferation of High-Security Biological Labs Must Be Controlled, and Should Be Tied More Closely to Broader Research and Public-Health Goals," *Nature*, November 17, 2009.

52. This subject has been treated extensively in two book-length publications and, therefore, is not further developed here. Leitenberg, *The Problem of Biological Weapons*, pp. 155–206; and Leitenberg, *Assessing the Biological Weapons and Bioterrorism Threat*, pp. 65–85.

53. SRS Technologies, "Quantification of Open Source Research Publications in Biological Sciences for Biological Weapons Development Utility," final report, prepared for Defense Threat Reduction Agency, June 16, 2003.

54. This citation is being withheld to prevent the further spread of information to those interested in developing *B. anthracis* as a weapon.

55. U.S. Government Accountability Office, "DOD Excess Property: Risk Assessment Needed on Public Sales of Equipment That Could Be Used to Make Biological Agents," GAO-04-817 N1, Washington, October 7, 2003. See Leitenberg, *Assessing the Biological Weapons and Bioterrorism Threat*, pp. 41–42.

56. In the same period that legislation to strengthen U.S. food inspection and regulation was being considered, legislation that would regulate and restrict tobacco products under the jurisdiction of the Food and Drug Administration was also finally enacted. When the U.S. Senate passed regulations governing the tobacco industry in June 2009, after decades of efforts to achieve such legislation, Dr. Margaret Hamburg, the new head of the FDA, said, "We now have an opportunity to really make a difference with what is probably the No. 1 public health concern in the nation and the world." Duff Wilson, "Senate Approves Tight Regulation over Cigarettes," *New York Times*, June 12, 2009. It was a particularly notable statement given that Dr. Hamburg had for the previous half dozen years been in the forefront of emphasizing the bioterrorism threat.

57. Gardiner Harris, "Infant Deaths Fall in U.S., Though Rate Is Still High," *New York Times*, October 16, 2008; and Editorial, "29th on Infant Mortality," *New York Times*, October 19, 2008.

58. "Reduction in Disease Prevention Budget at CDC Questioned by Lawmakers," *SeniorJournal.com*, March 12, 2007, http://seniorjournal.com/NEWS/Politics/2007/7-03-12-ReductionIn.htm.

59. Sarah A. Lister, "An Overview of the U.S. Public Health System in the Context of Emergency Preparedness," Congressional Research Service, Washington, March 17, 2005; Center for Arms Control and Non-Proliferation, "Federal Funding for Biological Weapons Prevention and Defense, Fiscal Years 2001–2009," Washington, revised May 27, 2008, http://www.armscontrolcenter.org/resources/fy2008_bw_budget.pdf; and Henry H. Wills and others, "Initial Evaluation of the Cities Readiness Initiative,"

RAND Corporation, Santa Monica, CA, 2009, http://www.rand.org/pubs/technical
_reports/2009/RAND_TR640.pdf.

60. For example, between 2003 and 2009, the National Institute of Allergy and
Infectious Diseases awarded 20 grants for research on *Clostridium difficile*, a bacterial
stomach bug, which, as noted, sickens more than 350,000 Americans annually and
kills 15,000–20,000 of them. In the same period, the institute awarded 306 grants for
research on *B. anthracis*. For details, see the online database of the National Institutes
of Health, http://crisp.cit.nih.gov. Total spending on grants likely follows the same
pattern, but we cannot say for sure, as those data are unavailable. On *C. difficile*, see
Parker-Pope, "Stomach Bug."

61. Constraints on space required the omission of a review of U.S. pandemic flu
vaccine production capacity. Readers can obtain this information by contacting the
author at mleitenb@umd.edu.

62. Dr. Kellman, the conference organizer, followed this initiative with a book
published in 2008 that presented the same argument. Kellman, *Bioviolence*, p. 1.

63. Committee on Prevention of Proliferation of Biological Weapons in States
beyond the Former Soviet Union, *Countering Biological Threats: Challenges for the Department of Defense's Nonproliferation Program beyond the Former Soviet Union* (Washington:
National Academies Press, 2009).

64. Ibid., p. 8.

65. J. G. Breman, "The Ears of the Hippopotamus: Manifestations, Determinants,
and Estimates of the Malaria Burden," *American Journal of Tropical Medicine and Hygiene*
64, nos. 1–2 Supplement (January–February 2001): 1–11. The figure of 1 million global
mortality for malaria that is reproduced universally was taken from a paper published
in the 1970s that referred to "at least one million fatalities . . . among children, in
Africa annually." In addition, these numbers derive from a World Health Organization
reporting system that accumulates data supplied by a handful of hospitals in only
30 countries, ensuring that the number is greatly undercounted.

66. Further details and sources can be found in Leitenberg, *Assessing the Biological
Weapons and Bioterrorism Threat*, pp. 1–5.

67. Laura MacInnis, "WHO Tells Governments to Focus on Health Care," Reuters,
October 14, 2008. In 2005, the World Health Organization revised its International
Health Regulations, which became binding law to its member states in June 2007.
The goal of these revisions was to protect against the international spread of epidemics
and other public health emergencies by enhancing the capacity of disease surveillance
and response in member states. Clearly, these are capacities lacking in many developing nations, particularly the poorest ones.

68. "The WHO reports that Africa's overall [gross domestic product] is estimated
to be 32 per cent lower as a result of malaria, equivalent to a loss of US$100 billion
annually. The HIV pandemic in Sub-Saharan Africa is just as devastating, and it is
expected that by 2010 per capita GDP in some of the hardest-hit countries will drop
by 8 per cent, with heavily affected countries losing more than 20 per cent. . . . Globally
the economic costs of tuberculosis (TB) to the poor are estimated to be $12 billion
per year." Tom Daschle and Tara O'Toole, "Biodefense in the 21st Century," paper
submitted to the Institute for Public Policy Research (UK), June 2008, p. 6. Their data
were taken from a 2003 report by the U.S. Institute of Medicine (NAS), "Microbial
Threats to Health: Emergence, Detection and Response"; and the World Health Organization, "Scaling up the Response to Infectious Diseases: A Way Out of Poverty,"
Report on Infectious Diseases, 2002.

69. Center for Arms Control and Nonproliferation, "Federal Funding for Biological Weapons," revised May 27, 2008.

70. W. Seth Carus, *Bioterrorism and Biocrimes: The Illicit Use of Biological Agents in the 20th Century* (Washington: National Defense University, 1998, 2001).

71. Nelson Hernandez, "Fort Detrick: Inventory Uncovers 9,200 More Pathogens: Laboratory Says Security Is Tighter, but Earlier Count Missed Dangerous Vials," *Washington Post*, June 18, 2009. In another ironic example, the state of Kansas, which has campaigned for several years to become the still-to-be-designated location for the National Bio and Agro Defense facility, a BSL-4 laboratory, was one of the 14 states earning the lowest grades in a national health preparedness survey. Karen Shideler, "Report Ranks Kansas Low in Public Health Preparedness," *Wichita Eagle*, December 30, 2001.

72. Yudhijit Bhattachargee, "Biosecurity: Discovery of Untracked Pathogen Vials at Army Lab Sparks Concerns," *Science* 324, no. 5935 (June 26, 2009): 1626.

73. Sam Hannanel, "Investigators Find Biological Research Labs Slow to Upgrade Security Criticized a Year Ago," Associated Press, August 5, 2009. Perhaps a more serious incident occurred in May 2009—a deliberate theft by a former researcher in the strictly controlled Canadian government's National Microbiology Laboratory in Winnipeg. The researcher, with full Canadian government security clearances, was on his way to a new position at a biodefense facility in the United States. His work involved producing a vaccine for the Ebola virus. To save time and effort, he took along 22 vials of material, some of which included Ebola genes. The material was noninfectious, but the incident demonstrated the ease of insider violation of regulations. Jen Skerritt, "Ebola Gene Theft a Shocker; Sparks Serious Questions about Security at City's Microbiology Lab," *Winnipeg Free Press*, May 14, 2009.

74. National Academy of Sciences, *Biotechnology Research in an Age of Terrorism* (Washington: National Academies Press, 2004), p. 5. See also Leitenberg, *Assessing the Biological Weapons and Bioterrorism Threat*, pp. 75–78.

75. "Mandate for Failure: The State of Institutional Biosafety Committees in an Age of Biological Weapons Research," Sunshine Project, Austin, TX, October 4, 2004. See also Leitenberg, *Assessing the Biological Weapons and Bioterrorism Threat*, pp. 82–83.

76. Laura Kahn, "Licensing Life Science Researchers," *Bulletin of the Atomic Scientists*, April 6, 2009.

77. Arturo Casadevall, Susan A. Ehrlich, David R Franz, Michael J. Imperiale, and Paul S. Keirn, "Biodefense Research: A Win-Win Challenge," *Biosecurity and Bioterrorism: Biodefense Strategy, Practice and Science* 6, no. 4 (2008): 1–2.

78. Elaine M. Grossman, "Science Groups Counter WMD Panel's Prescription for Stemming Biological Threats," Global Security Newswire, March 13, 2009.

79. National Science Advisory Board for Biosecurity, "Enhanced Personnel Reliability among Individuals with Access to Select Agents," May 2009; Yudhijit Bhattachargee, "Experts Want Scientists to Monitor Their Colleagues," *Science*Insider, April 30, 2009, http://blogs.sciencemag.org/scienceinsider/2009/04/experts-want-sc.html. A month later, a Defense Science Board report presented the remarkable insights that the theft of biological agents or toxins from a DOD lab was unlikely unless an insider was the thief, in which case theft was feasible, and that it was dubious that an insider could carry out weaponization of a biological agent except in the case where his laboratory work included the equipment that would be needed for the task. "Report of the Defense Science Board Task Force on Department of Defense Biological Safety

and Security Program," May 2009, pp. xi, 19, 40, http://www.acq.osd.mil/dsb/reports/2009-05-Bio_Safety.pdf.

80. Richard B. Marchase and Darrell G. Kirch, letter to the U.S. Working Group on Strengthening the Biosecurity of the United States, Washington, May 29, 2009, http://opa.faseb.org/pdf/2009/Biosecurity_FASEB_AAMC_5.29.09.pdf.

81. Kavita M. Berger and Alan I. Leshner, "Editorial: New Rules for Biosecurity," *Science* 324, no. 5931 (May 29, 2009): 1117.

82. "AAAS Report Warns That New Lab Security Measures Could Undercut Biological Research," All American Patriots website, June 1, 2009, http://www.allamerican patriots.com/48752834-aaas-report-warns-that-new-lab-security-measures-could-undercut-biological-resea.

83. Charles F. Dasey, "Medical Benefits of the Biological Defense Research Program," *Politics and the Life Sciences* 9, no. 1 (August 1990): 77–84.

84. Victoria Sutton, "Survey Finds Biodefense Researcher Anxiety—Over Inadvertently Violating Regulations," *Biosecurity and Bioterrorism: Biodefense Strategy, Practice and Science* 7, no. 2 (2009): 225–26. See also Committee on Assessing Fundamental Attitudes of Life Scientists as a Basis for Biosecurity Education, National Research Council, *A Survey of Attitudes and Actions on Dual Use Research in the Life Sciences: A Collaborative Effort of the National Research Council and the American Association for the Advancement of Science* (Washington: National Academies Press, 2009).

85. Martin Matishak, "After Delay, Senate Committee Approves Biosecurity Bill," Global Security Newswire, November 5, 2009, http://gsn.nti.org/gsn/nw_2009 1105_8558.php.

86. "Biodefense Research and the Biological Weapons Convention," in Leitenberg, *Assessing the Biological Weapons and Bioterrorism Threat*, pp. 68–85.

87. Brian Jenkins offered a similar recommendation regarding nuclear terrorism: "The first thing we have to do is truly understand the threat. Nuclear terrorism is a frightening possibility but it is not inevitable or imminent, and there is no logical progression from truck bombs to nuclear bomb." See James Kitfield, "Interview: How I Learned Not to Fear the Bomb," Global Security Newswire, October 20, 2008, http://www.nti.org/d_newswire/issues/2008_10_20.html#1D29B503.

Chapter 10

1. A growing body of work makes this point, including several chapters in this volume. John Mueller has written extensively on the subject. See especially, "A False Sense of Insecurity?" *Regulation* 27, no. 3 (Fall 2004): 42–46; and *Overblown: How Politicians and the Terrorism Industry Inflate National Security Threats, and Why We Believe Them* (New York: Free Press: 2006). See also Ian S. Lustick, *Trapped in the War on Terror* (Philadelphia: University of Pennsylvania Press, 2006); Benjamin H. Friedman, "Leap before You Look: The Failure of Homeland Security," *Breakthroughs* 13, no. 1 (Spring 2004): 29–40; Benjamin H. Friedman, "Think Again: Homeland Security," *Foreign Policy* (July–August 2005): 22–28; James Fallows, "Success without Victory," *Atlantic Monthly*, January–February 2005, pp. 80–90; and James Fallows, "Declaring Victory," *Atlantic Monthly*, September 2006, pp. 60–73.

2. On what counts as homeland security spending, see the section on "Homeland Security Mission Funding by Agency and Budget Account" in the Crosscutting Programs of the *Analytical Perspectives* volume of the federal budget. The most recent is at http://www.whitehouse.gov/omb/budget/fy2010/assets/homeland.pdf. As of

spring 2008, roughly half (49 percent of the fiscal year 2009 budget) of homeland security spending occurred within the Department of Homeland Security. Other departments that received significant chunks of total homeland security spending were Defense at 29 percent (mostly going to security for military installations), Health and Human Services at 7 percent, Justice at 6 percent, State at 4 percent, and Energy at 3 percent. Several departments got 1 percent or less. Steven M. Kosiak, "Overview of the Administration's FY 2009 Request for Homeland Security," Center for Strategic and Budgetary Assessments, March 27, 2008, p. 6, http://www.csbaonline.org/4Publications/PubLibrary/U.20080330.FY_09_HLS_Request_U.20080330.FY_09_HLS_Request.pdf.

3. The quote is from James Fallows's blog, "Year-End Pensee," January 15, 2009, http://jamesfallows.theatlantic.com/archives/year_end_pensee/. As Fallows has noted, a useful rhetorical gesture would be to change the name of the Department of Homeland Security to something like the Department of Civil Safety.

4. The length of the border figure comes from the International Boundary Commission's website at http://www.internationalboundarycommission.org/boundary.html. The number of foreign visitors comes from U.S. Department of Homeland Security, *Yearbook of Immigration Statistics: 2008* (Washington: Office of Immigration Statistics, U.S. Department of Homeland Security, 2009), p. 65, http://www.dhs.gov/xlibrary/assets/statistics/yearbook/2008/ois_yb_2008.pdf.

5. This point is not made to endorse the idea, embraced in different forms by the last two U.S. administrations, that U.S. foreign policy should aim to end these conditions abroad in the name of sapping terrorist motivation. Trying to do so invites policies with costs that vastly outweigh their benefits. The use of the phrase "mature liberal institutions" above rather than "democracy" is intentional. On the danger of violent politics in democratizing states, see Edward D. Mansfield and Jack Snyder, *Electing to Fight: Why Emerging Democracies Go to War* (Cambridge, MA: MIT Press, 2005). See also, Fareed Zakaria, *The Future of Freedom: Illiberal Democracy at Home and Abroad* (New York: W. W. Norton, 2003).

6. Brian Ross, "Secret FBI Report Questions Al Qaeda Capabilities," ABC News Online, March 9, 2005, http://abcnews.go.com/WNT/Investigation/story?id=566425&page=1.

7. On the limited number of terror prosecutions in the United States, see "Terrorist Trial Report Card," September 11, 2001–September 11, 2008, Center for Law and Security, New York University, http://www.lawandsecurity.org/publications/Sept08TTRCFinal1.pdf; Eric Schmitt, "F.B.I. Agents' Role Is Transformed by Terror Fight," *New York Times*, August 18, 2009, http://www.nytimes.com/2009/08/19/us/19terror.html?_r=1&hp; Dan Eggen and Julie Tate, "US Campaign Produces Few Convictions on Terrorism Charges," *Washington Post*, June 12, 2005, http://www.washingtonpost.com/wp-dyn/content/article/2005/06/11/AR2005061100381.html; and David Cole, "Are We Safer?" *New York Review of Books* 54, no. 4 (March 9, 2006): 15–18.

8. See, for example, Stephen Flynn, *The Edge of Disaster: Rebuilding a Resilient Nation* (New York: Random House, 2007).

9. Gail Makinen, "The Economic Effects of September 11: A Retrospective Assessment," Congressional Research Service, September 27, 2002, http://www.fas.org/irp/crs/RL31617.pdf; and Brian W. Cashell and Marc Labonte, "The Macroeconomic Effects of Hurricane Katrina," Congressional Research Service, September 13, 2005, http://assets.opencrs.com/rpts/RS22260_20050913.pdf.

10. The production that Germany and Japan maintained under allied bombardment during World War II demonstrates the point. On those cases and the theoretical trouble with strategic airpower theory, see Robert A. Pape, *Bombing to Win: Airpower and Coercion in War* (Ithaca, NY: Cornell University Press, 1996). A comparison between strategic airpower theorists and those claiming that the United States faces grave risk from cyberattack is made in James A. Lewis, "Assessing the Risks of Cyber Terrorism, Cyber War and Other Cyber Threats," Center for Strategic and International Studies, December 2002, http://csis.org/files/media/csis/pubs/021101_risks_of_cyberterror.pdf.

11. The best example is Daniel Benjamin and Steve Simon, *The Age of Sacred Terror* (New York: Random House, 2002).

12. Jihadism is a violent wing of the Islamist movement that grew in the Muslim world in the 20th century. The Islamist movement desires government by sharia but is not necessarily violent or revolutionary. Although there are Shiite Islamists, particularly in Iran and Iraq, it is Sunni Islamism that spawned the terrorists that target the United States today. Jihadists claim that they are a vanguard that will ignite the rest of the Sunni world to cast off secular rulers, via violence, restoring the caliphate, the ancient Islamic kingdom. Jihadists say that Islam requires each Muslim to fight against non-Muslims, Shia, secular rulers, and their supporters. Mary Habeck, *Knowing the Enemy: Jihadist Ideology and the War on Terror* (New Haven, CT: Yale University Press, 2006), pp. 28–29, 105–22.

13. On 9/11 as an aberration, see John Mueller, "Harbinger or Aberration?" *National Interest* 69 (Fall 2002): 45–50. Contrary to many claims, terrorism has been declining in frequency in recent years. See Andrew Mack, ed., *Human Security Brief 2007* (Vancouver: Simon Fraser University, 2008), pp. 8–20, http://www.humansecurity brief.info/HSRP_Brief_2007.pdf.

14. Jason Burke, *Al Qaeda: Casting a Shadow of Terror* (New York: Palgrave Macmillan, 2003), pp. 145–160. See also *The 9-11 Commission Report: Final Report of the National Commission on Terrorist Attacks upon the United States* (New York: W. W. Norton, 2004), pp. 59–60, 67.

15. Marc Sageman, *Leaderless Jihad: Terror Networks in the Twenty-First Century* (Philadelphia: University of Pennsylvania Press, 2008).

16. Mack, *Human Security Brief 2007*, pp. 8–20; Gilles Kepel, *Jihad: The Trail of Political Islam*, trans. Anthony F. Roberts (Cambridge, MA: Belknap Press, 2002); Audrey Kurth Cronin, *How Terrorism Ends: Understanding the Decline and Demise of Terrorist Campaigns* (Princeton, NJ: Princeton University Press, 2009); and Scott Shane, "Rethinking Our Terrorist Fears," *New York Times*, September 26, 2009, http://www.nytimes.com/2009/09/27/weekinreview/27shane.html.

17. Fawaz Gerges, *The Far Enemy: Why Jihad Went Global*, 2nd ed. (New York: Cambridge University Press, 2009), pp. 115–85.

18. John Mueller, *Atomic Obsession: Nuclear Alarmism from Hiroshima to Al-Qaeda* (New York: Cambridge University Press, 2009).

19. See Milton Leitenberg's chapter in this volume.

20. *The 9-11 Commission Report*, pp. 60, 151.

21. For an overview of terrorist attempts to use chemical and biological weapons, see Jonathan Tucker, ed., *Toxic Terror: Assessing Terrorist Use of Chemical and Biological Weapons* (Cambridge, MA: MIT Press, 2000).

22. An example of this claim is Gabriel Weimann, *Terror on the Internet: The New Arena, the New Challenges* (Washington: U.S. Institute for Peace Press, 2006), p. 127.

23. For a sampling, see Bruce Schneier, "Portrait of the Modern Terrorist as an Idiot," *Wired*, June 14, 2008, http://www.wired.com/politics/security/commentary/securitymatters/2007/06/securitymatters_0614.

24. Gallup Inc., "Terrorism in the United States," July 6–8, 2007, http://www.gallup.com/poll/4909/terrorism-UnitedStates.aspx#1. Question: "How worried are you that you or someone in your family will become a victim of terrorism—very worried, somewhat worried, not too worried, or not worried at all?"

25. Ibid. Question: "How likely is it that there will be further acts of terrorism in the United States over the next several weeks—very likely, somewhat likely, not too likely, or not at all likely?"

26. Again, this spending should not be confused with the DHS budget, which includes only about half the total homeland security spending. The figure for 2000 is from Veronique de Rugy, "What Does Homeland Security Spending Buy," AEI Working Paper no. 107, American Enterprise Institute, October 29, 2004, updated, April 1, 2005, http://www.aei.org/paper/21483. Later figures are from Kosiak, "Overview of the Administration's FY 2009 Request for Homeland Security."

27. Calculated from annual DHS "Budget-in-Brief" documents available at http://www.dhs.gov/xabout/budget; and "Federal Funding for Homeland Security: An Update," Congressional Budget Office, July 20, 2005, http://www.cbo.gov/ftpdocs/65xx/doc6566/7-20-HomelandSecurity.pdf. The figures include both discretionary and mandatory spending, with the former typically comprising about 80 percent of the total.

28. On the formation of the department, see Susan B. Glasser and Michael Grunwald, "Department's Mission Was Undermined from Start," *Washington Post*, December 22, 2005, http://www.washingtonpost.com/wp-dyn/content/article/2005/12/21/AR2005122102327.html; and Dara Kay Cohen, Mariano-Florentino Cuéllar, and Barry R. Weingast, "Crisis Bureaucracy, Homeland Security and the Political Design of Legal Mandates," *Stanford Law Review* 59, no. 3 (December 2006): 684–700.

29. Office of Management and Budget, "2008 Report to Congress on the Benefits and Costs of Federal Regulations and Unfunded Mandates on State, Local, and Tribal Entities," January 2009, p. 12, http://www.whitehouse.gov/omb/assets/information_and_regulatory_affairs/2008_cb_final.pdf. This range is likely significantly lower than the total cost of homeland security regulations because it does not consider nonmajor regulations and some indirect costs. Scott Farrow and Stuart Shapiro, "The Benefit-Cost Analysis of Security Focused Regulations," *Journal of Homeland Security and Emergency Management* 6, no. 1 (January 2009): 2, http://www.bepress.com/jhsem/vol6/iss1/25.

30. Mark G. Stewart and John Mueller, "Cost-Benefit Assessment of United States Homeland Security Spending," Research Report no. 273.01.2009, Centre for Infrastructure Performance and Reliability, University of Newcastle, Australia, January 2009, http://hdl.handle.net/1959.13/33120. As they note, they leave out the reasonable guess that the expected annual mortality from terrorism could be zero or only a handful, meaning the cost per life saved could be far higher. They also do not account for the fact that a variety of government activities—the wars, portions of the defense and intelligence budget—has counterterrorism value. That means homeland security spending can be credited with only a fraction of the lives saved annually from terrorism and that the cost-per-life-saved estimates ought to be multiplied. Those authors did similar analysis for specific airline security measures. Mark G. Stewart

and John Mueller, "A Risk and Cost-Benefit Assessment of United States Aviation Security Measures," *Journal of Transportation Security* 1, no. 3 (September 2008): 143–59.

31. If a policy costs more per life saved than the value of a statistical life, the government is valuing life more highly than people do in their behavior and could probably produce more health by regulating in other ways. Stewart and Mueller use $7.5 million per life saved, the middle of a range of estimates from $4 million to $11 million. That is an adjustment from a range of $3 million to $9 million in a 2000 article. W. Kip Viscusi, "The Value of Life in Legal Contexts: Survey and Critique," *American Law and Economic Review* 2, no. 1 (Spring 2000): 205. A related concept is risk-risk or health-health analysis, which says that at some cost, a regulation will cost more lives than it saves by destroying wealth used for health care and other welfare-enhancing activities. One calculation of that cost, from 2000, is $15 million. Robert Hahn, Randall Lutter, and W. Kip Viscusi, "Do Federal Regulations Reduce Mortality?" AEI-Brookings Joint Center for Regulatory Studies, Washington, 2000, http://aei-brookings.org/admin/authorpdfs/redirect-safely.php?fname = ../pdffiles/hlv.pdf.

32. There are many exceptions that cost far more. Cass Sunstein, *Risk and Reason: Safety, Law and the Environment* (New York: Cambridge University Press, 2002), pp. 29–33.

33. A similar view is expressed by Daniel Byman, "A Corrective That Goes Too Far," *Terrorism and Political Violence* 17, no. 4 (Spring/Summer 2005): 512.

34. I have not seen this view clearly articulated in print but have heard it in person from Jeremy Shapiro of the Brookings Institution. It is touched on in Jessica Stern, "Dreaded Risks and the Control of Biological Weapons," *International Security* 27, no. 3 (Winter 2002–2003): 99.

35. On al Qaeda's stated desire for overreaction, see, for example, John Mintz, "Bin Laden Lauds Costs of War to U.S.," *Washington Post*, November 2, 2004, http://www.washingtonpost.com/wp-dyn/articles/A16971-2004Nov1.html.

36. This topic is dealt with in somewhat cursory fashion because of space and because more knowledgeable authors have discussed it in detail elsewhere, including William Burns's chapter in this volume. See also Sunstein, "Terrorism and Probability Neglect," *Journal of Risk and Uncertainty* 26, no. 2–3 (March–May 2003): 23–38; and Cass Sunstein, *Risk and Reason*, pp. 51–52.

37. John Zaller argues that elite discourse guides war support, that the balance of arguments in the media determines the balance of public opinion on war. Zaller, *The Nature and Origins of Mass Opinion* (New York: Cambridge University Press, 1992). For a discussion of why the imbalance in elite opinion leads Americans to overrate national security dangers in general, see Benjamin H. Friedman, "The Terrible 'Ifs,'" *Regulation* 30, no. 4 (Winter 2007–2008): 32–44.

38. This is an extension of the argument that voters do not have incentive to learn their true interests. See Anthony Downs, *An Economic Theory of Democracy* (New York: Harper & Row, 1957).

39. The exploration of heuristics as an explanation for decisionmaking under uncertainty stems from prospect theory, a set of ideas from cognitive psychology influential in economics. Prospect theory tells us that people's decisions about risk depend on the context, the frame, in which they decide. The frame depends on how the risks are presented, prior assessments of the risk, and its characteristics, as opposed to its magnitude. Prospect theory says that people are more sensitive to gains and losses than absolute welfare. On prospect theory, see Daniel Kahneman and Amos Tversky,

"Variants of Uncertainty," *Cognition* 11, no. 2 (March 1982): 143–57; and Amos Tversky, Paul Slovic, and Daniel Kahneman, eds., *Judgment under Uncertainty: Heuristics and Biases* (Cambridge: Cambridge University Press, 1992). For a discussion of how this research relates to political science, see Jack S. Levy, "An Introduction to Prospect Theory," *Political Psychology* 13, no. 2 (June 1992): 171–86.

40. Cass Sunstein, *Laws of Fear: Beyond the Precautionary Principle* (New York: Cambridge University Press 2005), pp. 41–42.

41. Rose McDermott, *Risk-Taking in International Politics: Prospect Theory in American Foreign Policy* (Ann Arbor, MI: University of Michigan Press, 1998), pp. 29–31.

42. People in politics rhetorically adopt this position. Speaking of the terrorist danger to the United States, FBI Director Robert Mueller stated that we are "safer, but not totally safe"—as if total safety were an achievable standard. Al Goodman, "FBI: U.S. Safer, Not Totally Safe," CNN.com, May 10, 2005, http://www.cnn.com/2005/WORLD/europe/05/10/mueller.terrorism/index.html.

43. McDermott, *Risk-Taking in International Politics*, pp. 6–7.

44. Robert Jervis, *Perception and Misperception in International Politics* (Princeton, NJ: Princeton University Press, 1976), pp. 187–88.

45. Daniel Kahneman and Amos Tversky, "Prospect Theory: An Analysis of Decision under Risk," *Econometrica* 47, no. 2 (March 1979): 263–91.

46. Tversky, Slovic, and Kahneman, *Judgment under Uncertainty*, pp. 23–100.

47. Amos Tversky and Daniel Kahneman, "Extensional versus Intuitive Reasoning: The Conjunction Fallacy in Probability Judgment," *Psychological Review* 90, no. 4 (October 1983): 293–315; and Nancy Kanwisher, "Cognitive Heuristics and American Security Policy," *Journal of Conflict Resolution* 33, no. 4 (December 1989): 654–55.

48. For an analysis of odds of nuclear terrorism based on this insight, see John Mueller's chapter "The Atomic Terrorist?" in this volume, and his *Atomic Obsession*, supra, note 18. For a similar-style analysis that reaches more alarming conclusions, see Matthew Bunn, "A Mathematical Model of the Risk of Nuclear Terrorism," *Annals of the American Academy of Political and Social Science* 607, no. 1 (September 2006): 103–20.

49. Paul Bloom and Csaba Veres, "The Perceived Intentionality of Groups," *Cognition* 71, no. 1 (May 1999): 1–9; and Jervis, *Perception and Misperception*, pp. 319–23.

50. This tendency helps explain why reporters long falsely claimed that al Qaeda tends to release videos before attacks and that terrorists tend to attack around election time. On some problems with this latter claim, see Tim Noah, "The Electoral-Cycles Theory," *Slate*, March 4, 2009, http://www.slate.com/id/2212019/. More generally, this tendency of thought may help explain the paranoid mindset Richard Hofstader describes in *The Paranoid Style in American Politics: And Other Essays* (Cambridge, MA: Harvard University Press, 1996). Hofstader writes that the paranoid style of thinking in American politics is a belief in "the existence of a vast, insidious, preternaturally effective international conspiratorial network designed to perpetrate acts of the most fiendish character" (p. 14). The paranoid, Hofstader says, sees the enemy as ubiquitous, nearly supernatural, and imputes to him the antithesis of the flaws he sees in his own society (pp. 31–32).

51. Tversky, Slovic, and Kahneman, *Judgment under Uncertainty*, pp. 163–78; Sunstein, *Laws of Fear*, pp. 36–39; and Sunstein, "Terrorism and Probability Neglect."

52. Paul Slovic, "Perception of Risk," *Science* 236, no. 4799 (April 1987): 280–85.

53. Harvey Sapolsky, "The Politics of Risk," *Daedalus* 119, no. 4 (Fall 1990): 83–96.

54. Benjamin Page and Robert Shapiro, *The Rational Public: Fifty Years of Trends in American's Policy Preferences* (Chicago: University of Chicago Press, 1992), pp. 367–69.

55. This argument comes from John A. Thompson, "The Exaggeration of American Vulnerability: The Anatomy of a Tradition," *Diplomatic History* 16, no. 1 (Winter 1992): 23–44. See also John Schuessler, "Necessity or Choice? Securing Public Consent for War," paper presented to the Midwest Political Science Association, Chicago, April 15, 2004; and Michael Desch, "America's Liberal Illiberalism: The Ideological Origins of Overreaction in U.S. Foreign Policy," *International Security* 32, no. 3 (Winter 2007–2008): 7–43.

56. Theodore Lowi, *The End of Liberalism: The Second Republic of the United States* (New York: W. W. Norton, 1979), pp. 50–63, 127–165. On the use of fear to sell largely unrelated policies in U.S. foreign policy, see Jane Kellett Cramer, "National Security Panics: Overestimating Threats to National Security," PhD diss., Massachusetts Institute of Technology, 2002, p. 133. Policymakers exaggerate other threats for the same reason; terrorism is unique only in that its salience makes it particularly useful of late.

57. *National Security Strategy of Engagement and Enlargement* (Washington: White House, 1995), pp. 1–2, http://www.fas.org/spp/military/docops/national/1996stra.htm.

58. On executive dominance of the debate about Iraq and oversell, see Chaim Kaufman, "Threat Inflation and the Failure of the Marketplace of Ideas: The Selling of the Iraq War," *International Security* 29, no. 1 (Summer 2004): 5–48.

59. This conclusion is based on limited and preliminary accounts of former officials, so it could be wrong. See, for example, Scott McClellan, *What Happened: Inside the Bush White House and Washington's Culture of Deception* (New York: PublicAffairs Books, 2008), pp. 128–29; and George Tenet with Bill Harlow, *At the Center of the Storm: My Time at the CIA* (New York: HarperCollins 2007), p. 321.

60. For a discussion of efforts to justify drilling for oil in Alaska as a counterterrorism project, see Sheldon Rampton, "Terrorism as Pretext," *PR Watch* 8, no. 4 (Fall 2001), http://www.prwatch.org/prwissues/2001Q4/terror.html. To see alternative energy policies sold the same way, see, for example, Barack Obama, "Energy Security Is National Security," remarks to Governor's Ethanol Coalition, Washington, February 28, 2006, http://obamaspeeches.com/054-Energy-Security-is-National-Security-Governors-Ethanol-Coalition-Obama-Speech.htm. For the argument that free trade is a way to fight terrorism, see then United States Trade Representative Robert B. Zoellick, "Countering Terror with Trade," *Washington Post*, September 20, 2001. On foreign aid as an anti-terror tactic, see Howard LaFranchi, "Foreign Aid Recast as Tool to Stymie Terrorism," *Christian Science Monitor*, February 26, 2002, http://www.csmonitor.com/2002/0226/p02s01-uspo.html. The argument that Americans who use drugs unwittingly support terrorists was made by President George W. Bush, who said, "The traffic in drugs finances the work of terror." Remarks by the president in signing Drug-Free Communities Act Reauthorization Bill, Washington, December 14, 2001.

61. He made the case in an interview with Fareed Zakaria on CNN. "GPS with Fareed Zakaria," transcript, CNN, July 13, 2008, http://www.cnn.com/2008/POLITICS/07/13/zakaria.obama/.

62. For example, "A New Approach for Safeguarding Americans," speech by John Brennan, assistant to the president for homeland security and counterterrorism, Center for Strategic and International Studies, Washington, August 6, 2009, http://csis.org/files/attachments/090806_brennan_transcript.pdf.

63. This may simply reflect public opinion, a result of chasing the median voter, whose overwrought fears of terrorism are caused by the other explanations discussed

here. Or it might be a result of more complex strategic choices by the parties that may change. Democrats might decide, for example, that being dovish is not as risky as they thought.

64. See, for example, Jill Zuckman, "Democrats Take Bush to Task over Homeland Security Funding," *Chicago Tribune*, April 2, 2003; "America at Risk: GOP Choices Leave Homeland Vulnerable," report prepared by the Democratic staff of the House Select Committee on Homeland Security, October 2004; and Jonathan Weisman and Shailagh Murray, "Democrats Promise Broad New Agenda, Now in Control, They Plan to Challenge Bush," *Washington Post*, November 8, 2006, http://www.washington post.com/wp-dyn/content/article/2006/11/07/AR2006110701760.html.

65. "Road Map for Change: Imperative for Change, Phase III Report of the U.S. Commission on National Security/21st Century, February 15, 2001, http://govinfo. library.unt.edu/nssg/PhaseIIIFR.pdf.

66. Richard A. Clarke, *Against All Enemies: Inside America's War on Terror* (New York: Free Press, 2004), pp. 249–51; and Cohen, Cuéllar, and Weingast, "Crisis Bureaucracy," pp. 687–700.

67. William C. Clark, "Witches, Floods, and Wonder Drugs: Historical Perspectives on Risk Management," in *Societal Risk Assessment: How Safe Is Safe Enough?* ed. Richard C. Schwing and Walter A. Albers (New York: Plenum, 1980), pp. 287–318.

68. This is an example of what social scientists call path dependence, the idea that certain outcomes last even in the absence of their original causes, due to some self-perpetuating phenomenon. Paul Pierson, "Path Dependence, Increasing Returns, and the Study of Politics," *American Political Science Review* 94, no. 2 (June 2000): 251–67.

69. James Q. Wilson, "Innovation in Organization: Notes toward a Theory," in *Approaches to Organizational Design*, ed. James O. Thompson (Pittsburgh, PA: University of Pittsburgh Press, 1971), pp. 195–218; and Stephen Peter Rosen, *Winning the Next War* (Ithaca, NY: Cornell University Press, 1991), pp. 1–22.

70. On the infusion of values, see Philip Selznick, *Leadership in Administration: A Sociological Interpretation* (Berkeley, CA: University of California Press, 1957). On the confusion of national and parochial interests as an organizational pathology, see Jack Snyder, *The Ideology of the Offensive: Military Decision Making and the Disasters of 1914* (Ithaca, NY: Cornell University Press, 1984), pp. 15–34.

71. James Q. Wilson, *Bureaucracy: What Government Agencies Do and Why They Do It* (New York: Basic Books, 1989), pp. 25–26, 246–47. On the mission of military organizations, see Barry R. Posen, *The Sources of Military Doctrine* (Ithaca, NY: Cornell University Press, 1984), pp. 13–80.

72. See, for example, a DHS website, Ready.gov. Various efforts to promote vigilance and readiness exist. For example, "Ready Campaign Launches Social Media Initiative to Encourage Americans to Prepare for Emergencies," January 16, 2009, DHS press release, http://www.dhs.gov/xnews/releases/pr_1232126867101.shtm.

73. The Obama administration's secretary of homeland security, Janet Napolitano, has limited direct fearmongering but warns of complacency. Ginger Thompson, "A Shift to Make the Border Safe, from the Inside Out," *New York Times*, April 5, 2009, http://www.nytimes.com/2009/04/06/us/06napolitano.html. The department continues to promote vigilance and preparation, however.

74. Lists of homeland security grants are found at "State, Local and Tribal Grant Programs," U.S. Department of Homeland Security, http://www.dhs.gov/xopnbiz/grants/; and "FY 2010 Homeland Security Grant Program," Federal Emergency Management Agency, http://www.fema.gov/government/grant/hsgp/index.shtm#0.

NOTES FOR PAGES 200–201

75. On the confluence of interests called the military-industrial complex and how it affects public threat perception, see Stephen P. Rosen, ed., *Testing the Theory of the Military-Industrial Complex* (Lexington, MA: Lexington Books, 1973), pp. 23–24; Stephen Van Evera, "Militarism," unpublished manuscript, 2001, http://web.mit.edu/polisci/research/vanevera/militarism.pdf; and Friedman, "The Terrible 'Ifs.'"

76. Recent budget constraints led the Pentagon to shift funding from some conventional platforms to capabilities needed in current wars, limiting but not eliminating the intellectual connection between conventional platforms and counterterrorism. As a result, the incentive to hype terrorism is less. These cuts and the general pressure that the growth in ground force manpower is putting on the services' procurement budgets have caused some elements of the Air Force and Navy to resist the nation's focus on counterinsurgency as a counterterrorism tool. For brief treatments of the tension in the Pentagon between counterinsurgency and conventional missions, see Benjamin H. Friedman, "The Iron Triangle vs. Small Wars," *World Politics Review*, April 9, 2009, http://www.worldpoliticsreview.com/article.aspx?id=3586; and George C. Wilson, "Another Looming Disaster," *CongressDaily*, November 9, 2009, http://www.nationaljournal.com/congressdaily/foa_20091109_3681.php. For an expression of concern about the rise of the counterinsurgency missions from an Air Force perspective, see Charles J. Dunlap Jr., "We Still Need the Big Guns," *New York Times*, January 9, 2008, http://www.nytimes.com/2008/01/09/opinion/09dunlap.html.

77. For a critique of this idea, see Justin Logan and Christopher Preble, "Failed States and Flawed Logic: The Case against a Standing Nation-Building Office," Cato Institute Policy Analysis no. 560, January 11, 2006, http://www.cato.org/pub_display.php?pub_id=5358.

78. The Navy claims relevance to counterterrorism throughout its FY10 budget justification. *Highlights of the Department of the Navy FY 2010 Budget* (Washington: Department of the Navy, 2009). Those claims are summarized by Ronald O'Rourke, "Navy Irregular Warfare and Counterterrorism Operations: Background and Issues for Congress," Congressional Research Service, October 8, 2009, http://fas.org/sgp/crs/natsec/RS22373.pdf. The Navy also issues press releases such as "Navy Surges Ships to Deny Terrorists Use of Maritime Environment," *Navy Newsstand*, March 25, 2005, http://www.navy.mil/search/display.asp?story_id=18507. Examples of the Air Force's claim of counterterrorism and counterinsurgency relevance are John W. Bellflower, "The Soft Side of Airpower," *Small Wars Journal* (January–February 2009), http://smallwarsjournal.com/blog/journal/docs-temp/161-bellflower.pdf; and Charles J. Dunlap Jr., "Developing Joint Counterinsurgency Doctrine: An Airman's Perspective," *Joint Forces Quarterly*, no. 49 (April 2008): 86–92. An example of a press release heralding Air Force counterterrorism prowess is "March 10 Airpower: ISR Missions Critical in War on Terrorism," *Air Force News Service*, March 10, 2007, http://www.af.mil/news/story.asp?id=123044263.

79. Congress created 12 homeland security "centers of excellence" at universities that receive federal funding. A variety of other institutions have established homeland security centers. Every think tank now has homeland security experts. Several new think tanks are devoted exclusively to homeland security, including the ANSER Institute, which produces the *Journal of Homeland Security* (http://www.homelanddefense.org/journal) not to be confused with *Homeland Security Today* (http://www.hstoday.us).

80. Julia Neyman, "Colleges Embrace Homeland Security Curriculum," *USA Today,* August 24, 2004, http://www.usatoday.com/news/education/2004-08-24-homeland-usat_x.htm.

81. The idea of freedom of speech producing a free marketplace of ideas is from John Stuart Mill, "On Liberty," in *The Philosophy of John Stuart Mill: Ethical Political and Religious,* ed. Marshall Cohen (New York: Modern Library, 1961), pp. 185–319. An explanation of how the marketplace of ideas fails in national security politics is Stephen Van Evera, "Why States Believe Foolish Ideas: Non-Self-Evaluation by States and Societies," in *Perspectives on Structural Realism,* ed. Andrew K. Hanami (New York: Palgrave, 2003), pp. 163–198.

82. On these dynamics, see Sunstein, *Risk and Reason,* pp. 78–99.

83. Jack Snyder, *Myths of Empire: Domestic Politics and International Ambition* (Ithaca, NY: Cornell University Press, 1991), p. 41.

84. Friedman, "Leap before You Look," p. 29; and James Fallows, "What Would Bogey Do?" in "Are We Safe Yet?" *Foreign Affairs* Roundtable, September 11, 2006, http://www.foreignaffairs.com/discussions/roundtables/are-we-safe-yet.

85. Marcia Kramer, "Bloomberg on JFK Plot: 'Stop Worrying, Get a Life,'" WCB-STV.com, June 5, 2007, http://wcbstv.com/topstories/Terrorism.New.York.2. 244966.html. At one time, Senator John McCain expressed similar sentiments: "Get on the damn elevator! Fly on the damn plane! Calculate the odds of being harmed by a terrorist! It's still about as likely as being swept out to sea by a tidal wave! Watch the terrorist alert and go outside again when it falls below yellow. Suck it up, for crying out loud. You're almost certainly going to be okay. And in the unlikely event you're not, do you really want to spend your last days cowering behind plastic sheets and duct tape? That's not a life worth living, is it?" John McCain and Mark Salter, *Why Courage Matters: The Way to a Braver Life* (New York: Random House: 2004), pp. 35–36.

86. Thomas O. McGarity, *Reinventing Rationality: The Role of Regulatory Analysis in the Federal Bureaucracy* (New York: Cambridge University Press, 1991), p. xiv.

87. Sunstein, *Risk and Reason,* pp. 99–152.

88. McGarity, *Reinventing Rationality,* p. 271.

89. Sunstein, *Risk and Reason,* pp. 26–27; Robert W. Hahn and Paul C. Tetlock, "Has Economic Analysis Improved Regulatory Decisions?" *Journal of Economic Perspectives* 22, no. 1 (Winter 2008): 67–84; W. Kip Viscusi and Ted Gayer, "Safety at Any Price?" *Regulation* 25, no. 3 (Fall 2002): 54–63; and Stuart Shapiro, "Politics and Regulatory Policy Analysis," *Regulation* 29, no. 2 (Summer 2006): 40–45.

90. William A. Niskanen, "More Lonely Numbers," *Regulation* 26, no. 3 (Fall 2003): 22; and William West, "The Institutionalization of Regulatory Review: Organizational Stability and Responsive Competence at OIRA," *Presidential Studies Quarterly* 35, no. 1 (March 2005): 76–93.

91. Stuart Shapiro, "Politics and Regulatory Policy Analysis."

92. Alain C. Enthoven and K. Wayne Smith, *How Much Is Enough: Shaping the Defense Program, 1961–1969* (New York: Harper & Row, 1971), pp. 32–72.

93. On Chertoff's embrace of risk-management rhetoric, see, for example, Michael Martinez, "Chertoff Touts Risk Management Approach," *CongressDaily,* December 20, 2005, http://www.govexec.com/dailyfed/1205/122005cdpm1.htm. On the link between this approach and congressional demands for funds, see Cohen, Cueallar, and Weingast, "Crisis Bureaucracy," pp. 715–16. For one example of his alarmism, see Michael Chertoff, "Make No Mistake, This Is War," *Washington Post,* April 22,

2007, http://www.washingtonpost.com/wp-dyn/content/article/2007/04/20/AR2007042001940.html.

94. For example, the Office of Risk Management and Analysis was created in April 2007 in the National Protection and Programs Directorate. On this and other efforts to bake risk management into DHS, see David H. Schanzer and Joe Eyerman, "Improving Strategic Risk Management at the Department of Homeland Security," IBM Center for the Business of Government, 2009, http://www.businessofgovernment.org/pdfs/SchanzerdeRugyReport.pdf.

95. This subject has spawned a cottage industry of studies. See, for example, James Jay Carafano, "Spending Smarter: Prioritizing Homeland Security Grants by Using National Standards and Risk Criteria," Heritage Foundation Backgrounder no. 2033, May 10, 2007; "DHS Improved Its Risk-Based Grants Program' Allocation and Management Methods, but Measuring Programs' Impact on National Capabilities Remains a Challenge," Testimony of William O. Jenkins, director of homeland security and justice issues, before the Subcommittee on Homeland Security, Committee on Appropriations, House of Representatives, March 11, 2008; and Todd Masse, Siobhan O'Neil, John Rollins, "The Department of Homeland Security's Risk Assessment Methodology: Evolution, Issues, and Options for Congress," Congressional Research Service, February 2, 2007.

96. On the weakness of regulatory review in considering homeland security regulations, see Robert W. Hahn, "An Analysis of the 2008 Government Report on the Costs and Benefits of Federal Regulations," Regulatory Analysis 08-04, AEI Center for Regulatory and Market Studies, December 2008, pp. 8–9, http://aei-brookings.org/admin/authorpdfs/redirect-safely.php?fname=../pdffiles/phpnZ.pdf; and Farrow and Shapiro, "The Benefit-Cost Analysis of Security Focused Regulations."

97. Farrow and Shapiro, "The Benefit-Cost Analysis of Security Focused Regulations," pp. 3–5, 11–12.

98. Cindy Williams, "Strengthening Homeland Security: Reforming Planning and Resource Allocation," IBM Center for the Business of Government, 2008, http://www.businessofgovernment.org/pdfs/CindyWilliamsReport.pdf. Note that the Defense Department has the same failing. The shares of budget going to each military service have been virtually constant since the Kennedy administration. On constant service shares, see Jim Cooper and Russell Rumbaugh, "Real Acquisition Reform," *Joint Forces Quarterly*, no. 55 (October 2009): 62. In one sense, DHS's management is in a better position to force agencies to adhere to its decisions than is the Office of the Secretary of Defense. DHS agencies are weaker than the military services, with less pull in Congress, and congressional oversight of DHS is far more diffuse. On the other hand, because the tendency to overreact to terrorism via homeland security is probably greater than the tendency to overreact to the threats the services deal with, Congress may be less tolerant of technocratic resistance.

99. Enthoven and Smith, *How Much Is Enough*, p. 79.

100. Ibid., p. 6.

101. David B. Truman, *The Governmental Process: Political Interests and Public Opinion*, 2nd ed. (Berkeley: CA: Institute of Governmental Studies, 1993). See also, Wilson, *Bureaucracy*.

102. One recent study argues that the Bush administration created DHS to take funding and attention from DHS agencies' legacy missions. Cohen, Cuéllar, and Weingast, "Crisis Bureaucracy," pp. 714–55.

103. On competition of interests as a cause of innovative military doctrine, see Owen R. Cote Jr., "The Politics of Innovative Military Doctrine: The U.S. Navy and Fleet Ballistic Missiles," PhD diss., Massachusetts Institute of Technology, 1995; and Harvey M. Sapolsky, "The Inter-Service Competition Solution," *Breakthroughs* 5, no. 1 (Spring 1996): 1–3.

104. On the division of labor in the provision of homeland security, see Veronique de Rugy's chapter in this volume; and Matt Mayer, *Homeland Security and Federalism: Protecting America from Outside the Beltway* (Westport, CT: Praeger Security International, 2009).

105. Bruce Schneier, *Beyond Fear: Thinking Sensibly about Security in an Uncertain World* (New York: Copernicus Books, 2003), pp. 38–40; and Cass R. Sunstein and Richard Zeckhauser, "Overreaction to Fearsome Risks," Faculty Research Working Paper RWP08-079, John F. Kennedy School of Government, December 3, 2008, http://web.hks.harvard.edu/publications/getFile.aspx?Id = 330.

106. Sunstein and Zeckhauset, "Overreaction to Fearsome Risks," p. 13.

107. Robert Divine, *The Sputnik Challenge* (New York: Oxford University Press, 1993).

108. Ibid., p. 13.

109. On Democratic calls for more spending, see note 64. For analysts making the case, see *Emergency Responders: Drastically Underfunded, Dangerously Underprepared*, report of an Independent Task Force Sponsored by the Council on Foreign Relations, Warren B. Rudman, chair; Richard A. Clarke, senior adviser; Jamie F. Metzl, project director (New York: Council on Foreign Relations Press, 2003); and Jonathan Chait, "The 9/10 President: Bush's Abysmal Failure on Homeland Security," *New Republic* (March 3, 2003): pp. 18–23.

Chapter 11

1. Priscilla Lewis is codirector of the U.S. in the World Initiative (http://www.usintheworld.org), a project of Dēmos, a nonpartisan public policy research and advocacy organization based in New York City. This chapter was prepared in close collaboration with U.S. in the World codirector Sue Veres Royal. It reflects valuable insights from the issue experts, policy advocates, funders, and communications researchers who have participated in various ways in U.S. in the World's Managing the Fear Factor Project. Specific contributions from project participants have been noted wherever possible; necessarily, many informal contributions have gone unnoted—but not unappreciated.

2. This theory was developed in the late 1980s by Sheldon Solomon, Jeff Greenberg, and Tom Pyszczynski (now professors of psychology at Skidmore College, the University of Arizona, and the University of Colorado at Colorado Springs, respectively), who have published extensively in this area.

3. See, for example, Jeff Greenberg, Sheldon Solomon, and Tom Pyszczynski, "Terror Management Theory of Self-Esteem and Cultural Worldviews," *Advances in Experimental Social Psychology* 29 (1997): 139; and Jamie Arndt, Jeff Greenberg, Tom Pyszczynski, and Sheldon Solomon, "Subliminal Exposure to Death-Related Stimuli Increases Defense of the Cultural Worldview," *Psychological Science* 8, no. 5 (1997): 379–85.

4. As reported, for example, in Emanuele Castano, "In Case of Death, Cling to the Ingroup," *European Journal of Social Psychology* 34 (2004): 1–10; and in Jeff Schimel and others, "Stereotypes and Terror Management: Evidence That Mortality Salience

Enhances Stereotypic Thinking and Preferences," *Journal of Personality and Social Psychology* 77, no. 5 (November 1999): 905–26.

5. For example, see Tom Pyszczynski, Sheldon Solomon, and Jeff Greenberg, *In the Wake of 9/11: The Psychology of Terror* (Washington: American Psychological Association, 2003); and John B. Judis, "Death Grip: How Political Psychology Explains Bush's Ghastly Success," *New Republic*, August 27, 2007, http://www.carnegieendowment.org/publications/index.cfm?fa=view&id=19566.

6. Relevant experiments by Solomon, Greenberg, and Pyszczinski are summarized in Drew Westen, *The Political Brain: The Role of Emotion in Deciding the Fate of the Nation* (New York: PublicAffairs, 2007).

7. Axel Aubrun, Andrew Brown, and Joseph Grady, "Detecting Intentions, Managing Fear: How Americans Think about National Security," report produced by the Topos Partnership for the National Security Network and the U.S. in the World Initiative, Summer 2008, http://www.usintheworld.org.

8. See Jaak Panksepp, *Affective Neuroscience: The Foundations of Human and Animal Emotions* (New York: Oxford University Press: 1998); and Joseph LeDoux, *The Emotional Brain: The Mysterious Underpinnings of Emotional Life* (New York: Simon & Schuster, 1998).

9. Damage to the prefrontal cortex has been associated with impairment of the capacity for empathy. See, for example, S. G. Shamay-Tsoory, R. Tomer, B. D. Berger, and J. Aharon-Peretz, "Characterization of Empathy Deficits Following Prefrontal Brain Damage," *Journal of Cognitive Neuroscience* 15, no. 3 (April 1, 2003): 324–37.

10. Joseph LeDoux, *Synaptic Self: How Our Brains Become Who We Are* (New York: Viking Press, 2002).

11. A few mortality salience experiments have demonstrated that the negative effects of mortality reminders can be offset by asking subjects to "think carefully" before answering researchers' questions or by prompting subjects to consider the "common humanity" that we share with other people. See Jay Dixit, "The Ideological Animal," *Psychology Today*, January 1, 2007, http://www.psychologytoday.com/articles/200612/the-ideological-animal.

12. Aubrun, Brown, and Grady, "Detecting Intentions, Managing Fear."

13. "Public Perceptions of U.S. Global Engagement, Pre- and Post-9/11," U.S. in the World, *Talking Global Issues with Americans: A Practical Guide* (New York: Rockefeller Brothers Fund, 2004), p. 22, http://www.usintheworld.org.

14. The juxtaposition of "Stone Age brains" and modern dangers is the subject of Daniel Gardner's synthesis of research on risk, titled *The Science of Fear: Why We Fear the Things We Shouldn't—and Put Ourselves in Greater Danger* (New York: Dutton Adult, 2008). Gardner covers the points made here as well as many other relevant insights.

15. The observations here are based on an unpublished presentation delivered by Judith Lewis Herman, M.D., at a retreat organized by U.S. in the World in 2008. Dr. Herman is the author of *Trauma and Recovery: The Aftermath of Violence—from Domestic Abuse to Political Terror* (New York: Basic Books, 1992) and director of training at the Victims of Violence Program at Cambridge Hospital.

16. The tend-and-befriend model was developed by Shelley E. Taylor, distinguished professor of psychology at the University of California, Los Angeles, whose work focuses on how social relationships protect against stress.

17. Dr. Herman cites the work of Ann Wolbert Burgess and Lynda Lytle Holmstrom on recovery from rape, including "Adaptive Strategies and Recovery from Rape," *American Journal of Psychiatry* 136 (1979): 1278–82.

18. Neil Smelser, university professor of sociology emeritus at the University of California, Berkeley, has written on societal responses to terrorism in *The Faces of Terrorism: Social and Psychological Dimensions* (Princeton, NJ: Princeton University Press, 2007); and "September 11, 2001, as Cultural Trauma," in *Cultural Trauma and Collective Identity*, by Jeffrey C. Alexander, Ron Eyerman, Bernhard Gieson, Neil J. Smelser, and Piortr Sztompka (Berkeley and Los Angeles: University of California Press, 2004), pp. 31–59.

19. See, for example, Gardner, *The Science of Fear*; also David L. Altheide, *Terrorism and the Politics of Fear* (Lanham, MD: AltaMira Press, 2006); and Marc Siegel, *False Alarm: The Truth about the Epidemic of Fear* (Hoboken, NJ: John Wiley, 2005).

20. As Daniel Gardner, himself a journalist, reminds readers in *The Science of Fear*.

21. From unpublished remarks by Heather Hurlburt, executive director, National Security Network, at a retreat organized by U.S. in the World in 2008.

22. From unpublished remarks by Brian Jenkins, senior adviser to the president of the RAND Corporation, made at the same retreat.

23. Peter N. Stearns, *American Fear: The Causes and Consequences of High Anxiety* (New York: Routledge/Taylor & Francis Group, 2006).

24. See Axel Aubrun and Joseph Grady, with Andrew Brown, "Promoting Progressive Thinking about Policy in Fearful Times," report produced by the Topos Partnership for the U.S. in the World Initiative, in partnership with the National Security Network, 2009. Funded by the Open Society Institute and available at http://www.usintheworld.org.

25. This method of testing, called TalkBack Testing, was developed by Topos cofounders Axel Aubrun and Joseph Grady, based on principles and techniques of the cognitive and social sciences. In TalkBack Testing, subjects are presented with brief texts (roughly 80–150 words) and then asked several open-ended questions, at least one of which focuses on their ability to repeat the core of the message or pass it along to others—as in the game of telephone. The testing is designed to assess whether a given idea has the capacity to become an organizing principle for thinking and communicating about the issue.

26. Personal communication from Steven Kull, director of WorldPublicOpinion.org and the Program on International Policy Attitudes and director of the PIPA/Knowledge Networks poll of the U.S. public. Also see Steven Kull, "The Voice of the Public," in U.S. in the World, *Talking Global Issues with Americans*, pp. 14–20.

27. Personal communication from Meg Bostrom, cofounder of the Topos Partnership.

Chapter 12

1. I would like to thank Paul Slovic (Decision Research, University of Oregon), Ellen Peters (Decision Research, University of Oregon), Baruch Fischhoff (Carnegie Mellon University), and Tim Sellnow (University of Kentucky) for their helpful suggestions while writing this chapter. I would also like to thank Oleg Pavlov (Worcester Polytechnic Institute) for his input with the causal loop diagram depicted in Figure 12.1.

This research was supported by the National Science Foundation under grant numbers SES-0728934 and SES-0901036. It was also supported by the U.S. Department of Homeland Security through the Center for Risk and Economic Analysis of Terrorism Events under grant number 2007-ST-061-000001. However, any opinions, findings, conclusions, and recommendations in this document are those of the author and do not necessarily reflect views of the National Science Foundation or the U.S. Department of Homeland Security.

This chapter represents an expanded and more detailed version of an essay written by the author, "The Path Well Taken: Making the Right Decisions about Risks from Terrorism," *Cato Unbound*, January 5, 2009, http://www.cato-unbound.org/2009/01/05/william-burns/the-path-well-taken-making-the-right-decisions-about-risks-from-terrorism/.

2. Molly J. Hall, Ann E. Norwood, Robert J. Ursano, Carol S. Fullerton, and Catherine J. Levinson, "Psychological and Behavioral Impacts of Bioterrorism," *PTSD Research Quarterly* 13, no. 4 (2002): 1–7.

3. Paul Slovic, "Terrorism as Hazard: A New Species of Trouble," *Risk Analysis* 22, no. 3 (2002): 425–26.

4. Jennifer S. Lerner and Dacher Keltner, "Fear, Anger, and Risk," *Journal of Personality and Social Psychology* 81, no. 1 (2001): 146–59.

5. William J. Burns and Paul Slovic, "Predicting and Modeling Public Response to a Terrorist Strike," in *The Feeling of Risk: New Perspectives for Risk Perception*, ed. Paul Slovic (London: Earthscan, forthcoming in July 2010). This chapter was based in part on a paper, "Predicting Public Response to a Terrorist Strike," which was the winner of the Best Paper Award at the Society for Risk Analysis 2005 Conference.

6. William J. Burns, Paul Slovic, Roger E. Kasperson, Jeanne X. Kasperson, Ortwin Renn, and Srinivas Emani, "Incorporating Structural Models into Research on the Social Amplification of Risk: Implications for Theory Construction and Decision Making," *Risk Analysis* 13, no. 6 (1993): 611–23.

7. Mary Douglas and Aaron Wildavsky, *Risk and Culture: An Essay on the Selection of Technical and Environmental Dangers* (Berkeley, CA: University of California Press, 1982), pp. 192–206.

8. Kerry G. Herron and Hank C. Jenkins-Smith, *Critical Masses and Critical Choices: Evolving Public Opinion on Nuclear Weapons, Terrorism, and Security* (Pittsburgh, PA: University of Pittsburgh Press, 2006), pp. 153–59.

9. Dan M. Kahan, Donald Braman, Paul Slovic, John Gastil, and Geoffrey L. Cohen, "The Second National Risk and Culture Study: Making Sense of—and Making Progress in—the American Culture War of Fact," October 3, 2007, pp. 1–23, http://ssrn.com/abstract=1017189.

10. Roger E. Kasperson and others, "The Social Amplification of Risk: A Conceptual Framework," *Risk Analysis* 8, no. 7 (1988): 177–87.

11. Burns and others, "Incorporating Structural Models into Research on the Social Amplification of Risk."

12. Individuals who have received disaster response training will often exhibit risk-reducing behaviors as their perceived risk increases (e.g., make preparations, comply with emergency warnings, assist neighbors, make a conscious effort to return to normal activities when safe to do so). This observation is based on interviews conducted with individuals who have received Community Emergency Response Team training in the San Diego area and their response to wildfires before and after their training. Engaging in risk-reducing behaviors represents a more effective and sustainable approach to restoring a sense of control.

13. William J. Burns and Paul Slovic, "The Diffusion of Fear: Modeling Community Response to a Terrorist Strike," *Journal of Defense Modeling and Simulation: Applications,*

Methodology, Technology 4, no. 4 (2007): 1–20, http://www.scs.org/PUBs/jdms/vol4 num4/Burns.pdf.

14. Fynnwin Prager and others, "Exploring Reductions in London Underground Passengers Following the 2005 Bombings," *Risk Analysis* (currently under review).

15. The VIX index is often referred to as a measure of investor fear. It could also be thought of as an indicator of investor perceived risk. Technically, it is a measure of the expected volatility of the S&P 500 index options with higher numbers indicating more volatility during the next 30 days. CBOE Volatility Index (VIX), http://finance.yahoo.com/q?s=%5Evix (accessed November 6, 2009).

16. William J. Burns, "Comparing the Economic Consequences of Three Disasters: Accounting for Fear and Perceived Risk," paper presented at the 2009 Society for Risk Analysis conference, Baltimore, December 2009.

17. Melissa L. Finucane, Ali Alhakami, Paul Slovic, and Stephen M. Johnson, "The Affect Heuristic in Judgments of Risks and Benefits," in *The Perception of Risk*, ed. Paul Slovic (London: Earthscan, 2000), pp. 413–29; and Ellen M. Peters, Burt Burraston, and C. K. Mertz, "An Emotion-Based Model of Risk Perception and Stigma Susceptibility: Cognitive Appraisals of Emotion, Affective Reactivity, Worldviews, and Risk Perceptions in the Generation of Technological Stigma," *Risk Analysis* 24, no. 5 (2004): 1349–67.

18. Cass R. Sunstein, "Terrorism and Probability Neglect," *Journal of Risk and Uncertainty* 26, no. 2–3 (2003): 121–36.

19. John Mueller, *Overblown: How Politicians and the Terrorism Industry Inflate the National Security Threat and Why We Believe Them* (New York: Free Press, 2006), pp. 1–48.

20. Cass R. Sunstein, *Laws of Fear: Beyond the Precautionary Principle* (New York: Cambridge University Press, 2005), pp. 39–41, 64–88.

21. Franklin Delano Roosevelt, First Inaugural Address, March 4, 1933, http://www.americanrhetoric.com/speeches/fdrfirstinaugural.html.

22. Roxane Cohen Silver, E. Alison Holman, Daniel N. McIntosh, Michael Poulin, and Virginia Gil-Rivas, "Nationwide Longitudinal Study of Psychological Responses to September 11," *Journal of the American Medical Association* 288, no. 10 (2002): 1235–44.

23. Darren W. Davis and Brian D. Silver, "Civil Liberties vs. Security: Public Opinion in the Context of the Terrorist Attacks on America," *American Journal of Political Science* 48, no. 1 (2004): 28–46.

24. Herron and Jenkins-Smith, *Critical Masses and Critical Choices*, pp. 65–93.

25. Ben Sheppard, *The Psychology of Strategic Terrorism: Public and Government Responses to Attack* (London: Routledge, 2009), pp. 97–98.

26. Harumi Ito and Darin Lee, "Assessing the Impact of the September 11 Terrorist Attacks on U.S. Airline Demand," *Journal of Economics and Business* 57, no 1 (2005): 75–95.

27. Peter Gordon, James E. Moore II, Ji Young Park, and Harry W. Richardson, "The Economic Impacts of a Terrorist Attack on the U.S. Commercial Aviation System," *Risk Analysis* 27, no. 3 (2007): 505–12.

28. Adam Z. Rose, "A Framework for Analyzing the Total Economic Impacts of Terrorist Attacks and Natural Disasters," *Journal of Homeland Security and Emergency Management* 6, no. 1 (2009), article 9.

29. James A. Giesecke, William J. Burns, Anthony Barrett, Ergin Bayrak, Adam Rose, and Michael Suher, "Regional Economic Damage from Catastrophic Events: Evaluation and Comparison of Resource Loss and Fear Effects under a Hypothetical

RDD Attack Scenario," paper prepared for the 56th North American Regional Science Association International, San Francisco, November 2009.

30. The Los Angeles dirty-bomb study described was closely patterned after the radiological dispersal device depicted in the DHS National Planning Scenarios. In this study, a specific geographic location and time period were chosen. "Scenario 11: Radiological Attack—Radiological Dispersal Devices," July 2004, http://www.globalsecurity.org/security/library/report/2004/hsc-planning-scenarios-jul04_11.htm.

31. Sheppard, *The Psychology of Strategic Terrorism*, pp. 97–98.

32. Sunstein, "Terrorism and Probability Neglect."

33. Sunstein, *Laws of Fear*, pp. 39–41, 64–88; and Bruce Schneier, *Beyond Fear: Thinking Sensibly about Security in an Uncertain World* (New York: Springer, 2006), pp. 3–43.

34. Mueller, *Overblown*.

35. Dan Garner, *Risk: The Science and Politics of Fear* (London: Virgin Books, 2008), pp. 61–89.

36. Peter Schwartz, *Inevitable Surprises* (New York: Gotham Books, 2003), pp. 221–35.

37. John D. Sterman, *Business Dynamics: Systems Thinking and Modeling for a Complex World* (Boston: McGraw-Hill, 2000), pp. 3–39, 845–91; and Peter M. Senge, *The Fifth Discipline: The Art and Practice of the Learning Organization* (New York: Doubleday, 2006), pp. 3–91, 163–90. See also Kambiz E. Maani and Robert Y. Cavana, *Systems Thinking and Modelling: Understanding Change and Complexity* (Auckland, New Zealand: Prentice Hall, 2000), pp. 12–14 .

38. Martin E. P. Seligman, *Learned Optimism: How to Change Your Mind and Your Life* (New York: Pocket Books, 1998).

39. Schneier, *Beyond Fear*, pp. 3–43.

40. M. Granger Morgan, Baruch Fischhoff, Ann Bostrom, and Cynthia J. Atman, *Risk Communication: A Mental Models Approach* (New York: Cambridge University Press, 2002), pp. 19–33.

41. Baruch Fischhoff, Roxana M. Gonzales, Deborah A. Small, and Jennifer S. Lerner, "Evaluating the Success of Terrorism Risk Communications," *Biosecurity and Bioterrorism: Biodefense Strategy, Practice, and Science* 1, no. 4 (2003): 255–58; and H. Keith Florig and Baruch Fischhoff, "Individuals' Decisions Affecting Radiation Exposure after a Nuclear Explosion," *Health Physics* 92, no. 5 (2007): 475–83.

42. James Flynn, "Nuclear Stigma," in *The Social Amplification of Risk*, ed. Nick Pidgeon, Roger E. Kasperson, and Paul Slovic (New York: Cambridge University Press, 2003), pp. 326–52; Paul Slovic, "Perception of Risk," *Science* 236 (1987): 280–85; Paul Slovic, "Perception of Risk from Radiation," in *The Perception of Risk*; and Paul Slovic, James H. Flynn, and Mark Layman, "Perceived Risk, Trust, and the Politics of Nuclear Waste," *Science* 254 (1991): 1603–7.

43. Roz D. Lasker, *Redefining Readiness: Terrorism Planning through the Eyes of the Public* (New York: New York Academy of Medicine, 2004).

44. Ellen Peters and others, "Numeracy and Decision Making," *Psychological Science* 17, no. 5 (2006): 407–13; and Ellen Peters, Nathan Dieckmann, Anna Dixon, Judith H. Hibbard, and C. K. Mertz, "Less Is More in Presenting Quality Information to Consumers," *Medical Care Research and Review* 64, no. 2 (2007): 169–90.

45. Timothy L. Sellnow, Robert R. Ulmer, Matthew W. Seeger, and Robert S. Littlefield, *Effective Risk Communication: A Message-Centered Approach* (New York: Springer, 2008), pp. 19–32.

46. Rose McDermott and Philip G. Zimbardo, "The Psychological Consequences of Terrorist Alerts," in *Psychology of Terrorism*, ed. Bruce Bongar, Lisa M. Brown, Larry E. Beutler, James N. Breckenridge, and Philip G. Zimbardo (New York: Oxford University Press, 2007), pp. 357–70.

47. Yacov Haimes, "Risk Analysis for Homeland Security and Defense: Theory and Application," paper presented at Risk Symposium 2006, Santa Fe, NM, March 2006.

48. Peter Taylor-Gooby and Jens O. Zinn, "Current Directions in Risk Research: New Developments in Psychology and Sociology," *Risk Analysis* 26 (2006): 397–411.

49. Paul Slovic and Elke U. Weber, "Perception of Risk Posed by Extreme Events," paper presented at the Risk Management Strategies in an Uncertain World conference, New York, April 2002.

50. Lee Clarke, *Worst Cases: Terror and Catastrophe in the Popular Imagination* (Chicago: University of Chicago Press, 2006), pp. 1–24.

51. Tom Ridge, *The Test for Our Times: America under Siege and How We Can Recover* (New York: Thomas Dunne Books, 2009), pp. 83–120, 196–206, 226–41.

52. Beginning with the appointment of Secretary Chertoff, the Department of Homeland Security began to take an all-hazards approach to managing risk, which included an increased sensitivity to the use of probabilities and consequences. "National Preparedness Guidelines," U.S. Department of Homeland Security, September 2007, http://www.dhs.gov/xlibrary/assets/National_Preparedness_Guidelines .pdf.

53. The Department of Homeland Security has developed 15 disaster-planning scenarios. They cover terrorism, natural disasters, and an accidental flu outbreak. http://www.globalsecurity.org/security/library/report/2004/hsc-planning-scenarios-jul04.htm (accessed January 4, 2010).

54. Louise K. Comfort, ed., *Shared Risk: Complex Systems in Seismic Response* (New York: Pergamon, 1999), pp. 3–9.

55. R. Keith Sawyer, *Social Emergence: Societies as Complex Systems* (Cambridge: Cambridge University Press, 2005), pp. 145–69; and Joshua M. Epstein, *Generative Social Science: Studies in Agent-Based Computational Modeling* (Princeton, NJ: Princeton University Press, 2006), pp. 5–46.

Index

Page references followed by t or f
denote tables or figures, respectively.

Abadie, Alberto, 53
abstract thinking, fear factor
    considerations, 215–17
Abu Sayyaf, 18, 33, 57
academia, 201
Afghanistan, 73–75
    al Qaeda in, 73–74
    safe haven for terrorism, 64–65
    Taliban in, 52, 66
    use of U.S. military force in, 64–65,
        67–68, 87
Africa
    addressing problem of bioterrorism,
        177–78
    biological weapons programs, 164
air marshals, 118, 127
airline security and protection, 114–19,
    127–28
airports, 118
Al Aqsa Martyrs Brigades, 33
Al Gama'a al-Islamiyya (GAI), 18, 33
al Qaeda, 9, 16–19
    biological weapons, 164–66, 170–71
    characteristics, 188
    countermobilization strategy, 19–21
    disengagement from, 57
    education level of individuals, 52, 54
    enemies of, 140–41
    as "global insurgency," 19
    hypocrisy, 41
    implosion, 19
    interest in and progress toward
        nuclear capacity, 154–58
    Internet, 37, 190
    "lessons learned" studies, 15
    leverage strategy, 19
    limited capability in general,
        100–101, 187–90
    as lone organization targeting U.S.
        homeland, 100–101
    loose nukes and, 141
    martyrdom, 41

mobilization strategy, 13
Muslim victims of attacks, 18, 41
number of operatives in United
    States, 100
replacement of leaders, 70
suicide operations, 41
transition to insurgency, 19
U.S. Embassy bombings in Kenya
    and Tanzania, 64
war on terror and, 61
WMDs, 94–95
Al-Shabaab, 33
Alberts, Donald, 33–34
Albright, David, 156
Algeria
    French pull out, 33
    Harakat al-Dawlaal-Islamiyya, 15
    National Liberation Front (FLN), 11
Algerian war, 13
Allah's Brigade, 18
Allison, Graham, 139, 143, 159
American Association for the
    Advancement of Science, 181–82
American Science, 174
amplification of fear and risk, 236–41
anarchist movements and activities,
    12–13, 190
Ansar al-Islam, 33
anthrax *(B. anthracis)*, 161, 174
    Amerithrax incidents, 164–66, 169,
        170–71, 172, 178
assassination, 11, 64, 65, 70, 80
    "targeted killing," 69–71
Association of American Medical
    Colleges, 181
Atef, Muhammad, 165
atomic terrorism. *see* nuclear terrorism
Atta, Mohammed, 190
Aum Shinrikyo, 164, 169

Bacillus anthracis. see anthrax *(B.
    anthracis)*
Bandura, Albert, 32
Bangladesh, Jihad Movement, 18
Becker, Gary, 124, 125

305

military or police repression path, 16, 18
myths about, 14–16
negotiations path, 16, 17
optimal security provision, 124–28
patterns of ending terrorist groups, 2, 16–19
understanding terrorism's strategies, 9–14, 20–21
Defense, U.S. Department of, 90, 174, 175
delegitimization strategy, 13
demand side of terrorism, 50–51
democracies
leverage strategies and, 13–14
repression approach to ending terrorism, 18
developing countries, misdirecting public health efforts, 162, 176–78
Dhani, Ahmad, 42
diaspora communities, 38
disaster, coping with, 236, 237f
disengagement from terrorism, 56–59
displacement effect, 103–4
Divine, Robert, 209–10
Douglas, Mary, 234–35
Downsizing the Federal Government, 135
dual-purpose equipment exports, 175

Eastern Turkistan Movement, 18
economic development goal, 88–89
education level of organization members and recruits, 50–52, 54
Edwards, Chris, 135
Egger, Emmanuel, 146
Egypt, 18, 33, 63
Ehrlich, Paul, 36
Eisenhower, Dwight D., 209–10
emotion and reason, relationship between, 213
Enhancing Personnel Reliability among Individuals with Access to Select Agents, 181
Enthoven, Alain, 206
environmental conditions producing terrorism, 23, 35–38, 39
ethnic separatism, 33
Euskadi Ta Askatasuna (ETA), 11, 33, 52

Fadl, Jamal Ahmed al-, 155
Farris, Ayman, 190
fear
amplification versus resilience, 236–41

coping with, 219–20
cost of, 242–44
cultural influences, 234–36
effects of, 213–14
event characteristics, 232–34
in FDR's first inaugural address, 242
ignoring probabilities, 241
physiological state of fearfulness, 215–17
policy implications, 244–45
unreasoning fear, 242
fear factor management, 213–17, 226–28
affecting an individual's worldview, 217–18
cultural dimensions, 214, 220–22
developing successful messages, 228–29
individual psychological and cognitive dimensions, 214–20
influence on public thinking, 214, 222–28
misjudging risk and, 87, 218–19
mortality salience and, 214–15, 216, 217
overreaction, 226–28
resiliency against fear, 221–22
traumatized individuals and communities, 219–20
see also managing fear
fearmongering, 6, 183, 202–3, 213–14
Federal Aviation Administration, 127, 133
Federal Bureau of Investigation, 85, 90, 97, 170, 171
federal provision of homeland security, 128–32, 208–9
federalism, 207
Federalist Papers, 207
Federation of American Societies for Experimental Biology, 170, 181
Feith, Douglas, 167–68
financial networks, interdiction of, 85
Fischhoff, Baruch, 247
FLN (National Liberation Front), 11
foreign policy, global environmental terrorism factors, 37–38
Forest, James J. F., 2, 23
frames and themes for communication, 223–28
FrameWorks Institute, 217
France, first Algerian war, 13
Franz Ferdinand, Archduke, 11
Friedman, Ben, 5, 185

Contributors

Mia Bloom is an associate professor of international studies and womens studies at Pennsylvania State University and a fellow in the International Center for the Study of Terrorism. She is a former term member of the Council on Foreign Relations and a member of the Council of World Affairs.

William Burns is a research scientist at Decision Research and a consultant at the Center for Risk and Economic Analysis of Terrorism Events.

Veronique de Rugy is a senior research fellow at the Mercatus Center at George Mason University, an adjunct scholar at the Cato Institute, and serves on the board of directors of the Center for Freedom and Prosperity.

James Forest is the director of terrorism studies and an associate professor at the United States Military Academy.

Benjamin H. Friedman is a research fellow in defense and homeland security studies at the Cato Institute.

Jim Harper is the director of information policy studies at the Cato Institute and a member of the Department of Homeland Security's Data Privacy and Integrity Advisory Committee.

Audrey Kurth Cronin is professor of strategy at the National War College and senior research fellow with the Changing Character of War Programme at Oxford University.

Milton Leitenberg is a senior research scholar at the University of Maryland's Center for International and Security Studies.

Priscilla Lewis is codirector of the U.S. in the World Initiative, which was formerly a part of the New America Foundation and is now affiliated with Dēmos.

James Lewis is a senior fellow at the Center for Strategic and International Studies.

John Mueller holds the Woody Hayes Chair of National Security Studies, Mershon Center, and is professor of political science at Ohio State University.

Paul Pillar is visiting professor and director of studies of the Security Studies Program in the Edmund A. Walsh School of Foreign Service at Georgetown University. He retired in 2005 from a 28-year career in the U.S. intelligence community, in which his last position was national intelligence officer for the Near East and South Asia.

Christopher Preble is the director of foreign policy studies at the Cato Institute. Preble was a commissioned officer in the U.S. Navy and is a veteran of the Gulf War.

Cato Institute

Founded in 1977, the Cato Institute is a public policy research foundation dedicated to broadening the parameters of policy debate to allow consideration of more options that are consistent with the traditional American principles of limited government, individual liberty, and peace. To that end, the Institute strives to achieve greater involvement of the intelligent, concerned lay public in questions of policy and the proper role of government.

The Institute is named for *Cato's Letters*, libertarian pamphlets that were widely read in the American Colonies in the early 18th century and played a major role in laying the philosophical foundation for the American Revolution.

Despite the achievement of the nation's Founders, today virtually no aspect of life is free from government encroachment. A pervasive intolerance for individual rights is shown by government's arbitrary intrusions into private economic transactions and its disregard for civil liberties.

To counter that trend, the Cato Institute undertakes an extensive publications program that addresses the complete spectrum of policy issues. Books, monographs, and shorter studies are commissioned to examine the federal budget, Social Security, regulation, military spending, international trade, and myriad other issues. Major policy conferences are held throughout the year, from which papers are published thrice yearly in the *Cato Journal*. The Institute also publishes the quarterly magazine *Regulation*.

In order to maintain its independence, the Cato Institute accepts no government funding. Contributions are received from foundations, corporations, and individuals, and other revenue is generated from the sale of publications. The Institute is a nonprofit, tax-exempt, educational foundation under Section 501(c)3 of the Internal Revenue Code.

CATO INSTITUTE
1000 Massachusetts Ave., N.W.
Washington, D.C. 20001
www.cato.org